S0-BXB-665

Lawrence G. Hines
Dartmouth College

The Persuasion of Price

Introductory Microeconomics

Winthrop Publishers, Inc.
Cambridge, Massachusetts

Library of Congress Cataloging in Publication Data

Hines, Lawrence G
The persuasion of price.

Includes bibliographical references and index.
1. Microeconomics. I. Title.
HB171.5.H65 330 76-44295
ISBN 0-87626-661-8

17 Dunster Street, Cambridge, Massachusetts 02138

10 9 8 7 6 5 4 3 2 1

Contents

List of tables

List of figures

Preface

The distinguishing feature of this book is its emphasis upon application. This shows up in two ways: the micro principles are introduced in a less abstract, more familiar fashion than is the practice of many texts, which may assist the learning process and the applications anticipate and answer some student questions about what micro analysis has to do with the real world. A spill-over benefit from this emphasis upon application is the somewhat larger share of the students' attention span that it gives the instructor.

As do all micro texts, the present work covers the basics—demand and cost functions, price determination under various market conditions, factor returns, and the like—but it differs from other texts in its attention to micro aspects of public-sector allocation and long-run decisions in the market economy. The concern with long-run decisions is a natural development of the text's emphasis upon applications: many micro issues cannot be confined to the short-run analytical model.

Most introductory economics texts stress the substantial growth in the public sector since the Great Depression. This book does also, but concentrates mainly on the effects of government expansion upon resource allocation. These effects are shown to follow from government tax and spending decisions, programs of public investment, subsidies, and controls. In public investment, for example, the theoretical micro issues of benefit-cost analysis are examined against the background of how the federal agencies have employed this tool. Finally, as with many recent micro texts, a chapter is devoted to externalities and environmental issues.

In writing this book I have imposed upon friends, and my debt should be acknowledged even though it cannot be repaid. Blake Winchell, Dartmouth '75 economics honors major, has been a most perceptive and helpful critic of various drafts of this book. My professional colleagues, Professors Ben S. Branch, University of Massachusetts, Alan S. Gustman, Dartmouth College, and Thomas J. Finn, Wayne State University, have all saved me from public exposure *in errore*, as well as offering all too many suggestions for improving the manuscript. Dr. James J. Flannery, U.S. Department of the Interior, was so extensive in his critical review of the chapter on benefit-cost analysis that I was tempted to substitute his review for my chapter.

All of these friendly critics were full of good advice, and since good advice is no less difficult to take in writing a textbook than in more exciting endeavors, there should be no guilt by association for those listed above.

I can only hope, as did Samuel Johnson upon the publication of his dictionary, that my guilt will be limited to "a few wild blunders and risible absurdities."

Linda Baron, Theresa Scott, and Mary Volz have typed—and retyped—with skill and good disposition the various versions of this work, and have accepted my compulsive revising as if it were normal behavior.

The Persuasion of Price

I The framework of analysis

1 Introduction: why microeconomics?

*You can't always get what you want.—Mick Jagger**

Microeconomics is based on the unremarkable proposition that you can't always get what you want, or—as some are fond of saying—"There ain't no such thing as a free lunch."

Both of these statements emphasize that in spite of current impressive gains in affluence of some parts of the world, there is no evidence that economic pressures are about to wither away.

Not all the good things in life are free

Even a Rockefeller, his personal needs surfeited beyond caring, cannot ignore the effect of limited resources on the activities of men and nations. These resources, or factors of production—raw materials, manpower, land, and machinery and equipment—are the ingredients of economic output, and in their business affairs, the Rockefellers must organize their use of resources in conformity with their availability—economizing on those that are scarce and relying more heavily upon the relatively abundant. To do otherwise is to court inefficiency and, almost surely, to fall behind in the competitive struggle. Nations and households (families) are hardly less obligated to choose the abundant over the scarce.[1]

The United States, although profligate in its use of resources when compared with underdeveloped nations, cannot ignore opportunities to produce more rather than less with its resources. Indeed, in the developed, high-output nations, economic choices involve a larger number of options and therefore create more perplexing problems in determining what

* From the Rolling Stones' album, *Let It Bleed*, copyright by London Records, Inc., 539 West 25th St., New York, N.Y.

[1] Economists invariably describe any resource that commands a price as "scarce," by which they mean that the resource is not so readily available that everyone is satisfied. "Scarce" should not be equated with "rare" in the economics of resource allocation, as is sometimes the case in common usage.

should be produced. Nations such as Canada and the United States and those of Western Europe that are well endowed with natural resources, talented labor, and advanced technology nonetheless gain no respite from pressures to expand economic activity. Communities want more and better schools; the military wants additional personnel and more sophisticated weaponry; welfare recipients want higher payments; and middle-income groups want longer vacations, college education for their children, color TV, and recreational second homes. These wants spur competition for resources and force choice among different production options, giving up one kind of output to get another. The economic problem arises when there are scarce *means* (resources) to be apportioned among competing *ends* (wants).

This tradeoff, wherein ends are forced to conform to means, is carried out in advanced societies by an economic organization that institutionalizes choice. Whether this organization takes the form of a market economy such as is typical of the United States and Western Europe, or operates through the direction of a planning board, such as in the Soviet Union and China, there is no escaping the fact that there is but one route to maximizing output—allocation of resources according to the *scarcity principle.* This principle, which guides production and consumption away from the use of more scarce resources, is the cardinal force in directing economic activity.

The consequences of economic activity

Whether the economic decisions of a nation, a tribe, or a factory are made by a centralized agency (planning board), reflect individual choice expressed through the market system, or rely mainly upon established custom, two basic functions are involved: (1) *allocation of the limited resources*, and (2) *distribution of the limited output*.

Depending on how these two primary functions are carried out, a number of subfunctions follow more or less automatically. For example, decisions arise in resource use between the private and the public sectors of the economy; decisions also must be made between producing for immediate consumption and building machinery and equipment that will increase future output. In the market economy, the familiar choices that all consumers make to get the most from their limited incomes are major determinants of economic activity. The net result of all such decision making—some of which is greatly influenced by such institutions as banks and government agencies—determines the composition of economic output.

What an economy has to do

An economy's functions can be summarized in terms of *what* output is produced, *how* the output is produced, and *for whom* the output is produced. The second consideration—how production is carried out—depends in part upon deciding what is to be produced. The production techniques in an advanced economy are largely determined by cost considerations and the composition of the economy's output. The production of complex machinery, such as automatic washing machines and television sets, for example, requires a higher level of technology and more capital than can be commanded by the less developed nations.

Technology and a nation's standard of living rise together. But innovation alone is not enough. To initiate a diffusion of techniques and new products, there must be a receptive climate—cultural as well as economic and technical. Diffusion is more likely to occur between nations having similar cultures and experiencing roughly equivalent stages of economic development than between those where differences are great. Take, for example, the early Kwakiutl Indians of British Columbia, who periodically disposed of personal property through *potlatch,* a system whereby tribe members gave away items of wealth to demonstrate their affluence. Contrast this primitive economy with that of the inhabitants of Manhattan Island, New York, who from the first showed a much stronger attachment for property.

The planned economy: platform shoes or sausage

Most Soviet citizens stress that in material terms life has improved considerably over the last decade. . . .

Despite . . . government efforts to improve living standards, the economy remains a meat-and-potatoes affair and consumers are still accorded lower priority. The gap in living standard between the cities and the countryside is immense though efforts have been made to narrow it.

While women students at the best universities worry about platform shoes, stylish slacks and miniskirts, country people in rough clothes jam Moscow stores buying up long sausages to take to villages where even such relatively cheap meat is rarely available.[2]

---

[2] "Moscow Has Secured the Benefits of Detente Without Risking Open Society," *New York Times*, December 23, 1974, p. 16. © 1974 by The New York Times Company. Reprinted by permission.

Whether economic output is prized for the satisfactions it gives when used or when given away, the determination of what to produce is a basic function of any economy. Choices differ. The Kwakiutl Indians were at one time greatly attracted to output that was readily transferable, or—in a frenzy of display—easy to destroy during ceremonial rites. On the other hand, Manhattan Islanders did not find that the solidity and immobility of property interfered with either their tribal rituals or conventional behavior.

The law of scarcity: coercion of choice

The economies of both the Kwakiutls and the Manhattan Islanders fall under the restraint of the law of scarcity. Whether the choice involves canoes and jewelry or highways and school buildings, no economy has everything it wants. A simplified version of the production options an economy faces is illustrated in Figure 1.1 by the graph of production possibility curves for two products.

Production possibility curves show what combinations of output are possible when resources are fixed and what happens when resources

Figure 1.1 Kwakiutl Production Options

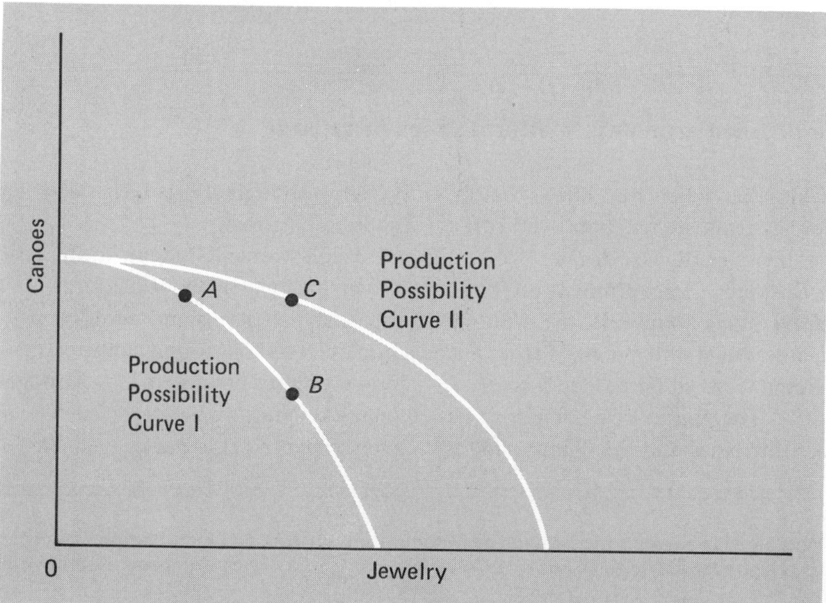

become more abundant or production techniques are improved. In Figure 1.1, Curve I shows that more canoes are produced at Point A than jewelry, and the reverse at Point B. Production Possibility Curve II shows an increase in the output potential of jewelry, following an improvement in production techniques such as the development of a more efficient method of processing silver ore.

A shift upward in the production possibility curve indicates higher output, which can come about from improved technology, such as mentioned above, or from more or better resources. In Figure 1.1, improved technique doubles the amount of jewelry that can be produced with existing resources, thus raising the jewelry component in the combinations represented by Curve II. At Point C on Curve II, for example, the tribe can produce as many canoes as at Point A on Curve I, but more jewelry. Clearly, Curve II illustrates a preferable combination.

The production possibility curves in Figure 1.1 are drawn with a bow, indicating that output is greater when resources are devoted more or less equally to the two production options. As more resources are concentrated on one production option, the productivity (output) of the added resources decreases. The effects of variations in the combination of labor, materials, and machinery and equipment on output and cost will be developed at length in Chapters 6 and 10. In the meantime, we can provisionally explain the bow in the production possibility curves as being caused by transferring good canoe-makers (but relatively poor jewelry-makers) to jewelry production, and shifting good jewelry-makers (but poor canoe-makers) to canoe production, as the demand for one or the other product changes. There is more to the curve than this, but at this time our main interest is in how resource scarcity imposes choice on individuals and nations.

Opportunity cost: output options forgone

The choice of a particular canoe-jewelry combination may seem less than momentous. But even if the illustration is trivial, the principle is not. The need to choose in the use of scarce resources is a principle applicable to all societies, although high-output societies are usually more dedicated to the acquisition of material wealth and therefore give higher priority to efficiency and output goals. The nonindustrial society illustrates the consequences of choice clearly, however, because it gives a less obstructed view of the nature of costs. The industrial society shows costs in monetary units—dollars, francs, yen—making comparison easy in deciding what resources to use in production, but concealing the real cost of production, the resources used up in producing the economy's output.

When cost is expressed in terms of forgone production instead of dollars or francs, it is called *alternative* or *opportunity* cost. *Opportunity cost is the output that is lost by using resources for one set of output choices instead of another.* For example, the opportunity cost of raising wheat on a plot of land is the output that might otherwise have been raised, such as corn.

In deciding upon output choices, a society must give up some things to obtain others. The Kwakiutl Indians could increase the production of canoes by forgoing output in spruce-root rain hats, argillite-grease dishes, whale's-tooth amulets, goat-hair blankets, and other accoutrements of the Kwakiutl good life. In industrial society, the opportunity cost of production is less apparent but no less important. Just as with the Kwakiutls' production possibilities, opportunity cost lies behind all output decisions. There are times of economic dislocation in advanced economies, however, as during large-scale unemployment, when output does not live up to the potential of the production possibility curve. As a result, output can be increased by employing resources that otherwise would have remained idle. The opportunity cost at such times is not forgone tape recorders, hi-fi sets, squash racquets, or spinning reels, but the idleness of workers.

Shifting resources from idleness to employment affects production possibilities in the same way that finding new resources moves production options upward from Point C to a point on Curve AB in Figure 1.2

Macroeconomics and microeconomics

Economics shows up in many places—in the production of ballet, the treatment of illness, the performance of rock concerts, the practice of religion, and flights to the moon. All of these activities use resources that are limited in supply and their use involves economic choices. At the "grass roots" of the economic process, such choices are the basis of economic activity. The branch of economics that covers this wide area is called *microeconomics*. Resource-using decisions by business firms, individuals, households, government agencies, colleges, baseball teams, labor unions, and charitable or nonprofit foundations all fall within the range of microeconomics. But, although the prefix *micro* means small, microeconomics should not be equated with a microcosm or, for that matter, with small minds. It is mainly by contrast with *macro*economics that the micro prefix becomes significant.

Macroeconomics views the economy as a whole, and is concerned with matters such as national income, gross national product, the general level of prices, employment, and investment and economic growth. Rather than

Figure 1.2 Reemployment in the Kwakiutl Economy

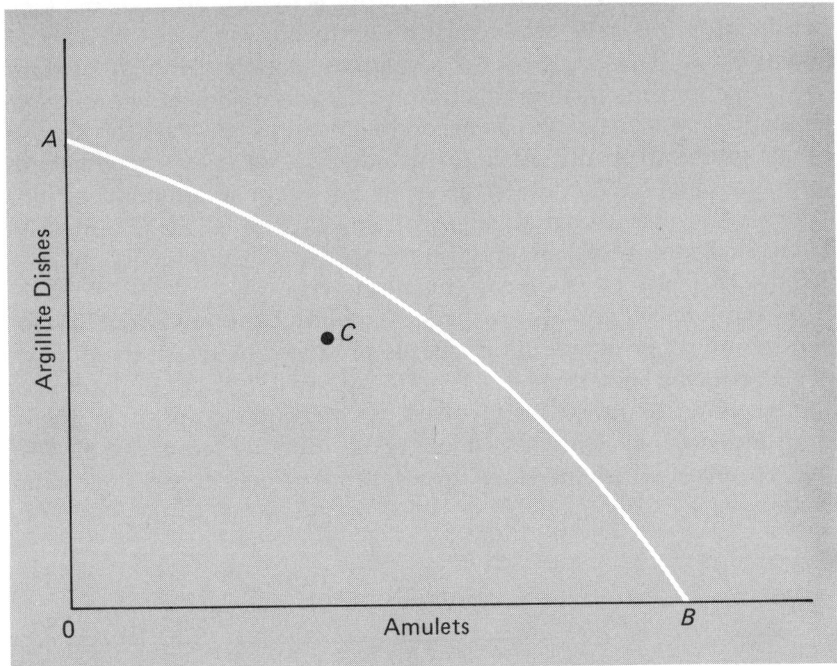

representing sharply separated fields, however, macro- and microeconomics are interrelated and interdependent, with microeconomic activity being the base upon which macroeconomic activity rests. Of the two branches of study, macroeconomics is the younger, having developed rapidly following the Great Depression of the 1930s. Today, however, both macro- and microeconomics have firmly established roles in the analysis of economic issues. In this book we explore the microeconomic branch.

Summary

Economics is the study of the problems, the opportunities, and the social arrangements that result from the need to choose how resources should be used. Since wants are abundant and resources are scarce, priorities have to be established to determine the composition of economic output and how this output is distributed.

Basically, an economic system performs three main functions: (1) *what* output is to be produced; (2) *how* the output is to be produced; and (3) *for whom* the output is to be produced. These functions may be carried out in different ways, depending on the social and economic arrangement employed. Such means include reliance upon custom and tradition in some preindustrial societies, dependence on the market system when prices are the main guides to production in many industrial societies, and greater use of administratively-determined goals in the planned economies. In all instances, however, whether the economy is that of the Baffin Island Eskimos or British socialists, the use of resources in producing one thing precludes their use in producing something else.

All economies, whatever the stage of cultural and industrial development, by the act of determining what is produced foreclose the opportunity of producing something else. This is the *opportunity cost* of production. Although opportunity cost is involved in all economic decisions, the advanced industrial systems have more choice options—opportunities—for using resources, which increases the relevance of the concept in economic considerations.

Key terms and concepts

Scarcity resources and output insufficient to meet all needs and requiring rationing by price or other means.

Economic Problem the choice decisions required to apportion limited resources among more abundant needs.

Production Possibilities synonymous with production options; the tradeoffs represented in production possibility curves.

Microeconomics the study of the factors affecting economic decision making by production units such as business firms or public planning agencies, and major consumption units such as individuals and households.

Macroeconomics the study of the behavior of the economy as a whole, as indicated by such measures as employment and output.

Discussion and review questions

1. Why do economists keep saying, "There ain't no such thing as a free lunch" when parents support children, governments provide welfare payments to the poor, and wealthier industrial nations extend aid to the underdeveloped nations?

2. A market economy allocates resources on the basis of scarcity. Why not allocate resources on the basis of technical efficiency or love?

3. A market-directed economy and an agency-directed economy both have to deal with the problem of scarce resources. How are their approaches similar? How are they different?

4. It is sometimes said that in the high-output economy decisions on resource allocation become both broader and harder. How can the choices of how to use resources be more difficult in such an economy than in one near subsistence?

5. The doctrine of opportunity cost says much the same thing as "There ain't no such thing as a free lunch." Are the principles the same? Are there cases where opportunity cost is both more apparent and more relevant than others?

6. In his book titled *Small Is Beautiful,* E. F. Schumacher argues that developing nations should not try to emulate the more advanced production achievements of the developed nations, but should approach advanced techniques of production on a smaller scale. Schumacher holds that success is more likely when development goals are less ambitious. How would you illustrate this proposition using production possibility curves?

2 The market: prices in action

*The economic organization is built up and controlled, in a way familiar in its broad outline to everyone, through the impersonal forces of price.**

Price is a great persuader. It can produce queues of hopeful purchasers at Washington Day sales or boycotts at meat counters. Such actions, in turn, generate waves that flow back through the marketing system to the producers, encouraging some firms to greater output and others to less, rewarding some occupations and undertakings more than others. All this activity keeps the economy in motion.

Price is the focus of this motion. Prices reflect the scarcity of economic resources, whether urban land, managerial talent, petroleum, or women welders. And scarcity dominates the decisions of consumers and producers—decisions that bring about a stream of adjustments in patterns of economic output and the continuing reorganization of combinations of capital, land, and labor factors used in production.

In the response to price movements, the two essential functions of an economy are carried out: (1) allocation of resources—land, labor, and capital—in rough conformity to the market decisions of consumers; and (2) distribution of income—the rewards for contributing to production—among those owning and controlling these resources. Price thus reflects and transmits decisions between producers and consumers, employers and employees, savers and borrowers.

The market system: quiet economic organizer

The market system attracts little attention. There is no administrative organization located in a suite of offices in Ottawa or Washington. Indeed, the market system is an abstraction—a system only in the sense that, in the pursuit of economic gain, consumers and producers alike make decisions

* Frank H. Knight, *The Economic Organization* (Chicago: University of Chicago, 1933), p. 32.

that influence and control economic activity. Unlike a socialist system, the market system depends on no supreme agency to plan and direct economic activity. The absence of a formal organization is frequently advanced by its advocates as evidence of its greater efficiency. Other systems are held to be less efficient because resources are employed in the government bureaucracy that decides and directs the allocation of resources in the economy.

The sovereign consumer

Whether the market system is superior to the planned economy in organizing economic activity is at times a matter of debate. But the role of the consumer is certainly more important in the market system, and this fact has led to the doctrine of *consumer sovereignty*, which assigns to the consumer the pivotal role in the market system. Production responds to the consumer's dictates as he chooses from among the various opportunities for spending income. Figure 2.1 depicts the role of the consumer as the chief decision maker in the market system.

If the consumer is in fact able to exercise economic choices in a clear and unequivocal way, without interference or constraint from other interests in the system, the direction of economic activity will be determined as illustrated in Figure 2.1. The consumer, as befits a sovereign, heads the activity and bids the system respond. This diagram oversimplifies how the market system works, endowing the consumer with more than actual

Figure 2.1 The Consumer and the Market System

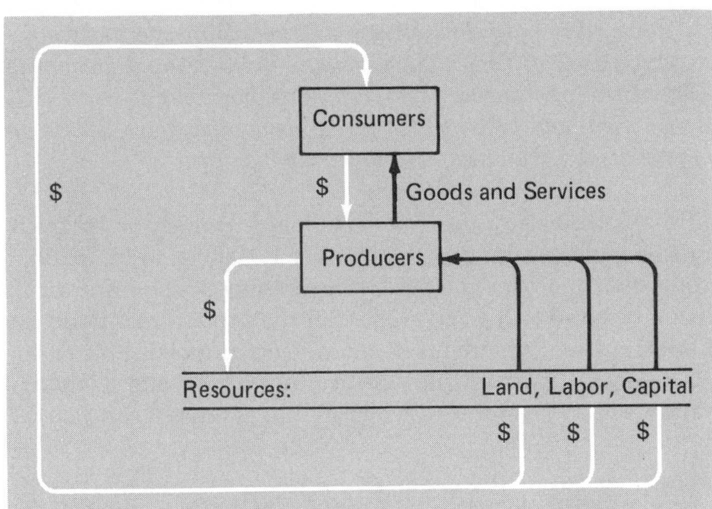

authority, but it does point up the interrelated nature of consumption and production.

The market system is a closed circular flow: expenditures by the consumer come from income created by the employment of labor and resources in the economy. Individuals are thus responsible for economic activity at two levels: (1) as resource owners (of labor if not other resources), and (2) as consumer/savers. As resource owners, they contribute to the economy's output in return for income payments; as consumer/savers, they apportion income between consumption and saving, thereby influencing the composition of the economy's output. These interactions take place without centralized direction or control, with individuals selecting from the array of consumption and occupational opportunities those that maximize their economic welfare.

Self-interest: the invisible hand

Some claim that the best of economic arrangements is brought about through the pursuit of self-interest—maximum output is achieved, rewards go to those who produce what others want, and the composition of output reflects buyers' choices. This is not a new notion. Indeed, it is one of the oldest propositions in economics, having been advanced by Adam Smith in his *Wealth of Nations*, first published in 1776. Smith put it this way:

> *As every individual . . . endeavours as much as he can both to employ his capital in the support of domestic industry, and so to direct that industry that its produce may be of greatest value; every individual necessarily labours to render the annual revenue of the society as great as he can. He generally, indeed, neither intends to promote the public interest, nor knows how much he is promoting it . . . . [H]e intends only his own gain, and he is in this, as in many other cases, led by an invisible hand to promote an end which was no part of his intention.*[1]

Adam Smith's conception of the "invisible hand," which he believed channeled resources into those undertakings most beneficial to the public, presumes not only that the consumer is the sovereign decision maker in the market system, but also that what's good for the consumer is good for society as well. Maximizing consumer self-interest may indeed come closer to promoting the general welfare than some other approaches, such as protecting producer self-interest through a tariff, but at times it can also fall

[1] *Wealth of Nations* (New York: Random House, Inc., Modern Library Edition, Edwin Cannan, ed., 1937), p. 423.

short of the social ideal. Specifically, market decisions do not coincide with the public interest (1) where the consumer does not in fact determine what the economy produces, (2) where consumer control of the allocation of resources is uneven and inequitable, or (3) where economic activity produces side effects, either gains or losses, that are not accounted for by market prices.

The invisible hand necessarily falters in its good work of guiding the economy in the public interest when the consumer's choices are uncertain. In some cases, the consumer's signals to the producer may be clear and insistent, for instance, as in the shift in demand during the 1974 energy crisis from larger cars to economy models.[2] Where the consumer is uninformed, misinformed, or uncertain, however, sovereignty is likely not to be asserted. Under these circumstances, the consumer may be persuaded to make purchases that mainly enhance producers' income.

Uninformed choice does not always mean that the consumer is at the mercy of the producer. Sometimes uncertainty in choice simply reflects the unimportance of the decision, as cigarette A versus cigarette B. In other cases, however, especially in the selection of the technical or professional services of plumbers, surgeons, television repairmen, or dentists, the consumer's lack of knowledge can have serious consequences. In encounters with specialists consumer ignorance may allow the seller to take advantage of the consumer—a surgeon may perform unnecessary or questionable operations or a plumber may install unneeded equipment.

Income inequality and the market

Even if production responds perfectly to consumer choice, the pattern of production that the invisible hand brings about may still fall short of the social ideal. Inequality in income and wealth gives some consumers more goods and services than others. No matter how accurately the market system reflects consumer choice, gross differences in income result in output decisions that are far from the social optimum. But the market system is unrivaled in organizing information. Sometimes its operation is compared with that of voting.

The market economy and the elective system are both unusually effective in condensing widely divergent views into a small number of actual choices. In the elective system and the market economy, voter and consumer choices affect subsequent political and market developments. But the analogy can be overdrawn. Even when responding only to the

[2] Only to shift back to somewhat larger models in 1976 and 1977 when the first shock of higher gasoline prices had worn off.

signals of the consumer, the market does not operate on the principle of "one person, one vote." In the market economy's "election," consumers have as many "votes" as they have dollars; the rich can outvote the poor and direct resources into areas of trivial or negative social worth—Bill Blass jackets and Porsche sports cars, for example—while poorer consumers have difficulty housing, clothing, and feeding themselves and their families. The use of resources to satisfy the more cosmetic needs of the wealthy may reflect well on the market economy's ability to respond to the consumers' votes, but the result can hardly be considered an achievement in social welfare.

Consumer behavior: filthy rich division

Sometimes the costly and off-beat ideas get plenty of publication but no purchasers. Abercrombie & Fitch in New York claims to have had some "serious" inquiries but no sales yet of a $30,000 movie it offers to turn out. But Neiman-Marcus, the Dallas department store, says it has roped in at least one buyer for a $3,500 plastic mouse ranch, featured in this year's Christmas catalog.

Neiman-Marcus also says it already has sold several His and Her Hoverbugs, advertised at $3,640 each. The craft moves on a cushion of air, a few inches off the ground or water. Sakowitz Co. in Houston has sold a pair of two-session piano lessons from Peter Duchin, each costing $3,750. Abercrombie & Fitch says it has sold a pair of collectors' guns for $9,500 and an antique Japanese sword for $2,750. All appeared in its Christmas catalog.[3]

Broad social objectives, particularly those modifying the existing distribution of wealth and income, involve actions that are not likely to be a by-product of consumer and producer decisions—the invisible hand notwithstanding. Even when it operates with flawless efficiency, the market economy cannot unfailingly be expected to bring about an improvement in the social welfare at the same time that it directs resources to areas of greatest private gain. In some happy circumstances, social welfare and private gain will coincide, as in the development of a more effective fire extinguisher or an improved antibiotic, but private gain is also obtained

[3] *The Wall Street Journal*, December 5, 1974, p. 1. Reprinted with permission of *The Wall Street Journal*, © Dow Jones & Company, Inc. 1974. All rights reserved.

from products that are designed to become obsolete and from the use of resources to persuade rather than to produce.

The market's operation falls short of the ideal in a number of areas, but alternative ways of organizing economic activity, such as by planning board, also encounter difficulties in reaching the socially-optimum economic arrangement. The question thus becomes: Which of the second-best ways (or less-than-second-best ways) of directing the economy is to be preferred? Are there criteria that can be used to determine whether the market economy is operating effectively?

Efficiency criteria

Efficiency means different things to different people. Take the case of the internal combustion engine. The engineer is likely to conceive of efficiency in terms of a performance goal such as horsepower in relation to engine size, or pollution discharge per housepower unit. The economist considers horsepower or pollution abatement in terms of cost. Economically, the most efficient engine will be the one that yields the most horsepower or the least pollution per dollar of resources used, not the maximum horsepower or greatest abatement without regard to cost.

Engineers, of course, are well acquainted with the need to compromise pure engineering goals to meet the competition of cost in the automobile market. Contrast, for example, the different design objectives specified for an automobile built to compete in the Indianapolis 500, and for a West German car to be used for transportation in a country where the price of gasoline may range up to $1.75 a gallon. What is an efficient design for one vehicle would be an absurdity for the other. Moreover, a whole range of economic and technical interactions may be involved in reaching the "best" solution for a given set of priorities. In the mid-1970s, modifications made in automobile engines to reduce pollution illustrate the interaction of cost and performance in product design and efficiency objectives.

The catalysts' requirements for unleaded gas introduces . . . another element of cost. Engines with high compression ratios are more efficient than those with low compression. But they require premium-grade fuel, with octane ratings as high as 100, and nearly all such fuel contains lead. If lead is removed, premium gasoline will become considerably more expensive. [If lead isn't removed, the catalysts will be impaired.]

The best trade-off of cost [economic efficiency] and performance [technical efficiency] appears to lie with octane ratings from 91 to 96; 91 gasoline will cost 2 cents more per gallon than conventional leaded gas. The true cost to the motorist, however, will be considerably higher than that, because he will be getting poorer gas mileage.

These costs would be offset to some extent, however, because the use of lead in gasoline imposes penalties of its own. Lead builds up undesirable engine deposits, and elimination of it is expected to lessen some maintenance costs—spark-plug replacement, for example—and perhaps lengthen engine life. Moreover, evidence indicates that airborne lead particulates can be harmful to health, so there are good reasons for reducing the amount of lead in gasoline anyway. Accordingly, the full costs of eliminating lead should not be charged against the catalytic converter.[4]

The concept of economic efficiency goes beyond the organization of resources by the producer; it involves the composition of output as well. Output composition—autos, houses, entertainment, and so forth—is optimum (or efficient) when the benefits or satisfactions from a given combination of goods and services are greater than those derived from any other arrangement. In the market view of economic efficiency, in terms of either cost or output composition, the prevailing income distribution is not questioned.

The Pareto optimum

Employing the market standard, optimum or efficient resource allocation is attained when it is impossible to make an individual or group better off without decreasing the economic welfare of some other individual or group. This indirect way of defining economic efficiency is generally called the *Pareto optimum* after the famous Italian economist, Vilfredo Pareto, who advanced the proposition shortly after the turn of the twentieth century. As the Pareto optimum is stated, it is value-free, that is, it makes no moral or ethical judgment about the desirability of the existing output or the goods-and-services distribution. One accepts the market as the final arbiter of what kinds and quantities of output should be produced. In terms of the Paretean criterion, a change in the economy's output or distribution is justified when the economic welfare of one part of society is enhanced

[4] C. G. Burck, "Let's Take a New Look at Automotive Pollution," *Fortune*, June 1973, p. 248.

The above quotation illustrates more than just automobile design options. It identifies what the economists term "externalities"—detrimental or beneficial impacts upon society or third parties—in the use of the automobile. In the above case, airborne lead is an external cost or detriment to society that is not accounted for by the market economy.

without diminishing that of other members of society. Since most social reforms consist of taking income by taxes from some individuals and giving it to others through government services, such activity falls outside the Paretean guidelines.

Perfection isn't efficient . . . or economical

In the early nineteenth-century American's system of manufacturing, there was already discernible the concern for economy which would distinguish the late twentieth-century form of the American system. The first American system aimed to make products just good enough for their purpose. The aesthetic-that-was-not-functional, the ornament that was merely traditional, had no place in the American scheme. For Americans, a high-quality machine was not one that was polished and ornamented, but one that worked.

From the point of view of the foreign observer it seemed that Americans had actually made a system for building products that were "imperfect." To most English eyes, products that were "just good enough" for their job, that lacked the extra polish and ornament, fell below the highest standard. The late twentieth-century American system went still further in outraging the Old World craftsman's ideal. For while the nineteenth-century system aimed to manufacture products that were *just good enough* for their purpose, the twentieth-century actually aimed to manufacture products that were no better than they needed to be.[5]

The market mechanism and collectivism

The distinction sometimes made between the way resource allocation takes place in a market economy as opposed to collectivist countries overstates the differences between the two systems. The traditional view is that the market economy depends mainly on price interaction between consumers and producers, while collectivism relies mostly on the direct decisions of a planning board that sets output quotas and establishes priorities for resource use. Increasingly, however, concern over cost and efficiency has led to greater use of the market mechanism in collectivist countries.

[5] Daniel J. Boorstin, *The Americans—The Democratic Experience* (New York: Random House, Inc., 1973), pp. 194–95.

Professor Charles E. Lindblom of Yale University remarks on the trend toward greater reliance on the market mechanism as follows:

Today the market mechanism is a device both for the organization of the relatively unplanned sectors of the American economy and for such central planning as is practiced in the United States. In Britain and Scandinavia, it organizes both the private and the socialized sectors of the economy. In Yugoslovia, it serves as an overall coordinator for an economy of publicly-owned enterprises. In many underdeveloped countries it is a powerful tool of development planning. It is the market mechanism rather than capitalism that the U.S.S.R. and its satellites are trying to employ—precisely to improve their planning . . . .

. Communist ideology was antagonistic to the very idea of the market. . . . [W]ith respect to formal planning and resource allocation, the overwhelming concern of Soviet policy was "balance" rather than what economists call optimality. Optimality involves careful evaluation of returns to production in alternative lines.[6]

As Lindblom acknowledges, there is a difference between the use of the market mechanism under capitalism and under collectivism. In the private sector of the capitalist economy, while responding to prices, consumers and producers collectively determine prices. Determining what and how much to produce follows more or less automatically from these decisions. No government agency sets production quotas or resource payments. Under ideal conditions, the market mechanism achieves efficiency in resource allocation—equalizing the benefits in relation to costs over the economy's range of undertakings—without the direction and control of centralized government.

The market mechanism does three things extremely well: (1) It gathers information and presents it as prices—made for instant comparison which can be used by both consumers and producers. (2) It organizes and directs production and distribution with a minimum of centralized control and cost. (3) It relies on a built-in incentive device—higher return or profit—to keep the producer alert to consumer desires.

The market mechanism can be adapted to the goals of a collectivist economy. The spread between price and cost can serve as a gauge of how well the goals of a collectivist industry or firm are achieved, instead of relying on physical output, and as an indicator of how efficiently resources are used in different collectivist industries. But even with freedom of choice, the authority of the consumer in the collectivist state is less than

[6] Charles E. Lindblom, "The Rediscovery of the Market" from *The Public Interest* (No. 4, Summer 1966), pp. 89–90, 92. Copyright © 1966 by National Affairs, Inc.

Capitalism or communism, more of some output means less of other

Some people may imagine that "cost" is a capitalist category, that money does not matter in a Soviet-style economy. How wrong they are! Brezhnev would make no such mistake. Investments, high farm prices, huge subsides represent real resources diverted to agriculture. The high level of military expenditures restricts the resources available to the rest of the economy. Yet more is urgently needed in other areas as well.[7]

under capitalism because the range of choice is restricted. Unless market socialism or collectivism differs very little from capitalism, the consumer-directed sector of capitalism is larger than under collectivism. The market mechanism may be employed in collectivism to direct and reward resources, but prices in such instances are likely to reflect the decisions of the planning-board more than consumer choice.

Something of the same thing occurs in a capitalist economy when legislatures pull resources from private consumption for public projects such as highways, educational services, space exploration, and national defense. Market collectivism differs in the way the public resource-using decisions are made, however, and in the larger role of the public sector in the economy. While collectivism may adapt the market mechanism to collectivist standards, capitalism sometimes uses private-market standards to decide whether to undertake public investment projects. Benefit-cost analysis by the United States federal government relies largely on the market standard.

Resource allocation in the private and public sectors of the economy

Although the areas of economic activity controlled by consumers and producers through private decisions, and by government through public decisions, are generally treated as if they are quite separate, there is much

[7] Alec Nove, "Will Russia Ever Feed Itself?" *The New York Times Magazine*, February 1, 1976, Sec. 6, p. 51. © 1976 by The New York Times Company. Reprinted by permission.

overlap between the two sectors. Government exerts a pull upon the economy's resources through market purchases, the employment of government workers, and contracts with private business firms. Although there is interaction between the public and private sectors, the purposes of the two sectors are different. The public sector is concerned more with broad social purposes such as equality of education, adequacy in welfare programs, and improvement in social security, whereas the private sector's main obligation is to organize the production and distribution of output within the framework of the market.

At times, however, public-sector decisions are tied to the efficiency standard of the private sector. In deciding whether certain public expenditures should be approved, for a flood-control project or an irrigation program, for example, Congress is likely to employ benefit-cost analysis in reaching its decision. Using market data to show the relationship between the benefits of a government undertaking and its costs, the conclusion is expressed in the form of a benefit-cost ratio. If the ratio is high in benefits relative to costs, say, 2.8/1, this is generally accepted as evidence for approving a government expenditure. But if the ratio is low in benefits relative to costs, say, .7/1, the expenditure is considered questionable. Benefit-cost studies are undertaken by the federal government for public projects, such as hydroelectric power production. In the case of a hydroelectric installation, for example, the benefits are the dollar value of the electricity produced and the costs are the outlays, also in dollar terms, for the construction and operation of the hydroplant. A project in which costs exceed benefits, as in the case of a .7/1 ratio, is considered unjustified because it would result in shifting resources from the private sector of the economy, where when there is full employment resources presumably yield at least one to one, to the public sector, where they yield less.

All of this may sound both precise and proper. Government activities are held accountable to an economic standard designed to identify and discourage less efficient undertakings. But whether benefit-cost analysis as it is commonly employed guides government to the optimum social resource use depends on analysts' success in quantifying benefits and costs and the extent to which these monetary measures express the social purpose. We will explore these issues more fully in Chapter 15.

Summary

Price is the focus of decision making in the market system. Different prices, which reflect consumers' appraisals and the conditions of scarcity, determine where and how resources are used in the economy under the market system. Price reflects and transmits decisions between producers and consumers, employers and employees, savers and borrowers. Price is both a cost and a reward, depending on who pays and who receives.

In the market system, there is no formal administrative organization responsible for carrying out economic decision making as is the case with the more structured kinds of economic organizations, such as the socialist system. As a result, consumers have a greater responsibility for the production decisions that take place. Such decisions are directed in large part by the consumers' decisions to buy some things and not others. The importance of consumers' roles in the market system has led to the doctrine of *consumer sovereignty*, which attributes to the consumers the major decision-making role in the market system: production responds to their dictates as they confer and withhold their financial favors.

In following their self-interest, consumers and procedures take actions that some observers believe maximize society's general economic welfare. Others are critical of market decisions in some areas, however; they contend that through advertising the producer can persuade consumers to actions that may not represent their own welfare, and that the operation of the market system results in inequality in income distribution and inequality in the direction of the economy: more income means more dollar votes in economic decision making.

There are different ways to judge the efficiency of a production unit or distribution arrangement. *Economic efficiency* in production means attaining a production goal using minimum inputs—that is, the lowest cost. In overall allocation of an economy's resources, the *Pareto optimum* is attained when a further modification in the distribution of resources improves the welfare of some people only by decreasing that of others.

Although the use of price as a basic guide to resource allocation is generally identified with private enterprise and the market system, it is also employed in planning-board direction of economic activity, as increasingly has become the case in the Soviet Union and its satellites.

Key terms and concepts

Resources the limited or scarce ingredients of economic output, such as labor, land, and machinery and equipment. Resources are sometimes called factors of production or inputs.

Capital machinery and equipment used in production.

Consumer sovereignty the doctrine that attributes the decisive force in determining economic output to consumers.

Market economy the system of allocating resources and determining output in response to consumers' and producers' reactions to prices and costs. Synonymous with *price system, market system,* and *market mechanism.*

Invisible hand Adam Smith's concept that by seeking private gain a producer satisfies the public interest even though not meaning to do so.

Efficiency criteria standards for judging the achievement of the economic system or a production unit.

Pareto optimum a criterion that considers economic efficiency at a maximum when the welfare of an individual or group cannot be improved by modifying the allocation of resources unless the welfare of another individual or group is decreased.

Value judgments judgments based on moral or ethical considerations such as whether the existing distribution of income should be changed.

Private sector that part of the economy directed by consumer-producer market decisions.

Public sector that part of the economy directed by political decisions.

Benefit-cost analysis a form of economic analysis in which project benefits and costs in dollar terms are expressed as a ratio, for example, 1.7/1, to indicate the desirability of undertaking a project.

Discussion and review questions

1. The major thesis of this book is that price is a great persuader. What is so great about its persuasion? Why is price any more persuasive than moral suasion or religious conviction? Is price really less of a persuader than these, but more involved in our everyday activities?

2. It is sometimes said that the market system is more efficient than an economy directed by a planning board. On what grounds can this contention be defended? On what grounds can it be criticized?

3. *Efficiency* can be variously defined. How does economic efficiency differ from technical efficiency?

4. Is there any truth to the statement that "What is worth doing is *not* necessarily worth doing well"?

5. The doctrine of consumer sovereignty confers upon the consumer the most important role in determining what is produced in the market economy. In the real world, the consumer's authority is diluted by other influences. What are these influences and how important are they?

6. Is there a difference between consumer sovereignty and freedom of choice? Can there be one without the other?

7. Are there some kinds of economic activities and some economic decisions that are more responsive to the direction of the invisible hand than others? How does self-interest direct the invisible hand in its good works?

8. Critics of Adam Smith's view of the operation of the market economy say the invisible hand doesn't really direct resources to achieve the greatest social welfare or public interest, but rather magnifies the inequalities in the prevailing distribution of income. Is this statement universally true, partly true, or wholly false?

9. Vilfredo Pareto advanced the proposition that the allocation of resources was at an optimum when the welfare of some members of society could not be improved without impairing that of others. How useful is this standard for deciding the desirability of various government programs such as flood-control projects and poverty programs?

10. In the public sector of a market-directed economy, the allocation of resources to some public undertakings, such as flood-control projects, must pass a benefit-cost test. Why are projects that pass this test said to justify a shift of resources from the private to the public sector of the economy, while those whose benefits do not exceed costs are said to be unwarranted?

3 The business firm

*Charles the Second, By the grace of God, King of England, Scotland, France, and Ireland, defender of the faith, &c. To All to whome these presents shall come, greetings. Whereas Our Deare and entirely Beloved Cousin Prince Rupert [and others] have . . . undertaken an Expedicion for Hudsons Bay in the Northwest part of America for the discovery of a new Passage into the South Sea and for the finding some Trade for Furrs, Mineralls, and other considerable Commodityes . . . have humbly besought us to Incorporate them and grant unto them and theire successors the sole Trade and Commerce of all those Seas, Streightes, Bayes, Rivers, Lakes, Creekes, and Soundes, in whatsoever Latitude they shall bee that lye within the entrance of the Streightes commonly called Hudsons Streightes together [with other lands]. . . . [The company] shall bee one Body Corporate and Politique in deed and in name by the name of the Governor and Company of Adventurers of England tradeing into Hudsons Bay.**

The Honourable Company, the Company of Adventurers Trading into Hudson Bay, still operates in Canada, making it the oldest trading corporation in the Western Hemisphere if not the world. Now engaged primarily in big-city retail sales, it retains vestiges of its more romantic past in posts at Rupert House at the bottom of James Bay and at more northerly locations. For the first three hundred years of its existence, the Company operated under its English charter, but in 1970 a Canadian charter replaced the original grant of Charles II, reflecting the changed pattern of ownership in the corporation and rising Canadian nationalism.

During the seventeenth and eighteenth centuries, the Hudson's Bay Company enjoyed a status unlike that of any other business firm. It was not only a repository of British authority in North America, but also a vehicle of economic penetration into the vast northern territories. Its his-

* The Royal Charter of the Hudson's Bay Company, A.D. 1670. (Original spelling retained, punctuation modernized.) Reproduced in E. E. Rich, *Minutes of the Hudson's Bay Company, 1671-1674* (Toronto, Ontario: The Champlain Society, 1942), pp. 131-132.

toric role aside, few business firms illustrate so well one of the main attractions of the corporate form of organization as the Hudson's Bay Company. The Company has enjoyed a perpetuity of life unaffected by the death of its founders and subsequent owners.

The corporation

Unlike other forms of business organization, the corporation has a legal identity of its own. The corporation is a legal person, created by the state, with a life independent of any particular set of stockholder-owners. As a legal entity, the corporation can protect its interests in court, suing for redress of injury or enjoining practices that are harmful to it. Assumption of legal responsibility is one of the great attractions of the corporate form, since this makes the corporation—not the stockholders—the object of damage suits for wrongdoing or penalties for infractions of the law in all save a few rare cases. For practical purposes, the property of the stockholders cannot be attached in payment of claims made against the corporation.

Limited liability

The limitation of the stockholder's liability is a major reason for the growth of the corporation during the late nineteenth and early twentieth centuries. In the individual proprietorship or partnership form of business, ownership carries with it *unlimited liability*, which means that the proprietor's and partners' property can be attached in the settlement of claims against the business. In the case of a partnership, for example, the partners are responsible individually for debts incurred by the firm, whether or not they have been a party to decisions that resulted in the liability.[1]

The case of the unwary partner, bilked out of hearth and home by an unscrupulous or obtuse business associate, is hardly a likely occurrence, however, if for no other reason than that partners are generally alert to their self-interest.[2] Nevertheless, limited liability—loss that does not exceed the stock investment—encourages widespread ownership of corpo-

[1] In the United States, qualifications for incorporation and partnerships are established by the states. The Uniform Limited Partnership Act, which is in force in a majority of the states, permits limited liability to be extended to partners if they are clearly distinguished from general partners.

[2] In most states, so-called homestead provisions protect partners against attachment of their dwellings for partnership liabilities.

rate stock. The stockholder-owner need know nothing about the corporation's business in order to share its financial gains. And if gains are not forthcoming, the poorly performing stock can always be sold and replaced by one that promises better returns.

It is possible for a partnership to accumulate sufficient capital for a large-scale enterprise, but today such cases are rare. The financial resources available to the successful corporation through the organized exchanges are more than abundant, while the partnership has to rely on a small number of wealthy participants and the earnings of the firm. The Carnegie Iron and Steel Company, which dominated the United States steel industry before the advent of the United States Steel Corporation, operated most effectively as a partnership, as did the J. P. Morgan Company, which put together the U.S. Steel Corporation in 1901. But most large businesses in an industrial society are public corporations. There are many private corporations—firms whose stock is not available to the general public—but increasingly corporations have "gone public" in order to tap the extraordinary financial resources that are available through the financial exchanges. The Hudson's Bay Company, for example, although established as a private corporation owned by fewer than twenty courtier friends of Prince Rupert in 1670, had within the next seventy-five years expanded to number stockholders around one hundred. On going public in the twentieth century, the Company issued over fourteen million shares of stock.

Private corporations, whose stock is not for sale on York Street in Toronto or Wall Street in New York, are necessarily at a disadvantage in raising large sums for investment. The public corporation can attract hundreds of millions of dollars to finance a successful venture. The American Telephone and Telegraph Company, for example, represents a capital investment of nearly thirty billion dollars in stock and an equivalent amount in bonds and other debt.

Not all the assets of corporations come from the sale of stock. Firms also grow by plowing earnings back into the business, as well as relying on stocks and bonds as a source of capital. Before we go further, however, such terms as "stock," "bonds," and "capital," although encountered in any newspaper's financial page, need to be identified more fully.

The varieties of investment

Capital is the foundation of the industrial system. The term *capital* can be used to refer to the actual agents of production—the machinery and

AT&T sells $552 million common stock—largest sale ever no strain on market

New York—American Telephone & Telegraph Co. quickly retailed 12 million new common stock shares valued at $552 million, the largest public sale of stock by a corporation ever.

AT&T's shares were priced at $46 each, matching the market price at its existing common. As in any public offering, however, the selling price included all brokerage fees.

Based on the selling price of $46 and the annual dividend rate of $3.40, the current return would be 7.4%. "It is a good yield for so safe an investment, and already there is speculation about a possible dividend increase early next year," one dealer said.

Many individuals and various institutions obviously agreed, as they snapped up the record issue almost immediately. Among the major buyers were bank trust departments, pension funds and mutual funds, according to Morgan Stanely & Co., a chief underwriter along with Goldman, Sach & Co., Merrill Lynch, Pierce, Fenner & Smith Inc. and Salomon Brothers.[3]

equipment, the plant and fixtures of production—or it can be applied to the money value of these economic assets. Different usages reflect different ways of looking at the same thing. Each serves a purpose.

In this chapter, we are concerned with the financial affairs of the business firm, and we shall express capital in dollar terms. In Chapters 11 and 12, in which we shall consider returns to factors of production, capital is viewed as a concrete agent of production, physically distinct from other factors. As might be expected, it is not always possible to rely upon a single term, especially when outlining the conflicting views of the economist, the accountant, and the newspaper columnist. The term *capital assets*, for example, which is frequently employed as a measure of a firm's financial resources, is a conglomeration of noncapital tangible factors such as land, as well as intangible items such as patents and mineral rights. But we can leave the finer distinctions for later; we are interested here in the way in which firms acquire capital.

[3] The sale of 12 million shares of common on October 1, 1975, raised AT&T's total common stock outstanding to 577 million shares.

"AT&T Retails $552 Million of Common in the Largest Such Corporate Sale Ever," *The Wall Street Journal*, October 2, 1975, p. 34. Reprinted with permission of *The Wall Street Journal*,

Stocks and bonds

Two important sources of capital are stocks and bonds. Stocks and bonds are financial instruments that have certain features in common but offer different approaches to capital accumulation. The stockholder is generally described as an owner of the corporation, whereas the bondholder is deemed a creditor of the corporation. This is a valid distinction, but the ownership role of the stockholder can be overdrawn since the courts have narrowly restricted the authority of stockholders to challenge corporate policy.

The stockholder usually holds voting privileges and the right to dividends—quarterly payments to stockholders, which in general reflect the corporation's earnings. One unacquainted with typical corporation annual meetings might reasonably assume that the question of dividend payments would be an issue decided by stockholder vote. This is not the case.

At times dissident stockholders raise issues that are embarrassing to management. Stockholders may attempt to unseat the incumbant directors and the top management of a firm, but this action is almost certain to fail unless supported by a large stockholder bloc or engineered by another firm in a takeover move. In the latter case, the massive job of contacting stockholders requires large-scale advertising as well as cultivation of the important stockholder blocs, for example, banks and insurance companies. For the average stockholder, who is likely to own less than fifty shares of GM's 287 million shares outstanding, the notion of the typical stockholder influencing corporate policy by vote is ridiculous.

The stockholder's legal rights

But if stockholders are owners of the corporation, why can't they take court action to force it to pay dividends commensurate with its earnings or obtain a judgment to pack off part of the firm's assets? Unfortunately, the legal prerogatives of stockholders are limited: Ownership rights do not permit the overturn of corporate policy—save through voting out a directorate and replacing it with one that appears more likely to follow a different policy. Stockholders cannot legally impose their will upon management or attach the assets of the firm in the exercise of their property rights. Stockholders' rights are quite limited—mainly to receiving dividends, *if* they are declared. And management frequently finds outlets for corporate earnings other than dividends. Funds may be channeled toward expansion of the firm, rewards to management, takeover struggles, or renovation of production facilities. If stockholders don't like the corporation's policies, they can make a nuisance of themselves at the annual meeting or take their investments elsewhere.

What if the stockholder does decide to try to change things at the annual meeting?

The annual meeting of the corporation: box lunch and business suits

Nothing is really decided at the large corporation's annual meeting. It is true that top management, the chairman of the board, and a sprinkling of corporate directors are in attendance, responding to questions and explaining corporate policy. Votes are held on issues that are usually identified in advance of the meeting—with management holding the proxies of most of the stockholders not present at the meeting. *Proxies*—signed statements that legally transfer voting rights from the stockholder to the proxy holder—are usually sent out by the management before the annual meeting.

Attendance at annual meetings is not an effective way to influence corporate decisions. Typically, about the only stockholders who attend annual meetings are those with little else to do such as the elderly, those who can't get out of it, such as management representatives, and those seeking publicity, such as women's rights advocates who point out that although women own most of the common stock in the United States, corporate directors are predominately male. All this is window dressing. When the proxy slips are returned and the blocs of institutional stockholders are lined up, management usually has enough votes to control corporate policy—no matter how much opposition may arise at the annual meeting.

The bondholder's rights

The average stockholder can sell stock if he or she disapproves of corporate policy. What about the bondholder? How much influence do bondholders have on corporation decisions? As with stock, the magnitude of the bondholder's investment determines such influence. Unlike common stock, which generally has no set dividend payment schedule, bonds represent a promise to pay a fixed obligation at a specific date, plus periodic interest payments. Legally, the bondholder has no way of participating in the decisions of the corporation unless there is default of bond interest or principal. On default, the bondholders can assert their prior claim to corporate earnings and assets before demands for stockholder dividends and most other debts are met.

Because they make this prior claim on the corporation's financial resources, bonds are generally considered a safer investment then stock, but during a period of prosperity and rising prices, the risk of business failure is less and stock dividends generally exceed the fixed interest payment on bonds. Moreover, higher prices and larger dividend payments are likely to cause stock prices to rise, and higher stock prices represent an increase in value that is convertible to cash through sale.

Some firms avoid bonds even during good times because of their inflexibility—bonds have a set obligation date and fixed interest payments. Other firms find it necessary to use bonds to raise capital. Firms with an indifferent record of dividend payments and new firms without an established dividend record may have difficulty in selling stock. Although generally relying less on bonds to raise capital than on stock, most large firms employ both. When the United States Steel Corporation was formed, Andrew Carnegie, whose Carnegie Steel Company was the nucleus of the new firm, took payment in bonds rather than stock. J. P. Morgan, who headed the syndicate that brought U.S. Steel into existence, rewarded himself with stock, as did many others who transferred property to the new corporation. Indeed, the payments in stock to the Morgan Company for its services were so generous, as were inducements to other firms to enter the combination, that the stated value of U.S. Steel's stock at the time of issue substantially exceeded the value of the new corporation's physical assets. As a result, the stock was said to be *watered,* that is, overpriced for the assets it represented. The term *watered* was coined by Daniel Drew, who had been a drover before becoming a stock broker. He found the motives for the overissue of stock to be similar to those of the drover who watered cattle to increase their weight just before a sale.

In 1901, U.S. Steel common stock was issued between $40 and $50 per share, but within a few years the stock had fallen to below $9 on the New York Stock Exchange. Part of the decline in price was undoubtedly due to a market recession, but its massive overissue was certainly a major factor as well. With the return of prosperity, however, U.S. Steel eventually was able to assert its leadership of the steel industry and squeeze much of the water from its stock.

Business failure and its consequences

For some firms, the inability to meet financial obligations brings about a more or less abrupt departure from the business scene. The grocery store with too few customers, the small printing plant that can't meet competi-

Business failure? Just keep producing

West Bromwich, England—Another specialty auto maker has gone to the wall. . . . The concern makes the Jensen Interceptor and the Jensen-Healey sports cars.

The receivership doesn't necessarily mean that Jensen will stop producing. A spokesman said the step had been taken to protect creditors. The company, he said, has liabilities of the equivalent of about $9.5 million and assets of about $8.8 million.

There is "a full order book and no unsold cars," the company said.[4]

tion, and the poorly managed furniture store are all likely to end in bankruptcy court and a sheriff's sale. Not so the larger undertakings such as the Franklin National Bank and the Penn-Central Railroad. The big firm usually continues business during receivership much the same as before.

Who directs during receivership?

The directors of a corporation reflect the financial power structure, both stockholders and bondholders, whether the firm is prospering or under the receivership of the court. Under receivership, however, the power structure is tilted toward the bondholders. This may cause control to be superimposed upon corporate management from the outside. Or, it may simply augment the authority of the representatives of the bondholders who are already in the directorate. In short, stocks and bonds are more than sources of capital. They are also instruments of corporate control.

The variety of financial instruments

Stocks and bonds are issued in different kinds and denominations. Some are ingenious creations designed to exploit the money market and control the business firm. To prevent dilution of control, which may occur

[4] "Jensen Motors Ltd. Has Receiver Named," *The Wall Street Journal*, Sept. 16, 1975, p. 17. Reprinted with permission of *The Wall Street Journal*, © Dow Jones & Company, Inc. 1975. All rights reserved.

if the corporation issues a large amount of *common stock*, a firm may sell *preferred stock*. When the term *stock* is used without a prefix, as earlier in this chapter, the reference is to common stock, which generally represents the larger value of the firm's stock issue. Preferred stock may entitle the holder to a vote in corporate affairs, but increasingly, preferred stockholders are nonvoting. Unlike common stock, preferred carries a fixed dividend which generally accumulates for later payment if passed in any year. In addition, preferred stockholders rank just behind bondholders as claimants on the firm's earnings and assets.

Some preferred stock guarantees dividends only if common stock dividends are paid, with no obligation for the corporation to make up skipped dividends on the preferred stock. Such a stock is called *noncumulative preferred* stock. With noncumulative preferred stock both common and preferred dividends may be passed, and then in a later year the payment to common stockholders may be raised above the customary level. Employed in this manner, noncumulative preferred stock is a vehicle for discriminating in favor of the common stockholders.

Generally preferred stock is nonvoting and common stock is voting stock, but common stock is sometimes issued without voting rights. A classic case of using nonvoting common stock to exercise control occurred during the early years of the automobile industry in the case of the Dodge Brothers Company.

In 1925, the New York banking house of Dillon Reed & Company reorganized the Dodge Company, reissuing the firm's preferred stock and four-fifths of its common stock as nonvoting. By retaining $2.5 million in *voting* common stock, Dillon Reed was able to control an investment of approximately $130 million. In a somewhat similar case in 1929, the Cities Service Company, a Midwest public utility, issued preferred stock that had twenty times the voting power of its common stock. This special bloc of preferred stock was acquired entirely by the H. L. Doherty Company, which ensured that H. L. Doherty would control Cities Service—at a price, incidentally, of just one dollar per share for the twenty-vote stock. The original one-vote common stock had previously been sold for a price from $20 to $60. Through such manipulation, a little bit of ownership brought a great deal of control. In more recent times, the regulations of the Securities and Exchange Commission, established in 1935, have made such disenfranchisement of majority stockholders much less likely, and most exchanges will not list nonvoting common stock.

Bonds: a form of indebtedness

Bonds generally have a maturity date of ten years or more and guarantee annual interest payments of a specified percent. Common stock is more flexible than bonds as a means of raising capital because a firm is not legally obligated to pay dividends on common stock, although a firm that persistently skips dividends is sure to be abandoned by investors.

To many, a bond is the symbol of upper-income affluence, a conservative and secure investment. But not all bonds are the same—nor are they equally secure. Bonds are issued with different maturity dates, different rates of interest, and various repayment guarantees. In the simplest case, a bond may be marketed as a general credit obligation of the business firm. Such bonds are called *debentures* and are said to be *unsecured* because of the absence of special financial backing.

A business with a steady income and a record of financial probity will usually find a ready market for its debentures; firms with less stable earnings that encounter financial difficulty will find a more limited market for their securities. To persuade reluctant investors to buy, special inducements or guarantees may be built into the stocks and bonds. If common stock promises uncertain performance, preferred stock may be issued with a *convertible feature*, which permits the investor to exchange preferred for common stock after the success of the business venture has been demonstrated. Or, stock may be issued with *warrants*, which allow the holder to buy additional stock at a fixed price. If the market price of the stock rises above the price fixed by the warrant, the option to buy at the warrant price constitutes a clear gain to the stock purchaser.

Bonds may also carry special inducements to the investor. Since bondholders are the first claimants on a firm's assets in the event of financial distress, a bond may be backed by tangible corporate property. Such bonds are said to be *secured* and the property pledged is specified. Some Boston & Maine Railroad locomotives bear metal plates, for example, designating them as security for a bond issue held by the First Bank Corporation of Boston. If further protection is desired by bond purchasers, a *closed-end* secured bond may be issued, which prevents the property pledged from being used as collateral for other bond issues.

The corporate conglomerate

A conglomerate is a combination of firms engaged in largely unrelated businesses. International Telephone and Telegraph, ITT, is a conglomerate. It not only dominates international telephone and telegraph services between the Western Hemisphere and Europe, but it owns and operates the Sheraton Hotel chain, a large household finance corporation, Avis Car Rental, a real estate development corporation, and many other lesser affiliates. Why are corporate conglomerates formed? What are the advantages, economic or otherwise, of bringing together under one controlling

James Joseph Ling: conglomerate king

After several ups and downs, Ling's small electronics firm grew to have an annual gross of $1.5 million. In 1955 he decided to sell stock in it to the public; when Wall Street underwriters just laughed at him, he and some associates sold the stock themselves, handing out prospectuses from a booth at the Texas State Fair. They peddled 450,000 shares at $2.25 each. . . . Armed with the cash, Ling made his first corporate acquisition—LM Electronics, a West Coast firm on which his down payment was $27,500—and changed his own company's name to Ling Electronics. . . . In 1958 he gained entry to Wall Street when White, Weld and Company undertook a private placement of Ling Electronics convertible bonds. Then the deals came faster and more bewilderingly. In 1959 he took over Altec, University Loudspeakers, and Continental Electronics; in 1960, Temco Electronics and Missiles; in 1961, Chance Vought Corporation, an aviation pioneer. By the end of 1962, he controlled an aerospace and electronics company (by then called Ling-Temco-Vought) capable of competing for contracts with any other in the country. Then, in 1964, he suddenly launched what he whimsically called Project Redeployment, in which he began selling to the public shares in the companies he had acquired. . . . He would sell off, say, a quarter of the shares of a Ling-Temco-Vought subsidiary; the magic of Ling's name would propel the price of the shares well up in the market, and the three-quarters that Ling had retained would be temporarily worth far more than it had been a few days or weeks before. . . . In 1965, Ling-Temco-Vought ranked number 204 on the *Fortune* directory of the largest U.S. industrial companies; in 1967, 38; finally in 1969, 14.[5]

organization firms that share no common ground in production or marketing?

A combination made up of firms producing the *same* product may bring about production economies and market control, but a conglomerate unites firms producing *different* products. A conglomerate may benefit the

[5] Ling is no longer head of Ling-Temco-Vought. In 1970, he was forced out by the company's creditors, in part the result of a spectacular but abortive cash tender offer of $425 million for Jones and Laughlin Steel. By 1975, the reorganized LTV had slipped to 37 in the *Fortune* 500.

affiliated firms—or, at times, feed upon them—but in broader areas such as national policy and financial management, the conglomerate exercises its greatest influence. The conglomerate movement, which reached such heights in the United States in the 1960s, did not create either a new or a superior form of business organization. But it did change the power structure in many US industries.

During the mid-1960s, conglomerate takeovers were sometimes vigorously resisted by firms marked for acquisition, and campaigns for the stockholders' favor frequently attracted attention beyond the financial pages. The conglomerate usually held the advantage over the target firm—especially during the heyday of the movement when conglomerate stock prices were high. A takeover attempt usually involved (1) the selection of a firm for acquisition—generally, but not necessarily, a firm smaller than the conglomerate; (2) quiet market purchases of the firm's common stock as a base for acquisition; and (3), a *tender offer* to the firm's stockholders that was designed to persuade them to exchange their common stock for securities of the conglomerate, thus ultimately shifting control to the conglomerate.

The tender offer

Various arrangements may be employed in a tender offer, but it is typical for the conglomerate to exchange convertible debentures for the common stock of the firm to be absorbed. To the stockholders of the target firm, the tender offer is attractive because of the spread between the market price of the target firm's stock and the value of the conglomerate's convertible debentures.

Whether the conglomerate sustains its favorable market record, indeed whether it holds together as a business organization, depends on how well the affiliated firms perform over the years. In some cases the flamboyant promotion talents of conglomerate organizers are not equally suited to later management of the captured firms. In other cases, a takeover battle may leave the captured firms in something of an administrative shambles. For months the firm's management has been preoccupied with plans and maneuvers to block the takeover. When the battle is over, dissidents must be weeded out, the new affiliate must be made responsive to the conglomerate, and efficient operation of the firm must be restored.

Why conglomerates?

When Mallory, the famous British mountaineer, was asked why he wanted to climb Mount Everest, he is said to have replied, "Because it is there!" This is really not an answer at all, but a facile evasion of the question. So with the case of the conglomerate. Its sudden appearance in the business community has been held to be an extension of the drive for profits—if not long-run profits for the stockholders, at least short-term gain for the promoters. But this is only a surface reaction; a fuller explanation is needed.

The spread of conglomerates in the 1960s was not due to the quest for profits alone, though this motivation was important. The earlier combination movement in the first half of the twentieth century played a part in the later events. By exhausting most of the opportunities for mergers within an industry that did not violate federal antitrust laws, later combinations were forced across industry lines. Equally important, the economic climate of the 1960s was favorable to the formation of conglomerates. These were times of corporate affluence, necessary to underwrite the costly acquisition battles. In all this university schools of business may have played a part, encouraging the notion that their graduates were equipped to meet successfully the broadest managerial challenges. This was not always true, as sometimes became all too apparent, but by then the thrust of the conglomerate movement had been blunted by other developments. Finally, compliant accountants and a receptive securities market gave strong impetus to the movement as it got underway. When conglomerates' stock prices were eventually brought in line with earnings, many fell by the wayside.

Successful or not, the spread of conglomerates raised anew a familiar question in economics: What is the dominant goal of the business firm—profits, size, sales?

Does the business firm maximize profits?

The above question is a semantic trap. For theoretical simplification economists sometimes assume that a business firm's primary motivation is the pursuit of profit. Profit, the excess of business income over costs, may be abundant or nonexistent depending on such factors as market competition, demand for the firm's output, and production costs. Even with a strict interpretation of profit maximization, however, it does not follow that business firms concentrate on profit to the exclusion of other considerations. Business firms may favor more income rather than less income, just as do most individuals, but the social and legal framework also conditions the firm's pursuit of profit. The business firm cannot ignore the norms of society, although some critics argue that these norms are insufficiently regarded. Most business policies raise ethical issues that are quite as important as their economic considerations. At this point, our interest in business behavior is to ask the narrower question: What are the major goals or objectives of the business firm?

The acknowledged purpose of the business firm is to make money. In making money, other benefits are generated as well, such as income and employment for workers, satisfaction for consumers, and prestige for business leaders. But these benefits are the by-products of money-making, although they are quite as important from society's standpoint. The business system generates these desirable by-products only when the income from sales covers cost. But aside from the necessity of covering cost, all business firms will not pursue profit with equal dedication. Some firms respond more to indirect indicators of business success, such as sales or the firm's capacity rank in the industry; others seek monetary gain with single-purpose enthusiasm; and still others trade profits for other goals—a higher growth rate, industry leadership, or product innovation.

No firm is immune to the rule of survival—income must exceed outgo—but as income rises businesses vary in their emphasis on nonprofit objectives. The firm's decisions are influenced by who gets the profit. In the individual proprietorship, for example, the decision maker is the sole recipient of the firm's gain, so profit may have highest priority. Even here, however, other goals may intrude: a farmer's pride in erosion-free fields, the abatement of pollution by a socially-conscious manufacturer, or concessions in the hiring of the underprivileged by a humanitarian employer.

The expanding responsibilities of corporate management

As it evolved, the corporation gradually began to encounter a greater number of demands emanating from outside the classic marketplace. Around the time of the nation's birth, when the small, atomistic firm described by Adam Smith fought it out in a rowdy free market, the sole obligation of the business enterprise was to produce goods and charge what the traffic would bear. Conflicts between this narrow economic interest and broader social expectations began to arise in the late nineteenth century, but did not become pervasive until the 1930's. . . . [Now] every choice a corporation makes . . .—to close a plant, to fill a swamp, to hire a quota of blacks—affects thousands of people who have no voice in the classical marketplace but who are increasingly creating new market conditions through social pressure, moral suasion, and law. Simply trying to gauge the corporation's responsibility to these diverse interests is still a relatively new job for management. It may also be the most complicated.[6]

---

[6] C. G. Burck, "The Intricate 'Politics' of the Corporation," *Fortune*, April 1975, p. 110.

The goals of management

Corporate decision making is much more complex than decision making in the individual proprietorship. For the most part, corporate decision making lies with management when all goes well, and increasing sales are among management's highest priorities. As Professor William Baumol of Princeton University has pointed out, the firm with expanding sales revenue is likely to be popular not only with customers, but also with bankers, distributors, and stockholders. Baumol contends that "personal self-interest could well induce the managers of a firm to seek to maximize sales, since executive salaries appear to be far more closely correlated with the scale of operations of the firm than with its profitability. . . . The volume of sales approaches the status of a prime business objective."[7]

In all organizations—business, government, academic, and so on—prestige and power are most often associated with large operations. The head of a large government agency or a big corporate division will almost always be paid more than a counterpart in a smaller unit, and the president of a larger corporation will normally be more handsomely rewarded than the chief executive of a smaller concern. The message is clear: corporate executives and agency heads have a strong incentive to encourage expansion. This does not mean that their self-interest is exclusively and crassly material. The power and authority that goes with leadership positions may be quite as important to the business executive as monetary reward, but in most cases prestige, power, and salary go together.

Where does this leave the stockholder in the corporate power structure?

The stockholder and the corporate power structure

Although a firm's stockholders may number in the millions, stockholders are mainly spectators in the firm's decision-making process. Fragmentation of ownership prevents the typical stockholder from exercising any significant influence in decisions made at the corporation's annual meeting. Adolf A. Berle, Jr. and Gardner C. Means demonstrated this over forty years ago in a study that examined the separation of control from ownership in the American corporation.[8] When stockholders are widely scattered, the management of a corporation can dominate decision making through the use of the proxy in all but the most exceptional cases.

[7] W. J. Baumol, *Business Behavior, Value and Growth* (New York: Harcourt Brace Jovanovich, Inc., 1967), p. 46.
[8] *The Modern Corporation and Private Property* (New York: Commerce Clearing House, 1932).

Moreover, since the courts have held that stockholders have no legal claim to the assets of the corporation and cannot force a particular policy upon the firm, other than through their voting power, corporate decision making is almost always firmly in management's hands.

The institutional power blocs

In their pioneer study, Berle and Means documented the disenfranchisement of corporate stockholders, which continues to this day. But recently investor power blocs have arisen with the growth of mutual funds, insurance companies, foundations, pension funds, and increased bank participation in corporate investment. Together such institutions hold upwards of one-third of the value of the stock listed on the New York Stock Exchange. They exert an influence on corporate affairs out of proportion to this very substantial ownership.

The separation of ownership and control that was brought about by widespread stock ownership has increased the leverage of bloc holdings, especially with mounting security purchases by institutions. Pension funds, employee's contributions toward retirement, are a rapidly growing source of institutional investment. When the labor force and the economy expand, retirement funds grow even more rapidly. This expansion is further accentuated by organized labor's growing concern over retirement security.

Mutual funds have also increased in popularity during the past decade. By spreading investment, the mutual fund presumably insulates the small investor from the risk of poor market performance of a limited investment. And in addition to diversifying investment, the mutual fund purports to bring superior knowledge and talent to the investment decision. At times results have fallen notably short of these expectations, however, especially when mutual funds have been manipulated for the enrichment of insiders, as with the promotions of Cornfeld and Vesco.

The rise in institutional investing has also increased the authority of the banking community in corporate affairs. As administrators of trusts and pension funds, and as agents of foundations and mutual funds, banks have assumed a critical role in determining economic growth in the American economy.

Management of the corporation—will the entrepreneur please stand up?

In the individual proprietorship, the proprietor is the manager-operator, owner, and decision maker. In the corporation, these functions are spread among different individuals who increasingly are persons with specialized knowledge and training. As a result, the corporate decision-making process may be quite blurred at times, especially when committee decisions supplant those of individuals.

But if one can identify the entrepreneur—whether individual or committee—the locus of decision making can be established.

The entrepreneur has been variously described in the economic literature. The entrepreneur is the driving innovator, canny trader, or over-achieving promoter-organizer whose talents are not wasted on such mundane tasks as apportioning scarce resources to reach a stable equilibrium in a market without rivals. Rather, the entrepreneur flourishes in an environment of dynamic uncertainty—and turns it to advantage. J. A. Schumpeter, a distinguished former Harvard University economist, describes the entrepreneur as follows:

The function of the entrepreneur is to reform or revolutionize the pattern of production by exploiting an invention or, more generally, an untried technological

---

The well-developed entrepreneur down on the farm

Sorenson is known as an exceptionally resourceful man, with a keen nose for bargains. Recently, for example, he managed to buy eight bins, formerly used by the federal government to store surplus grain, for a total of $2,000. New bins of comparable size would have cost him five times as much. He also buys and sells second-hand tractors and other equipment the way Wall Street traders buy and sell hot stocks.

What gives Sorenson a special edge . . . is his ability to recognize and seize new opportunities to improve his profits. Some farmers are extremely reluctant to innovate, but Sorenson has repeatedly shown the courage and foresight to experiment with new technologies. Back in the Forties, he was one of the first farmers in this area to use nitrogen-based fertilizers on corn—a move that promptly raised his per-acre yield by 25 percent. And he is perennially among the first to try the bigger and better farm machines turned out by the manufacturers. "The cost of manpower is always a critical factor," he explains. "I'm always looking for ways of substituting machinery for labor."[9]

---

[9] Arthur M. Louis, "It Takes An All-Around Expert to Run an Iowa Farm," *Fortune*, July 1975, p. 88.

possibility for producing a new commodity or producing an old one in a new way, by opening up a new source of supply of materials or a new outlet for products, by reorganizing an industry and so on. . . . To act with confidence beyond the range of familiar beacons and to overcome that resistance requires aptitudes that are present in only a small fraction of the population and that define the entrepreneurial type as well as the entrepreneurial function. This function does not essentially consist in inventing anything or otherwise creating the conditions which the enterprise exploits. It consists in getting things done.[10]

The entrepreneur gets things done in areas that the methodical business manager overlooks or is reluctant to enter. The entrepreneur is the supreme economic opportunist, alert to the prospect of gain throughout the market economy, whether in the promotion of conglomerates, the besting of business rivals, or the introduction of a new product.

The entrepreneur need not own a business firm. J. P. Morgan was certainly an entrepreneur when he put together the United States Steel Corporation, and the majority of present stockholders of U.S. Steel, although acknowledged as owners, do not share in the entrepreneurial function in any important way. Institutional investors exercise direction and control that at times may involve excursions into the entrepreneurial area, but most directors—unless also firm executives—are not likely to be sufficiently acquainted with corporation affairs to exercise much impact on policy. Therefore the management of the firm is the "entrepreneur in residence."

Some firms afford less opportunity to exercise the entrepreneurial talent than others. Electric utilities, for example, are likely to be so circumscribed by government regulations and controls, as well as being protected from competition, that decision making is largely routine. Creativity may be called for in encounters with regulatory commissions and legislatures, but these dealings really exceed the entrepreneurial function.

Whether entrepreneurship is well developed in a firm depends in large part upon the opportunities for its exercise as well as the talent and temper of the business leaders. Whether the role of the entrepreneur is emphasized in economic analysis depends upon the economic arrangement being investigated. A competitive equilibrium model of firm behavior does not offer much of a stage to display the range of entrepreneurial talent, whereas the less orderly environment of the marketplace provides the able and alert entrepreneur the chance to turn uncertainty to advantage.

[10] Joseph A. Schumpeter, *Capitalism, Socialism, and Democracy* (New York: Harper & Brothers, 1942), p. 132.

Summary

The business firm is one of the important sources of economic decisions in the market economy. Such decisions involve product price, output, advertising, product quality, employment policy and raw materials purchase, research and development, and the organization and operation of the firm. One important function of the firm is to attract investment that can provide plant, machinery, and equipment. This function is carried out in somewhat different ways depending on the nature of the firm.

Three main forms of organizing firms are found in the modern economy: the individual proprietorship, the partnership, and the corporation. The individual proprietorship is most frequently encountered in smaller economic undertakings, such as retail sales and farming, while the corporation is almost inevitably the choice of large-scale undertakings, although it is also used for smaller operations. The partnership, although sometimes found in larger firms, is usually confined to the small and intermediate range of undertakings.

Limited financial liability is a major reason for the popularity of the corporate form in large-scale business. Because those who own stock in a corporation are not responsible for the financial obligations of the firm beyond the extent of their stock investment, the corporation is an attractive investment for those who do not wish to take an active part in the firm's affairs. As a result, this "passive ownership" has led to such widespread corporation stock ownership that typically the individual stockowner holds an inconsequential portion of the outstanding stock of a large corporation, thus exerting little control over the firm's policy. This has brought about the separation of ownership and control in the large corporation, generally lodging decision-making authority with the corporate managers and with institutions holding large blocs of stock, such as mutual funds and insurance companies.

The main financial instruments of the corporation are stocks and bonds. Stocks represent an ownership share in the firm; bonds constitute a credit obligation of the firm. There are many variations of stocks and bonds, but the main differences are the voting rights and dividend privileges of stocks and the fixed interest rate and maturity of bonds. Additionally, bondholders do not generally participate in the affairs of the corporation unless the corporation passes a payment of interest or principal.

The formation of conglomerate corporations, most extensive during the 1960s but continuing occasionally in the present, involves a combination of previously independent firms producing different products and services. The causes of the movement toward conglomerates are diverse: promoters' profits, enhancement of conglomerate stock value, diversity of corporate investment, and the exercise of entrepreneurial talent. The entrepreneur, sometimes identified as a separate factor of production, is distinguished from the usual business manager by his capacity to turn uncertainty to the advantage of the firm he directs. The entrepreneur is alert to the prospect of gain throughout the market economy, whether in the promotion of a conglomerate, the besting of business rivals in a price war, or the introduction of a new product.

Key terms and concepts

Corporation a form of business organization mainly characterized by the widespread issue of stock, limited liability, and perpetuity of life.

Individual proprietorship a single owner-operated business enterprise.

Partnership a form of business organization in which partners own and generally operate the firm and where each partner is fully liable for the acts of the others. The life of the partnership is dependent upon the continued participation of all partners.

Capital the money value of the business firm's economic assets, such as machinery, equipment, buildings, and franchises.

Proxy a legal transfer of voting rights, as from the stockholder to the recipient of the proxy, for example, the management of the corporation.

Common stock an ownership share in a corporation. Common stockholders generally have the right to vote at annual meetings and receive unspecified dividends.

Preferred stock an ownership share in a corporation. Preferred stockholders generally do not have the right to vote at annual meetings and are usually paid a specified dividend.

Cumulative preferred stock an ownership share in a corporation in which a specified dividend payment must be made up if skipped.

Noncumulative preferred stock an ownership share in a corporation that specifies that dividend payment need not be made up if skipped.

Bonds a credit obligation of a business firm, usually issued with a maturity or due date of ten or more years at a specified rate of interest.

Debentures bonds issued as general obligations of the business firm.

Secured bond a credit obligation of a business firm that guarantees the bond by designating a piece of property as security if payment is defaulted. Sometimes such instruments are called mortgage or collateral trust bonds.

Closed-end secured bond a credit obligation of a business firm that designates a piece of property as security in case of bond default and prohibits the security from being used for additional bond issues.

Conglomerate a form of corporate combination made up of affiliates from different industries.

Tender offer an inducement to the stockholders of a corporation to exchange their stock for cash or other financial instruments.

Warrants a certificate issued by a business firm that extends to the holder the right to purchase stock at an established price even though the market quotation is higher.

Convertible stock or debentures financial instruments that may be exchanged at the will of the holder for other stocks or bonds of the business firm.

Mutual funds firms that purport to decrease the risk for the small investor by spreading the investment of many small investors over a wider area.

Entrepreneur a business leader with superior ability to respond to opportunities for economic gain by capitalizing on uncertain conditions in the market economy.

Discussion and review questions

1. The corporation differs from other forms of business organization in possessing a legal identity separate from that of its owners. Why has this legal feature of the corporation greatly stimulated their growth and what effect has it had upon the ownership-management relationship?

2. Would you rather have a checking account with a bank organized as (a) a partnership with unlimited liability, or (b) a corporation with limited liability? (Assume there is no Federal Deposit Insurance program.) Would you rather invest in (a) a bank organized as a partnership with unlimited liability, or (b) a corporation with limited liability?

3. A stock issue increases the *equity* capital of a firm. What are the advantages and disadvantages of equity ownership for a stockholder? What are the advantages and disadvantages for the corporation of increasing its equity capital?

4. For the most part, bondholders have a prior claim on the financial assets of the corporation over other investors such as stockholders, if the firm goes bankrupt. What other features of bonds may make them attractive to investors? In what respects may bonds be unattractive to the issuing firm?

5. Why are there few large firms today in the form of partnerships, such as the J. P. Morgan Company and the Andrew Carnegie Company?

6. The financial history of the United States has been studded with ingenious kinds of stock issues. What has been their purpose?

7. The corporate conglomerate movement was the result of the convergence of a number of forces in the 1960s. What were the more important of these forces and why did they not continue? Why have not all firms been absorbed in some kind of conglomerate? Why do some firms resist being absorbed?

8. In making a tender offer, does the takeover firm operate through the stock market or the newspapers? Can there at times be a conflict of interest between the stockholders and management over the acceptance of such offers? How does a firm oppose a takeover?

9. It is sometimes said that explaining business behavior in terms of maximizing profits is too simplistic. If business firms do not maximize profits, what are their goals? If they do not maximize profits, does this mean that other considerations are more important?

10. In what areas is a business administrator responsive to much the same pressures and problems as a government administrator or college administrator? In what areas are they different?

11. What is the nature of the power structure in the modern corporation? How has it changed since the time of the Berle and Means study in the early 1930s?

12. Where is there more opportunity for the exercise of entrepreneurial talent—in a well-established, mature industry, or in a young, dynamic, developing industry? Are there some business environments in which no entrepreneurship can be exercised?

II The determination of price

4 Demand and supply I: the basic ingredients of price

You can't repeal the law of supply and demand.—Anonymous.

From the ancient Middle East bazaar to today's Brooklyn butcher shop, the merchant's typical defense against the consumer's complaints about high prices has been a response very close to the above aphorism: "You can't repeal the law of supply and demand."

The law of supply and demand is definitive and conclusive. Even those unskilled in debate can turn an argument to their advantage if they invoke "supply and demand" with sufficient authority. The law lends itself to authoritative assertion, but as a generalization it covers more than its compactness suggests. Much of this chapter is devoted to examining how the law operates and what lies behind the concept.

What is demand?

A demand schedule is part of all individuals' decision-making equipment whether they know it or not.

For both the Kwakiutl Indians of British Columbia and the Manhattan Islanders of New York City, consumption and production impose the necessity of choosing among opportunities to use resources for different purposes and at different times. Choice in the modern economy involves encounters between buyers and sellers, transactions in which economic output is exchanged at market-determined prices. No demand schedule is in sight during these transactions, however, nor do buyers and sellers usually display the full range of their purchase and sale options, although haggling, which is an essential element of some markets such as the Middle East bazaar or a New England auction, exposes more of the demand and supply relationship than is usually revealed. Generally, only the outcome of market transactions—the realized price—attracts much attention. The varied forces that determine price lie behind the market expressions of demand and supply. These subsurface forces are responsible for whether price is high or low, stable or fluctuating, predictable or uncertain. But before the forces that shape demand and supply can be explored, the question what is demand must be settled—not out of a passion for definitions, but because demand is a concept that lends itself to various interpretations. We will save time later if we agree now on the meaning of supply and demand.

Demand is willingness plus ability to buy. No matter how much an individual wants a new car or an old coin, he or she has no influence on the market for these items, that is, exerts no demand, unless desire is combined with the financial capacity to make the purchase. Some rather obvious consequences follow from this conception of demand, but one of the most important is that need alone plays no part in the generation of demand. The demand for air conditioners, for example, is likely to be substantially greater in middle-class suburbs than in the ghettos, not because the ghetto mean temperature is lower but because suburban income is higher.

Demand also covers a range of consumer reactions that extends beyond the specific market transaction that establishes the price of a good or service. It includes what buyers would purchase at different prices as well as the purchases that actually take place. Economists conceive of demand as a schedule or range of price-quantity relationships such as that shown in Table 4.1 and Figure 4.1. (Both of these illustrations are hypothetical.)

Table 4.1: The demand for home heating oil

Price of Oil	Quantity Demanded
$1.00 per gallon	3 million gallons
.70 per gallon	3½ million gallons
.50 per gallon	4 million gallons
.30 per gallon	5 million gallons
.10 per gallon	7 million gallons

The demand schedule and the demand curve both say the same thing. They cover the full range of potential consumer reactions to price, both at and beyond the realized price of the market. But sometimes, by expressing demand as a smooth, continuous relationship between prices and quantities, we lose track of reality in the symmetry of the hypothetical illustration. This is not a very important qualification of demand curves, but it should be recognized that some commodities and services are not available in highly divisible units and infinitely variable prices. Shoes are sold in

Figure 4.1 The Demand for Home Heating Oil

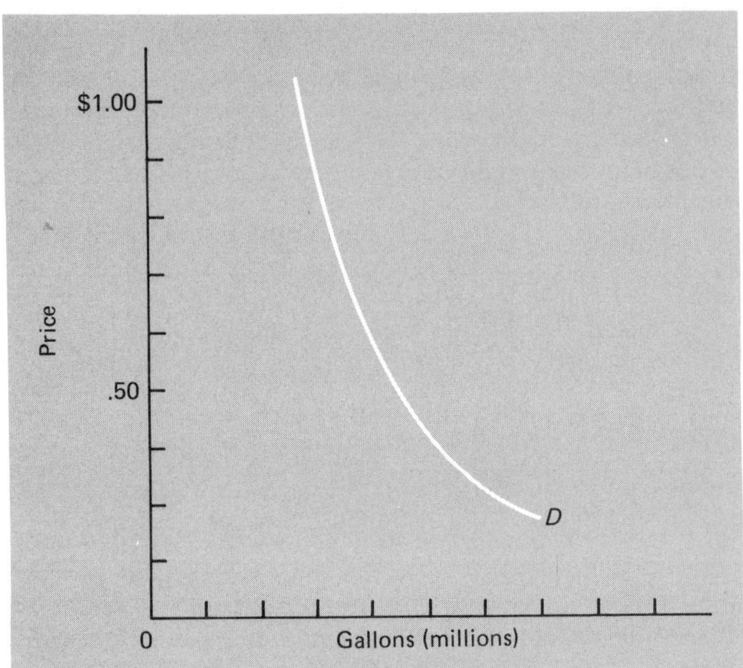

established price categories, $22.50 and $14.50, for example, rather than in continuous gradations from $10.00 to $25.00 a pair. The connecting prices shown in a curve may give the false impression of a continuous stream of demand at all price intervals, but the absence of continuous price-quantity gradations does not change the basic factors of price determination. Since home heating oil is infinitely divisible and the price per gallon is normally quoted down to the tenth of a cent, a continuous curve is appropriate. Moreover, the demand curve in Figure 4.1 is a *collective* curve. A collective curve includes all the actual and potential purchasers of home heating oil at various prices for one market area.

Although the demand curve covers a range of prices, only one price can prevail in a market. Market prices may change from time to time as the underlying forces of demand and supply are modified, but if two prices prevail simultaneously, then there are two markets, not one. Such a situation prevailed in Paris following World War II when there was an official and a black market price for the French franc. Different markets also exist in any city where a bank will lend money at different rates depending upon the security and credit of the borrower.

Change in demand or change in amount demanded?

The above heading may strike one as double talk. Actually, the issue is whether demand is represented by a single point on the demand curve or covers the full range of the curve. Each point on a demand curve represents the same basic demand function. The amount consumers stand ready to buy varies not because demand changes, but because price changes.

Changing price—and price alone—charts the course of the demand curve, typically encouraging larger sales at lower prices and lesser sales at higher prices. The different points along the demand curve represent changes in the *amount* demanded, whereas a change in demand involves a shift in the total curve. In schedule terms, a change in demand occurs when more or less of a good or service is purchased at the same price; a change in the amount demanded takes place when more or less goods or services are purchased at *different* prices. This distinction is illustrated in Figure 4.2 where the movement from Point A to Point B on Curve I represents an increase in the amount of home heating oil demanded, and the shift from Curve I to Curve II constitutes an increase in demand.

Figure 4.2 Change in Amount Demanded (Point A to Point B); Change in Demand (Curve I to Curve II)

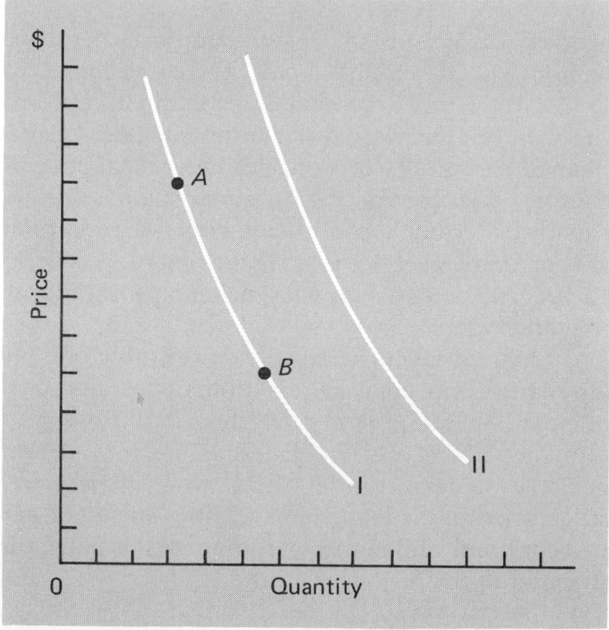

A shift or change in demand may be caused by variations in consumer income, product quality, or the prices of competitive products, any of which brings about a reevaluation by consumers of how much of a particular commodity they want to buy. These factors will be examined at greater length in the discussion of price determination in this and the following chapter, but here we should note that stability in demand and supply decreases over time because of the greater likelihood of a change in one or more of the factors that affect consumer behavior. Before examining the causes of changes in demand, however, we need to take a closer look at the shape of the typical demand curve.

Pet rocks aren't about to roll over and play dead

Rock Bottom Productions in Santa Clara, Calif., figures it sold one million "Pet Rocks" in less than 90 days before Christmas, not bad for a $4 item that consists of a small rock sitting on straw in a cardboard box plus an instruction booklet for the rock's care and training. Following up its marketing coup, Rock Bottom started selling pet rocks in Canada, aims for distribution in Europe and the Far East. The company also plans a line of pet rock T-shirts and a poster with caricatures of "famous" rocks (Goldirocks, for one). A licensee is already starting to market a pet rock food (rocksalt) and shampoo (an ordinary detergent to give a clean coat and prevent the frizzies.)

The pet rock idea spawns some imitations plus extensions of the fad. The Oregon Department of Geology and Mineral Industries offers to prepare a genealogy of anyone's pet rock for $1 plus postage. Lake Superior State College in Michigan plans an all-breed National Pet Rock Show.[1]

The downward sloping demand curve

Most demand curves slope downward to the right. There are special exceptions to this rule—the demand curve may be perfectly horizontal or even perfectly perpendicular—but the typical consumer reaction is to buy a smaller amount of most goods or services at a higher price, and a larger amount at a lower price. Figure 4.3 shows the inverse relationship between price and quantity that brings about the negative inclination of the demand curve.

[1] *The Wall Street Journal* Jan. 8, 1976, p. 1. Reprinted with permission of *The Wall Street Journal*,

Figure 4.3 The Setting for Demand and Supply Curves

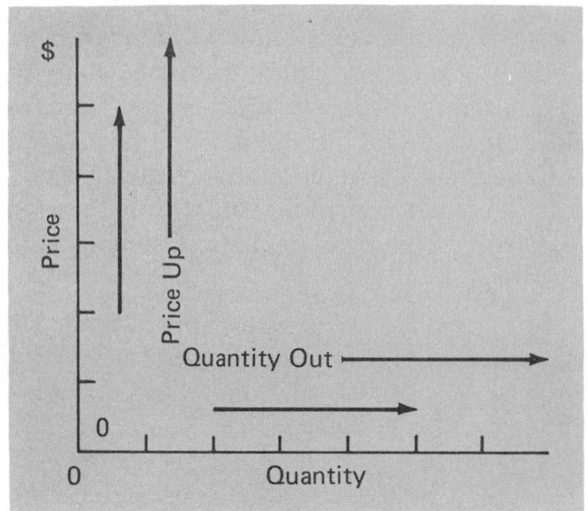

The concept of utility

In a sense, it is unnecessary to present an elaborate explanation for the reason the typical consumer buys more when the price is low and less when it is high. This phenomenon is substantiated by the most casual empiricism, the observation of what takes place in the marketplace. Economists have not attempted a psychological explanation for the consumer's behavior, but they have recast the consumer's reactions in accord with the concept of diminishing marginal utility. *Utility* is the satisfaction an individual derives from the consumption of a good or service.

Utility should be distinguished from value and price; it is an ingredient of both, but before economic value or price can arise, there must be utility *and* scarcity. No matter how useful are the sun's rays or the ocean's water, for example, unless limited in some way they have no economic value or price. As a combination, the sun and the sea are always limited, but their utility is greater during the winter for those living in inland regions of the Northern Hemisphere. Then the absence of the satisfactions (utility) of sun and sea are most apparent, and therefore prices at resorts where they can be obtained are highest.

The principle of diminishing marginal utility

As an individual acquires more of a given item of consumption, whether neckties or concerts, the satisfaction from additional consumption diminishes and other things become relatively more desirable. As more ties are acquired or more concerts attended, *total* utility increases, but as tie purchases or concert attendance increase, they afford less satisfaction than earlier concerts or ties. There are exceptions to this generalization, of course. Some ties and concerts are clearly superior to others, yielding more utility, but if marginal utility did not eventually fall with additional purchases of a given good or service, one would presumably go on acquiring one item, such as shirts, to the exclusion of other purchases. Consumers balance, or apportion, their budgets; no one accumulates a wardrobe consisting of forty-five pairs of socks and two shirts, or ninety-seven ties and three pairs of socks. While there may be a few tie or shirt freaks who delight in the display of bizarre or abundant shirts or ties, the typical consumer spreads purchases more evenly.

The downward slope of the demand curve conforms to the principle of *diminishing marginal utility.* Where consumption is severely limited and the consumer is unable to make certain purchases, such as of performances of the Metropolitan Opera Company or the Harlem Globetrotters in East Thetford, Vermont, the opportunity to see such artists would yield exceptionally high utility and, consequently, command a high price. But if East Thetford were to be selected as the summer quarters of the Met or the Globetrotters, frequent public performances would result, and if the consumer's capacity to enjoy successive performances did not increase, the marginal utility of such entertainment would decline. The artistic performances of the Globetrotters and the Met, just as less talented offerings, would face a downward slanting demand curve.

Price and utility are both involved in the consumer's spending decisions. They interact to shape the consumer's choices so that satisfactions from expenditures are greatest when the marginal return from a dollar spent on one thing is essentially the same as for that spent on another; that is, when an *additional* dollar spent on ties, gasoline, or shirts will yield approximately the same utility or satisfaction. If the marginal utility from a dollar spent on different purchases is not the same, the consumer satisfactions will be increased by purchases that bring more utility per dollar. The optimum relationship is expressed in the following equation.

$$\frac{\text{Marginal Utility of } X}{\text{Price of } X} = \frac{\text{Marginal Utility of } Y}{\text{Price of } Y}$$

$$\ldots = \frac{\text{Marginal Utility of } N}{\text{Price of } N}$$

In this equation *X* and *Y* represent commodities as varied as xylophones and autos, and services such as public transportation and hair styling. The designation N is a catchall category that covers the totality of the consumer's purchases.

If the consumer's balancing act depicted above is successful, the utility increment from one dollar expenditure will be the same as that from another, whether the expenditure is for a good or a service, an expensive or an inexpensive item. The precision of the utility adjustment shown above is likely to be encountered, however, in only the most compulsive utility calculator. Some consumers will balance utility more carefully than others because of differences in life style, value standards, and income. As an individual moves up the income scale, for example, opportunities for expenditure will increase, while differences in the utility return among various purchases may become less important. But all of this assumes a rational and at least moderately calculating consumer, one who knows his or her own interest and how best to maximize it. How well does this apply to your behavior as a consumer?

The marginal approach

The *marginal approach* is important beyond its application to diminishing utility. It is employed in other areas of demand and cost analysis. Unlike *average* and *total,* two familiar concepts from grade-school arithmetic, the measure of marginal change focuses upon the critical zone in which decisions are made. Average spreads change evenly over all the contributions to the total so that the impact of different ingrediens is concealed. This is demonstrated by the possibility of drowning while standing up in a pool of water averaging 3½ feet when the depths involved are areas 1 foot and six feet deep—unless you are Wilt the Stilt. The total tells us even less about the character of various components. *Marginal analysis,* by contrast, *traces change through successive applications of factors to production or through expenditures for consumption.*

The margin as a stream of change

How far consumption expenditures or production outlays may be carried is the essence of economic decision making. Such decisions are sometimes said to be made *at the margin,* that is, involving the last units purchased or produced. As will be demonstrated in Chapter 7, marginal analysis provides the most direct way to determine the optimum point of output or consumption. But the margin is best conceived as a *stream* of successive increments, rather than as a single decision point. Table 4.2

Butter the low-priced spread? It's all a matter of supply and demand and cows and cold weather and sugar prices

Wholesale butter prices Friday dropped eight cents a pound to 62½ cents. Some Midwestern grocery chains are featuring butter specials as low as 69 cents a pound, about 15 cents or more below prices a week ago. In some areas, butter is selling for the first time at prices below some grades of margarine, which are as high as 90 cents a pound.

Butter prices normally drop just before Christmas, mainly because the heavy holiday baking has been completed . . . [and] cold weather makes cows produce more milk. . . . Industry sources say demand for fluid milk has slowed in some key producing areas, causing more milk to go into butter production. . . .[T]he use of butter in food and baking industries has been cut by consumer resistance to high prices caused by soaring sugar costs.[2]

illustrates marginal change in comparison with changes in the average and total.

A glance at Table 4.2 is sufficient to show the difference of the marginal concept. With successive Met performances, total utility increases by a

Table 4.2: The arithmetic of the marginal concept[3]

Met Performances	Total Utility	Average Utility	Marginal Utility
1	10	10	10
2	18	9	8
3	24	8	6
4	28	7	4
5	30	6	2

[2] John Valentine, "Butter Isn't Always High-Priced Spread," *The Wall Street Journal*, December 23, 1974, p. 7. Reprinted with permission of *The Wall Street Journal*, © Dow Jones & Company, Inc. 1974. All rights reserved.

[3] The numerical statement of utility in Table 4.2 should not suggest that it is possible to measure and compare utility among different individuals in the same way that height can be compared by reference to the foot or income through the use of the dollar. This cannot be done because there is no standard for utility, but an individual can rank or order his or her reactions to successive purchases. This issue is considered further in the Appendix to this chapter.

decreasing proportion; the amount of this increase, or the difference between total utility for three and four performances, is the marginal utility. It is also apparent from Table 4.2 that the average, total, and marginal measures are simply different ways to organize or present basic information. Given the number of Met performances and any one of the three figures—total, average, or marginal utility—one can derive the other two figures.

But there's more to marginalism than the mechanics of computing marginal utility. Marginalism is a way of thought, a method of economic problem solving, quite as much as it is a measure of the change in economic variables. We do not mean to suggest that all doors open for the marginalist's "key," or that marginalism is used everywhere. Marginalism's great contribution is that it gives focus and direction to economic analysis. It will repeatedly be encountered throughout the book.

The slope of demand

Curves that stand on end

For most products and services, there is a considerable range in use: more or less gasoline will be purchased depending upon price and vacation plans; haircuts will be frequent or occasional according to lifestyle and price; and attendance at football games will depend on the weather, the price of tickets, whether the game is on television, and a multitude of other considerations. For some forms of consumption, however, there is no such flexibility. Building codes often prescribe specifications for certain constructions such as foundations and chimneys, and the prescription of medication may be unvarying in kind and amount. In other instances, an initial purchase makes other purchases largely inevitable. Having bought a car dictates the replacement of defective tires, for example, and the acquisition of skis presupposes the purchase of bindings.

Instead of the typical downward-sloping demand curve, previously illustrated, in some cases demand will be perpendicular. Figure 4.4 shows a perpendicular curve. The reason for such a curve is obvious. The diabetic, for example, requires a precise injection of insulin to maintain health; without bindings, skis are primarily conversation pieces. In both cases, a specific amount of a given produce is required; more is useless or detrimental. If consumers purchase such items, they are usually insensitive to price, neither increasing nor decreasing purchases if price changes.

Figure 4.4 The Demand for Ski Bindings (of those who have skis)[4]

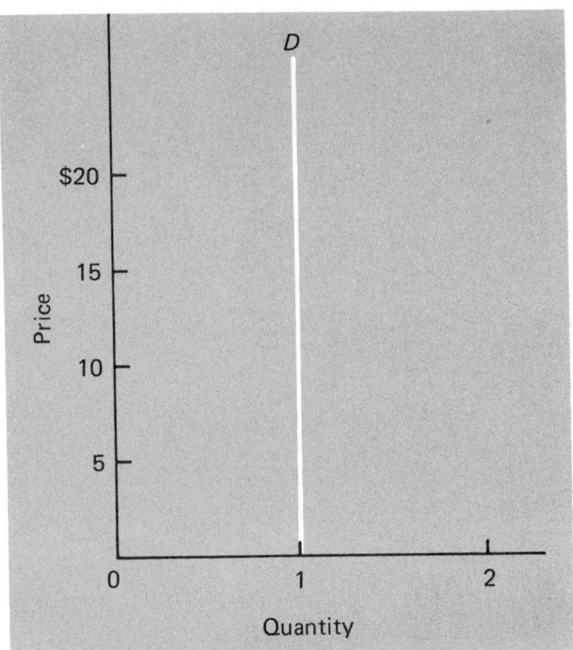

Horizontal curves

When a product is sold by many producers—most small grain crops, for example—the seller faces a demand curve that appears not to change whether all or part of his crop is offered for sale. The mill and elevator operator will buy all the wheat a farmer delivers for sale at the current market price, whether offered one, two, or three thousand bushels. None of these offers is large enough to affect the market price. Although the market demand curve for the whole world's wheat slopes downward, there is no effect upon market price for that portion sold by the individual farmer. Thus the demand curve for one farmer's wheat extends horizontally over the full range of his output, as shown in Figure 4.5.

Unlike the demand curve in Figure 4.4, which illustrates a freak case, the horizontal demand curve in Figure 4.5 plays a major role in the economic analysis of the behavior of the economic firm. At this point,

[4] If skis, bindings, poles, and other paraphernalia employed in sliding downhill are purchased as a package—as is frequently the case with beginners—the price sensitivity of the package will be much the same as that of skis, that is, downslanting rather than perpendicular.

Figure 4.5 The Demand for Wheat (as seen by the farmer selling his output)

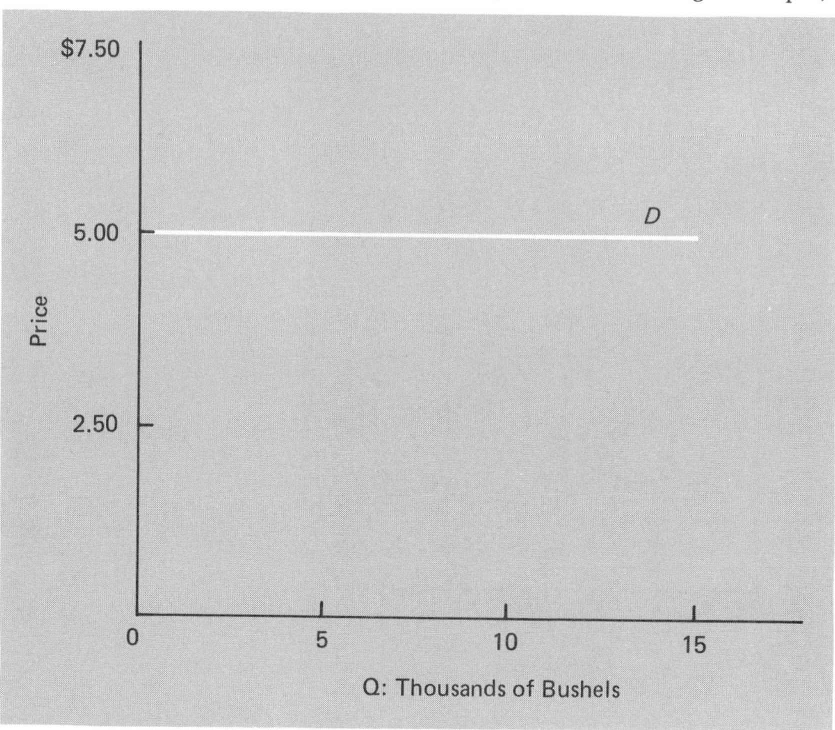

however, we need only emphasize that the collective downward slanting demand curve for the world wheat supply in no way conflicts with the horizontal demand curve that represents one seller's conception of the market for his or her output. The two curves focus on different parts of the market; the collective demand curve focuses upon the aggregate effect and the horizontal curve upon the negligible impact of the single seller upon the total supply in the market.

When we change our perspective from that of the single wheat farmer selling a small portion of the total wheat supply to the collective demand for all wheat produced, the demand curve encompasses prices above and below $5 per bushel and a range of quantity that dwarfs the single-farm output.

The collective market demand for wheat, Figure 4.6A, employs the same price scale as the farmer's view of the market, Figure 4.6B, but the scale of quantity is measured in millions of bushels rather than in thousands. The actual market price and quantity of wheat represented by the options on the demand curve depends on how supply interacts with demand.

Figure 4.6 The Demand for Wheat

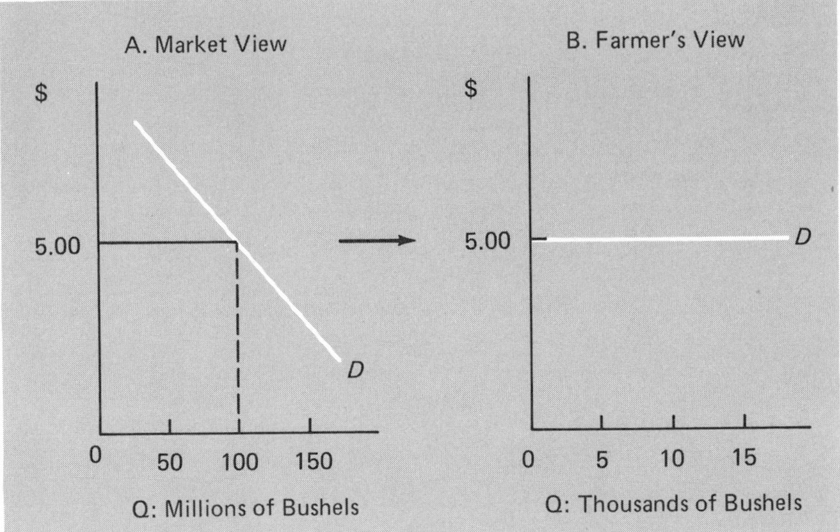

What is supply?

Supply is a cluster of offers to sell various amounts of goods or services at different prices. As in the case of demand, supply is best expressed as a schedule or curve. Supply is more than an output point: It is the total range of offerings at corresponding prices. A *change in supply* is a revision of the whole schedule or a shift in the whole curve, as from Curve *S* to Curve S_1 in Figure 4.7. A *change in the amount supplied* consists in movement along a given curve, such as from Point A to Point B on Curve S. In short, the terminology of supply is the same as that for demand and its price-quantity relationship is plotted against the same axes as demand.

The upward-sloping supply curve

Unlike the demand curve, which slopes downward, the typical supply curve slopes upward, indicating that the seller is persuaded to offer larger amounts on the market as price increases. The usual explanation for the upward-sloping supply curve is that the higher prices cover any increased costs of added output, and at the same time raise the producer's return from sales. The conventional upward-sloping supply curve applies for a period of time that is long enough for the producer to make output adjustments, including cases where supply has already been produced and

Figure 4.7 The Short-run Supply of Gasoline in a Very Small Town

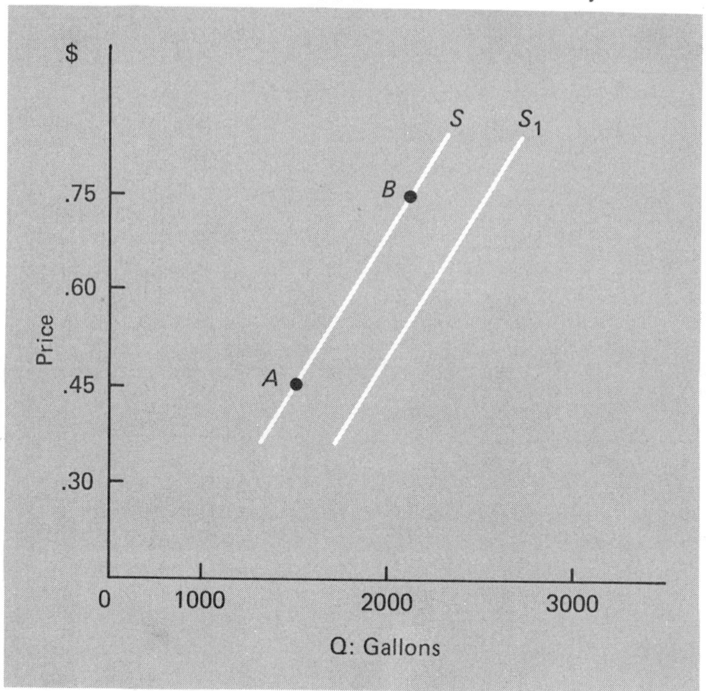

is being withheld from the market until the price is right. If there is not enough time for the producer to change the production schedule, however, the amount offered for sale will be fixed, as shown in Figure 4.8. Inflexible supply occurs when the supply curve covers a period of time too short for producers to respond to market changes, such as one day in the life of the Fulton Fish Market.

Fish, as any fisherman knows, are not instantly available—no matter what the price. But over time, success in commercial fishing is likely to correspond at least roughly with market price. If the Fulton Fish Market and the Boston Wharfside Market raise their prices for flounder and cod, fishing fleets in the Georges Bank off the Atlantic Coast will intensify their efforts. As a result, instead of the fixed, one-day catch illustrated in Figure 4.8, the supply of fish will be represented by a series of price-quantity relationships similar to those of the curves in Figure 4.7. The difference in the two diagrams is based on the ability of the producer/seller to adjust output to price change. There is no such adjustment in Figure 4.8 and limited adjustment in the previous illustration. In Figure 4.7, a longer period for adjustment is allowed than in Figure 4.8, but it is nonetheless a "short-run" time period.

Figure 4.8 Supply of Fish in Fulton Fish Market, Friday, September 22, 1976

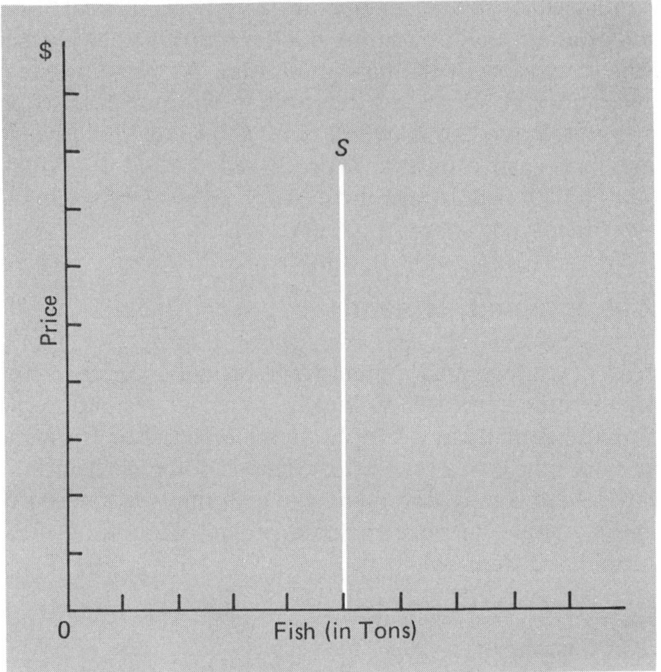

The not-so-short short run

In a *short-run* period, producer/sellers can make limited supply changes in response to price, but cannot significantly enlarge or decrease production facilities or change production techniques. Changes possible in the short run are limited to hiring or laying off labor, increasing or cutting back on raw materials and other direct ingredients of production—in other words, modifications that do not involve changes in production facilities. To make changes in the basic machinery and equipment of production requires more time than the "short-run." It will probably come as no shock to learn that economists call this more extended period the *long run*. In the long run, if production facilities are expanded or contracted along with manpower and materials, the supply curve may change both its position and its shape. Before these long-run effects can be considered, however, there is much more to be said about the basic nature of supply and demand.

The upward thrust of the short-run supply curve is the result of increasing pressure for large output when the production facilities cannot be expanded. Take the case of the fishing fleet previously mentioned. In the short run, the number or size of the fishing trawlers cannot be changed, but within limits, more or less men and gear can be put into use. A minimum crew must be on board to operate a trawler and carry on fishing, but the total operation will be more efficient—output per worker will be greater—if the crew exceeds the base minimum. At the same time, the size of the crew cannot be increased indefinitely without decreasing efficiency. More pressure upon the trawler's limited facilities will cause output per crew member—fish caught and processed—to fall off. Thus, although the total amount of fish caught increases, unit costs rise. This is reflected in the upward slope of the supply curve.

The meeting of supply and demand

When the forces of supply and demand are brought together, the result of this union determines price. Graphically, price determination can be shown by bringing the demand and supply curves together on the same price-quantity diagram. Since the demand curve slopes downward and the supply curve upward, there is only one point at which the two curves can intersect and, therefore, only one price that can prevail. Figure 4.9 illustrates the law of supply and demand.

Figure 4.9 The Price of Gasoline

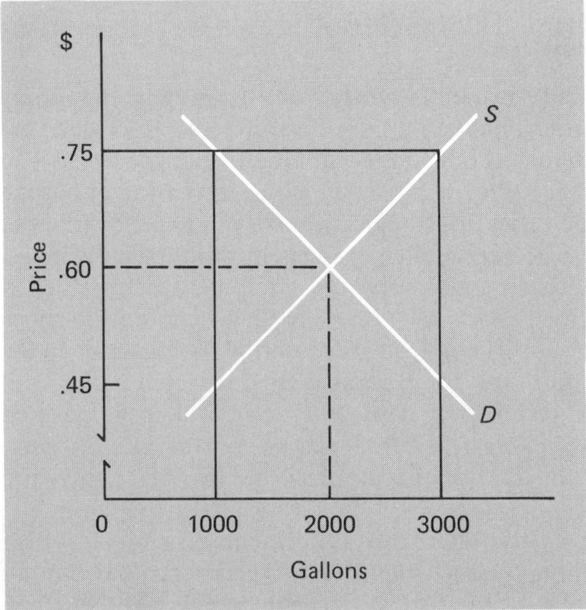

The narrow-minded market

A price of 60¢ can be established if there is no outside interference with the market process under the conditions represented in Figure 4.9. A price above or below 60¢ quoted in this market will not prevail. A lower price will rise and a higher price will fall. At 75¢, for example, 1,000 gallons of gasoline are demanded, but suppliers offer 3,000 gallons for sale; the market is out of adjustment. Unsold stocks of gasoline will accumulate at 75¢ a gallon and exert a downward pressure on price. Price will fall and the quantity demanded will rise until equilibrium is established at 60¢. At 60¢ the forces of demand and supply are in balance and the market is in equilibrium. As long as there is no change in demand and supply—no shift in either of the two curves—most movements away from the 60¢ price will be temporary, generating forces that bring about its reestablishment.

Price control under phase 4—buyer be gouged!

[Under Phase 4 price controls in 1973,] producers and distributors of a host of items ranging from basic commodities such as steel, paper, textiles, and chemicals to manufactured goods as common as nuts and bolts, paper clips and masking tape have come up with devices to extract the last possible dollar from purchasers.

Techniques range from outright breaking of contracts to more subtle approaches such as discontinuing a product and replacing it with an almost identical "new model" priced sharply higher. Some approaches seem to be perfectly legal under Phase 4 rules. Some approaches are obvious violations. But most fall into a gray area somewhere between. What they all have in common, though, is that they take advantage of apparent shortages to put through sharp price increases, often 15%, 20%, or 25%. . . .

It's no great surprise to economists or businessmen that controls work less well the longer they last and the tighter the supply and demand equation becomes. The government obviously can't police every business transaction. Therefore, price controls work effectively only when buyers and sellers want them to work.[5]

---

[5] R. E. Winter, "Taking Advantage," *The Wall Street Journal*, November 2, 1973, p. 1. Reprinted with permission of *The Wall Street Journal*,

Ration by price or by coupon

Although there may be times when the law of supply and demand may be challenged—as during wartime when certain food items are in very short supply—much mischief can result from ignoring how the market works. A prime function of the market is to ration or distribute the existing supply of economic output among consumers. The prospect of sharply rising gasoline prices created by shortages may encourage the adoption of price controls to forestall rising prices. But if price controls roll prices back to 45¢ a gallon instead of maintaining a price of 60¢ to clear the market, the amount offered for sale will be reduced to 1000 gallons at the same time that consumers attempt to buy 3000 gallons, as shown in Figure 4.9.

Shortage by price control

The control price of 45¢ creates a supply shortage, which is the result of establishing a price below the market level. This shortage is illustrated in Figure 4.9 by the difference between what suppliers offer at 45¢ and what consumers attempt to buy. Since a controlled price of 45¢ inhibits the allocative or rationing function of the market, supplementary rationing must be devised to avoid the irritations of long queues of customers, weekend station closings, and generally deteriorating customer-operator relations. What the market normally brings about through adjustment of price must be achieved under price controls by administrative procedures such as the distribution of coupons designating gasoline needs. Rationing attempts to restrict the consuming public to less gasoline that it would otherwise purchase at 45¢ a gallon.

Determining who gets how much gasoline requires conscious administrative decisions that the market makes automatically by ignoring considerations other than price. Having partially neutralized the impact of price upon the allocation of gasoline by placing the commodity under price controls, it is no longer possible to stimulate the movement of supplies from one region to another by changing price. Past consumption figures are likely to determine physical allocations under price control, with adjustments where quotas are considered inequitable or inappropriate. But such adjustments require time, talent, and discretion—none of which is ever abundant. Administrative control cannot match the market in reaction time. Moreover, if price control does not cover the total market area, supplies will gravitate to the uncontrolled portion where prices are higher, further accentuating the shortage in the controlled region. During the energy crisis of 1974, for example, price control in the United States caused petroleum supplies normally earmarked for the American market to be diverted to the uncontrolled, higher-priced European market. As Figure 4.10 shows, in effect, the supply curve in the American market was shifted back from Curve S to Curve S_1 showing that supply became less at a price below 60¢ per gallon.

One might conclude from the above discussion that interference with the market process is all bad. This is not the case. There are times when inequities in the market distribution of scarce commodities—such as in the aforementioned case of food during wartime—can be lessened by price control and rationing, especially if such a program has widespread support among producers and consumers. But poorly enforced half-way measures such as the Phase 4 control program during the early 1970s are likely to be more disruptive than beneficial to the economy.

Figure 4.10 Diversion of Supply to an Uncontrolled Market

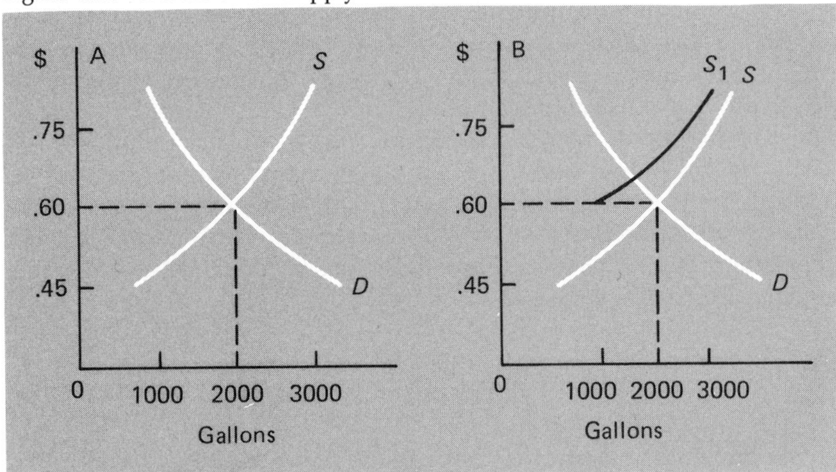

Summary

The law of supply and demand, frequently invoked as an explanation for the prevailing market price, considers only the consumers' offers to buy different amounts of product or service at various prices and the producers' offers to sell different amounts of products or services at different prices. In other words, the demand and supply curves and the schedules upon which they are based express purely price-quantity relationships. Normally, the demand price-quantity relationship is inverse, with purchases decreasing as price increases, and the supply price-quantity relationship is positive, with offers to sell increasing as the price increases.

When the demand and supply relationship is expressed in curve form, the demand curve slopes downward and the supply curve slopes upward. When one curve is superimposed on the other, on axes of price and quantity, the intersection establishes a single price. This price is an equilibrium price since there is no impetus for change as long as the conditions represented by the downslanting demand curve and the upslanting supply curve are in effect. If a price other than that established by the intersection of the two curves is introduced into the market—say, one lower than the intersection price—then the amount demanded at the lower price will exceed the amount supplied and market forces will drive the price back to the previous equilibrium point.

The demand curve normally slants downward, which indicates that consumers' willingness to purchase a good or service decreases as they acquire more. This decreased willingness to buy is usually explained by the *principle of diminishing marginal utility.* Utility is the capacity of a good or service to provide satisfactions for an individual. Utility is not an unvarying, measurable, or comparable aspect of goods and services, however; rather it indicates the consumer's attribution to the purchase. This attribution varies from one consumer to another; it also varies for the same consumer in acquiring different amounts of goods and services. In balancing the pattern of purchases so that satisfactions or utility are greatest, the consumer adjusts the purchases so that the

$$\frac{\text{Marginal Utility of } X}{\text{Price of } X} = \frac{\text{Marginal Utility of } Y}{\text{Price of } Y} = \ldots \frac{\text{Marginal Utility of } N}{\text{Price of } N}$$

When the marginal utility from a dollar spent on different purchases is the same, the consumer has attained the highest satisfaction level that can be obtained from a given budget.

Changes in the amount of money a consumer has to spend and changes in the availability of other products affect a consumer's marginal utility. These factors cause shifts in consumer behavior. Demand curves change, represented by movement to the left or right by the whole curve, as a result of changes in the income of the consumer, changes in the price of substitute products, changes in the quality of the product demanded and that of substitutes, and changes in consumers' attribution of the worth of the purchase. Supply curves shift as a result of higher or lower costs of production. Shifts or changes in demand and supply should be distinguished from a "change in the amount" demanded or supplied. A change in demand or supply is represented by a shift in the total curve, while a "change in the amount" demanded or supplied involves movement along the existing demand or supply curve.

Key terms and concepts

Demand willingness plus ability to buy.

Change in demand or supply a shift in the whole schedule or curve.

Change in amount demanded or supplied a movement from one point to another on the same schedule or curve.

Utility satisfactions attributed by the consumer to a good or service.

Diminishing marginal utility the decrease in additional satisfactions obtained from consumption of successive units of a good or service.

Marginal utility the change in total utility resulting from additional consumption of the same good or service.

Short run a period of time sufficient for the producer to hire or lay off labor or increase or decrease materials purchased, but not to make extensive changes in production facilities such as redesigning machinery and equipment or modifying plant capacity.

Long run a period in which any desired change can be made in production arrangements.

Discussion and review questions

1. How does the law of supply and demand compare with a law of the physical sciences, such as Boyle's law or the law of gravity? What is the difference between a tendency and a law?

2. Why isn't the demand for air conditioning in the ghettos greater than in the middle-class suburbs?

3. A demand curve expresses only two variables—price and quantity. Why doesn't it also express other factors such as income or product quality?

4. Demand consists of things individuals will buy at different prices as well as things they do buy at a particular price. Does an increase in demand take place if a larger amount of a product is purchased when the price falls?

5. A downward-sloping demand curve is generally explained on the basis of the principle of diminishing marginal utility. What evidence can be cited that utility diminishes? How would consumer behavior be affected if utility did not diminish?

6. Can a product or service have utility without a price? Under what conditions is this possible?

7. In balancing purchases, the calculating consumer will equate the marginal utility of one item in relation to its price with similar ratios for other purchases. What happens when prices change? What happens when there is a change in the quality of one of the purchases?

8. Economists make much of the marginal or incremental approach to supply and demand analysis. What does this approach consist of and why is it thought to provide more meaningful analysis in some areas than other approaches?

9. Some kinds of purchases involve what is called the *joint demand* of commodities that are used together. What happens to the demand for one jointly-demanded product when the price of its counterpart increases? What happens when one decreases in price? Can joint demand lead to highly inelastic demand for one of the jointly-demanded products?

10. A wheat farmer may never have seen a horizontal demand curve, but personal market experience would confirm this typical blackboard illustration. Does a wheat farmer's political activity also conform to the horizontal demand curve?

11. Why does the supply curve slope upward? Why does supply not generate a horizontal slope?

12. If price doesn't ration consumer demand, how can such rationing be achieved? What are the advantages and disadvantages of nonprice rationing?

Appendix: the indifference curve approach to demand theory

Whether consumer choice is explained by the use of utility, satisfactions, or some other concept, the question of how the reactions of the consumer are to be measured has troubled economists since before the turn of the twentieth century. Textbooks describe consumer decisions as choices or tradeoffs among different goods and services having varying utilities, pointing out that the utility consumers attribute to some things is greater than that of others.

The question is: How can the utility attributed by the consumer to different purchases be distinguished?

Cardinal and ordinal measurement of utility

Utility cannot be used to gauge consumers' reactions to certain products in the same way that feet are used to record distance or a pound to measure weight. The foot and the pound are invariant standards, making *cardinal* measurement possible. With such standards, distance and weight can be established precisely and expressed in terms of how much more or less one measurement is than another. Sometimes textbooks give the impression that cardinal measurement of utility is possible by using formulations such as *utils* and showing the marginal utility of successive units of consumption as areas blocked off under the demand curve.

The inference that a *util* is the physical measure of utility is clearly erroneous. Utility—consumer satisfactions—can be compared among consumers only in an imprecise way. But it is possible for the consumer to rank his or her own reactions to different purchase options in order—first, second, third, and so on. That is, an individual can measure utility *ordinally*. The consumer can tell whether some things bring more satisfaction than others and may be able to tell roughly by how much more, but not by reference to a standard that extends the comparison to other consumers' reactions.

To escape the cardinal measurements implied in traditional demand theory, the indifference curve approach conceives consumer behavior in a different way. In allocating limited income, the consumer is faced by a wide range of options for spending money—choices among different combinations of purchases. Table 4.3 is an indifference schedule of tradeoffs between vacation days in the mountains and at the seashore, an example of the options faced by consumers in deciding how to spend income.

In the hypothetical schedule in Table 4.3, the consumer is equally satisfied with eight days in the mountains and two days at the seashore or with two days at the seashore and eight days in the mountains, as well as various in-between combinations. In other words, the consumer is *indifferent* to the holiday combinations listed in Table 4.3 since each represents equivalent satisfaction. When this schedule is expressed as a curve in Figure 4.11, any point on the curve is the satisfaction equivalent of any other point.

Table 4.3: Holiday indifference schedule

Mountains	Seashore
8 days	2 days
6	2½
4	4
2½	6
2	8

Common characteristics of indifference curves

Indifference curves are convex to the origin

The indifference curve in Figure 4.11 is a linear expression of the data of Table 4.3. Most indifference curves have certain features in common. As shown in Figure 4.11, they are bowed, a condition which is more formally described as being "convex to the origin." The origin of the diagram is the zero point at the intersection of the horizontal and vertical axes. The bow or convexity will be deep or shallow depending on whether the indifference curve options are close substitutes. For example, if mountain and seashore holidays are perfect substitutes, the indifference curve will be a straight line, rather than a bowed line. The bow in Figure 4.11 indicates that mountain and seashore vacations are not perfect substitutes and, moreover, the relative desirability of either declines as its quantity exceeds that of the other in the indifference combination. Conversely, the desirabil-

Figure 4.11 Holiday Indifference Curve

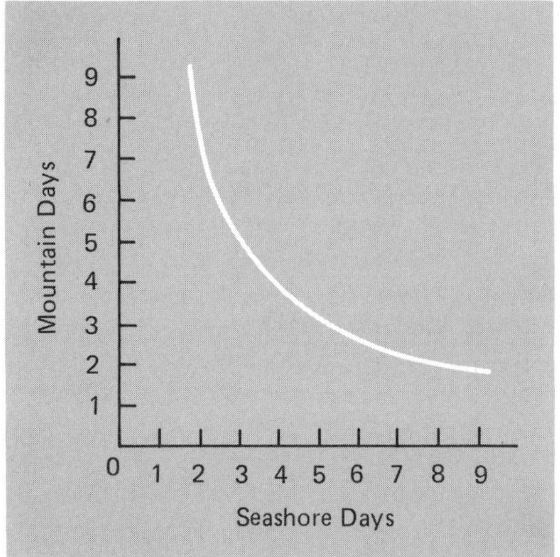

ity of each increases as the amount is diminished in the combination. This is shown in Figure 4.12 along with the application of the concept of the marginal rate of substitution.

The marginal rate of substitution

The marginal rate of substitution (MRS) expresses the consumer's evaluation of the worth of one of the purchase options—either seashore days or mountain days—in terms of the other. In other words, the MRS measures what the consumer is willing to give up of one of the indifferent components to obtain more of the other. It is a rate of tradeoff.

In Figure 4.12, if we start at eight mountain days and two seashore days and move down the indifference curve to five mountain days and three seashore days, it is apparent that three mountain days have been sacrificed to obtain an additional day at the seashore. As the seashore-mountain allocation ratio comes closer to 4–to–4, however, only two mountain days are given up to obtain an additional day at the seashore. Since the indifference curve in Figure 4.12 is symmetrical, the MRS is reversed as seashore days exceed mountain days in the indifference combinations. More seashore days are sacrificed to obtain an additional day in the mountains—one mountain day for two seashore days when moving from 4–to–4 and three seashore days for one mountain day when moving from 8–to–2.

More than one indifference curve will be needed to show the full range of holiday options confronting the prospective vacationer. More combina-

Figure 4.12 The Marginal Rate of Substitution

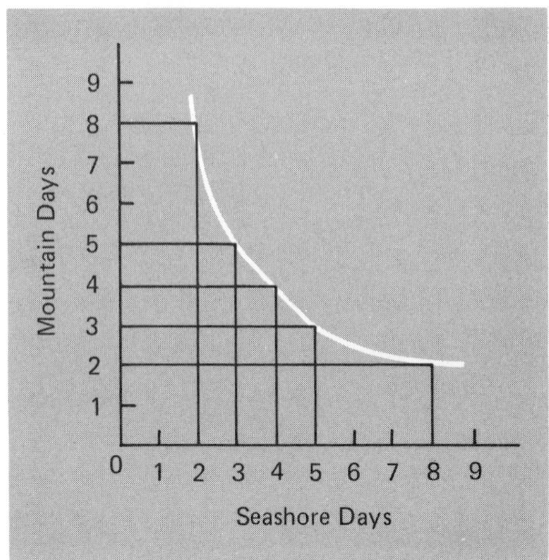

tions of vacation time are illustrated in Figure 4.13, by adding indifference Curves II and III to the original diagram. Indifference curves further from the origin, such as Curves II and III, represent higher levels of consumer satisfactions.

Figure 4.13 The Indifference Map

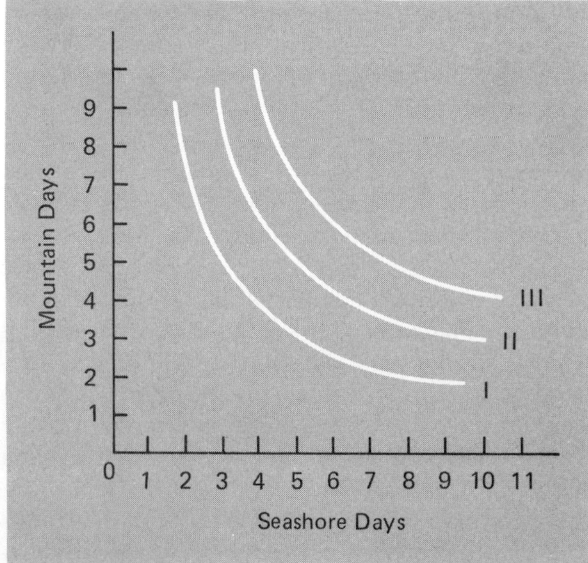

The case of Budiran's ass—choice between perfect substitutes?

Jean Buridan, a French philosopher, *circa* 1295–1356, has become associated with the case of the ass that starved to death in indecision between two equally succulent bales of hay. Actually, Buridan did not devise this illustration; it was suggested by one of Aristotle's examples and used by Buridan's critics in refuting Buridan's theory of will. What conclusion do philosophers draw from this case? Nicholas Rescher comments as follows:

[I]n case of strictly symmetrical preference (two essentially similar dates, two glasses of water, two bales of hay), the knowledge or information at our disposal constrains us to regard the objects of choice as equally desirable because each reason for valuing one applies, *mutato nomine*, to the other(s). So far as the factor of their value or desirability for us is concerned, our knowledge regarding each object is precisely the same. Problems of choice with symmetrical valuation can therefore be regarded as merely a species within the symmetrical knowledge genus, so that here too a random selection rather than any proper "choice" is the rationally justified procedure.[6]

Indifference curves do not cross

Any point on a higher indifference curve—II with respect to I and III with respect to I and II—increases consumer satisfaction, since the superior curve affords at least as much of one option and more of the other. When a nest of indifference curves is used to show a wider range of combinations than can be illustrated by a single curve, the graph is called an *indifference map*. The curves that make up this map cannot cross without contradicting the proposition that a superior indifference curve yields greater satisfactions throughout its full course than does a lower curve. Figure 4.14 illustrates the illogic of intersecting indifference curves.

In Figure 4.14, Points A and B lie on indifference Curve II, and Points A and C lie on indifference Curve I. Points A and B on Curve II indicate combinations that yield the same satisfactions. The same is true of Points A and C on Curve I. This leads to the conclusion that Point B is equal to Point C, since things equal to the same things are equal to each other. This is patently absurd, however, since the C combination consists of twice as much beach time—eight days compared with four days for B—while both

[6] Nicholas Rescher, "Jean Buridan," *The Encyclopedia of Philosophy*, Paul Edwards, ed. (New York: The Macmillan Company and The Free Press, 1967), Vol. 1, p. 428. Reprinted with permission.

Figure 4.14 Intersecting Indifference Curves—A Conceptual Error

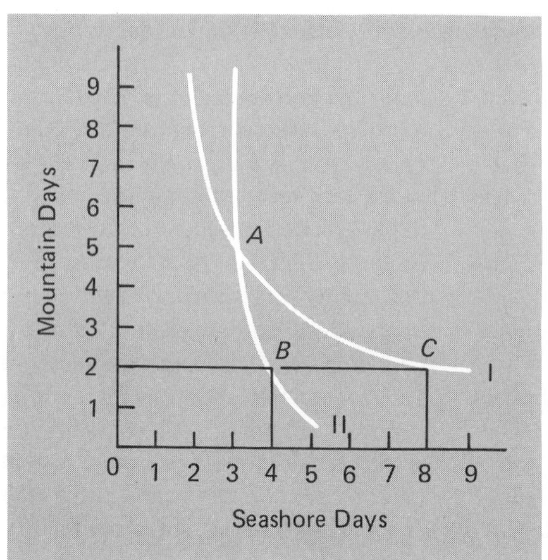

B and C afford equal mountain days. We can only conclude that the indifference curves in Figure 4.14 are misdrawn; the two curves should not cross but should fit together like nesting bowls.

So far we have elaborated the thesis that the consumer's welfare is increased by attaining a higher indifference combination. What determines how far the consumer can move up the indifference map? Mainly the prices of the various indifference combinations and the amount of money the consumer is willing to pay for them. This is shown by the *budget line*.

The budget line: what the consumer is willing to spend

The budget line is the straight line, MS, in Figure 4.15. This line shows how much vacation can be purchased if the consumer spends all of the budget of $250 on either option or on a vacation combination in between the two options. Assume a consumer who is attracted to a lower middle-income seaside resort and a spartan mountain retreat each offering ten days of vacation for $250. Ten days at either place does not maximize the consumer's satisfactions, however, as shown by the intersections of the budget line with Curve I at Points A and B and the line's tangency with Curve II at Point C. Point C represents the optimum adjustment, the combination that maximizes the consumer's welfare given the resort rates and the amount of money budgeted.

Figure 4.15 Maximizing Consumer Satisfactions

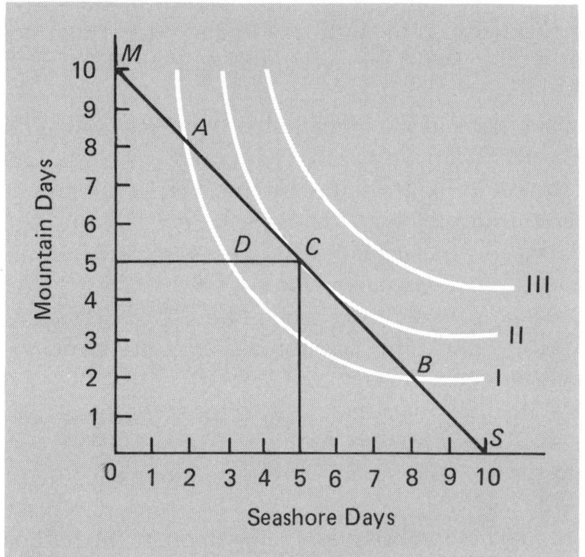

All vacation combinations that lie on or to the left of the budget line, including Points A, C, B, and D, are within the range of purchase by the consumer. All combinations to the right of the budget line, such as those of Curve III, cost too much. To reach Curve III, the consumer would have to spend more money than is allocated to vacations by the budget line in Figure 4.15. We can reinforce the point that C represents the best position for the consumer by noting that C is superior to any of the other combinations, A, D, or B. Points A, D, and B lie on Curve I and are of equal satisfactions. C has the same mountain days as D, five, but two more seashore days, making it a superior choice to D—and also to A and B, which are equivalent in satisfactions to D.

The marginal utilities from a day at the seashore and a day in the mountains are equal at C on indifference Curve II. This equilibrium can be related to consumption decisions not covered in Figure 4.15 by the formulation employed earlier in the chapter,

$$\frac{MU_m}{P_m} = \frac{MU_s}{P_s} = \ldots \frac{MU_n}{P_n}$$

in which m is mountain days, s seashore days, and n represents other consumption. Given market prices and the consumer's income and preferences, this balancing of marginal utilities brings the consumer the maximum benefit from consumption.

Changes in price and income

The position of the budget line on the indifference map depends upon the prices of the combination items and the amount of money allocated by the consumer for their purchase.

If the price of one of the items in the combination increases while the budget allocation remains unchanged, less of that item can be purchased at the higher price. This is shown in Figure 4.16A by the shift in the budget line from MS to MS′, which indicates that the fixed budget will buy less seashore vacation after its price increases. If seashore rates go down rather than up, the budget line will move farther out along the horizontal axis, which shows that more seashore vacation can be obtained from a given expenditure. Changing prices affect the consumer's welfare, generally through high prices that curtail consumption and low prices that increase consumption. In Figure 4.16A, an increase in seashore vacation rates decreases the consumer's satisfactions from Curve II to Curve I, decreasing seashore days from five to three while mountain days remain unchanged at five.

A change in income is also likely to change the position of the budget line. An increase in an individual's income makes possible larger expenditures for consumption, although there is no certainty of where the increase will be used. If more money is allocated to vacations, however, the budget line will be moved to a higher position on the indifference map. This is shown in Figure 4.16B where the budget line shifts from MS to M′S′,

Figure 4.16 Changes in Price and Budget

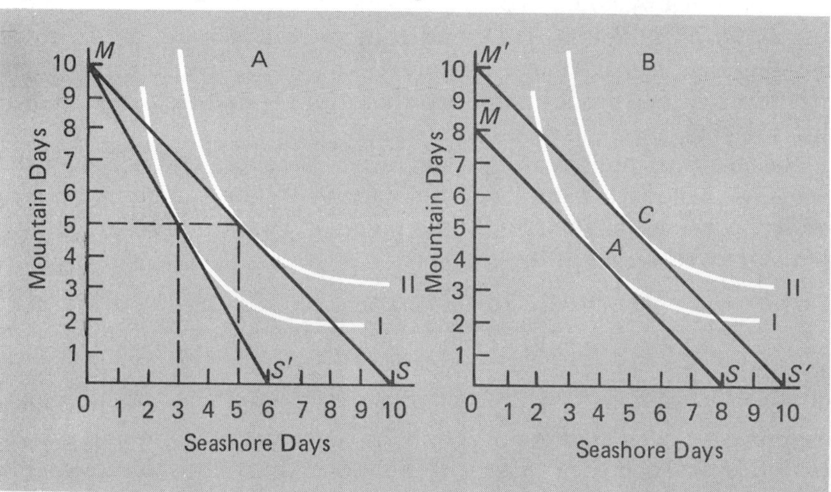

raising the consumer's welfare as indicated by the tangency of M'S' with Curve II at C.

So what can indifference curves do that demand curves can't?

Demand curves show the consumer's reaction to changes in the price of a particular good or service. The other goods and services that vie for the consumer's dollar must be conceived as represented by similar but separate demand curves elsewhere in the market economy. By contrast, the indifference curve approach is based on the presumption that choice involves comparison with other purchase options as well as with price. And the triviality of the choice combinations—seashore and mountain vacations, meat and potatoes, opera and hockey—should not divert attention from the significance of the principle.

In addition to bringing demand theory a step closer to reality, the indifference curve approach extends the range of propositions that can be analyzed graphically. Take the case of a cash welfare subsidy versus a subsidy-in-kind, a money payment to a low-income family rather than, say, low-cost public housing. Either subsidy is a benefit to those eligible, but the money grant has a more nearly neutral effect upon the recipient's pattern of consumption. Thus it represents a more desirable form of subsidy to the recipient.

In Figure 4.17, income is measured on the vertical axis and housing on the horizontal axis. The original budget line, BS (before subsidy), shows the amount of housing, OS units, that could be obtained if all the family

Figure 4.17 Subsidy in Cash and Kind

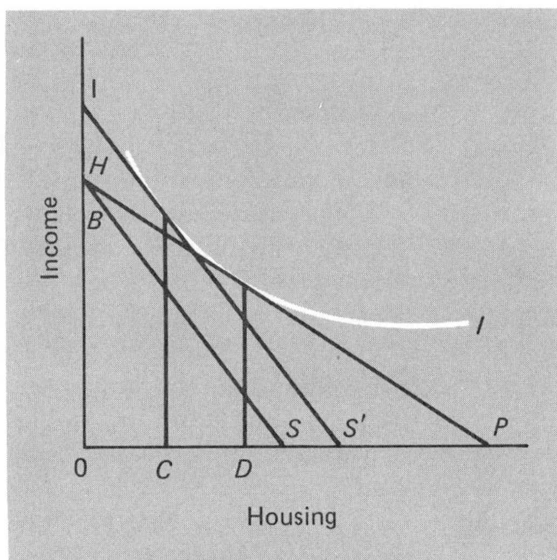

income were spent on housing. HP (housing project) shows the decrease in the price of housing that is brought about by the housing subsidy—eligibility for the low-cost housing project. The family rents OD units of housing at the subsidized price.

IS′ (income subsidy) shows the change in the family's budget line when the subsidy is given in cash rather than in kind. With the cash subsidy, the family rents OC units of housing, less than with the housing subsidy, which indicates that housing is forgone for other consumption with the greater freedom of choice of the cash subsidy.

Summary

Utility, the satisfactions attributed by the consumer to purchases, cannot be gauged by an absolute standard or by comparing one individual's to another's. Utility can be ranked in terms of an individual's reactions to different purchases. The ranking, called *ordinal* measurement, requires only a determination of whether one purchase yields more or less satisfaction than another, not how much more or how much less. The indifference-curve approach to consumer behavior relies upon the ordinal or ranking method in constructing sets of purchase combinations that have equal satisfactions for the consumer. An indifference curve describes these combinations—for example, ten pairs of shoes and five shirts, seven pairs of shoes and seven shirts, five pairs of shoes and ten shirts—each combination affording the consumer equivalent satisfactions so the consumer may be said to be indifferent among them.

Indifference curves may also be thought of as tradeoffs between different purchase options: food and clothing, opera performances and hockey games, vacations in the mountains and vacations at the seashore, and the like. Normally, as a combination becomes more heavily weighted with one of the items—say, shoes in the shoes-shirts tradeoff—additional shoes are less desired than additional shirts; the reverse is true when shirts are more abundant in the combinations. This results in indifference curves that are convex to the origin; that is, they look like an archer's bow with the string side away from the zero intersection of the axes. The indifference curve is sharply bowed or more nearly flat depending upon the *marginal rate of substitution*, which is the consumer's evaluation of the worth of one of the purchase options in terms of the other.

To the consumer, a higher indifference curve—one that combines larger amounts of both items—yields greater utility or satisfactions. The maximum consumer welfare is attained at the point at which the budget line touches the highest indifference curve. The *budget line* shows how much of each of the combination items can be purchased when all of the budget is spent on either of the items and various combinations of the two items. It is a straight line extending from one axis to the other.

An increase in the budget allotment raises the budget line parallel to the previous line, indicating that larger amounts of the combination items may be purchased. A decrease in the budget moves the line downward. When the price of one item changes relative to that of the other item in the combination, the budget line shifts further from the zero point when the price of the item falls and comes closer to zero as the price increases. The budget line moves toward the zero point when the price of one of the items rises because the fixed budget outlay will buy less at the higher price; when the price falls for one of the items in the combination, the budget line moves further from the zero intersection because a given outlay will buy more at the lower price.

Key terms and concepts

Cardinal measurement the determination of quantity, such as weight or length, by reference to an absolute standard, such as a pound or a foot.

Ordinal measurement the determination of the order or rank of events or reactions, such as an individual's satisfaction from different purchases. Events that can be measured cardinally, such as a 100-yard dash, can also be measured ordinally.

Indifference curve the linear expression of sets of consumption combination of two goods or services that are equivalent in satisfactions.

Indifference map a collection of indifference curves.

Budget line a linear expression of the purchase options with a fixed money outlay and given prices.

Marginal rate of substitution what the consumer is willing to give up of one of the indifferent combinations to obtain another unit of the other.

Discussion and review questions

1. How does the measurement of utility differ from the measurement of distance or weight? What is the significance of this for demand theory?

2. How do indifference curves avoid the problem of the measurability of utility? In doing so, do they restrict or extend the range of economic analysis?

3. The marginal rate of substitution is the tradeoff rate between two purchases. What will cause this tradeoff rate to change?

4. How do symmetrical preferences affect Buridan's ass?

5. What can indifference curves do that demand curves can't?

5 Demand and supply II: the dimensions of price

*Firewood has been selling, of late in New York City, for one dollar a stick. Piles of it. Right off the sidewalk. Split from small logs of oak or ash or maple. Split. Split again. Four pieces, four dollars. The bulk rate is around a hundred dollars a cord in the suburbs and a hundred and fifty dollars a cord in the city. From such prices, understandably, the less fortunate have turned aside. The Harvard Club is burning artificial logs made of wax and compressed sawdust.**

More than a change in the lifestyle of the Harvard Club resulted from the 1974 energy crisis in the United States. Sharp increases in fuel prices caused by the Middle East oil producers' embargo swept through households and industry, lowering thermostats and speed limits; depleting dealers' stocks of small cars and building up inventories of larger models; relaxing air pollution standards and returning coal to favor, encouraging record oil shale lease bids and a federal announcement of a goal of energy self-sufficiency by 1985.

These extraordinary developments were not accompanied by an orderly unfolding of the short-run forces of demand and supply. During the 1973–1974 winter, reaction to higher prices for heating oil was limited largely to turning down the thermostat, rather than shifting to other fuels. Changes to other fuel sources—such as natural gas or coal—require time for furnace modifications, and, in any case, supplies of alternative fuels were far from abundant. In consequence, the intersection of near perpendicular supply and demand curves, such as Curves D_1 and S_1 in Figure 5.1, took place at a much higher price during the embargo. Indeed, the supply curve during this period was shifted somewhat to the left by the reduction in foreign crude oil exports to the United States. Over time, the behavior of producers and consumers came closer to conforming to the demand and supply reactions described by the traditional short-run Curves D and S in

* John McPhee, *Pieces of the Frame* (New York: Farrar, Straus & Giroux, Inc., 1975), p. 193.

Figure 5.1 Middle East Oil Embargo

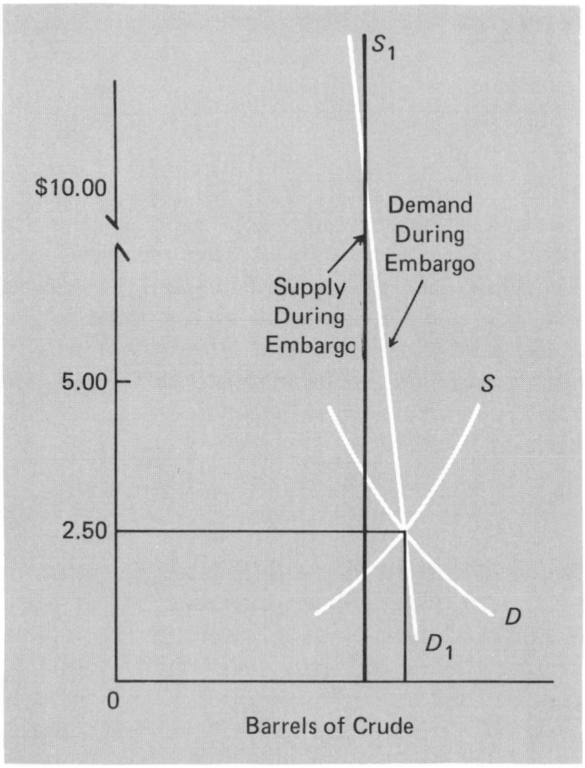

Figure 5.1, but in the meantime the price of crude oil rose spectacularly by approximately 400 percent.

The time periods covered by Figure 5.1 require some explanation. The pre-embargo demand and supply situation for crude oil is shown by the conventional Curves D and S, which intersect to establish price at $2.50 per barrel. The embargo changed all this, moderately cutting back exports from the Middle East to the United States but drastically increasing price. From October 1973 to March 1974, domestic oil producers and non-Middle East foreign sources of supply were unable to make up the deficiency. This situation is indicated by the supply Curve S_1. Although the United States supplies the larger part of its own petroleum needs, the reduction in the foreign supply had a dramatic effect on price. The embargo pushed the supply curve to S_1—which shows less oil to be available at a much higher price—and during the period of the embargo there was no significant addition to supply from other sources.

The embargo was not leak-proof, however, and some oil from the

Middle East did reach the United States via Europe, but this had little effect upon the price. Oil consumption in home and industry was reduced during the embargo, mainly at the sacrifice of home comfort and industrial output, but without as much shift to other fuels as might have been expected during the short run, represented by the less steeply inclined curve D. The embargo period was of less duration than the short run and was introduced at the start of the heating season in October. The timing of the embargo further reduced the consumer's ability to respond to higher oil prices by turning to substitute fuels.

The embargo shifted demand to Curve D_1 raising the price of crude oil to $10.00 per barrel.[1] During the embargo, demand and supply were both highly unresponsive to price changes. The consequences of this situation are apparent in Figure 5.1, but what is not so apparent is that the embargo created a most unusual environment for price determination. The purpose of this chapter is to examine closely the demand and supply characteristics in commonplace cases as well as in unusual situations such as the 1974 Arab oil embargo.

The meaning and measurement of price elasticity

The concept of the elasticity of demand and supply provides a precise measurement of the reaction of consumers and producers to price change. Indeed, in economics, the term *elasticity* is used in a very specific way and it is not enough to express the concept in general terms, as in the preceding discussion. Such general observations help to explain the nature of elasticity, but they do not establish the precise meaning of the concept and the range of its application.

Starting with elasticity of demand, three categories of price elasticity can be distinguished: elastic, unitary, and inelastic demand.[2]

Elastic demand occurs when a price change brings about a *greater than proportional* change in purchases; for example, when a 10 percent decrease in price causes a 20 percent increase in sales. (Elastic demand might just as well have been illustrated by an increase in price and a decrease in sales.)

Unitary demand involves a *proportional* change in purchases resulting from a given price change; for example, when a 10 percent increase in price causes a 10 percent decrease in purchases.

[1] The price of imported crude oil actually rose by somewhat more than 400 percent to over $10.00 a barrel during the embargo. Most of domestic crude oil production was controlled at $5.25 per barrel during this period and there was no appreciable movement of low-price crude to the higher price market because of the cutback in supply. Figure 5.1 ignores the split in the supply side but does not seriously misrepresent the market forces involved.

[2] Note that the noun *elasticity* covers all the subcategories, *elastic, unitary,* and *inelastic*. It is *not* synonymous with the adjectival form, *elastic* demand.

Inelastic demand occurs when a price change brings about a *less than proportional* change in purchases; for example, when a 20 percent increase in price causes a 10 percent decrease in sales.

Proportional change, which can be contrasted with *absolute* change, has been emphasized above, and is best explained by reference to the demand curve in Figure 5.2. The straight-line demand curve in Figure 5.2 is drawn so that price and quantity vary in equal absolute units—purchases fall or rise by amounts equal to the opposing change in prices. In other words, the *absolute* change in demand is the same for the whole curve and, as a consequence, the slope of the curve is unchanged from $10 to $1. But in spite of this absolute relationship, there is a different proportional relationship for each price-quantity intersection on the demand curve.

As price falls from $10 to $9, for example, purchases increase from one unit to two. The absolute change—one for one—is the same for this segment of the demand curve, but the proportional change in price is only 10 percent in contrast with a 100 percent change in quantity. Clearly, according to the previously stated definition of elastic demand, the relative change in purchases—100 percent—greatly exceeds the change in price—10 percent—so demand is highly elastic. If we move to a lower portion of the curve, say for the price-quantity intersects at $3 and $2, the propor-

Figure 5.2 Elasticity of Demand

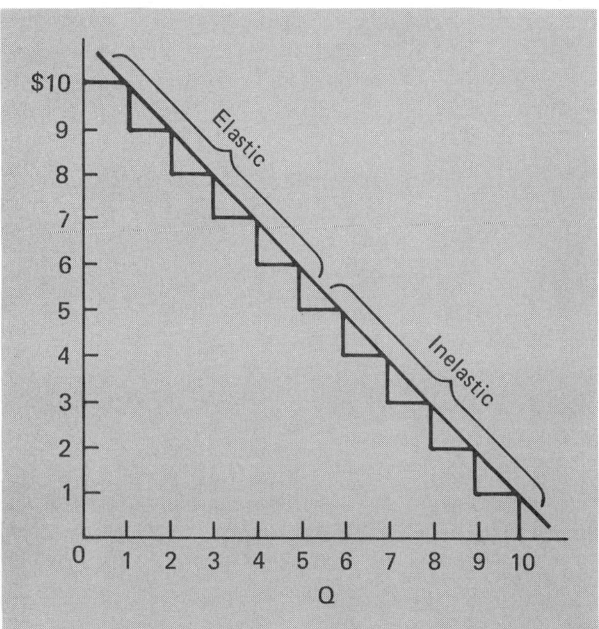

tional change in price is 33 percent as price falls in contrast with a lesser increase in purchases of about 11 percent from 8 to 9. As a result, this part of the curve is inelastic. Finally, at the midpoint, the curve in Figure 5.2 is unitary; the segment above is elastic and that below is inelastic.

There should be no doubt about the conclusions to be drawn from the above case. (1) Absolute change in the price-quantity relationship alone tells little about the nature of a curve's elasticity. (2) The slope of a demand curve is an unsatisfactory indicator of elasticity except in the atypical cases of perfectly elastic and inelastic demand. The second conclusion deserves special emphasis because at first glance it seems entirely logical to associate elastic demand with a relatively flat curve and inelastic demand with a more steeply inclined curve. Save for the exceptions noted above, however, virtually all demand curves have elastic and inelastic portions, although these segments need not be distributed equally as in Figure 5.2.

Elasticity as a coefficient

If we establish the price-quantity relationship of unitary demand as being equal to 1 because a given percentage change in price produces an equivalent percentage change in purchases, elastic demand may be expressed as being greater than 1 and inelastic demand as less than 1. To express elasticity as a coefficient makes it possible to compare the consumers' reactions to price changes for different commodities.

To compute elasticity coefficients, the percentage change in quantity is divided by the percentage change in price.[3]

$$\text{Elasticity of Demand} = \frac{\text{Relative (\%) Change in Quantity}}{\text{Relative (\%) Change in Price}}$$

If elasticity of demand is > 1, then demand is elastic.

If elasticity of demand is $= 1$, then demand is unitary.

If elasticity of demand is < 1, then demand is inelastic.

Although the procedure and data requirements for deriving elasticity coefficients are generally uncomplicated, to obtain the information necessary to measure consumers' reactions to price *alone* is another matter. The measurement is difficult because consumer purchases are influenced by many factors other than price—income change, new products, modification in product quality, price changes in other economic output, alterations in lifestyle, and so forth—while a demand curve expresses only the con-

[3] The coefficient of elasticity is usually expressed as a positive figure even though its sign is negative. Our interest is in the absolute value of the coefficient, that is, how much it is more or less than 1.

sumers' reactions to price change. In a given curve, other factors are assumed to remain unchanged. If this is not the case, the demand curve must be reconstructed. An increase in consumer income, for example, may shift the whole demand curve to the right, resulting in a new set of price-quantity relationships.

Since elasticity of demand measures a segment of the demand curve, it is subject to the same limitations as the demand curve. Data used to derive coefficients must be unaffected by income changes, by price changes in substitute products, and the like, and unaffected data are hard to obtain from market transactions covering an extended period of time. The longer the time covered by the price-quantity observations, the greater the influence that nonprice factors exert upon consumer purchases. As a result, the reliability of elasticity coefficients derived from statistical models may be quite short lived. In recognition of this, we should view the coefficients in Table 5.1 as approximations rather than as precise measures.

The estimates of elasticity coefficients in Table 5.1 deserve more than a passing glance, but before we look at them more carefully, let us consider briefly a lazy way to measure elasticity of demand. This is called the *total revenue* approach.

Total revenue and elasticity of demand

Total revenue equals price times quantity. When price changes and total revenue changes in the same direction—increasing as price goes up or decreasing as price goes down—that portion of the demand curve spanning the price movement is inelastic. If the opposite occurs—if total revenue increases when price falls or decreases when price rises—the demand for that segment of the curve is elastic.

The total revenue method of measuring elasticity can be checked against Figure 5.2, since it has already been established that the upper reach of that curve is elastic and the lower reach inelastic. We saw in Figure 5.2 that lowering price from $10 to $9 caused total revenue to rise from $10 to $18. Similarly, lowering price from $8 to $7, increased total revenue from $24 to $28. Past the midpoint of the curve, however, the price-to-total-revenue relationship is reversed. As price dropped from $3 to $2, total revenue decreased from $24 to $18, indicating that this area of the curve is inelastic. Finally, it follows that if price changes without affecting total revenue—if price falls from $5 to $4 and sales increase from 4 to 5, for example—demand for that segment of the curve is unitary.

Sales and elasticity

The total revenue approach is more than a lazy way to compute elasticity. It answers the important question: What happens to sales reve-

Table 5.1: Selected estimates of price elasticity of demand

Category	Elasticity of Demand	
Food		
Cabbage	0.4	
Potatoes	0.3	
Peas, fresh	2.8	
Peas, canned	1.6	
Tomatoes, fresh	4.6	
Tomatoes, canned	2.5	
Nondurable Goods	*Short-run*	*Long-run*
Shoes	0.9	
Stationery	0.5	
Newspapers and magazines	0.4	
Tires and related	0.8	1.2
Services		
Auto repair and related	1.4	0.4
Radio and television repair	0.5	3.8
Entertainment and Travel		
Motion pictures	0.87	3.7
Legitimate theater and opera	0.2	0.31
Foreign travel by U.S. residents	0.1	1.8
Public Transportation		
Taxicabs	0.6	
Intercity bus	0.2	2.2
Local public transportation	0.6	1.2
Utility Services		
Electricity	0.1	1.8
Fuel and ice	0.7	
Telephone	0.25	
Water	0.2	0.1
Miscellaneous		
Jewelry and watches	0.4	0.6

Source: For the food category, D. M. Shuffett, *The Demand and Price Structure for Selected Vegetables* (Washington, D.C.: U.S. Department of Agriculture, 1954. Technical Bulletin No. 1105). For all other categories, H. S. Houthakker and L. D. Taylor, *Consumer Demand in the United States: Analyses and Projections* (Cambridge, Mass.: Harvard University Press, 1970). Fractions have been rounded.

nue when prices change? As shown in Figure 5.3, if demand is elastic, sales revenue increases as price is lowered and decreases as price rises. With inelastic demand, the opposite occurs; sales revenue rises when price increases and falls when price decreases. In the demand curves illustrated in Figure 5.3, the panels hatched with minus signs (the smaller rectangle in Figure 5.3A and the larger rectangle in Figure 5.3B) show the respective losses in revenue caused by lowering price in the two areas. The panels hatched with plus signs (the larger rectangle in Figure 5.3A and the smaller rectangle in Figure 5.3B) show the increase in revenue from lowering price. The two cases demonstrate that when demand is elastic, a price reduction results in a gain in total revenue; when demand is inelastic, a similar price reduction causes a loss in total revenue.

The above example does not mean, however, that the seller can improve his or her economic position by following the simple maxim of raising prices when demand is inelastic and lowering them when it is elastic. The seller must also take into account what happens to cost when output and sales vary. Henry Ford's success in building a large and profitable industrial firm was based in part upon the elastic demand for the automobile, but innovative, low-cost production techniques made it possible for Ford to exploit the mass market for cars. Needless to say, this happy combination of increased sales and lower cost is not inevitable. We will take up the subject of cost of production in Chapter 6, but in the meantime, we have yet to answer the question of why the demand for some things is more responsive to price than the demand for others.

Figure 5.3 Total Revenue and Elasticity of Demand

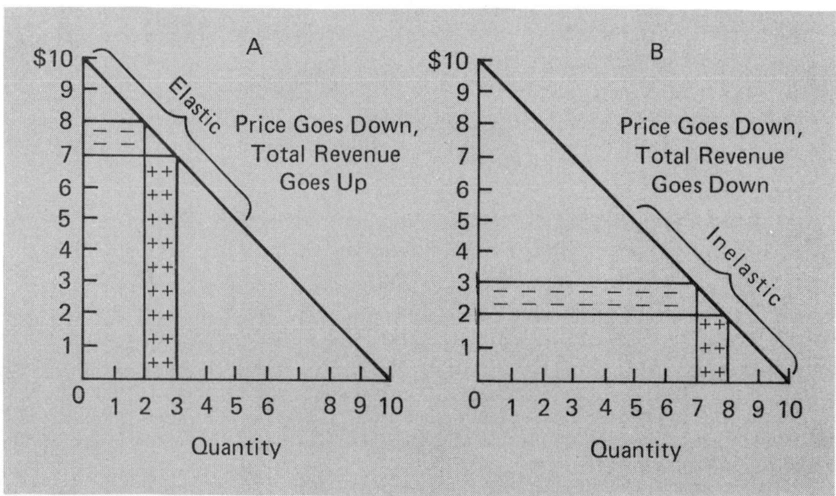

The high price of sugar? It's all a matter of supply and demand and import quotas and bad weather and poor forecasting

Early . . . [in 1974,] a Congressional committee reported euphorically, "Consumers have been secure in the knowledge that sugar will always be available on grocery shelves and that its cost will be a very small part of the family budget." . . . [In November, 1974,] an official of the U.S. Cane Sugar Refiners' Assn. drew a sharp contrast: "The supply situation is so tight that if a guy in Reston, Va., spills a 5-lb. bag, it has a bullish effect on the market." . . . What happened?

The basic reason . . . is a classic situation of commodity scarcity. The delicate balance between sugar production and sugar consumption was originally upset in 1970–72, when consumption for the first time outstripped production. Since then, however, consumption has consistently run ahead of a rising production rate and world stocks are now at a historic low.

For U.S. consumers, the squeeze has been made worse by the expiration of the Sugar Act in December, 1974. This law . . . guaranteed a supply of sugar, occasionally at prices below the world market even when sugar was short. That was because quota nations saw the U.S. as a sure market in overproduction times. Without the quota system, and its assurance of supplies, the U.S. is now compelled to compete in the world sugar market for more than 50% of its needs. In this, the last year under the act, Agriculture Secretary Earl Butz overestimated U.S. production and consumption. Bad weather and a switch to more lucrative crops cut production by 2.1 million tons. . . . The boom in the world price was sparked partly by Butz's January estimate of U.S. needs at 12.5-million tons, up from 11.7-tons projected late last year. That alone caused a 50% rise in world price.[4]

The causes of elasticity

In describing price elasticity, we have emphasized the extremes of elastic and inelastic demand. Actually, most demand curves blend gradually from elastic to inelastic and the part of the curve relevant to the determination of price usually excludes the upper and lower ranges, the extremes of both elastic and inelastic demand. And, except in the rare case of perfect inelasticity, the consumer is never completely insensitive to price. Price plays a more important role in some purchases than in others, and it is seldom unimportant. Even though the following discussion of the causes of elasticity also makes use of sharp contrasts, one should not assume that all consumption is a choice among extremes.

[4] "Why Sugar Prices are Zooming," *Business Week,* November 16, 1974, p. 113.

Substitutes and elasticity

If a single factor were chosen to explain why the demand for some goods and services is more sensitive to price than for others, that would certainly be the *availability of substitutes*. Take the case of the demand for home heating oil during the embargo by the Arab states. Clearly there are substitutes for fuel oil, such as coal, wood, and natural gas. But during the limited period of the embargo, ready change to other fuels was not possible. Consumers increased home insulation, closed off rooms, adjusted furnaces to operate more efficiently, and reduced thermostat settings in reaction to the rise in the price of fuel oil, but few substitute fuels were brought into use during the winter season following the rise in the world price of petroleum.

There is a substitute for most things. There are substitutes for products that are quite similar, brands of cigarettes and various headache remedies, and for things that are quite different, vacations in Europe, power boats, and second homes. Demand for these things is most likely to be elastic. But for things that have no acceptable substitute—insulin for the diabetic, eyeglasses for the myopic, and the automobile for the Electrolux sales representative—demand is inelastic. Generally an item for which there is no acceptable substitute is called a necessity, but linking the concept of elasticity to necessities involves certain pitfalls. Some things at first glance appear to be necessities—for example, food—but the demand for pork chops or veal chops is not inelastic. Food is a necessity, of course, but pork chops are not. Most foods are substitutes and those that compete for a part of the consumer's budget are generally elastic: butter and margarine, meat and fish and poultry, various cereal breakfast preparations, and fresh, frozen, and canned goods. Turn back to Table 5.1 for evidence to support this assertion.

The food category in Table 5.1 covers a wide range of estimates, from a highly elastic 4.6 coefficient for fresh tomatoes to an inelasticity coefficient of 0.3 for potatoes. None of the food items listed is a "necessity," but potatoes are probably the best candidate for this category. Potatoes are a low-cost food, an important item in the food budget of low-income consumers. Even if the potato price rises, they still are one of the better food buys.

Expenditure impact and elasticity

Some consumer items don't cost enough to induce a change in purchase habits when prices rise or fall. Cabbage and potatoes certainly fit this category for the middle- and upper-income groups. Even for the lower-income groups, potatoes and cabbage provide one of the cheapest ways to stock the family larder, despite increasing prices. Their elasticity coefficients are low—relatively inelastic—0.3 for potatoes and 0.4 for cabbage, according to the study reported in Table 5.1.

Habitual purchases that involve small outlays, such as the purchase of a daily newspaper or a cup of coffee, are also generally insensitive to price. If the price of a newspaper falls, there is little point in buying more than one. If the price rises, say from 5¢ to 10¢ or from 10¢ to 15¢, the impact of the additional 5¢ on most budgets is insignificant even though the percentage increase is huge. Only when the price of a daily paper rises to the point where the weekly or monthly outlay becomes significant, say when the price per copy reaches 35¢, will there be an incentive for most consumers to reorganize their buying practices, possibly encouraging joint newspaper purchase or increased reliance upon other media for news. In Table 5.1, the 0.4 elasticity estimate for newspapers and magazines largely reflects this insensitivity to price, especially since the demand for magazines is probably less inelastic than the demand for newspapers, and thus raises the combined elasticity coefficient.

The budgetary impact of purchases is not limited to such trivial cases, however. If it were, there would be little justification for more than passing mention of such instances. In some cases, expenditures may be small only by comparison with the aggregate outlay for the finished product, an automobile or a house, for example. The construction industry draws on a myriad of skills and materials—window locks, double-pane glass, masons, painters, ceramic tile, plumbers, and so on—the cost of any one of which represents only a fraction of the total expenditure for the final product. The result is that demand may be inelastic for the ingredient inputs, but not necessarily for the whole.

Increasing the price for window locks or the wages of plumbers, while other input prices remain unchanged, will not cause much reduction in the use of window locks or plumbers; nor will a decrease in the price of window locks or the wages of plumbers result in substantially larger total outlays for building construction. Elasticity of demand is the single most important factor in determining the price practices of the construction materials industry and the wage policies of the building trades. The bargaining leverage of building trade unions is far from unlimited, however, since contractors certainly recognize that a favorable contract negotiated by the plumbers will lead to similar demands by other building trade unions.

Time and elasticity

The effect of price change is not always immediately apparent. Supplies have to be used up before they are replenished; there is a time lag in converting some products to new uses, such as conversion of oil-using furnaces to natural gas—and sometimes related activities have to be rearranged before the consumer can respond to a price change, such as an off-season rate for airline travel. When the consumer has time to reorganize this pattern of consumption, however, price becomes a more important consideration and demand may move from inelastic to elastic. This is the case of the demand for motion pictures, which Table 5.1 shows to be moderately inelastic in the short run, having a coefficient of 0.87, but in the long run demand becomes highly elastic, with a coefficient of 3.7. From these figures we can deduce that, over time, substitute entertainments, including abstinence from movie going, become alternatives to movies.

In Table 5.1, we can see a shift from inelastic short-run demand to elastic long-run demand in tire sales, radio and television repair, motion picture entertainment, foreign travel, the use of buses and public transportation, and the purchase of electricity. And among the elasticity estimates of Table 5.1, two cases are noteworthy in their unresponsiveness to the time factor—auto repair, which remains inelastic at 0.4 in the long run as well as the short run, and the demand for water, which becomes more inelastic in the long run. The insensitivity of auto repairs to price is self-evident: Substitutes for the auto do not become more attractive over time. Moreover, the purchase price of the auto is usually large compared with the cost of most repairs, so that to delay repair is to forgo the use of an expensive investment without escaping the ultimate need for making the repair. Under these conditions, the distinction between the short and long run is unimportant in decision making.

The bizarre case of the long-run price inelasticity for water is perplexing. It is self-evident that the demand for water can hardly be other than inelastic, largely because of its small outlay in purchase relative to other household and industry purchases. Compared with other expenditures, water purchases have little impact upon the household budget. But this explains why the demand for water can be expected to be inelastic in *both* the short and long run, not why the demand for water is more inelastic in the long run. Without further attempts to probe this minor mystery, it may be well to turn to the other side of the diagram: supply.

Elasticity of supply

In most respects, the concept of elasticity of supply is a replay of elasticity of demand. The supply coefficient is derived in the same way and, consequently, supply is elastic or inelastic depending on how readily output responds to price. There are differences between demand and supply curves, of course. Graphically, supply curves are the reverse of demand curves: Supply is positively correlated with price, increasing with higher price, decreasing when price falls, whereas demand is inversely related to price.

The significance of the positive price-quantity relationship to the elasticity of supply is considered below, but we will put off our basic explanation of the shape of the supply curve until Chapter 6, where the short-run cost function is examined in detail. In the meantime, we will cover some familiar ground in considering elasticity of supply.

To compute elasticity for supply, we use the same procedure as for elasticity of demand.

$$\text{Elasticity of Supply} = \frac{\text{Relative (\%) Change in Quantity}}{\text{Relative (\%) Change in Price}}$$

And, identical with demand elasticity, the elasticity of supply coefficient is related to 1 in expressing the response to price.

If elasticity of supply is > 1, supply is elastic.

If elasticity of supply is $= 1$, supply is unitary.

If elasticity of supply is < 1, supply is inelastic.

The elasticity of supply coefficient measures the same properties as does the demand coefficient, but the elastic and inelastic properties of supply curves are more easily identified than their demand counterparts. In neither case is it possible to be certain that a curve is elastic or inelastic by its slope alone. But, if the supply curve has straight segments that can be projected to the price or quantity axis, as Curves S_1 and S_2 in Figure 5.4, a glance is sufficient to tell whether supply is elastic or inelastic. In Figure 5.4, for example, a price change from \$18 to \$20 brings a greater than proportional change in quantity for Curve S_1, an increase from 8 to 10 units. The same price change, \$18 to \$20, for Curve S_2 brings a less than proportional change in quantity, 23 to 25. Curve S_1 is elastic; Curve S_2 is inelastic. Any straight-line supply curve that extends or can be projected to the price axis, as does Curve S_1, is elastic. A similar curve that extends to the quantity axis, as does Curve S_2, is inelastic. Note that one curve is elastic and the other inelastic even though the slope of the two curves is the same.

If, instead of extending to either the price or quantity axis, the curve takes the unusual course, passing through the intersection of the price-quantity axes as do Curves S_2, S_3, and S_4 in Figure 5.5, the elasticity of

Figure 5.4 Slope and Elasticity of Supply

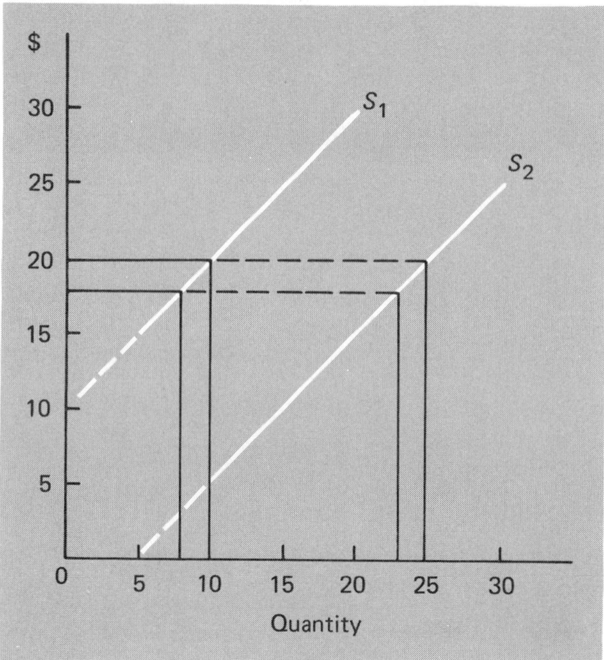

Figure 5.5 Elasticity of Supply

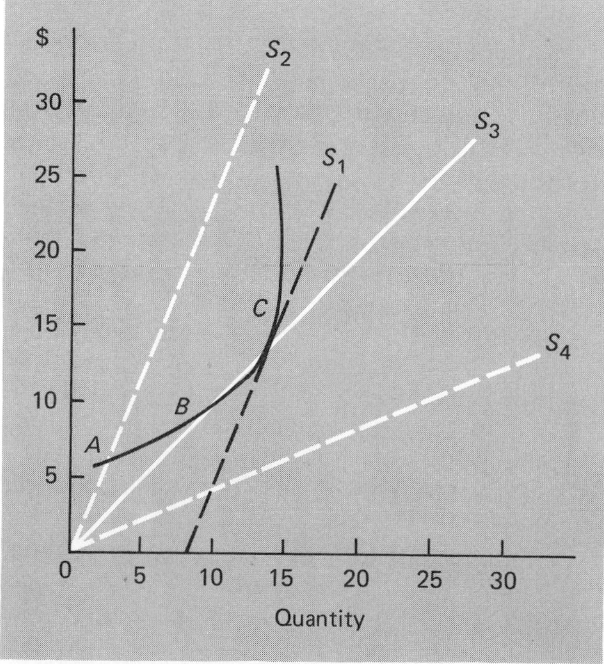

supply is unitary. In each case, the change in supply for Curves S_2, S_3, and S_4 is proportional to the change in price. If the supply curve is straight, it will have the same elasticity of supply throughout, unlike the straight-line demand curve. If a curve is not a straight line, for instance, Curve S_1 in Figure 5.5, we can make a projection from the supply curve to determine the elasticity of various segments of the curve. Three different points or segments have been identified on Curve S_1, A, B, and C, which can be shown by projection to be elastic, unitary, and inelastic, respectively. Segment A projects to the price axis and Segment C to the quantity axis, whereas Point B is tangent to a line that extends to the intersection of the price and quantity axes.

Beyond demand and supply: slightly

Demand and supply curves and elasticity coefficients provide a precise but incomplete picture of market forces. Economists recognize that the real economic causation lies behind prices, even though they spend much time working with supply and demand relationships that do not go much beyond the price dimension. As pointed out earlier, "other things" have a way of intruding upon the simplicity of the price-quantity relationship, and because some of these other things are difficult or impossible to measure, changes in life style or variations in product quality, for example, they are given less attention than the more measurable factors. Some can be measured, however, although it may not be so easy as it first appears. Income is one such factor.

Income elasticity

Income, one of the critical determinants of consumer decisions, stands about midway between the more measurable and the less measurable factors that affect demand. In the modern economy, income rarely takes a form other than money payment, which is easily measurable, but tracing the effect of income upon purchase decisions raises perplexing conceptual issues and at times difficulties with data. Similar to supply and demand elasticities, income elasticity is the measure of the relationship between income and purchases. The formula for computing the income elasticity coefficient follows the familiar form:

$$\text{Elasticity of Income} = \frac{\text{Relative (\%) Change in Quantity Purchased}}{\text{Relative (\%) Change in Income}}$$

As in previous applications, an income elasticity coefficient greater than 1 indicates that expenditures on an item rise proportionately more than income. In other words, the good or service is more important to the expenditures of upper-income than lower-income groups. Income elasticity of less than 1 occurs when expenditures for a particular item fall off more than proportionately as income rises. Such items are likely to be relatively more important in lower-income than upper-income budgets. When the income elasticity coefficient is equal to 1, expenditures change proportionately with income—a 10 percent increase (or decrease) in income results in a 10 percent increase (or decrease) in purchases, for example.

Necessities and the income effect

Goods and services that a consumer cannot or will not do without are likely to be represented by more nearly equal *absolute* outlays in the budgets of the rich and poor, thus reflecting an inelastic income coefficient. Luxury purchases, which tend to rise with income, are income elastic. Expenditures for some necessities such as food, fuel, and medical services, generally do not rise proportionately with income because a given amount of each is required, less causes greater hardship, and more serves little purpose.[5] Many luxuries, such as trips to Europe, attendance at private schools, and the purchase of first editions, are simply beyond the budgets of the lower-income groups. These kinds of purchases are made mainly by higher-income individuals. The work of Professors Houthakker and Taylor is instructive in this regard, although presenting the coefficients in Table 5.2 as measures of income elasticity probably goes farther than they would. Houthakker and Taylor, the authors of the estimates in Table 5.2, are careful to point out that although income is a major explanatory variable in the coefficients shown, they have not been able to isolate this factor completely.

Fuel, food, and physicians' services show appropriately low income elasticity coefficients, 0.38, 0.51, and 0.75, respectively, whereas furniture, new cars, and private education show high income elasticity, 1.48, 2.45, and 2.46, respectively. Table 5.2 has a few surprises, however, such as the income elasticity of alcoholic beverages and water, but for the most part, the results confirm the casual observer's expectations.

To measure the effect of a factor such as income on consumer behavior, other influences have to remain unchanged. Otherwise, we do not

[5] Here we are not referring to the traditional "food, shelter, and clothing" because the latter two categories afford the upper-income groups an opportunity to display their wealth quite as much as meeting a basic need.

Table 5.2: Estimates of income elasticity for selected items

Item	Coefficient	Item	Coefficient
Alcoholic beverages	1.54	Fuel	0.38
Food	0.51	Drugs	0.61
Tobacco	0.63	Physician's services	0.75
Clothing	1.02	Dentist's services	1.41
Housing	1.04	New cars	2.45
Furniture	1.48	Books	1.44
Electricity, gas	0.50	Radio and TV	1.22
China	1.41	Private education	2.46
		Water	1.02

Source: Table 6.5, H. S. Houthakker and L. D. Taylor, *Consumer Demand in the United States: Analyses and Projections* (Cambridge, Mass.: Harvard University Press, 1970), pp. 260–63.

know whether one factor or another is singly or jointly responsible for the change that takes place. In the case of income elasticity, for example, the price of the item under consideration as well as the prices of substitutes must remain unchanged in order for the elasticity coefficient to be confined to the income effect. This doesn't mean, however, that the economist, like the blind person confronting the elephant, must forever be confused by relying on too narrow a part of the whole. By measuring first one factor, then another—price, income, prices of competing items—we can obtain something approaching a balanced picture of the forces shaping consumers' decisions.

The impact of changes in the price of competing products upon sales of other products can also be expressed as a coefficient of elasticity. The measure of the responsiveness of sales of one product, say butter, to a change in the price of another, say margarine, is called *cross elasticity*.

Cross elasticity

The standard elasticity relationship, in which a change in quantity is compared with a change in price, is modified slightly to measure cross elasticity of demand.

$$\text{Cross Elasticity for A} = \frac{\text{Relative (\%) Change in Quantity of A}}{1\,\%\ \text{Change in Price B}}$$

Note that we compare the change in the amount purchased of one item with a 1 percent change in price of another item. If these items are close substitutes, purchases of either will go up as the price of the other increases and down as its price decreases. For example, butter purchases will rise when the price of margarine goes up, and decrease when the price of margarine falls. As a result, the cross elasticity for substitutes such as butter and margarine will have a positive sign. If the products are complements rather than substitutes, if the purchase of one leads to the purchase of the other, for example, as green's fees and golf balls, or fishing rods and fishing tackle, sales of the complementary product are more responsive to the price changes of the other product. In this case, the cross elasticity coefficient will be negative. Of course, some products or services are neither complements nor substitutes, for example, dental services and beer, and in such cases cross elasticity is zero, which indicates that outlays for dental services are unaffected by changes in the price of beer.

Consumers' decisions are but part of the forces of price determination; producers' actions are also important. In Chapter 6 we shall turn to the role of the producer in price determination.

Summary

Elasticity of demand measures the change that takes place in purchases as a result of a change in the price of a commodity or service. If the change in the purchase is more than proportional to the change in price—whether price goes up or down—the demand is *elastic*; if the change in the purchase is proportional to the price change, the demand is *unitary*; and if the change in the purchase is less than proportional—whether price goes up or down—the demand is *inelastic*.

Various factors influence the elasticity of demand for a commodity or service, but the most important consideration is the availability of substitutes. If a product has close substitutes, such as margarine for butter, the demand for that product will be more sensitive to price change because an increase in its price will cause a shift in purchases to the substitute and a decrease in price will attract customers away from the substitute. If a good or service has no substitutes, such as an emergency appendectomy, demand will be highly inelastic, generally insensitive to price change. Other factors also influence the consumer's reaction to changing price. Such factors might include whether the price of the item is very high or very low, whether the purchase takes a large or small part of the consumer's budget, or how long the consumer has to adjust to the price change.

Very high and very low prices contribute to insensitivity by the consumer to price change since even when modified a very high price limits consumption to those with abundant income or those who value the item highly. A very low price reduces the importance of further price change in the consumer's decision because it is already low. If the price of a product or service is a small part of the consumer's budget—such as newspapers, shaving cream, bobby pins, or toothpaste—the consumer is likely to be insensitive to a price change, even one that is proportionately large. When the outlay is substantial, however—such as the purchase of a house or a trip to Europe—a small proportional change represents a large absolute sum, and the consumer is more likely to modify purchases with a change in price. Finally, the more time the consumer has to adjust to a change in the price of the product or service, the more responsive the consumer is likely to be. As a result, some inelastic short-run situations will be elastic or less inelastic in the long run.

The elasticity of supply is measured in the same way as demand elasticity. Changes in the amount offered for sale are related to the change in price. The seller's response to the price change determines whether supply is elastic or inelastic. Generally, supply is more likely to be elastic when the output of a good or service can be increased or decreased with ease, and inelastic when production facilities are inflexible. Supply elasticity will vary from industry to industry, but as with demand elasticity, the longer the time available for adjustment to the price change, the more likely it is that supply will be elastic. The concept of elasticity can also be used to measure how sensitive purchases are to the level of income and the extent to which two products are substitutes for each other.

Key terms and concepts

Price elasticity (or **demand elasticity**) the measure of the responsiveness of purchases to a change in price. The coefficient of price elasticity is derived by the formula

$$\frac{\text{Relative (\%) Change in Quantity}}{\text{Relative (\%) Change in Price}}$$

If the coefficient is greater than 1, demand is elastic; if equal to 1, demand is unitary; and if less than 1, demand is inelastic.

Total revenue the quantity of sales times price.

Total revenue and elasticity If total revenue is inversely related to a change in price, demand is elastic; if total revenue remains the same when price changes, demand is unitary; if total revenue is directly related to price change, demand is inelastic.

Supply elasticity the measure of responsiveness of a quantity offered for sale to a change in price. The coefficient of supply elasticity is derived by the formula

$$\frac{\text{Relative (\%) Change in Quantity}}{\text{Relative (\%) Change in Price}}$$

If the coefficient is greater than 1, supply is elastic; if equal to 1, supply is unitary; and if less than 1, supply is inelastic.

Income elasticity the measure of the responsiveness of purchases to a change in income. The coefficient of income elasticity is derived by the formula

$$\frac{\text{Relative (\%) Change in Quantity}}{\text{Relative (\%) Change in Income}}$$

If the coefficient is greater than 1, the purchase is income elastic; if equal to 1, the purchase is neutral, or unrelated to income change; and if less than 1, the purchase is income inelastic.

Cross elasticity the measure of the change in purchases of one product caused by a change in the price of another product. The coefficient of cross elasticity is derived by the formula

$$\frac{\text{Relative (\%) Change in Quantity of A}}{\text{1\% Change in Price of B}}$$

If the coefficient sign is positive, Products A and B are substitutes; if the sign is negative, Products A and B are complements.

Discussion and review questions

1. By raising the world petroleum price fourfold, the Middle East oil producers increased their sales revenue tremendously. Why didn't the price increase reduce

the amount of petroleum demanded more than it did or increase substantially the supply of petroleum from non-Middle East sources?

2. What are the prospects of the United States attaining energy self-sufficiency by 1985?

3. Was the impact of the petroleum price increase distributed more or less equally throughout the world? Was it distributed more or less equally within the United States or in Canada? What were the responses of Canada and the United States to the petroleum price increase?

4. The single most important cause of elastic and inelastic demand is the presence or absence of substitutes. How do substitutes affect elasticity of demand?

5. What other factors affect the elasticity of demand? From your own experience as a consumer, identify cases of elastic or inelastic demand.

6. What difference does it make whether elasticity is measured as a proportional change or an absolute change?

7. The elasticity measure expresses the change in purchases as the result solely of changes in price. What problems does this lead to in the interpretation of statistically derived elasticity coefficients?

8. Why is demand over the long run likely to be more elastic than demand over a shorter period of time?

9. The slope of the curve may provide a clue to the elasticity of demand, but it is not a reliable guide in some cases. Why is this so?

10. Economists frequently observe that Henry Ford exploited the elastic demand for automobiles in promoting the growth of the Ford Motor Company. Are there more recent examples of similar developments? What about electronic calculators?

11. The coefficient of elasticity of supply is derived in the same way as that of price elasticity, but it is easier to judge whether supply is elastic or inelastic from supply curves than it is to judge price elasticity from demand curves. Why is this?

12. Income elasticity measures the sensitivity of purchases to changes in income. Do necessity and luxury purchases differ in regard to income elasticity? What kind of purchases are insensitive to income changes?

III Markets and costs

6 Production costs: the short run

For the first time since the massive Russian grain deal of 1972, wheat markets in the U.S. and abroad appear to be returning to normal.

*Which is to say that while supplies of some kinds of wheat remain abnormally small, enough of the golden grain is pouring into world trade channels to cool the speculative fever that pushed U.S. wheat prices up as much as 137 percent in eight months ending in February. There is no danger of a glut reappearing soon—at least not this year—but gloom-and-doom predictions of $1 loaves of bread are equally farfetched.**

The Russian grain deal of 1972, in which the Communist traders took some of their capitalist counterparts and the American consumer to the cleaners, sent shock waves throughout the world wheat market from the moment the magnitude of the transactions became known until years later when supply finally caught up with demand. It all began with a drought in Russia's main wheat-producing areas in the summer of 1972. *The New York Times* recounts the sequence of events as follows:

Toward the end of June [1972], some of the wheat in the Volga basin was already beginning to shrivel. . . . Perhaps as much as 5 percent of all grain lands in Russia were now in danger of being ruined.

So it was that on the Fourth of July, 1972, a slender graying Russian named Nikolai Belousov received a courtly, aristocratic American businessman named Michel Fribourg in his suite at the Regency Hotel in New York City. . . . At the end [of their meetings] they sealed, with a handshake and a toast in vodka, an agreement by Continental [Grain Company] to sell the Russians about $460 million worth of grain. Fribourg believes the deal was the largest single transaction a private businessman had ever negotiated up to that time.

* Stephen Josefix, "World Wheat Markets Seem to Settle Down After Two Hectic Years," *The Wall Street Journal*, April 5, 1974, p. 1. Reprinted with permission of *The Wall Street Journal*, © Dow Jones & Company, Inc. 1974. All rights reserved.

That was just the beginning. Over the next five weeks, Belousov kept buying, buying, buying—from Fribourg and five other American grain export companies.[1]

Although the Russian grain deal was carried out by private American traders, it was hardly an example of untrammeled free-market bargaining. The US government not only paid a subsidy to the American traders for the wheat sold to Russia, but extended credit to the USSR that enabled it to make the purchase at a below-market interest rate. Only the Soviet purchasing agent and a few upper-level US Department of Agriculture officials knew the extent of the Soviet purchases and at the time of the transactions the US officials did not appreciate their market impact.

The effect of the extraordinary deal soon became apparent, however. When the American traders entered the market to cover their commitments to Russia, supplies of wheat were drawn down well below normal domestic inventories and a year-long climb raised the price of wheat from slightly less than $60.00 a ton (about $1.63 a bushel) to $180 a ton.[2] During the same period, virtually all available shipping space was placed under contract to move the grain to Russia, and Houston, Texas, the port of shipment, was tied up for over a year with Russian grain loadings.

The short and the long of it

The Russian grain deal imposed on the American wheat market a large and traumatically abrupt increase in demand at a time when the growing season was so far advanced that there was no way to increase the wheat supply during 1972. Indeed, the Russian purchases were so large that supply adjustments in the following year could not redress the imbalance, and only the anticipation of a heavy yield in the 1974 season brought the price of wheat back within its normal range. Although operating on demand instead of supply, the initial price effect of the wheat deal was the same as that created by the oil embargo—a spectacular increase. Unlike the oil embargo, however, adjusting the seasonal wheat supply to increase demand or building back depleted wheat inventories is much easier than replacing the Middle East's oil contribution to the American market. Figure 6.1 traces the immediate or *momentary* reaction to the increased demand for wheat in the United States market that resulted from Russian purchases and the subsequent seasonal adjustment in supply and demand.

[1] Joseph Albright, "Some Deal," *The New York Times Magazine*, Nov. 25, 1973, p. 36. © 1973 by the New York Times Company. Reprinted by permission.

[2] The high momentary price of wheat during this period came in February 1974, when the Chicago futures price—the price quoted for delivery of wheat at a later date—rose to a record $6.45 a bushel, approximately four times the 1972 price quoted the Russians.

Figure 6.1 The Russian Wheat Deal

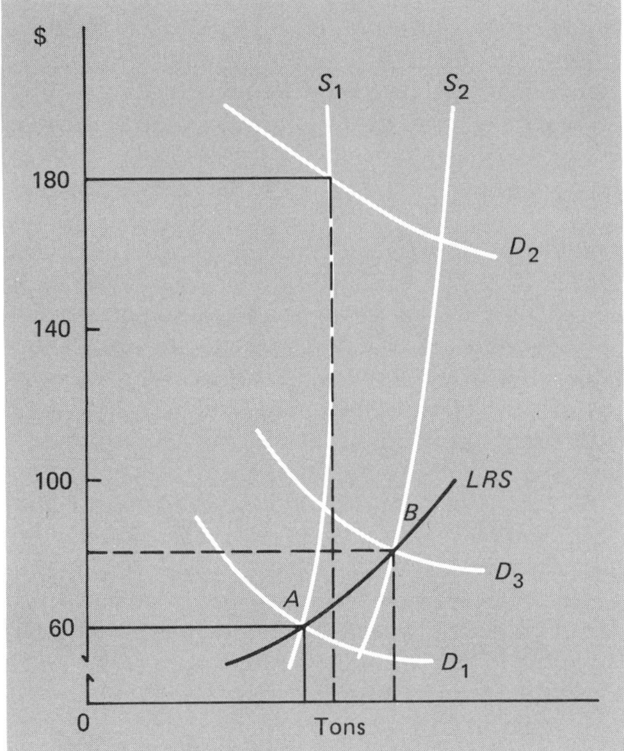

The seasonal supply curves shown in Figure 6.1, Curves S_1 and S_2, are steeper than for the typical short-run supply situation. This is because output cannot be changed much over the growing season. The seasonal output of wheat is largely determined at planting time by the acreage that is seeded. During the growing season, output can be influenced somewhat by the intensity of cultivation and the addition of inputs such as fertilizer and insecticides. To change significantly the output of wheat, however, more or less land must be brought under cultivation, and this must await the next planting period. As a result, wheat price changes take place through a sequence of seasonal adjustments represented by the movement of Curves S_1 and S_2 at different times, with the short-run or seasonal demand and supply intersections tracing the long-run supply function of wheat production, as Curve LRS in Figure 6.1.

The first step in the market's adjustment to the Russian purchase was a drastic increase in price from $60 a ton to $180 a ton. This increase was the result of the upward movement of demand from Curves D_1 to D_2 when short-run or seasonal supply could not be increased. The second step was the seasonal adjustment in supply, shown by Curve S_2, and a reduction in demand to Curve D_3. There were no Russian purchases during this second period. Curve D_3 lies above Curve D_1, because demand remains at a higher level in building back wheat inventories depleted by the sale to the Soviets, and the intersection of Curves D_3 and S_2 establishes a seasonal price that is above the original \$60 equilibrium price but below the \$180 momentary price.

The sequence of short-run adjustments traces the long-run costs of expanding wheat production over the seasons. If a line is drawn to connect the short-run points of equilibria, Points A and B in Figure 6.1, it traces the long-run supply curve for producing wheat. This long-run curve shows costs rising as additional land is brought under cultivation to expand wheat production. The long-run concept will be explored at greater length in Chapter 10. Here the difference between short-run and long-run cost is only briefly acknowledged.

All short-run supply curves rise, but not all long-run curves behave this way. In the case of wheat farming, for example, the long-run supply curve may rise because there is a limited amount of high-quality land available. To increase output poorer land must be used, which in turn raises the long-run cost of producing wheat. Even if there is no reduction in the quality of land diverted to wheat production, the price of the land is likely to be bid up in attracting it from other economic uses.

The long-run supply function is introduced here to emphasize that the two functions, short-run and long-run, are based on different factors. While we can rely on the short-run curve to rise more or less steeply, except in unusual circumstances, the long-run curves may rise, fall, or remain constant. Briefly, the main difference between the short run and the long run is that all of the factors of production—land, labor, and capital as well as techniques of production—can be modified in the long run, while only some of these can be changed in the short run. The limitation of output in the short run was one of the earliest observations of economists, and to this day the short-run constraint finds formal expression in the *principle of diminishing returns.*

The principle of diminishing returns

The principle of diminishing returns has been around so long—since at least the eighteenth century—that it has become almost common property, equally at the service of editorial writers, politicians, and economists.

Fixed capital? Well, it can be moved in less time than built

Detroit—General Motors Corp., desperately trying to increase the availability of more economical engines in its cars, repurchased from American Motors Corp. a 12-year-old six-cylinder engine manufacturing line that GM disposed of in 1968. The line has been standing idle in an AMC plant for some 2½ years.

GM sold the V-6 line to Jeep Corp., now an AMC subsidiary, in 1968 for about $5 million, but "had to pay a slight premium" to get it back. GM is expected to incur several million dollars in additional expenses moving the bulky equipment, refurbishing it and revamping the engine it will produce to meet today's performances and pollution control requirements.

Still, sources said the accord is probably a bargain for GM. One source estimated such a line if purchased new would cost $50 million today. But more important, it would take two or more years to be built and delivered to GM—far too long a time to help with GM's immediate dilemma.[3]

It is hardly unexpected that the principle has acquired a variety of meanings and a more expansive treatment than economists accord to it.

During the heyday of the Classical economists in the early nineteenth century, the principle of diminishing returns was cast on a grand scale as a limiting factor in the growth of world economic output. Thomas Malthus drew support from the proposition for his view that population, if unchecked, had the capacity to outrun the world's food supply. The consequence for the world economy, as for Mr. Micawber in *David Copperfield* when his expenditures exceeded his income, was misery.

But unlike Mr. Micawber, economists did not take the view that "something would turn up" to set aside the impact of diminishing returns. Fortunately, however, something did turn up—technological innovation and capital accumulation—which averted the full thrust of diminishing returns. But from the early nineteenth century until now, the principle has been a persistent economic fact of life, diluted in its impact yet still vital.

Returns mean physical output not dollar value

Although diminishing returns is one of the foundation principles of economics, it is expressed in terms of physical units—bushels of wheat,

[3] C. B. Camp, "GM Buys Back 6-Cylinder Engine Unit," *The Wall Street Journal*, April 5, 1974, p. 10. Reprinted with permission of *The Wall Street Journal*, © Dow Jones & Company, Inc. 1974. All rights reserved.

pairs of shoes, tons of steel—rather than in the language of price and cost. The implications of diminishing returns are important today, but before relating this concept to the present we should note its early application.

John Stuart Mill and the principle of diminishing returns

John Stuart Mill, a giant among the philosophers and economists of the nineteenth century, explained the principle and its application as follows:

After a certain, and not very advanced, stage in the progress of agriculture, it is the law of production from the land, that in any given state of agricultural skill and knowledge; by increasing labour, the produce is not increased in an equal degree; doubling the labor does not double the produce; or, to express the same thing in other words, every increase of produce is obtained by a more than proportional increase in the application of labour to the land.

This general law . . . is the most important proposition in political economy.[4]

Mill leaves no doubt about the central role of diminishing returns in economics and its impact upon the world's agricultural output. His message was obvious: The supply of agricultural land was largely fixed, but population continued to increase, portending a decline in material welfare as the fixed land supply was cultivated more intensively and less bountifully. Although Mill was careful to point out that diminishing returns occurred under conditions of unchanging agricultural techniques, the nineteenth century was not a time of innovation in either agriculture or industry. The prospect for raising economic output was grim. Not until the industrial revolution did the development of improved techniques of production and the use of steam power increase world output, first in industry and later in agriculture. With these changes, diminishing returns no longer raised the specter of world impoverishment.

The principle has been largely set aside in its broader application, but it is far from dead. It remains the primary consideration in short-run output decisions of firms that are able to employ different resource combinations to vary output. The world has not yet been trapped by declining marginal output—although recently the limits-to-growth school has revived this issue—but throughout most of time production has been subject to some constraints. What John Stuart Mill said about the decline of marginal output as labor factors are added to a plot of land still holds.

[4] John Stuart Mill, *Principles of Political Economy* (London: Longmans, Green; Sir W. J. Ashley edition, 1909), p. 177.

Conceivably, any of the primary factors of production—land, labor, or capital—can remain unchanged long enough to impose an output limitation on production. This occurred in the United States in 1972, when acreage planted in wheat could not be increased during the growing season in response to the Russian's large grain purchase. If the time period is very limited, virtually all factors of production are fixed, but two factors—land and capital—are generally even less flexible than others. Before the Industrial Revolution, not only was agriculture the dominant economic activity, but capital was a relatively unimportant factor in a way of farming that had changed very little since the time of the Romans. Land, the limiting factor, was fixed in extent over the longer time span as well as over the shorter seasonal period.

When science and technology turned to agriculture, first with steel plows, cultivating and harvesting machinery, and much later with genetically improved crops, inorganic fertilizers, and pesticides and herbicides, agriculture finally broke free from the limitation of land. The land-man relationship was broadened to include other inputs such as fertilizer and farm machinery, which greatly raised farm output. Whether in the nineteenth or twentieth century, however, if land is fixed and another factor is increased, average output will rise initially, reach a high point—the point of diminishing returns—and then fall. This relationship is shown in Figure 6.2, which expresses changes in output as a function of inputs of labor.

Diminishing returns is not the only significant point illustrated in Figure 6.2. Even though average returns turn down at Point D, total output continues to rise well beyond the point of diminishing returns. Note the behavior of total output, Curve TP in Figure 6.2A. Pushing output beyond the point of diminishing returns, either for the firm or the nation, is hardly the economic equivalent of sailing off the edge of the earth. Indeed, quite the contrary. *In the operation of the typical firm, production will be carried beyond the point of diminishing returns.* The reason the firm behaves in this manner, and the extent to which production is carried beyond diminishing returns, depends on the importance of fixed factors in the production arrangement. We will consider the fixed factors further when the transition is made from product curves to cost curves. For the moment, however, it is enough to warn against assuming that diminishing returns imposes an output straitjacket on the firm.

Why do returns diminish?

Actually, not all production arrangements encounter diminishing returns. Production equipment and processes that are highly specialized,

Figure 6.2 Diminishing Returns

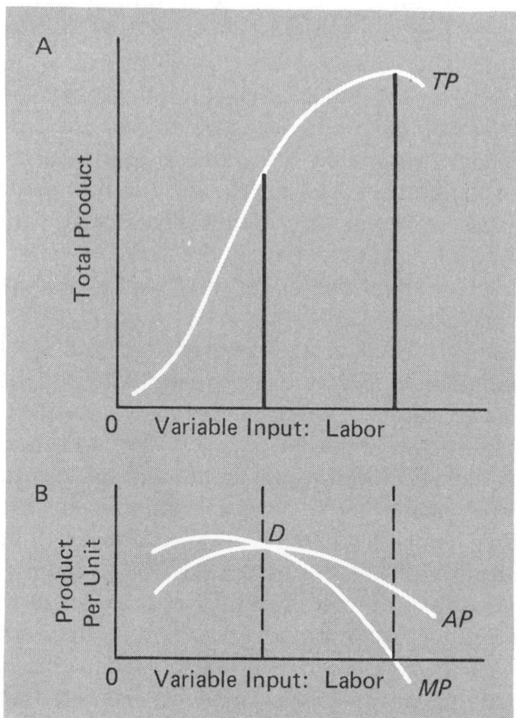

such as typewriters and assembly lines, have input relationships—typist to typewriter and operator to assembly-line task—that are largely invariant, especially in the short run. In order to increase output, more typists are employed on more typewriters, not more typists with one typewriter. As additional typists and additional typewriters are employed, there is no cause for a decline in average output and, therefore, returns do not diminish. Returns—physical product or output—eventually fall off when one factor is held constant and successive units of another factor are applied to increase total output. For this to happen, the relationship between these factors or inputs must be flexible, even while one of the factors remains fixed.[5] If these conditions prevail, as they do by definition in the short run, the input-output relationship will be that illustrated in Figure 6.2.

Returns diminish because some factor combinations produce more per

[5] The principle of diminishing returns is sometimes called the law of *variable proportions* to emphasize the conditions necessary for the reduced output rather than the cause of its decline.

unit of input than others. Take a given area of land that is large enough to be cultivated intensively by ten men or just barely planted and harvested by two. With two men (the variable inputs), the land (the fixed factor) is underutilized; there is too much fixed factor for the variable input. With ten men, the situation is reversed. Not only can planting and harvesting be undertaken with greater care by ten men, but lavish cultivation can be carried out during the growing season. In terms of the diagram in Figure 6.2, ten farm workers can carry production well beyond diminishing returns toward the point of maximum total output. As production is pushed beyond diminishing returns, the fixed factor continues to be spread more thinly among the increasing variable inputs until eventually even total output takes a downward turn. This relationship is shown hypothetically in Table 6.1.

Table 6.1: Diminishing returns in agriculture[6]

Variable Input (Man days)	Total Returns (Tons of wheat)	Marginal Returns (Tons of wheat)	Average Returns (Tons of wheat)
1	8	8	8
2	20	12	10
3	34	14	$11\frac{1}{3}$
4	48	14	12
5	60	12	12
6	70	10	$11\frac{2}{3}$
7	78	8	$11\frac{1}{7}$
8	84	6	$10\frac{1}{2}$
9	88	4	$9\frac{7}{8}$
10	90	2	9
11	90	0	$8\frac{2}{11}$
12	88	−2	$7\frac{1}{3}$

Optimum output and marginal returns

Well before the maximum total output is reached, a firm will find it uneconomical to continue to increase production by adding more variable inputs. If the firm were to determine its output schedule in terms of variable input only, in other words, if it were to produce to the point at which a unit of output requires the smallest contribution of labor, it would stop at the point of diminishing *average* returns. But it takes more than

[6] The marginal and average columns in Table 6.1 are both derived from the first two columns. Average returns are obtained by dividing output by input, and marginal returns are the successive increments to total returns. For example, as variable inputs are increased from two to three, total returns rise from twenty to thirty-four tons of wheat, making the marginal contribution of the third variable input fourteen tons of wheat.

variable factors for most production; it takes capital, raw materials, land, and other ingredients. When these inputs are represented graphically as physical entities, as the labor input in Figure 6.3, output can be related to only one input at a time. When work hours and capital equipment are converted to dollar value, however, all these factors can be recorded on the same graph, but without such a conversion we can only appraise indirectly the influence of the factor(s) that are not accounted for in the graphical illustrations of Figures 6.2 and 6.3.

Variable input per unit of output is least at the point of diminishing average returns, but with every increase in output—from an output of one to the maximum capacity of the farm or factory—less and less fixed factor is used per unit of output. Variable factor per unit of output increases after the point of diminishing returns, but the fixed factor is spread more thinly. If unhampered in reaching the most efficient use of both variable and fixed inputs, the firm will carry production to the point at which the economy from spreading the fixed factor over added output is just compensated for by the diseconomy from adding variable inputs beyond the point of di-

Figure 6.3 The Stages of Returns

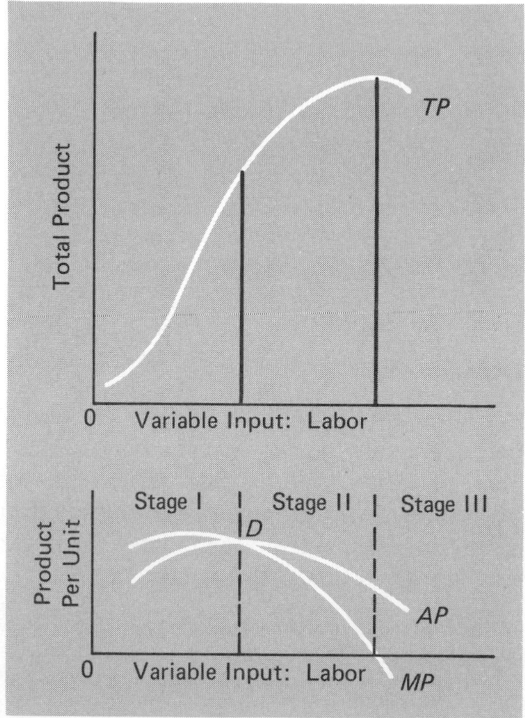

minishing returns. Sometimes, of course, this optimum input combination cannot be attained because there is insufficient time. We will turn to this case later. Our first interest is in establishing the basic nature of the firm's output and cost curves.

In Figure 6.3 there are now three curves describing output that follow strikingly different paths—the total, the average, and the marginal curve. The curves differ but their relationship is fixed: the marginal curve cuts the average curve at the latter's highest point and the total returns curve peaks where the marginal curve reaches zero. The curves are a "family" unit; they are all derived from the same data, but the data for each curve are arrayed in a different way—as an increment, as an average, and as a total. The marginal product curve (MP) intersects the average product curve (AP) at the latter's highest point because when an increment to output produced by the added variable unit is greater than average output, the average is raised. When the marginal increment is less than the average output, the average is pulled down. Since the average product curve is rising when the marginal curve is above it and falling when the marginal curve is below, it follows that the two curves can intersect only at the zenith of the average product curve.

The stages of production

Three output stages can be identified in Figure 6.3 to illustrate the operation of the principle of diminishing returns and its effect upon the firm's production decisions: Stage 1, *rising returns,* in which average returns increase up to the point of diminishing returns; Stage II, *diminishing returns,* in which total returns continue to rise although marginal and average returns decline (the point at which marginal returns reaches zero and total returns is greatest marks the division between Stages II and III); and Stage III, *negative returns,* in which all returns—marginal, average, and total—are on the decline.

How far is production carried?

Production will not be carried into Stage III unless the firm misjudges the consequences of such a decision. In this stage, total output actually decreases as more inputs are added. At the other extreme, Stage I also represents a generally untenable range of production options, although the reasons are not so apparent. This leaves Stage II as the area within which the firm is most likely to operate.

As the firm adds variable inputs in Stage I, it benefits from increasing productivity of the variable factors as these inputs are added up to the point of diminishing average returns. Assuming its price does not fall from increasing output, the firm will carry production at least to the point of diminishing average returns. But why should production be carried beyond diminishing average returns?

The increased output brought about by adding variables up to the point of diminishing average returns explains why production is carried to this point, but why is it extended beyond? Assuming the firm can adjust to the optimum input-output relationship, production will be carried further beyond the point of diminishing average returns as the fixed factor grows more important in relation to the variable factor.

The optimum factor relationship is reached when the gains from spreading the fixed factor are just balanced by the reduced returns from adding variable factors beyond the point of diminishing average returns. Since Figure 6.3 does not show the influence of the fixed factor upon output, however, we must infer that a more costly fixed factor will push output further beyond the point of diminishing returns. Precisely what this output will be cannot be shown with the returns diagram, but requires the use of cost curves to record the outlays for both the fixed and the variable factors. The development of cost curves is the next step in the analysis of the firm's decision-making process.

The short-run cost function—basis for output decisions

The firm's output decisions involve two main considerations: the costs of production and the selling price of output. Costs of production are only a step away from the above discussion of factor returns.

What is cost?

Cost can be expressed in a number of ways—in money terms, in the resources employed in production, or in the output forgone when scarce resources are used to produce some things instead of others. For economists, the principle of diminishing returns is only a slightly concealed cost function—where output is high per unit of input, cost is low; where output is low per unit of input, cost is high. This function is shown in Figure 6.4. At the point of diminishing average returns, Point D, the curve peaks, and per unit cost for the variable input is lowest.

Figure 6.4 Variable Cost and Diminishing Returns

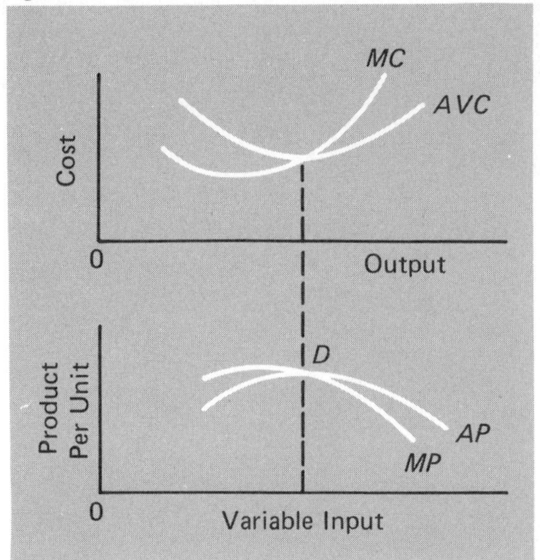

From returns to cost

Basically, the shape of a cost curve depends on the relationship between output and input: cost falls as output per unit of input increases and rises as output per unit of input decreases. For the average variable cost and marginal cost curves to reflect the shape of the average product and marginal product curves in reverse, as shown in Figure 6.4, the price of inputs must not change as different amounts of labor and materials are employed. The total wage bill will increase as more labor is employed, of course, but unless the wage rate remains the same when the firm increases or decreases employment, the variable and marginal cost curves will not correspond to the basic shape of those reproduced in Figure 6.4.

The shift from physical input units to dollar units increases the coverage of the cost diagram. Both variable factors and fixed factors can be shown on the same diagram when they are measured in dollars, as in Figure 6.5. In this figure, the marginal and average variable cost curves are joined at their origin, to indicate that they represent different ways of expressing the same data. The relationship between the marginal cost and average variable cost curve is the same as that between the marginal returns and average returns curves: when the marginal curve is below the average curve, it pulls the average down; when the marginal curve is above the average curve, it pulls the average up.

Figure 6.5 Average Variable Cost, Marginal Cost, and Average Fixed Cost

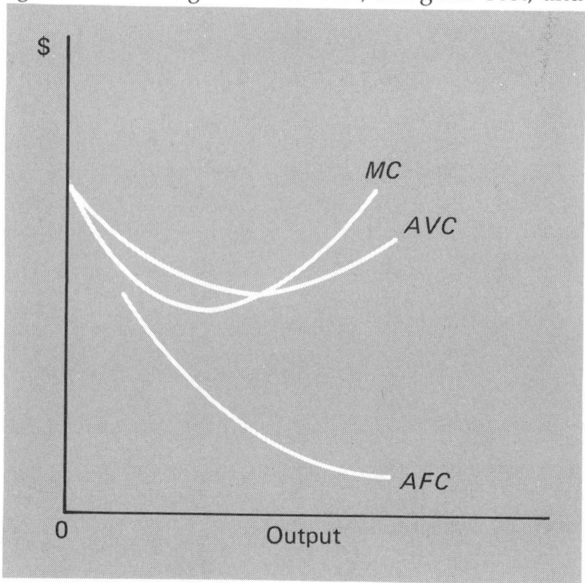

Fixed cost shown as a curve

Fixed cost is shown as a curve in Figure 6.5, which demonstrates that this outlay for capital and other fixed expenditures represents the same *absolute* amount whether production is large or small. Fixed cost decreases continuously when averaged over increasing output, as shown in Table 6.2. The smooth curves of Figure 6.5 do not reflect the data of Table 6.2.

Preview of cost concepts

Table 6.2 shows the full range of costs that are encountered by a firm in the short-run. They can be distinguished as follows:

$$\text{Marginal Cost} = \frac{\text{Increase in Total Variable Cost}}{\text{Increase in Output}}$$

$$\text{Average Variable Cost} = \frac{\text{Total Variable Cost}}{\text{Total Output}}$$

$$\text{Average Fixed Cost} = \frac{\text{Total Fixed Cost}}{\text{Total Output}}$$

$$\text{Average Total Cost} = \text{Average Variable Cost} + \text{Average Fixed Cost}$$

Since marginal cost and average variable cost are derived from the marginal product curve and the average product curve, we already know something about them before they appear on the cost curve diagram. Average fixed cost, however, has until now remained in the wings. It deserves a fuller explanation.

Table 6.2: The short-run costs of output

Output	TFC	AFC	TVC	AVC	TC	ATC	MC
0	$100				$100		
1	100	$100	$100	$100	200	$200	$100
2	100	50	175	87	275	137	75
3	100	33	275	92	375	125	100
4	100	25	400	100	500	125	125
5	100	20	550	110	650	130	150
6	100	16	725	121	825	137	175
7	100	14	925	131	1025	146	200
8	100	12	1150	143	1250	156	225

Average fixed cost: forever downward

Marginal cost and average variable cost are locked together, born of the same data, flat or steep in their togetherness. Fixed cost is another matter, a separate and independent entity in the firm's cost function that is unrelated to marginal and variable costs. Whether the firm produces much or little, total fixed cost is an unchanging sum. But when this sum is averaged over increasing output, the per unit cost declines continuously. If a firm's total fixed cost is $100,000 and it produces 50,000 hats, for example, the per unit fixed cost for each hat is $2.00. If it produces 100,000 hats, the per unit fixed cost is $1,00, and if the output of hats is raised to 200,000, average fixed cost is $.50.

Although the total fixed cost does not change during the short run, it is spread thinner and thinner as output increases. Even though average variable cost rises after the point of diminishing returns, average total cost is held down for awhile by the decline in average fixed cost. Average total cost thus is a blend of fixed and variable costs.

Average total cost

When only the physical returns from inputs of variable factors are known, minimum long-run cost output for the firm cannot be located precisely in Stage II of the returns diagram. Now, however, by referring to the average total cost curve in Figure 6.6, the firm's lowest cost of production can be identified. This point, labeled LTUC for "lowest total unit cost," identifies the least cost of production that is within the firm's range of output in the short run.

Figure 6.6 The Optimum Cost Point

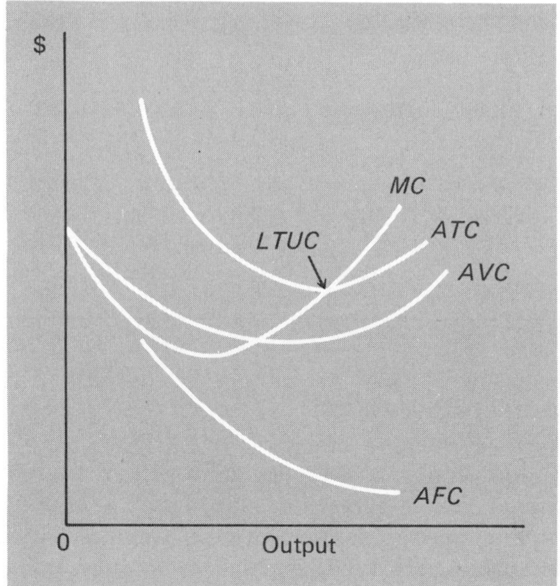

Because cost is lowest at Point LTUC does not mean that a firm will always carry production to this point and no farther. As will be shown later, sometimes the firm's output will be less than that at Point LTUC and occasionally it will be more, depending upon market conditions and the ability of the firm to adjust to these conditions.

To summarize, the average total cost curve is a composite of average variable cost and average fixed cost over the range of the firm's output. The point of diminishing average returns coincides with the low point on the average *variable* cost curve (*not* the average total cost curve) at the marginal cost intersection. The point of lowest total unit cost lies above and to the right of this point on the average total cost curve. As output is carried beyond the point of diminishing average returns to Point LTUC, the upward push of average variable cost is equalized by the downward pull of average fixed cost.

A further note on average fixed cost

The independence of average fixed cost deserves reemphasis. AFC may lie above, below, or in the same plane on the cost diagram as average variable cost. Its position depends on the relative magnitude of the two inputs. In a capital-intensive process, such as an oil refinery or a steel strip mill, the fixed cost ingredient in average total cost will dominate, resulting

Figure 6.7 Fixed Cost Dominant

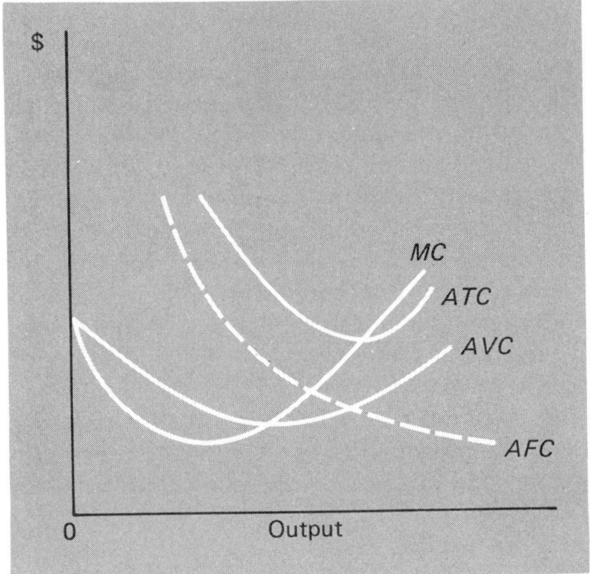

in a fixed to variable cost relationship similar to that in Figure 6.7. In a labor-intensive process, such as a small-contractor logging operation or a lens grinding establishment, the element of fixed cost for capital equipment will be substantially less than the outlay for labor and materials.[7] As a result, the average fixed cost curve will lie below the average variable cost curve, as depicted earlier in Figure 6.6. Fixed and variable cost curves may also lie in the same plane when outlays for variable and fixed inputs are roughly equivalent. When they do lie in the same plane, however, AVC and AFC intersect and confuse an already complicated diagram. For this reason, in the illustrations that follow the fixed cost curve will be placed below the variable cost curve, unless the purpose is to show the influence of a large element of fixed cost on the firm's output policy. For the most part, in subsequent chapters our attention will be focused on the average total cost curves and the marginal cost curves. In most cases, we will drop average variable cost and average fixed cost curves from the diagram.

[7] The above illustrations of capital-intensive and labor-intensive processes may require elaboration. A modern petroleum refinery is a highly automated, computerized operation, with the role of labor confined largely to reading dials and making adjustments in controls. Labor cost is low compared with capital cost. The small logging contractor employs a chain saw and a pick-up truck, but labor is the more important ingredient in the operation. Larger logging operations employ heavier equipment, such as machines that pinch off trees at their base instead of chain saws, tractors for removing the trees from the forest prior to cutting them into sections, and hydraulic loaders for stacking the harvested logs. Large logging operations are, of course, not labor-intensive.

Summary

The principle of diminishing returns is the basis of the short-run period of analysis in economics. The principle was originally applied on a much larger scale in which the growth in population was related to the world's supply of land. Presently it is used by economists to explain the shape of the variable cost curve of the firm during the short-run period. In economics, the short run is a period of time in which the firm can increase or decrease its variable factors, such as its labor force and raw materials, but not its fixed factors, such as land and capital equipment. If there is flexibility in a firm's production arrangements, it can change output in the short run by increasing or decreasing its variable factors. The firm's total output increases as additional variable factors are combined with the fixed factors and average output initially rises and then falls. When plotted on a diagram with variable inputs on the horizontal axis and output on the vertical axis, the zenith of the average product curve is the point of diminishing returns.

The principle of diminishing returns expresses a physical relationship that has important economic implications. In the case of the variable product curve, for example, the highest output per unit of input is the lowest cost per unit of variable input. This assumes that the per unit charge for the variable inputs does not change as more or less are used—for example, the wage rate remains the same as labor inputs are added—so that where output is greatest per unit of input, cost is least. As a result, the shape of the average variable cost curve follows the course of the average product curve in reverse: going up when the product curve goes down and down when it goes up.

The average variable cost curve expresses the relationship between output and input in one way; the marginal cost curve shows the output-input relationship is another way. The marginal cost curve is derived from the average cost curve by tracing the change in total cost that takes place as additional variable factors are added to increase firm output. Since the marginal and average curves are derived from the same data, they bear a fixed relationship to each other: when the marginal curve is below the average, increased production lowers the average; when the marginal curve is above the average, increased production raises the average. As a result, the marginal curve crosses the average curve at the latter's lowest point, which is also the point of diminishing average returns.

Short-run firm costs are not confined to variable costs. They also include fixed costs, which are outlays for factors of production that require time-consuming planning, remodeling, or expansion in plant and equipment to change output capacity. During the short-run period, the outlay for the fixed factors remains unchanged. When this unchanging sum of fixed cost is spread over increasing output, average fixed cost decreases. Since all firm costs in the short run are either variable or fixed, average total cost is the addition of the two. Average total cost, when expressed as a curve, is a blend of variable and fixed costs. For example, the average total cost curve exceeds average variable cost by the contribution of average fixed cost. The average fixed cost curve is a rectangular hyperbola, declining continuously as output increases, and when averaged fixed cost is added to average variable cost, the low point on the average total cost curve occurs above and to the right of the low point on the average variable cost curve. The low point on the average total cost curve can be identified as *LTUC*—lowest total unit cost—to distinguish it from the low point on the average variable cost curve. As in the case of average variable cost, however, the marginal cost curve intersects the average total cost curve at the latter's lowest point.

If the firm is to cover all costs—fixed as well as variable—it must produce beyond the point of diminishing returns. Average total costs are lowest at the point at which the marginal cost curve intersects the average total cost curve at LTUC, which is sometimes identified as the optimum output point. This output is considered optimum because per unit cost is lowest at this point.

Key terms and concepts

Short run the economic time period during which a firm can adjust output by using more or less variable factor in combination with a fixed factor.

Long run the economic time period during which any factor of production can be increased or decreased, the technique of production modified, and new firms can enter the industry or old ones leave.

Variable factors or inputs productive resources employed by the firm such as labor and materials that can be increased or decreased in the short run.

Fixed factors or inputs productive resources employed by the firm such as capital or land that *cannot* be modified in kind or amount in the short run.

Capital machinery and equipment employed by the firm in production.

Law of diminishing returns when variable inputs are successively added to a fixed factor, average output initially rises, reaches a peak—the point of diminishing returns—and then declines.

Average returns short-run total returns or output divided by the variable inputs employed in their production.

Marginal returns the incremental change in short-run total returns resulting from adding or reducing variable factors.

Law of variable proportions law of diminishing returns.

LTUC the lowest point on the average total cost curve.

Average total cost average variable cost plus average fixed cost.

Average variable cost total variable cost divided by output.

Average fixed cost total fixed cost divided by output.

Marginal cost the incremental change in total cost resulting from the production of successive units of output.

Discussion and review questions

1. The Russian grain deal of 1972 had both immediate market effects and longer-range impacts. How did the market react to the grain deal during these periods? What would you have done differently if you had been in charge of the US Department of Agriculture during the negotiations? If you had been a private US trader?

2. The wheat season—from planting to harvest—illustrates a short-run production period in which land is a fixed factor. Wheat output can be varied during this period, but not very much. What kind of changes can be made during the short-run wheat production period by increasing or withdrawing other factors to modify output?

3. The principle of diminishing returns describes physical input-output relationships. How is this principle relevant to economic considerations? Specifically, what causes diminishing returns?

4. In the early nineteenth century, the principle of diminishing returns was interpreted very broadly in predicting declining food output. The predictions did not

come about. Why not? Has the principle of diminishing returns become more relevant in its broader application in recent years?

5. What are the reasons for the predictions of the neo-Malthusians such as the limits-to-growth believers? How do economists generally appraise these predictions?

6. When applied to firm output on a smaller scale, what conditions must prevail in order for diminishing returns to occur? Illustrate from your own knowledge two or three instances where the conditions necessary for diminishing returns are satisfied.

7. Why are there no diminishing returns in the long run?

8. Do diminishing returns occur in *all* short-run situations?

9. What conditions must prevail in order for cost curves to be essentially a reversal or mirror of product curves?

10. It seems illogical for the firm to carry production past the point of diminishing returns. Why does the firm do so?

11. Why does average fixed cost wander all over the diagram with different production arrangements, while average variable cost and marginal cost maintain a set relationship to each other?

12. What is the relationship between the short-run industry supply curve and the firm's marginal cost curve?

7 The producer at the mercy of the market: competition

The price of milk has gone up throughout the country between 10 and 20 cents a gallon.

*Beef prices are coming down . . . the price has dropped to levels near those of last year.**

The same thing that caused rising milk prices brought about falling beef prices. Reductions in dairy herds in the fall of 1973 decreased the output of milk and increased the supply of beef. The basic reason for the curtailment of dairy operations during this period was an unfavorable cost-price relationship for dairy farmers. Dairy feed prices had risen sharply during the summer of 1973, more so than milk prices, making the sale of dairy herds in the high-priced beef market increasingly attractive. As herds were reduced, the supply of milk decreased and that of beef increased, thus boosting milk prices and decreasing beef prices.

The most obvious conclusion to be drawn from the above case is that economic events are sometimes quite interdependent—what happens in one part of the economy affects economic activity elsewhere. An equally significant message is the supremacy of the market in establishing milk and beef prices. Individually, consumers and producers in some fields, such as the dairy and beef industries, have little control over prices through their purchases and sales. Producers are at the mercy of the market; they cannot drive prices up even if they withhold their entire output and prices will not fall if they offer their total supply for sale. In like manner the individual consumer, even the largest household, is unable to create a price ripple in the milk and beef markets.

If producers get together and restrict output, however, prices will be affected. But when there are many suppliers, it is difficult for producers to arrange restrictive agreements—quite aside from their illegality. Over the years, the government has imposed output restrictions and price controls

* Ann-Mary Currier, "Beef Prices Dip, Milk Goes Up." *The Boston Globe*, October 4, 1973, p. 35.

in many areas of agriculture—most states control the retail price of milk, for example—so that something less than untrammeled competition prevails in some agricultural markets. But in spite of such intervention, important areas of the agricultural sector are largely competitive.

What makes one industry competitive and another not?

The kinds and causes of competition

In examining the economic behavior of firms and industries, economists have advanced a number of concepts that distinguish among different degrees of competition. These include perfect competition, pure competition, free competition, workable competition, imperfect competition, and monopolistic competition. Some of these concepts, such as perfect competition, are highly abstract rather than descriptive of real market situations. Others, such as pure competition, have a limited application to the American economy. And at the other end of the competitive spectrum, the concepts imperfect and monopolistic competition are designed to explain the market behavior of the real world.

In examining decision making by the firm, the logical starting point is the competitive short run, mainly because it is simpler and involves more straightforward cost-price responses than some of the more complex monopolistic market arrangements. Although the short run is the main focus of this chapter, the long run necessarily enters the discussion at times in establishing the territory of the two concepts.

Pure competition

The competitive short-run concept employed here is that of *pure competition,* which has important parallels in the market economy. Perfect competition involves a less realistic model of firm behavior, in which knowledge is all-encompassing, decisions flawless, and responses instantaneous. For the not-so-perfect competitive short run, the following, less rigorous conditions of pure competition are closer to reality.

Many producers and consumers

With many producers, an output change by one does not have an appreciable impact upon market supply and, therefore, upon price.

Another consequence is that with many producers, collusion to limit output is difficult to arrange and maintain. Under such circumstances, firms accept market decisions as beyond their control and unrelated to whether they *individually* increase or decrease output. The firm views the competitive market as a horizontal demand curve for its product, with price unchanged by its actions. This view of the market, noted first in Chapter 4, is illustrated again in Figure 7.1.

In like manner, there must be enough consumers in the market so that one or a few do not dominate purchases and dictate the producers' sale price, as may occur where a few large firms are the sole market for a product or service. Competition depends on more than a large number of producers and consumers, however. It requires a high degree of similarity in products or services offered for sale.

Identical products

If products are different, even if the difference is trivial—a color shade or brand name—some consumers will find in such distinctions a basis for preference. When this happens, it is no longer possible to lump the output of all producers together on the same supply curve. Nor can we add the demand of consumers on a single collective curve; that is, industry demand and supply curves cannot be drawn. When the products of all producers are identical, a single price prevails in the market. If products are different, preferences generate different prices and reduce the area of competition. If all farmers raise the same type of wheat, for example, the range of competition extends across the total wheat supply. But if both

Figure 7.1 The Competitive Firm's Demand Curve

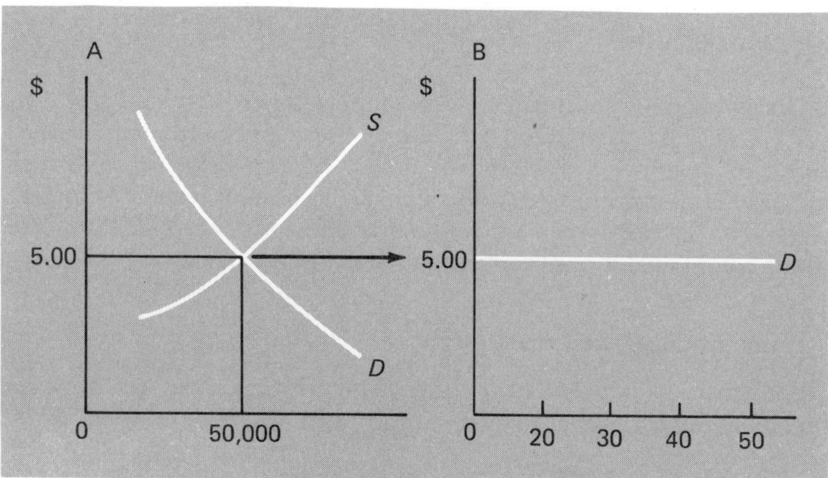

hard- and soft-kernel wheat are grown, which have different markets, then the range of competition is restricted and individual demand and supply curves must be constructed for each type of wheat. As commodities are made more distinctive, either by brand name or by basic design, the substitution of one for another decreases in direct proportion to the success of differentiation.

Since most manufacturers in an advanced economy attempt to distinguish their product from that of their competitors, identical products are most frequently found in agricultural or raw material markets, where a given type of wheat, coal, ore, or petroleum is much the same whether sold by one firm or another. When a commodity's characteristics are measurable, standard classifications and specialized markets generally arise with such designations as Number 2 soft red wheat, Mesabi Bessemer grade iron ore, Number 1 yellow soy beans, Number 2 bunker fuel oil, and AA grade exterior plywood.

In an industry that consists of many firms producing identical products, the competition between firms is generally intense. Even though the number of producers may be large enough to prevent collusive restriction of output, however, a sharp increase in the demand for a commodity may bring a higher-than-competitive return if there are production bottlenecks.

For supply to keep pace with demand there must be a free flow of resources to all the firms in an industry. These requisites of competition, mobility of resources plus freedom of entry, cut across both the short- and long-run periods. Both are necessary for effective competition.

Mobility of resources and freedom of entry

In the short run, a manufacturing firm, farm enterprise, or retail establishment is unable to modify its fixed factor or change its production techniques to meet an increase or decrease in product demand. The firm adapts by adding labor and raw materials, or by laying off workers and cutting back on materials. In a competitive industry, the firm does not change its output to influence price, but responds to a price change with output modifications. In adjusting to market price, marginal cost is the firm's guide to output, adding variable inputs and increasing output as price rises and restricting inputs and decreasing output as price falls. When resources are mobile, the short-run adjustment follows the course of the firm marginal cost curve, reacting to changes in market prices that are brought about by movements in the industry demand and supply curves. The firm-industry relationship is shown in Figure 7.2, in which different market prices are established by increasing demand from Curve D_1 through Curve D_3. The firm's short-run supply response in turn increases from 50 through 150 units of output.

Figure 7.2 Firm Input Mobility

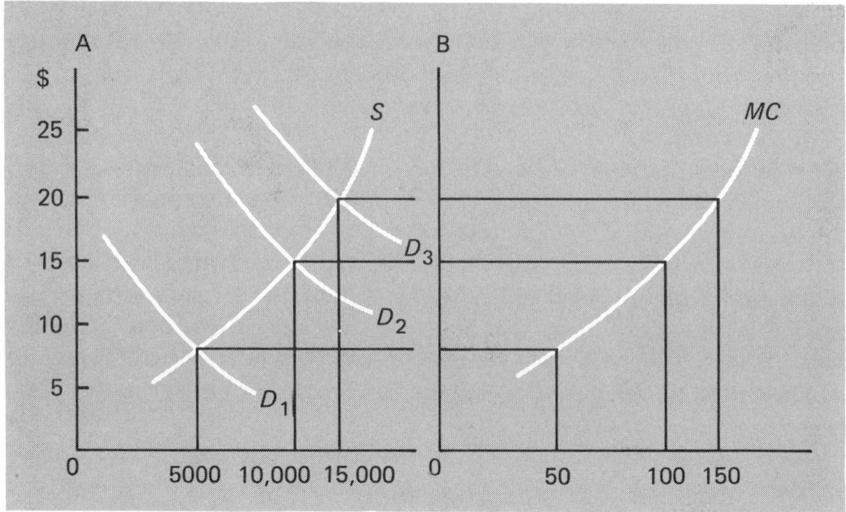

Marginal cost equals supply

The firm's marginal cost curve is shown in Figure 7.2B to emphasize its controlling role in the firm's response to market price, and to show graphically the relationship between the marginal cost curve, which is the firm's supply curve, and the industry supply curve in Figure 7.2A. The industry or market supply curve is a summation of the marginal cost curves for all the firms in a given industry or market above the intersection of marginal cost and average variable cost. We will discuss the reasons for this in some detail later in the chapter.

Since the industry supply curve is a composite of the marginal cost curves for all the firms in the industry, it does not necessarily correspond precisely to a particular firm's marginal cost curve. Finally, although it may be completely obvious from what has been said, the output scales for the firm and the industry are also quite different, as Figure 7.2 shows. The industry supply schedule covers all of the firms in the industry. The units on its horizontal axis consequently represent a much larger magnitude of output than that of the firm.

Mobility and the long run

Mobility of resources in the short run permits the firm to increase or decrease variable inputs while fixed factors remain unchanged. Long-run resource mobility allows for expansion or contraction of any and all

Marginalism in the air, or why it pays to fly planes less than half full

Continental Airlines, Inc., . . . [in 1962] filled only half the available seats on its Boeing 707 jet flights, a record some 15 percentage points worse than the national average.

By eliminating just a few runs—less than 5%—Continental could have raised its average load considerably. Some of its flights frequently carry as few as 30 passengers on the 120-seat plane. But the improved load factor would have meant reduced profits.

For Continental bolsters its corporate profits by deliberately running extra flights that aren't expected to do more than return their out-of-pocket [marginal] costs—plus a little profit. This philosophy leans heavily on marginal analysis . . . . Put most simply, marginalists maintain that a company should undertake any activity that adds more to revenues than it does to costs—and not limit itself to those activities whose returns equal average or "fully allocated" costs.

The approach, of course, can be applied to virtually any business, not just to air transportation. It can be used in consumer finance, for instance, where the question may be whether to make more loans—including more bad loans—if this will increase net profit. Similarly, in advertising, the decision may rest on how much extra business a dollar's worth of additional advertising will bring in, rather than pegging the advertising budget to a percentage of sales—and, in insurance, where setting high interest rates to discourage policy loans may actually damage profits by causing policy-holders to borrow elsewhere.

The difficulty comes in applying the simple "textbook" marginal concept to specific decisions. If the economist is unwilling to make some bold simplifications, the job of determining "true" marginal costs may be highly complex, time-wasting, and too expensive. But even a rough application of marginal analysis may come closer to the right answer for business decision makers than an analysis based on precise average-cost data.[1]

factors—those fixed in the short run as well as the variable inputs. Long-run mobility thus takes a number of different forms: modification in the size of individual firms, changes in the number of firms in the industry, or combinations of the two. In some industries, such as retail gasoline distribution, growth takes place mainly by opening more filling stations rather than by enlarging existing stations. Similarly, long-run reductions in supply usually involve the selective closing of stations. Other industries, such

[1] "Airline Takes the Marginal Route," *Business Week*, April 20, 1963, pp. 111-12.

as iron and steel and auto manufacturing, grow by increasing the output capacity of existing firms—expanding Bethlehem Steel, US Steel, General Motors, or American Motors. When was the last time a *new* US automobile company successfully marketed a car? (Kaiser-Frazer did during the post-World War II era, although its success was short-lived.) From a broader perspective, the Japanese postwar entrance into world auto production represents an unusually successful case of market penetration, although in a car size that had generally been ignored by American producers.

Long-run mobility through the entry of new firms (or, in the case of adjustment to decreased long-run demand, through exit of firms) is a more reliable indicator of competitive conditions than firm expansion or contraction. In any market situation—competition, monopolistic competition, or monopoly[2]—a firm can employ more or less of such variables as labor and raw materials unless there are shortages or restrictions on the use of these inputs. But whether the response of the firm constitutes a competitive or monopolistic adjustment depends upon long-run resource availability. The precondition for competition is resource availability, extending to firm entry, so that output restriction does not drive up prices. In competition, mobility coerces firms to produce at the least cost point (LTUC) where the long-run and short-run forces of competition come together in a stable price-cost equilibrium. One of the necessary conditions for such an equilibrium is knowledge by producers and consumers of the product and marketing conditions.

Knowledge of product and market

Both producers and consumers need to be informed for the competitive system to work well. Neither group can act in its economic self-interest if it is ignorant or misinformed about market opportunities.

For the consumer, inadequate information about products and services—at times involving misinformation or irrelevant information—leads to a randomness in purchase signals to the producer and shifts power to the producer. When competition is vigorous, however, the consumer is protected from producer manipulation. Part of vigorous competition comes from large, standardized product markets. The sale of wheat, iron

[2] Tentatively, the main type of market arrangements discussed in this chapter can be distinguished as follows: competition involves a large number of firms producing identical products, monopolistic competition consists of a smaller number of firms producing products that are similar but not identical, while monopoly occurs when a single firm produces a product that has no close substitutes. These brief characterizations will be developed further as our discussion proceeds.

ore, soybeans, magnesium, bauxite, and sow bellies is worldwide, for example, and although this does not thereby ensure competition, it extends the range from which supplies can be drawn and enlarges the area of buying and selling.

Knowledge of product and market not only contributes to the rational behavior of consumers and producers, it is necessary in order for self-interest to bring about an optimum allocation of resources within the economy. The presumption of Chapter 2 of efficient resource allocation in a competitive market economy can now be related to the structure of firm cost and changes in demand. In doing so, we will trace short-run market price changes and show how the firm adjusts to these changes.

But let us turn first to a question held over from our previous discussion of the mobility of inputs: why does the firm produce where marginal cost equals price?

Marginal cost and firm output

The firm takes its price cue from the market and adjusts its output so that marginal cost equals price, as is shown in Figure 7.2. The firm follows this practice whether price is high or low, whether it makes a profit or, within limits, a loss.

Why?

Because by producing where marginal cost is equal to price, the firm makes the greatest possible profit—if price is favorable—or the least possible loss—if price is too low. In other words, the firm maximizes profit or minimizes loss by equating marginal cost and price. But this doesn't sound reasonable: How can a firm be better off economically if it pushes output to the point where price and marginal cost are equal? In Figure 7.3 this is the case at 500 units of output. Why not produce where price is *above* marginal cost, say at 499 units of output, and thereby receive more for the sale of the output than it costs to produce?

Few maxims would appear to be more self-evident than that it is desirable to sell a product for more than it costs to produce. Indeed, this proposition is eminently sound when applied to total cost and total revenue, or when average cost and average revenue are related. But it does not hold true for marginal cost and price. The reason is that the marginal cost curve traces a sequence of incremental costs for a corresponding range of firm output. A high cost for the 500th unit produced, for example, does not necessarily mean high production costs for the 499th, 498th, and 497th units. The firm will expand production so long as one additional unit of output will add more to revenue than to cost. This

Figure 7.3 Short-Run Equilibrium Where Marginal Cost = Price

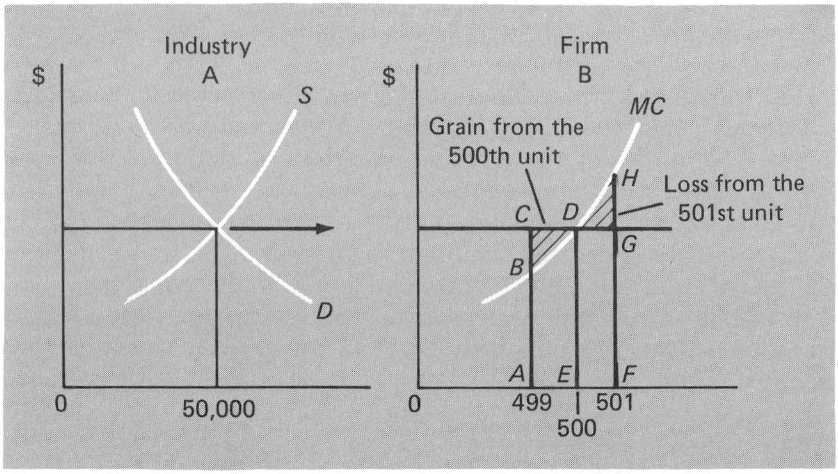

expansion will continue until marginal cost (MC) equals price. When MC = price at the 500th unit of output in Figure 7.3, further production causes marginal cost to rise above price.

By expanding the firm segment of Figure 7.3B, we can demonstrate the MC = price principle by comparing the changes in marginal cost and price. Since price remains unchanged throughout the range of the firm's output, the same increment of revenue is obtained from the sale of an additional unit of output whether it is the 499th, the 500th, or the 501st, but each additional unit of output costs more. The cost-revenue relationship in Figure 7.3 can be summarized as follows:

1. *Increasing output from 499 units to 500 units*
   Adds to revenue ACDE
   Adds to cost ABDE
   By producing the 500th unit, revenue exceeds cost by BCD.
2. *Increasing output from 500 units to 501 units*
   Adds to revenue EDGF (= ACDE)
   Adds to cost EDHF
   By producing the 501st unit, cost exceeds revenue by DHG.

Only the MC = price rule is illustrated in Figure 7.3. The diagram does not reveal how well off the firm is at the various outputs. By adding the firm's average total cost curve to the diagram, however, as in Figure 7.4B, it is easy to see whether the firm is making or losing money. The areas of "gain" and "loss" identified in Figure 7.3 refer only to the relationship between marginal cost and revenue, *not* to the overall profit or loss of the firm.

"Best off" during times of profit and loss

In seeking to maximize profit or minimize loss, how does the firm adjust output? Figure 7.4 illustrates three "best-off" output situations.

As price moves from $1.00 to $1.30 to $1.60, three successive periods of short-run equilibria are established, during which the firm equates MC and price. In each case, given the prevailing price-cost relationship, the economic forces affecting the firm are in balance. As price moves from $1.00 to $1.30 to $1.60, caused by shifts in industry demand from Curve D_1 to Curve D_2 to Curve D_3, the firm expands output from 500 units to 750 units to 900 units. The industry response to price change is 100 times that of the firm, reflecting the collective reaction of all the firms in the industry to the price change. With each higher price, the firm's economic well-being improves, moving steadily from the lowest price at which the firm can stay in business—where price is equal to marginal cost at average variable cost—to a profit at a price well above LTUC.

The firm at a loss

When the firm produces at a price below LTUC, as it does when the price is $1.00, cost exceeds price, but the firm is better off than if it shut down. In Figure 7.4, an output of 500 units at $1.00 represents the shut-down point. If price falls below $1.00, the firm will cease production because when price falls below average variable cost, the firm loses more by continuing to produce than by ceasing operations. The reason for this will be approached gradually.

The obvious question is: Why does the firm produce at all when price is below LTUC and it cannot cover all of its costs? The answer lies in the firm's cost structure and in the nature of the short run.

Remember that the short run isn't forever. For a limited time, the firm can produce at a loss with price below LTUC, but this cannot continue indefinitely. For the short run, the firm is actually better off operating at a loss in those cases in which price covers variable cost *plus something toward fixed cost* than it would be by shutting down. This is illustrated by the case of Northeast Airlines, which for years operated in the red before it was absorbed by Delta Airlines. Northeast didn't ground its flights during the years it was losing more than $10 million annually. To have done so would

Figure 7.4 The Firm in Short-Run Equilibria of Profit and Loss

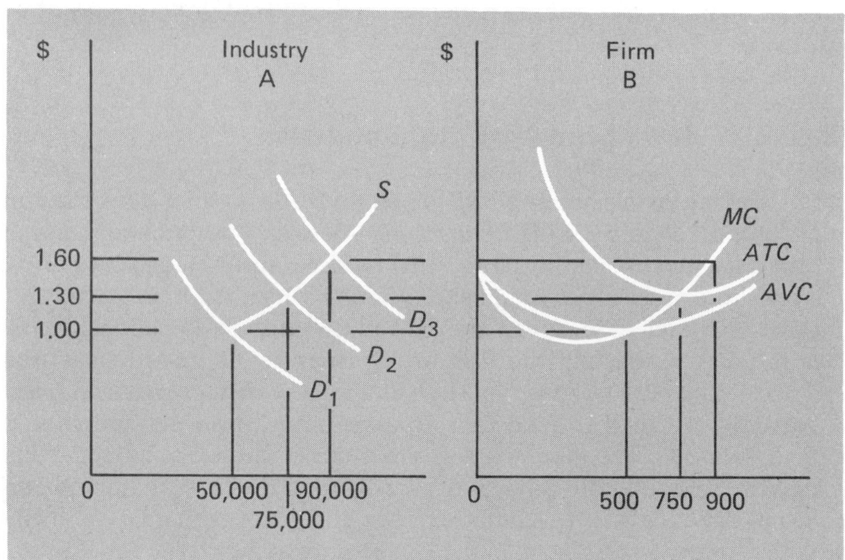

have brought about even greater losses. An oversimplified, semihypothetical illustration will show that economically Northeast Airlines had to keep flying.

Annual variable cost	$50 million
Annual fixed cost	40 million
Annual total cost	90 million
Annual revenue	80 million
Operating loss	$10 million

By continuing operations, Northeast Airlines lost $10 million annually. If it had ceased operations it would have lost $40 million. It is of course better not to have a loss, but if loss is inevitable, a small one is preferable to a large one. Northeast could not escape its fixed costs by shutting down. Variable costs, such as outlays for manpower and materials, are closely correlated with firm output. Fixed costs—such as interest on capital, rent, property taxes, salaries of key personnel, and maintenance charges—continue whether the firm is producing or not. Northeast Airline's fixed costs included its aircraft, hangers, maintenance facilities, and office, ticket counter, and passenger lounge space. Most of these facilities were financed partly by bonds issued with fixed interest and due dates or by long-term leases that were established for years ahead. These changes would have continued whether Northeast had shut down operations or flown its normal schedule.

But a firm's fixed charges, although they can be disregarded in short-run decisions, must eventually be paid if the firm is to avoid being placed under court receivership. For a time, a firm can operate in the red, as long as it can live off its own capital or persuade its creditors that it will eventually recoup its losses. When the long run comes around and fixed inputs have to be replaced, however, the firm will be hard put to finance new equipment unless it can liquidate past indebtedness. If unsuccessful, it will drop from sight because of its inability to maintain its capital structure or it will be absorbed by a firm that covets its market or needs its losses to reduce its corporate tax payments.

The unforgiving long run

In a competitive market, the long run deals harshly with what the short run tolerates. Only a price at LTUC, or $1.30 in Figure 7.4, will prevail in the long run. Any other price under competition—either $1.00, which involves a loss, or $1.60, which brings a profit—will be pushed up by the exit of firms, or pushed down by an inflow of production capacity. We have already noted the inability of the firm to replace worn-out machinery and equipment when its total costs are above price in the long run. An opposing force—the influx of productive capacity—confronts firms in an industry where price is significantly above LTUC. In the competitive long run, profit is self-destructive.

The great bank fiasco of recent times: the Franklin National failure—or the necessity of covering marginal cost

At the time of . . . the Franklin National Bank crisis in May 1974, Franklin held close to $300 million in municipal bonds with an average yield of only 4 percent. That yield was about 3 to 3.5 percentage points below the bank's average cost of money and about 7 percentage points below its marginal cost. Just comparing average yield with average cost, the bank was losing about $10 million a year on its municipal-bond holdings.[3]

---

[3] Sanford Rose, "What Really Went Wrong At Franklin National," *Fortune*, October 1974, p. 121.

What economists mean by profit

Everyone knows what *profit* means, and this gives economists a difficult time because their version of the concept is different from popular usages.

The owner-operator of a small retail clothing store, for example, considers profit to be what he or she has left after making payments to others—employees' wages, the cost of inventory, taxes, and other outlays. The owner-operator is not likely to consider as a cost what he or she could have earned working as a shop manager for someone else, or what the store he owns would bring in rent if leased to another enterpriser. But the salary and rent that the owner-operator might have received from others are costs of the use of his services and his store. As such, these costs—sometimes termed *implicit* costs—should be deducted from revenue in computing profit.

From society's standpoint, the output that is forgone when resources are used to produce one thing instead of another is a cost of what is produced, just as the cost to the owner-operator of the retail clothing store is what he could have earned working for someone else and renting his store for other purposes. But instead of acknowledging the alternative return from owned resources, the owner-operator is likely to consider everything he or she keeps as "profit." Large firms, employing more sophisticated accounting procedures, impute a cost for the use of resources that they own in order to know whether income covers full cost and not just out-of-pocket expenditures. But even large firms tend to consider profit to be what the firm keeps.

To the economist, profit arises only after the full costs of production are deducted from revenues, implicit costs for owned resources as well as out-of-pocket expenditures. The implication of this view may not be immediately apparent. It is that profit does *not* result from superior management or more productive resources. In a competitive system, such talent and productivity are rewarded by higher return.

If profit does not arise from superior management, choice location, or higher quality raw material, what does this leave? Two things—fortuitous market conditions, as represented by Curve D_3 in Figure 7.4, or restraint in output, which is to say monopoly control. The second cause of profit—monopoly—will be discussed in Chapter 8. The first—fortuitous market conditions—is responsible for profits in competition only in the short run.

Because of freedom of entry, profit in a competitive industry is a temporary phenomenon. Its presence attracts additional investment into the industry in the long run, thereby increasing supply and eliminating profit by bringing price down to LTUC. When this happens, the industry is in long-run equilibrium; firms cover their costs but at a return that does not attract further investment to the industry.

Barring changes in market demand, the firm-industry equilibrium rests at a stable, no-profit adjustment. Although the full range of the firm's response to profit carries the analysis into the long-run period, which is the subject of Chapter 10, we can't leave the firm in short-run limbo.

The steps to long-run equilibrium for the firm are traced in Figure 7.5. The starting point is short- and long-run equilibrium for the firm and industry where marginal cost is equal to price at OA. Firm output is 500 units, and industry demand and supply are equal at OA with an output of 50,000 units. This short- and long-run equilibrium is disrupted by an increase in demand from D_1 to D_2 which raises the market price to OB, causing the firm to increase output to 700 where marginal cost equals OB. The firm and industry are now in short-run equilibrium, firm output having increased by 200 units and total industry having increased output by 20,000 units. As long as new firms do not enter the industry and existing firms do not expand, which can occur only in the long run, supply curve S_1 remains in effect. But the increase in price raises the return in this industry above that of other competitive industries, thus bringing short-run profit to the firms in this industry.

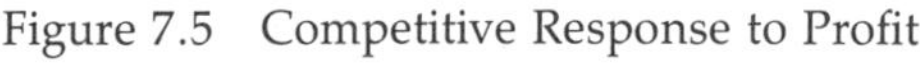

Figure 7.5 Competitive Response to Profit

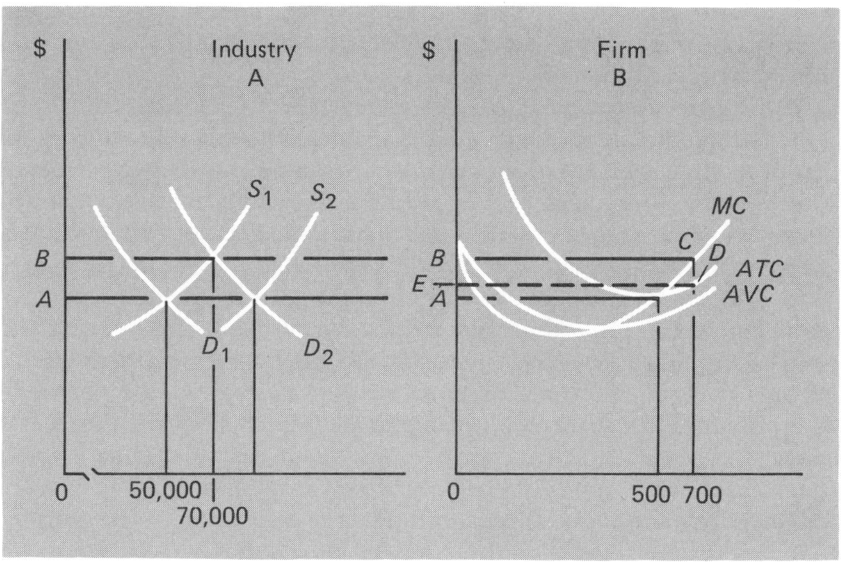

Marginal cost equals price again

Firm profit is shown in Figure 7.5B as CD (or BE) per unit of output, and EBCD represents total profit. Note that per unit profit is the difference between ATC and price for *700* units of output, not for 500 units at LTUC. Although numerous outputs yield profit when price is OB, the maximum profit occurs when 700 units are produced because this is where MC equals price. The price-cost relationship illustrated in Figure 7.5 presents a number of output options that are profitable, but the firm is best off at 700 units of output.

The move from short-run to long-run equilibrium in Figure 7.5 is illustrated as occurring without affecting either the size of the firm or its cost structure. For this to happen, expansion of the industry must take place by more firms entering the industry rather than existing firms enlarging, and without increasing the demand for factors and raising their cost to the industry. The long-run case illustrated here is that of *constant cost.* Other long-run cost functions will be considered in Chapter 10; here our interest is in the process of adjustment rather than the character of the cost function.

We left the firm and industry in short-run equilibrium with a price of OB and a profit of EBCD. But profit attracts investment in the long run, causing supply to shift to Curve S_2. The intersection of Curves D_2 and S_2 pushes price back to OA, causing the firm to contract its output to 500 units, at which level it experiences neither profit nor loss. With this adjustment there is no incentive either for the industry to expand or for firms to be forced out. The industry has returned to long-run stable equilibrium.

Logically, this chapter ends at this point, neatly resting on its long-run equilibrium, but inevitably, in some stubborn minds, the question will arise: How do firms survive if they do not make profits? Actually, the issue of whether profits are necessary for economic survival is partly one of semantics—what is meant by the term *profit*—but the question is persistent because those who receive profits are understandably most eloquent in their defense. But remember that by *profit* economists mean a return that is *in excess* of that required to keep the firm economically well off. If happiness is a 12 percent return on investment, reflecting the yield of resources in competitive ventures, then this is the cost of using and keeping the resources employed in a given industry. To the business owner, this 12 percent is "profit," but the economist views it as a *cost*—what has to be paid out to produce. As such it is a legitimate ingredient of the firm's cost curves.

Whichever view of profit is held, however, the real issue is the effect of its payment upon resource allocation. The economist's usage directs attention to this issue.

Summary

How a firm behaves in the market economy depends upon whether it controls the price of its product by its output decisions or whether the market is unaffected by these decisions. If the firm has no influence on the price of the product that it sells, this is circumstantial evidence that the firm is one of many in a competitive industry. In economics, there are different concepts of competition used to describe different market conditions and to serve as analytical models. Pure competition is employed as an introductory concept because of its simplicity and because there are parallels between this model and the market economy.

With pure competition no firm can dominate the process of price determination. There are many producers and consumers; the product offered for sale is the same from all the producers; and there is freedom of movement of resources in and out of the competitive industry and no barriers to firm entry. This is not a small order, and only approximations of pure competition are encountered in the modern economy, but the model is a useful frame of reference in the analysis of price determination.

If there is pure competition in a market, the firm adjusts its output to the prevailing market price by carrying output to the point at which its marginal cost is equal to the market price. At this output, the firm's profit will be greatest or its losses least. Thus, whether the firm is making money or losing money, so long as it stays in business it will be best off by producing where marginal cost and price are equal. If the firm curtails output and produces where price exceeds marginal cost, it will lose the gain that it could obtain by increasing output, which brings in more when sold than it costs to produce. If the firm carries output beyond the point at which MC equals price, however, it adds more to cost than it does to revenue since this output costs more to produce than it sells for. The MC = price rule holds whether the market price is above or below LTUC.

The firm responds to price changes in the short run by increasing output when price rises and decreasing output when price falls. The marginal cost curve traces the firm's output reactions to changing price; thus the marginal cost curve is the firm's supply curve. Only the portion of the marginal cost curve above its intersection with average variable cost is the firm's supply curve, however, since when price drops below average variable cost, the firm is economically better off if it shuts down. For the short run, the firm can operate at a loss so long as price is above average variable cost because by doing so it covers all variable cost and a portion of its fixed outlays. If it shuts down, none of the fixed outlays—which would nonetheless continue—would be covered. When price falls below average variable cost, however, the firm loses money not only on the fixed factors but also on the variable factors. The economic message is clear: cease operations.

If the firm produces at a price above LTUC in the short run it makes a profit. Profit is defined more narrowly by the economist than by the accountant or businessman. For the economist, profit is what is left after deducting all costs, implicit as well as explicit. There are two main causes of profit: fortuitous market conditions, such as an increase in demand, and monopoly control of pricing, such as the OPEC manipulation of the world crude oil price.

Key terms and concepts

Competition a market condition in which neither producers nor consumers individually can significantly affect an industry's output or price.

Mobility of resources the response of factors of production such as labor and capital to price change by moving to areas of higher price and retreating from areas of lower reward.

Freedom of entry the unrestricted opportunity for a firm to place on the market a product identical or similar to that already sold by other firms.

Equilibrium a balance of economic forces—either within the economy, industry, or firm—in which there is no pressure to modify the existing resource allocation.

Short-run equilibrium in competition, the point at which price is determined by the intersection of demand and supply in the industry and firm output by the equity of marginal cost and price. In monopolistic competition and pure monopoly, short-run equilibrium involves the equity of marginal cost and marginal revenue.

Long-run equilibrium in competition, output for the firm at which marginal cost equals price at LTUC and demand is equal to supply for the industry. In monopolistic competition, the output at which marginal cost is equal to marginal revenue and average cost is equal to average revenue. In pure monopoly, the output at which marginal cost is equal to marginal revenue and average cost is less than average revenue.

Profit in competition and monopolistic competition, return above that necessary to cover the full cost of inputs, such as land, labor, and capital, that results from short-run fortuitous circumstances. In the case of monopoly, profit is the return above costs that results from restriction of output.

Discussion and review questions

1. What areas of the economy do you consider to be most competitive?

2. What are the requisites of pure competition, and to what extent do you find them in the real world?

3. In pure competition, the firm demand curve is horizontal but the industry demand curve is downslanting. Since the industry is made up of firms, why is there this difference?

4. Why is it not possible to construct a single demand curve and a single supply curve for all wheat produced in the United States and Canada?

5. What is meant by saying that the short-run firm adjustment follows the course of the marginal cost curve? What is the upper and lower range of the firm short-run adjustment?

6. The firm marginal cost curve is best understood as a supply curve. How does the firm marginal cost curve relate to the industry supply curve?

7. Why does it pay to fly airplanes less than half full?

8. What factors of production are mobile in the short run? What factors are not mobile?

9. In pure competition, why is the firm forced to produce where marginal cost equals price (marginal revenue)?

10. Why does the firm produce at all when its costs are higher than the price of its product?

11. Why does the firm continue to produce as long as the price of its product covers average variable cost?

12. Why do economists define profit differently from the way in which the concept is generally understood in the business community?

8 Something less than competition I: the causes

*They've gone off on a kick that'll make them big goddamn trust-busters. That was all right fifty years ago. Fifty years ago it was a good thing for the country. It's not a good thing for the country today.—Richard M. Nixon.**

San Francisco, July 25 (AP)—A Federal jury found the A & P supermarket chain guilty today of fixing prices in buying fresh meat and assessed the giant company a total of $32,712,081 in damages. The Great Atlantic and Pacific Tea Company was found guilty of conspiring to fix prices at both the wholesale and retail levels.†

It is almost a century ago that trust-busting got its somewhat uncertain start in the United States with the passage of the Sherman Antitrust Act in 1890. The promotion of competition in the American economy has since become the accepted national policy, although the history of the Sherman Act is one of uneven enforcement.

The trust and the Sherman Antitrust Act

During the development of large-scale industrial capitalism in the United States in the late nineteenth century,[1] the monopoly practices that accompanied this growth became increasingly oppressive to small business, Midwestern farmers, and the consumer. In this period, control of

* "Richard M. Nixon Tapes on the Kleindienst—ITT Affair," *The Wall Street Journal*, July 22, 1974, p. 3. Reprinted with permission of *The Wall Street Journal*, © Dow Jones & Company, Inc. 1974. All rights reserved.

† *The New York Times*, July 26, 1974, p. 43. © 1974 by The New York Times Company. Reprinted by permission.

[1] Monopoly market control by no means originated with industrial capitalism. In the year 1700, for example, 70 percent of the beaver pelt supply was destroyed by fur companies in Montreal in order to prevent a fall in price.

price and output was achieved through the *trust,* a legal arrangement that enforced output restrictions and price maintenance on the part of participating firms. Prior to the Sherman Antitrust Act, agreements to fix prices were not illegal, although they could not be enforced as contracts under common law. For this reason, and to avoid the uncertainty of whether firms would hold to a price agreement, trusts were formed. The formation of the trust transferred, or entrusted, the voting stock of the participating firms to one of the firms for a period of five years or so. The trust organization spread widely as a means of controlling output and price. As the early vehicle of price fixing, the term *trust* has become synonymous with monopoly practices in general and has remained in our language even when the object of antimonopoly prosecution is not a trust, but a more modern form of business organization.

The Sherman Act was aimed mainly at preventing restraint of trade, collusive price-fixing, and other restrictive practices, but its antimonopoly scope was quite broad. Early interpretation of the law by the Supreme Court weakened it greatly, however, and later court decisions and supplementary Congressional legislation were required to restore the act's original purpose. The major responsibility for its enforcement lies with the federal government's special Antitrust Division of the Department of Justice, but a novel feature of the Sherman Act is the "triple-damage" provision that affords a party injured by monopoly practices the right to sue for three times the actual loss incurred. The framers of the Sherman Act hoped that this exceptional damage penalty would discourage monopoly practices, and thus reduce the need for litigation and enforcement by the federal government.

The triple-damage provision has not much influenced business behavior, however, although it has occasionally been invoked against a business firm. The $32,712,081 damage suit against the Great Atlantic & Pacific Tea Company (A & P) in 1974 involved a triple-damage suit. The court found that A & P was so able to dominate meat purchases in some markets that it controlled prices. (This form of market control is called *monopsony*—monopoly in purchase by a single buyer. If the sale of a commodity is dominated by a small number of buyers, the control by purchasers is called *oligopsony*.) Market control by buyers generally attracts less attention than a seller's monopoly, although in certain markets—tobacco auctions, for example—the number of large buyers is limited, leading to public exposure of the buyers' greater influence in the pricing process. And in the early summer of 1974, the player hold-outs in the National Football League carried picket signs that charged the clubs with being "oligopsonists"!

Clearly, economics is relevant!

The compromise of competition

It would be wrong to give the impression that the American economy has descended from a state of early competitive grace to one of latter-day monopolistic sin. From the very onset of capitalism, producers have seldom overlooked an opportunity to restrict supply and raise price, and frequently the opportunities were more abundant in the earlier period of industrial development than they are now. Some of the best examples of restraint of trade and corporate domination are found in the era of the early industrial giants—Rockefeller, Carnegie, Betcha-A-Million Gates, Judge Gary of steel price-fixing dinners fame[2], and the supreme financial overlord, J. P. Morgan. This was a time when power built up fast as markets expanded and new industries developed. A certain ruthlessness toward business rivals, which sometimes led to their summary elimination, called attention to the compromise of competition. The niceties of later approaches to market control, such as the combination movement of the 1920s, accomplished much the same thing, but without exposing the corporate tooth and claw. Early or late, however, producers have been alert to ways of controlling market supply to reduce the intensity of competition.

Raw materials control

Before World War II, the Aluminum Company of America (Alcoa) and its subsidiary, Aluminium of Canada, were the only producers of virgin aluminum in the Western Hemisphere. This classic case of monopoly—a single producer with a unique product—was firmly grounded in patents and large-scale ownership of raw materials. Patent control of the electrolitic process of producing aluminum was the basic source of Alcoa's market control, making the acquisition of bauxite deposits, the raw material from which aluminum is refined, of little purpose to other firms.

Alcoa is no longer a pure monopoly. The structure of the aluminum industry was abruptly altered by World War II, and neither patents nor high-grade bauxite ownership enabled Alcoa to retain control of the market. Actually, Alcoa's patent rights to the electrolitic process expired, and a way to use lower-grade bauxite was developed, but the company's lonely supremacy in the industry was abruptly altered by the enormous increase in production capacity during the 1940s. The Defense Plant Corporation, a federal wartime agency, built aluminum plants and leased them to private

[2] Elbert Henry Gary, county judge before becoming corporation lawyer and first chairman of the board of directors of the United States Steel Corporation, imposed the Corporation's will upon the steel industry through the "Gary dinners." At these gatherings, industry policy was discussed and informal agreements were reached with other firms in the industry.

firms during the war to meet the extraordinary aluminum needs of the aircraft industry.

After the war, the federal government followed a policy of disposing of these plants wherever possible to firms other than Alcoa, such as the Reynolds and the Kaiser concerns. The postwar structure of the aluminum industry changed from that of a single firm to a few firms, but the effect of the change was greater than the modest increase in the number of firms would suggest. Although there were only a few firms in the industry, the industry's increased production capacity was far greater than it would have been after a period of peacetime growth. This increased capacity sparked healthy competition for postwar markets. The industry changed from pure monopoly to oligopoly, but to an oligopoly that was more competitive than might be expected.

A large investment in a processing facility such as a multimillion-dollar aluminum plant, petroleum refinery, or steel mill, is not undertaken unless a raw material supply can be assured for the life expectancy of the investment. But a firm's raw material policy may serve as more than a guarantee against running out of the ingredients of production; a firm may acquire such a large share of existing raw material supply that entry into the market by other firms is both difficult and costly. The early history of the United States Steel Corporation illustrates this point.

Formed in 1901, US Steel brought together in one corporation about half of the steel capacity in the United States, but substantially more than half of the high-grade Lake Superior iron ore deposits. Overwhelmingly the dominant firm in the industry, with the largest holdings of low-cost Mesabi ore, for many years after its formation US Steel represented a formidable barrier to the entry of new firms. Over the years, however, US Steel's capacity share in the industry has declined. This was the result not so much of the infiltration of new firms into the steel industry, but of the expansion of firms already in the industry. Although shorn of some of its power, US Steel is still the acknowledged price leader in the industry. We will consider how it exercises price leadership later in the chapter in our discussion of collusion and mutuality of interest.

Patent control

The history of Alcoa illustrates the role of patents as a source of monopoly power, but two additional points need to be made about patents as a basis for monopoly.

First, patents are granted for innovative production techniques or new products that are presumably beneficial to mankind. As a stimulus and reward, the innovator is given exclusive marketing rights to such developments. In effect, the patent holder is granted a monopoly and exempted from antitrust prosecution for the life of the patent. The inevitable question is: Where is the public interest? In promoting innovation and thereby decreasing competition, or in encouraging competition at the expense of reducing innovation? Unfortunately, it is not possible to generalize in this instance. Whether such a trade off of advantages and disadvantages occurs frequently and, if so, whether the public interest is best served by granting patents or preventing monopoly depends on the particular case.

Second, although a patent establishes a legal monopoly over a product or process, it is illegal to employ this privilege to exert control over unpatented products or processes. For example, at one time the United Shoe Machinery Corporation (USMC) leased its equipment to shoe manufacturers on an all-or-none basis. One of its products, the lasting machine, was clearly superior to competitors' models. But to obtain the use of the lasting machine, a shoe manufacturer has to lease the full line of USMC equipment, most of which was no better than competitors' machinery. By leasing its lasting machine as a part of a package deal, USMC captured much of the shoe machinery market. This practice was eventually prohibited by the US Supreme Court as a restraint of trade.

Large firm market control

A large firm, whether an efficient producer or not, can manipulate the market in a way that its smaller rivals cannot hope to do. In oligopoly, not only does the large firm have an appreciable impact on market supply, but in a nationwide or worldwide market it can sell below cost in one region to discipline or encroach upon the market of a competitor, while holding price at a profitable high in other areas. The early practices of the Standard Oil Company show how the large firm may turn operations over a broad market area to its advantage.

During the infancy of the petroleum industry, the market for crude oil was highly unstable and frequently glutted from new oil discoveries, which were difficult to predict and harder to control. By contrast, the refining and retailing end of the business offered safe investment and stable return. "Coal Oil Johnny," John D. Rockefeller, chose safety and stability. Under Rockefeller's direction, the Standard Oil Company became the industry giant. The leverage that redounded from its dominance of the industry was legendary—and probably apocryphal in some instances. In negotiating freight rates on oil shipments with the Pennsylvania Railroad, for example, the Rockefeller company is said to have obtained a rebate not only on every barrel of oil it shipped over the railroad, but a rebate as well on oil shipped by competitors. Seldom has a large firm's power been exercised with such ingenuous indirection.

Nationally, a large firm may pursue an aggressive policy in one market, while following a less sanguine approach in other sales territory. The large firm may even cut price below cost in one market, while it maintains its overall profitability through higher prices elsewhere. The small firm that is confined to a limited market area can make no effective competitive response to such tactics. Bankruptcy or absorption by the larger firm are the likely alternatives if this divide-and-conquer policy is pursued to finality. This piecemeal approach to market penetration has frequently been cited as one of the tactics that Rockefeller's Standard Oil Company used to gain early dominance of the US petroleum industry, although revisionist historians question the extent to which this tactic was actually used. In any case, indictments against such illegal practices still occur from time to time especially in retail chain marketing.

Mutuality of interest

If the number of firms in an industry is small, as is the case in the auto and steel industries, vigorous price competition is most unlikely. Firms do not have to agree overtly *not* to compete, nor do they have to meet clandestinely to fix prices; it is enough that a firm recognizes that a price cut on its part will be noted by its rivals, since the immediate consequence of under-cutting the established industry price is to draw customers from other firms. There are few signals to which the business firm's antennae respond more alertly than price changes. When a firm cuts prices, its competitors' sales orders drop, sales managers' quotas go unfulfilled, and production managers' output schedules are cut back. Competitors immediately suspect that a rival has cut price and the response is to match or exceed the price cut. But such retaliatory behavior brings the industry lower prices and less return on investment. Since all the firms involved know this beforehand, the initial price cut is not likely to take place.

The *mutuality of interest* of the small number of firms generates an abhorrence of price cutting as a means of enlarging a firm's share of the market. Instead, competition takes a less robust, nonprice form: advertising, product differentiation, and special services. This does not mean that prices remain unchanged when the number of firms in an industry is small, but rather that price modifications are extended across the industry. When a price change occurs in response to economic forces, such as rising production costs or demand, the adjustment affects the whole industry, when the firms are producing much the same product.

How to compete—genteely

In any industry, a few companies compete for ever-larger shares of the market according to certain well-established but unstated rules. The principal rule is that price competition, except on very limited occasions, is an anti-social practice, and one to be strictly avoided, since it threatens to destroy the whole club. Similarly, the products offered by members are more or less identical; introducing radically new technology is considered unsporting. Instead, these companies compete in the less volatile arenas of cost-cutting (through automation and the removal of factories to low-wage areas) and product differentiation (beating out the competition by means of more attractice and convenient packaging and more arresting advertising). Since a dollar in advertising is likely to have a quicker payoff than a dollar invested in the product itself—how much better than a Camel can you make a Chesterfield?—the "breakthroughs" in the consumer products tend to be trivial changes tailored to advertising campaigns.[3]

The not-so-different differentiated product

Most products and services that are branded and advertised are more alike than different: autos, restaurants, tennis rackets, shoes, outboard motors, double-thickness glass windows, airline service, rugs, refrigerators, gasoline, and a multitude of items beyond the ken of most of us. When products are alike, the sensitivity of producers to the market decisions of their rivals is acute, accentuating the mutuality of interest. But the way in which mutuality of interest is expressed depends on the structure of the particular industry. If there is not much difference in the size or efficiency of the firms in an industry, competition will be vigorous or restrained depending largely upon the number of firms. If the number of firms is small but they are varied in size, however, as is the case in the iron and steel industry and the auto industry, mutuality of interest is likely to take the form of price leadership.

Price leadership—a blend of dominance and mutuality of interest

Price leadership requires the acceptance by the industry of a "spokesman" firm that establishes price and initiates change—up or down—with

[3] Richard Barnet and Ronald Müller, "Global Reach," *The New Yorker*, December 2, 1974, p. 59.

more or less immediate compliance by the rest of the firms in the industry. A classical case of price leadership has existed for many years in the steel industry in the United States, for which the US Steel Corporation is the price leader. From time to time, the leadership role of US Steel is challenged by the industry's number two firm, Bethlehem Steel, which may initiate some price changes, or by smaller firms, which sometimes shade prices during a recession to increase their share of the market or boost prices during steel shortages to increase revenues. But for the most part, US Steel's leadership is unchallenged.

The industry accepts US Steel's leadership in pricing because it is the largest firm in the industry and can enforce its decisions on smaller firms by undercutting their markets. Mainly, however, US Steel's price leadership is successful because of the mutuality of interest of all firms in the price policy fostered by US Steel.

How price leadership works

Steel pricing involves two steps: establishing a *base* price and an *extra* add-on price. Base prices are quoted on steel ingots, billets (bars), sheets, beams, and the like. Some steel products, such as rods for concrete reinforcement and building I-beams, are standardized base-price items, but most steel is sold on special order and milled to customers' specifications. Custom orders include cold-rolled steel of high malleability for auto bodies, enameled sheet steel for the canning industry, high-carbon steel for cutting tools, stainless steels of many different compositions for various purposes, *ad infinitum*.

If the container industry orders galvanized steel, for example, the price will be made up of a base charge for the sheet steel and an extra add-on charge for galvanizing. For every base price, there are hundreds of extra prices for the multitude of special treatments that steel can undergo. Normally, the base steel price will be revised annually, and this practice usually attracts attention during periods of inflation—sometimes prompting government attempts to roll back such increases. Extra prices may change on short notice, usually without fanfare, most frequently at quarterly intervals. Generally only a few of the hundreds of extra prices will be changed at any one time. To change an extra price, US Steel simply sends its customers a loose-leaf replacement for the page in the "extra" book that covers a particular process, such as galvanizing or enameling. A few days or weeks later, all the other firms in the industry send *their* customers loose-leaf replacement sheets embodying identical price changes. The result is industry-wide uniformity of price for thousands of base-extra combinations of steel products. The practice effectively holds price competition in check.

Ford the follower

Detroit—Ford Motor Co., which previously proposed plans for a tentative price increase of about 8%, or some $418, at retail on its 1975 model cars and trucks, said it currently plans to raise prices more than that and closer to the almost 10%, or $500, boost that General Motors Corp. will tack onto its 1975 vehicles.[4]

Price leadership can occur even in an industry in which firms do not produce identical products. Industries as different as chewing gum and automobiles provide examples of strong price leadership, with the Wrigley Company and General Motors Corporation assuming the leadership roles in their respective industries. In the auto industry, pricing is a complex activity that involves announced price schedules, dealer trade-in practices, and company-dealer bonuses and sales incentives that sometimes encourage dealers to shade published prices. As everyone knows, General Motors is the dominant firm in the US auto industry. Not only is it the largest single producer, with about one-half of the industry's total capacity, but over the years it has been by far the most profitable firm in the industry. Indeed, it has been one of the most profitable manufacturing undertakings in all of history. Traditionally, Ford or Chrysler announces its price changes and the final adjustment is made when GM makes its position known.

That Ford Motor Company and Chrysler Corporation in the auto industry, or National Steel Corporation and Jones and Laughlin Corporation in the steel industry—all multimillion dollar corporations—should docilely submit to the dictates of another firm in the matter of prices, at first glance strains credulity. But as stated earlier, price leadership is really an expression of mutuality of interest, rather than a ruthless disregard for the welfare of other firms in the industry. For the leadership practice to work, the spokesman firm must proclaim a price that the rest of the industry will accept, or what is essentially the same thing, choose a price that can be enforced. In the last analysis, the price leader's authority rests on the leader's ability to encroach upon a dissident firm's market by price cutting to keep the firm in line.[5]

[4] *The Wall Street Journal*, August 21, 1974. Reprinted with permission of *The Wall Street Journal*, © Dow Jones & Company, Inc. 1974. All rights reserved.

[5] In unusual circumstances, the spokesman firm may not be the actual price leader, as would be the case if American Motors announced prices for the automobile industry.

As long as the firms in the price-led industry are content to forgo price competition as a way of establishing their share of the market, industry stability with profit may be sufficient inducement to follow the leader's pricing. Moreover, if price wars and widely fluctuating prices are the alternative to price leadership, it is all the easier for the dominant firm to convince the rest of the industry to follow its lead, especially if the industry is one of heavy fixed costs. Price wars in such industries are likely to be economically disastrous because huge losses on fixed charges take place if prices are cut to just cover variable costs. Prolonged sales below total cost invite bankruptcy, and nothing so gauche (or illegal) as overt collusion is required to dissuade firms from this form of economic suicide as an alternative to the orderly world of price leadership.

But this is not to say that crude, forthright collusion to fix prices does not take place at times. Nor is it necessary to turn back to the days of the "robber barons" to illustrate this point. Recent behavior by the manufacturers of heavy electrical equipment provides sufficient evidence that collusion is not a thing of the past.

Collusion: General Electric, Westinghouse, and phases of the moon

Heavy electrical switchgear is not associated in most minds with phases of the moon. Indeed, in most minds it is probably not associated with much of anything, but in the 1950s General Electric, Westinghouse, Allis Chalmers, and a number of lesser-known manufacturers of electrical equipment devised a schedule of collusive bidding that was keyed to the moon's phases.[6] Astrology was not involved, but simple, crass conspiracy to fix prices. Which firm was to be the "low" bidder was determined in advance and rotated among the conspirators in accord with lunar cycles. In meetings among producers in the middle 1950s, General Electric emerged as the price leader in the collusion. Mr. Baddia Rashid, chief of the trial section of the Antitrust Division of the US Department of Justice, describes General Electric's role as follows:

Between the November, 1955 meeting and the April, 1956 meeting, General Electric has unilaterally put into effect a price increase. The rest of the companies

[6] Collusive price arrangements covered a variety of heavy electrical equipment—power transformers and turbine generator units, as well as switchgear—but the most elaborate arrangements for price-fixing involved switchgear, mainly circuit breakers that protect equipment from overload.

therefore met in April of 1956 to decide what they would do . . . . They had a discussion and decided that with respect to some products they would all follow G.E.'s prices; with respect to other products they would not follow it.

When this was agreed upon General Electric thereafter retracted its price increase with respect to those products that the other companies did not agree to.[7]

While top GE executives were extolling the competitive way, presumably unknown to them other executives—vice-presidents and division chiefs of GE and personnel of other firms in the electrical equipment industry—were negotiating agreements that effectively eliminated competition in an important segment of the industry. But why did collusion and price fixing take place in one segment of production and not, for example, in lamp bulb or refrigerator production? Two factors were primarily responsible: (1) the overcapacity of production facilities for heavy electrical equipment, and (2) the small number of producing firms. Because there was a small number of producers dominated by GE and Westinghouse, agreements were easy to reach and the meetings of the conspirators attracted little attention. Many meetings were actually held during the conventions of the industry's trade group, the National Electrical Manufacturers' Association.

The industry "white sale"

In spite of attempts to discourage price cutting, however, in January 1955, the supply of heavy electrical equipment was so considerable that price cuts up to 50 percent took place in some lines. During this so-called "white sale," GE and Westinghouse gained most of the business, thereby inducing the smaller firms to accept the protection of stable and higher, agreed-upon prices, rather than unstable and lower, market-determined prices. At the same time, by cornering much of the market for heavy electrical equipment, GE and Westinghouse risked attracting investigation and prosecution by the Justice Department's Antitrust Division. In short, the climate was right for agreement. Since this segment of the industry suffered from overcapacity, however, any agreement had to cover more than price. Supply had to be controlled in order to fix price. This meant that sales quotas had to be allocated among the producing firms, including new market entrants, and market territories had to be assigned. It became apparent almost at once that taking over the market function was no part-time job. Indeed, one of the most prominent lessons of this affair is

[7] John Bridge, "The Problem of Price Fixing—Antitrust Violators Schemed to Only Limited Success," *The Wall Street Journal*, January 1961, p. 12. Reprinted with permission of *The Wall Street Journal*, © Dow Jones & Company, Inc. (1961). All rights reserved.

that it is extremely difficult to suppress market forces. Repeatedly, competition had to be curbed in order to maintain above-market prices.

Eventually, the conspiracy was unmasked. In 1960, twenty-nine companies were charged with conspiring to restrain trade. All pleaded guilty. Sentences were handed down under Section 1 of the Sherman Act, which declares illegal "every contract, combination in the form of trust or otherwise, or conspiracy, in restraint of trade or commerce among the several States, or with foreign nations." Fines were levied both on the companies and on the individuals who had engaged in conspiracy, and modest jail terms were imposed on those primarily responsible for the price fixing. General Electric, for example, was fined a total of approximately one-half-million dollars and three of its executives were sent to jail. Eight others received suspended sentences.

The jail sentences, although light, represented something of a departure from the court's usual approach in antitrust cases. Nor was this the end of it. For the larger companies involved in the conspiracy, the fines levied were not much of a penalty, but when the defendants pleaded guilty, their customers—mainly public utilities and government agencies—brought suit against them under the Sherman Act's triple-damage provision. These suits were settled out of court and the extent of the damages paid is unknown, but there is no doubt that by comparison the court fines were inconsequential. In the final analysis, circumventing the market proved to be not only difficult but costly.

The market approach to overcapacity is itself not without economic distress and disorganization, including cutthroat pricing. And, the larger the element of fixed cost in an industry, the more severe are the throes of readjustment. Although the market solution to overcapacity may bring temporary economic dislocation, ultimately it improves resource allocation and increases consumer welfare. But this does not necessarily mean that smaller production units will replace or be able to compete better with larger units. Oftentimes larger firms have lower costs than smaller firms, and when this is the case, competition may actually bring about its own destruction.

Economy of sale as a cause of monopoly

When the American economy was young but unmistakably on the road to large-scale industrial capitalism, a supporting development was taking place in the public utility industry. In the United States, many so-called "public" utilities such as the airlines, railroads, power companies, and the telephone service, are actually privately owned. The significant economic characteristic of such large operations is that they have a distinct cost advantage over smaller undertakings.

There are two factors at work that favor the larger public utility: (1) its lower per-unit capital cost because of more intensive use of such factors as railroad track and equipment, for example, and (2) lower cost per unit of output because the costs of production go down for some larger installations. Figure 8.1 illustrates both factors. The average cost curves for the smaller firm ATC_A, and the larger firm ATC_B, show the effect of reduced cost per unit up to LTUC, but ATC_B—although the same shape—describes a cost range well below that of the smaller firm.

Why should a large firm have lower costs than a small firm? It doesn't in all cases. In some instances its costs may even be higher, but for public utilities, economy of scale is the typical cost pattern. *Economy of scale* is a shorthand designation for the lower per-unit cost of production that is sometimes the result of enlarging the size or scale of a unit of production. Large turbines generate electric kilowatts at a lower cost than smaller turbines, for example, and larger pipes (or tanks) require less material relative to volume than smaller installations. As a result, if larger firms can take advantage of such scale economies, they can produce—and sell—at a lower price.

Expressed diagrammatically, Firm B (the larger firm in Figure 8.1) can

Figure 8.1 Firm Economy of Scale

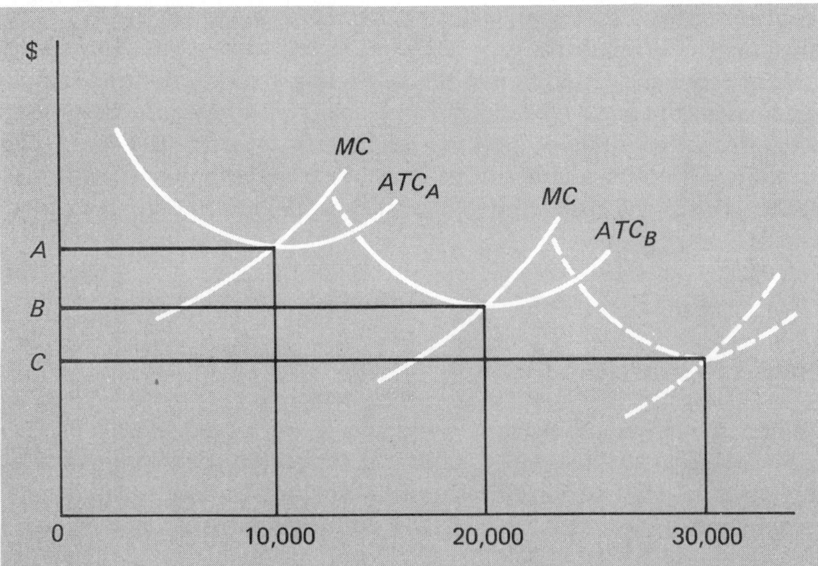

sell its output profitably at a price that is below the cost of production for the smaller firm, if the market is sufficiently large. At any price below OA, for example, the cost of production for Firm A is not fully covered by price, but Firm B can more than cover its costs as long as price is above OB. Moreover, any price from OB to just below OA causes economic distress for the smaller firm, without in any way inconveniencing the larger firm. Indeed, if price is held within this range, the smaller firm will be forced out of business. When there are pronounced economies of scale in production, smaller firms cannot survive the destructive nature of competition. Under such circumstances, to attempt to enforce competition is not only futile, it eventually leads to monopoly.

The smaller firm is not likely to be helped by an expansion of the market either. Unless it can achieve a quantum increase in size that puts it within the output range of the larger firm, it will remain a high-cost producer. For example, if Firm A and Firm B in Figure 8.1 expand capacity by equal amounts of 10,000 units, the smaller firm still suffers a cost disadvantage.

Because monopoly may be the consequence of economies of scale, when this takes place it is sometimes called a *natural* monopoly to distinguish it from monopolies based on resource ownership, patents, and other means of controlling the market. The enforcement of competition is not appropriate in the case of a natural monopoly, for two reasons. First, competition in this case does not bring about a number of small-size production units. Second, the consumer will suffer uneconomically high prices if the scale of production is held down. The public interest is best served by permitting one firm to monopolize a market area and then regulating it to prevent price gouging. The prospect of government regulation, however, raises complex economic and legal considerations, and necessitates commission hearings and court reviews. The regulatory approach thus has its own problems in the pursuit of efficiency.

The above discussion of economies of scale is barely the first word on this subject. The topic will be treated at greater length in Chapter 10, along with other long-run cost factors.

Summary

The cornerstone monopoly legislation in the United States is the federal Sherman Antitrust Act of 1890. The Sherman Act was designed mainly to prevent restraint of trade, such as collusive price-fixing and other restrictive business practices, although its antimonopoly scope is broad. During the years immediately following its passage, the Sherman Act was not effective in promoting competition in the American economy primarily because of the interpretation of the concept of interstate commerce that the Supreme Court applies in its ruling on the act. The Court held that the Sherman Act did not apply to economic activity such as manufacturing, that took place primarily within a state. Later decisions overcame this initial diversion of purpose, but the enforcement of the act has waxed and waned from one administration to another.

There are forces and structures in a market economy that discourage competition as well as influences that promote competition. Control of important sources of raw materials, such as bauxite ore for aluminum refining or nickel deposits, may severely curtail the competition in the affected industries. Patent control of production processes, such as the electrolytic process of producing aluminum and the Polaroid-Land method of instant photographic development, provide the holders with legal immunity from competition for the life of a patent. If a firm is the largest in an industry, such as the United States Steel Corporation and the original Standard Oil Company, it may dominate an industry through price leadership and other less obvious practices.

If the number of firms in an industry is small, *mutuality of interest* will encourage a pricing policy that avoids vigorous competition. Mutuality of interest may be expressed in several ways: in a predetermined division of the market rather than competing for shares, in emphasizing service and product differences rather than price competition, and in accepting rather than challenging the price established by the dominant firm in the industry.

Restraint of trade may also be brought about by collusion, the illegal agreement among firms to limit production, fix prices, allocate sales territory, or otherwise avoid competition. Collusion is most likely in industries in which the number of firms is small and in which the mutuality of interest in holding to a higher price has been eroded by the attraction of temporary gain for the firm that breaks away. Additional pressure for price cutting in such circumstances arises when there is overcapacity of production facilities, as was the case in the electric switchgear industry in the 1950s.

Promoting competition by discouraging or preventing monopoly is not always successful, quite aside from the effectiveness of the government's regulatory approach. Indeed, in an industry where a larger firm has lower costs because of economy of scale, competition does not operate satisfactorily since the larger firm can undercut the price of smaller competitors and drive them from the field. After competitors have been eliminated, the remaining large firm can raise price above the competitive level without fear of retaliation or encroachment of entering firms. To prevent this kind of monopoly development in cases in which the product is an important consumer product or service, such as electricity, a single firm is legally franchised to sell in a particular area under the control of a regulatory commission.

Key terms and concepts

Monopoly a single seller in a market.

Monopsony a single buyer in a market.

Oligopoly a small number of sellers in a market.

Oligopsony a small number of buyers in a market.

Mutuality of interest recognition by producers that it is to their economic interest to avoid price competition.

Price leadership the initiation of price modifications for an industry by the dominant firm, usually but not inevitably the industry's largest, and conformity to this price by other firms in the industry.

Economy of scale the cost function in which larger firms have lower total average costs than smaller firms.

Natural monopoly the emergence of monopoly control by one firm as a result of economy of scale.

Discussion and review questions

1. Why did the trust form of business organization flourish in the United States in the late nineteenth century? Why is it seldom used now as a form of large-scale business organization?

2. What is the difference between a trust and a conglomerate? Why aren't conglomerates prosecuted under the Sherman Antitrust Act? How do conglomerates differ from the ordinary corporation?

3. A unique feature of the Sherman Antitrust Act is its triple-damages provision, which was designed to reduce government's need to prosecute firms for monopoly practices. How was this provision supposed to work and how well has it succeeded?

4. In the players' strike of 1974, why were the member clubs of the National Football League called oligopsonists? Was this a fair charge?

5. In its early years, Alcoa possessed at least two bases for monopoly power. How important are these sources of monopoly power now? Why did price leadership not arise in the aluminum industry in the United States after World War II?

6. Why did "Coal Oil Johnny" succeed where others failed?

7. What is meant by *mutuality of interest* and how does it explain the acceptance of price leadership in an industry? What kind of environment is conducive to price leadership?

8. How does a differentiated product affect competition? What if a product is differentiated, but is not really different? Does this mean that the industry is actually one of pure competition?

9. What are base prices and extra prices in the steel industry? How are prices determined in the iron and steel industry? Should the process be changed by government intervention?

10. Why did collusion take place in the electric switchgear industry during the 1950s, rather than some form of price leadership?

11. What is the market solution to overcapacity in an industry? Why are some firms more anxious to avoid the market solution than others?

12. Why cannot competition be relied upon to protect the consumer when firms encounter significant economies of scale in production? What is the alternative to competition?

9 Something less than competition II: the kinds and consequences of monopoly restraint

*And [Joseph] gathered up all the food of the seven years, which were in the land of Egypt. . . . And all countries came into Egypt to Joseph for to buy corn; because that the famine was sore in all lands. . . . And Joseph gathered up all the money that was found in the land of Egypt.**

People of the same trade seldom meet together, even for merriment and diversion, but the conversation ends in a conspiracy against the public, or in some contrivance to raise prices.†

Joseph's corner of ancient Egypt's grain supply and the eighteenth-century British tradesmen's propensity to collude indicate the deep-seated nature of the incentive to restrain trade. Indeed, the heritage of precapitalism is anything but vigorous competition, even though the church, the courts, the press, and early legislative bodies generally tried to check monopoly excesses. The results were mixed at best.

Twentieth-century capitalism has evolved its own forms of market control, on the whole less predatory than earlier types, but nonetheless effective. Instead of attempting to eliminate competitors by cutthroat pricing and aggressive marketing practices, modern business strategy is more subtle. Competition, if not actually genteel, is at least restrained, usually avoiding price cutting. Instead, firms emphasize product differentiation and use advertising to establish a hold on the market. The result is eco-

* *Genesis*, 41:48, 52; 47:14.

† Adam Smith, *The Wealth of Nations* (New York: Random House, Inc.; Modern Library Edition, Edwin Cannan, ed., 1937), p. 128. *The Wealth of Nations* was first published in Edinburgh, Scotland, in 1776.

nomic behavior that is neither highly competitive nor extremely monopolistic, but a blend of competitive and monopolistic elements. And the blend varies from industry to industry in the modern economy. Some industries rely heavily on advertising to promote their product and others do not; price leadership is the norm in some cases and not in others; there are so few competitive firms in some industries that the result is close to monopoly, while in others an abundance of firms generates nearly competitive conditions. The range of market control is considerable, and therefore Table 9.1, which compresses the differences in types of market control into a few categories, suffers from oversimplification. But it provides a starting point for examining the main kinds of producer control.

Pure monopoly

Pure monopoly, although at the opposite end of the spectrum of producer control, has some things in common with pure competition. Pure monopoly—a single seller—is a simple form of organization that is infrequently encountered in most markets. Of all the different types of producer control, monopoly concentrates more power over price in the seller than any other marketing arrangement. But this does not mean that all monopolists are equally powerful and profitable. The British East India Company, which monopolized trade between England and the Far East for almost 250 years as a result of a charter grant from Parliament in 1600, has very little in common with the present-day, small-town clothier who sells Botany suits. The clothier is a monopolist of sorts, but a Botany franchise is an anemic power-base at best compared with the East India Company's sole proprietorship of the sale of exotic wares in the markets of England and the Continent.

The size of the market and the availability of substitute products are critical determinants of monopoly power. If there are no close substitutes for monopolist products, demand is less elastic and monopoly control of the market is greater. The phrase "demand is less elastic" should not be interpreted to mean that the monopolist generally sells in an inelastic area of the demand curve. There are instances of inelastic demand, such as the diabetic's reaction to the price of insulin, but in addition to being rare, prices in such cases are likely to be held in check by competition or government regulation. (Perfectly inelastic demand, although largely hypothetical, is illustrated later in Figure 9.2, along with the competitive firm demand and the more traditional monopoly demand curve.) Monopoly demand can be best explained in terms of the concept of *marginal revenue.*

Table 9.1: The range of market control

Market Type	Main Characteristics	Where Found	Extent of Price Control by Firms
Pure Competition	Many producers and identical products.	Numerous agricultural commodities, e.g., cotton, wheat, and corn, and selected retail markets.	None
Oligopoly—			
Imperfect Competition	Few producers to more than few and essentially identical products.	Steel, plywood, aluminum, sulfur.	Varies—roughly proportional to firm's share of the market.
Monopolistic Competition*—Differentiated Oligopoly	Few producers to more than few and differentiated products.	Automobiles, aspirin, soap, cigarettes, canoes.	Varies—dependent on firm's share of market and success in product differentiation.
Pure Monopoly	Single producers and unique product.	Nickel, aluminum (before World War II), and various public utilities, e.g., telephone, airlines, electric power.	Complete control of price through output, except where regulated by government agencies.

*According to legend, Procrustes, a highwayman in ancient Greece, entertained himself by adjusting his victims to an iron bed by stretching them if they were too short and compressing them if they were too tall. In every classifier there is a little Procrustes, which shows up in the above table in the treatment of oligopoly. Aside from the question of whether oligopoly as a term can properly be stretched to "more than a few," some classifiers place monopolistic competition and imperfect competition nearer to the "many" end of the market spectrum than to the "few" end.

Marginal revenue

Marginal revenue measures the change in total revenue that results from increasing or decreasing sales. It is usually expressed as the increment to total revenue from the sale of an additional unit of output, but it is more meaningful when conceived as a stream or flow of revenue increments that changes as price is varied. The fourth column in Table 9.2

Figure 9.1 Marginal Revenue and Average Revenue

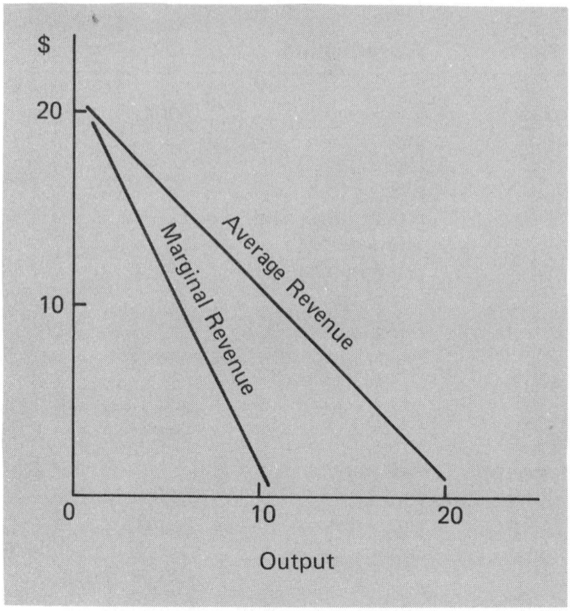

illustrates this flow. The average revenue and marginal revenue curves shown in Figure 9.1 are linear representations of the data presented in the first and last columns of Table 9.2.

Marginal revenue is one of the main considerations in the firm's decision to increase or decrease production. By comparing the potential

Table 9.2: Marginal revenue

Price (Average Revenue)	Quantity	Total Revenue	Marginal Revenue
$20	1	$20	—
19	2	38	18
18	3	54	16
17	4	68	14
16	5	80	12
15	6	90	10
14	7	98	8
13	8	104	6
12	9	108	4
11	10	110	2
10	11	110	0

added revenue (the marginal revenue increment) with the potential added cost (the marginal cost increment), management can determine whether the extra output will pay for itself. The monopolist—or any firm for that matter—is best off when output is carried to the point where marginal cost equals marginal revenue. This is not a new principle. It is the same principle as that followed by the competitive firm, which carries output to the point where marginal cost equals price, since for the competitive firm, marginal revenue is identical with price. This identity between price and marginal revenue in the case of the competitive firm's demand curve can be explained by reference to Figure 9.2.

Whether the demand curve is the horizontal price line of pure competition, the downslanting curve of monopoly, or the highly unusual, perfectly inelastic perpendicular demand curve, marginal revenue can be derived for each of these curves. In the case of the downslanting demand curve, however, marginal revenue diverges from demand or average revenue, as shown in Figure 9.2B.

The three illustrations in Figure 9.2 employ the designations AR (average revenue) and MR (marginal revenue). Average revenue is recorded in the first column in Table 9.2 and is identical with the graphic price-quantity relationships expressed in the demand curve. Average revenue is also

Figure 9.2 Demand and Marginal Revenue

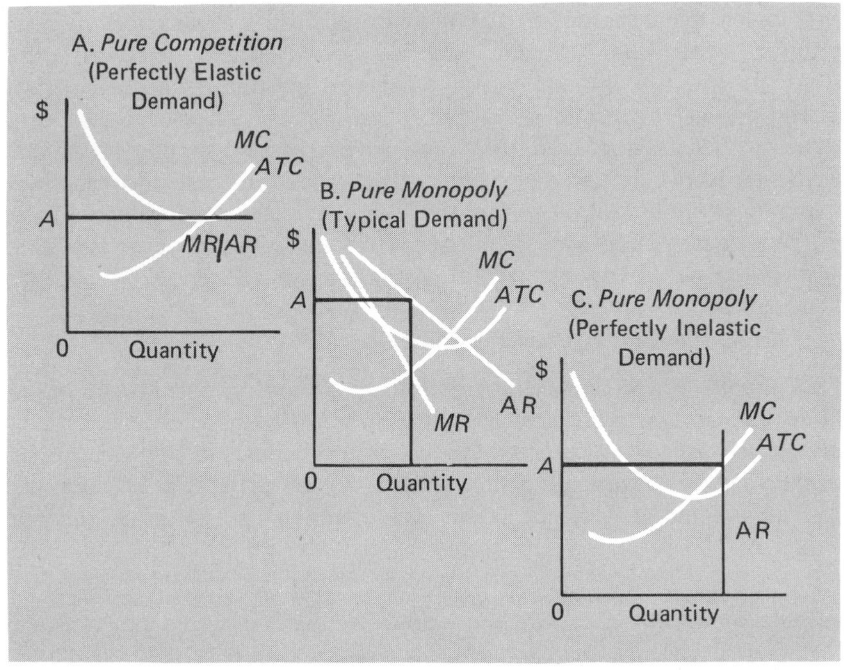

called demand because if total revenue is divided by the quantity sold, the resultant average is the same as the price column. For example, employing the data in Table 9.2, dividing 1 into $20 equals $20; dividing 2 into $38 equals $19, and so on. In the case of perfectly elastic and perfectly inelastic demand, however, average revenue and marginal revenue are the same. In Figure 9.2A, the perfectly elastic firm demand curve of pure competition shows price unchanged whether the competitive firm sells all or part of its output, so when sales increase or decrease, the amount added or deducted is equal to the price OA, and the marginal revenue curve is the same as the firm demand AB.

The case of the perfectly inelastic demand curve—the perpendicular curve in Figure 9.2—is admittedly a freak case.[1] Normally, marginal revenue traces the change in total revenue that results from changes in sales, but the perfectly inelastic demand curve shows unchanging sales whether price is high or low. Even the Middle East oil producers who raised crude prices 400 percent in 1973-1974 experienced some reduction in sales. In Figure 9.2, prices above OA more than cover firm costs, and the higher the price within the upward range of the perfectly inelastic curve, the greater the monopolist's profit. In this unusual situation, the monopolist will be restrained mainly by noneconomic considerations, such as concern for consumers' welfare or fear of prompting government regulation.

Unlike the extreme case above, the monopolist with the typical downslanting demand curve does not have everything his way. Indeed, in most cases, the monopolist is obliged to sell in the elastic portion of the demand curve rather than its inelastic segment. Facing a downslanting curve, the monopolist *cannot* sell whatever amount he wishes without affecting price; increased sales mean lower prices, higher prices mean decreased sales. Moreover, unit costs of production for the monopolist vary as output is increased or decreased, just as in the case of competition. The monopolist is best off where the cost of the last unit produced is just equal to the revenue added by its sale. This familiar proposition is restated for monopoly as follows: marginal cost = marginal revenue.

Marginal revenue: elasticity indicator

The intersection of marginal revenue and marginal cost not only establishes price and output for the monopolist, but the marginal revenue curve serves also as an indicator of the elastic and inelastic segments of the demand curve. Employing the total revenue approach to determine elasticity—demand is elastic when total revenue and price are inversely

[1] One critic urged that I exclude this case on the ground that it raises more questions than it answers. His advice is sound, but I am attracted to it because students sometimes ask about it and, although somewhat contrived and certainly limited, it completes the full range of demand possibilities.

related and inelastic when total revenue and price are positively related—it can be demonstrated that the demand curve in Figure 9.3 is elastic from a price of $20 to $10 and inelastic from $10 to $1. Total revenue first increases as price declines to $10, and then falls as price continues to decrease. We can express this in terms of incremental change rather than aggregate revenue change: When marginal revenue is positive (greater than zero), demand is elastic; when marginal revenue is negative (less than zero), demand is inelastic. Marginal revenue is thus an instant indicator of whether a segment of a downward-slanting demand curve is elastic or inelastic, as illustrated in Figure 9.3.

Although it is natural to assume that a monopolist can set price at virtually any point he wishes, to be best off economically output must be set where marginal cost equals marginal revenue. Thus the monopoly follows the same general rule of policy as the competitive firm, which equates marginal cost and price. Marginal revenue replaces price for the monopoly because the firm faces a downslanting rather than a horizontal demand curve.

The monopoly produces where MC equals MR because if production stops short of this point, marginal revenue is greater than marginal cost and the firm forgoes revenue that could be obtained from additional sales. It does not carry production beyond the point where MC equals MR, however, because to do so adds more to costs than is brought in revenue, and—as in competition—it does not carry production below the shut-down point where marginal cost equals average variable cost.

Figure 9.3 Marginal Revenue and Elasticity of Demand

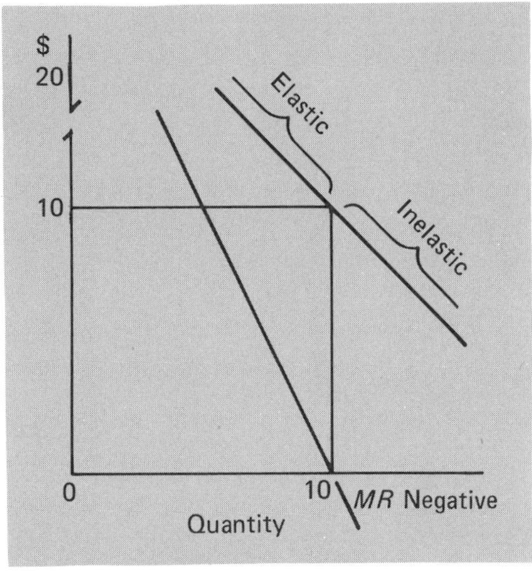

If the monopoly with a downslanting demand curve follows the MC = MR rule, it necessarily sells in the elastic segment of the demand curve, *not* in the inelastic portion. This may seem out of character for a firm that presumably controls the market, but the monopolist, as any other firm, seeks to maintain the price-output combination that produces the greatest profits or the least loss. To do so, the monopolist equates MC and MR as shown in Figure 9.4.

Although the firm is not likely voluntarily to carry output beyond the point where marginal cost is equal to marginal revenue, it is conceivable that something approximating this might happen under public utility regulation. If the utility regulatory commission establishes price at OA and output at OD in Figure 9.4, the firm is required to sell in the region of inelastic demand and experiences negative marginal revenue.

Profit or loss at MC = MR

We know that the firm will be best off where MC = MR, but whether this means maximizing profit or minimizing losses can be most easily shown by relating average cost and average revenue, as in Figure 9.5.

The average cost of OF units of output is OA (which is equal to FD), and the price per unit is OB (which is equal to FC). Price exceeds cost per unit of output by AB, which yields a total monopoly profit of ABCD on OF units. Unlike the case of pure competition where profit may occur in the short run but not in the long run, in the case of monopoly, profit is likely in

Figure 9.4 The Price-Output Choice Under Monopoly

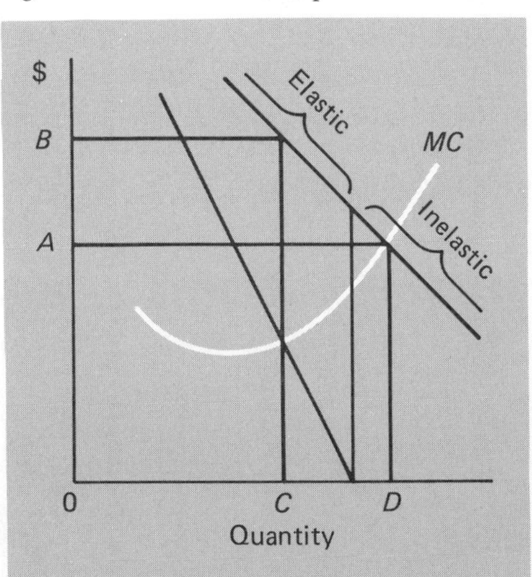

Figure 9.5 Monopoly in Short-run Equilibrium

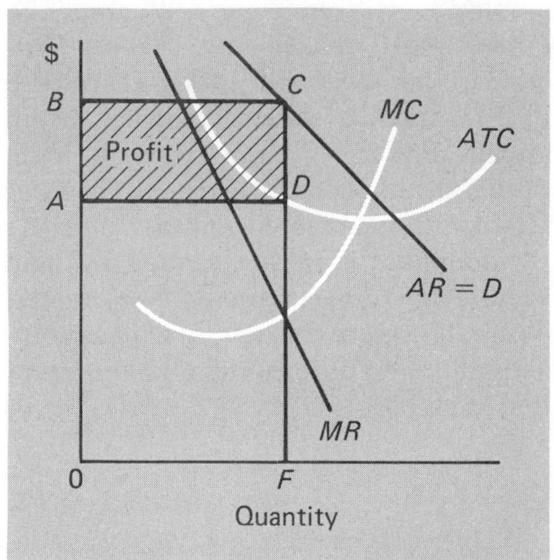

the short run and certain in the long run. The occasional short-run profit of the competitive firm is brought about by a windfall of increased demand, a dislocation that reduces supply, or some event that is fortuitous for the seller but bad news for the buyer. Monopoly profit differs from such transient, competitive good fortune both in cause and durability. Monopoly profit derives from output restriction, a direct consequence of producer control of the market. The persistence of profit depends on the monopolist's ability to exclude rivals from its market.

Monopoly *cum* oligopoly

If the market supply is increased by entering firms, the monopolist's power will be checked and profits will decrease. Precisely how much prices fall and profits suffer from entrants, however, depends on whether the sharing of the market adds significantly to supply. On the whole, the fewer the entrants, the more closely their behavior will resemble that of monopolists; the larger the number of oligopolists, the less distinguishable price and output are from competition.

Oligopoly: market control by the few

Oligopoly means market control by a small number of producers or sellers, but the question arises: What is a small number? In some markets there are fewer sellers than in others, and sometimes a market controlled by a few sellers is largely indistinguishable from a monopoly. Just where the division occurs between oligopoly (small numbers) and competition (large numbers) cannot be pinpointed at five, ten, twenty, or thirty firms. The distinction depends on whether the seller can influence price by withholding or offering output on the market. In the steel industry, twenty firms may not be enough to impair producer control, whereas in the electrical appliance industry only ten firms may produce vigorous competition. The structure of an industry is as important as the number of firms in determining producer control. A dominant firm surrounded by many smaller satellite firms is more likely to approximate monopoly pricing than the same number of equal-sized firms. Therefore, the nature of oligopoly is less definitive than that of pure competition or pure monopoly. The following discussion of *duopoly* illustrates this point.

Duopoly

The two-seller case has received lavish attention in the economic literature, and has provoked various conclusions. Depending upon the assumptions made about the duopolists' recognition of their actions upon each other, the establishment of price and output can be either abruptly forthright—the sellers recognizing their mutuality of interest and immediately turning to the monopoly adjustment—or a meandering series of reactions to each other's output decisions on the assumption that the rival's policy is independently determined. Between these two behavioral extremes—mutuality of interest and independence of action—the recognition of a rival's impact on the market is more realistic. Indeed, only an incredibly unobservant duopolist would overlook the market behavior of a compeer. Since this is the case, the realistic market approach by duopolists is to share monopoly output and monopoly gain. In doing so, however, the monopoly price is determined through the use of a combined marginal cost curve for both duopolists, which is equivalent to the marginal cost of a monopolist. Market sales are also shared on a predetermined basis, such as the respective capacity of the two firms.

Figure 9.6 illustrates a duopoly with equal capacity and mutuality of interest. Curve MC_{A+B} is the marginal cost curve for the two duopolists, which represent, in effect, a single producing unit. OC is the price established by the intersection of marginal cost and marginal revenue. If the duopolists share equally in market sales, OA will be sold by one firm and AB (which is equal to OA) by the other. Sales equality is not a necessary consequence of duopoly, however; various other divisions of the market between two sellers can occur. Usually the sales distribution is based on the output capacities of the duopolists, although other factors may be involved, such as which firm entered the market first.

Figure 9.6 Duopoly Pricing Recognizing Mutuality of Interest

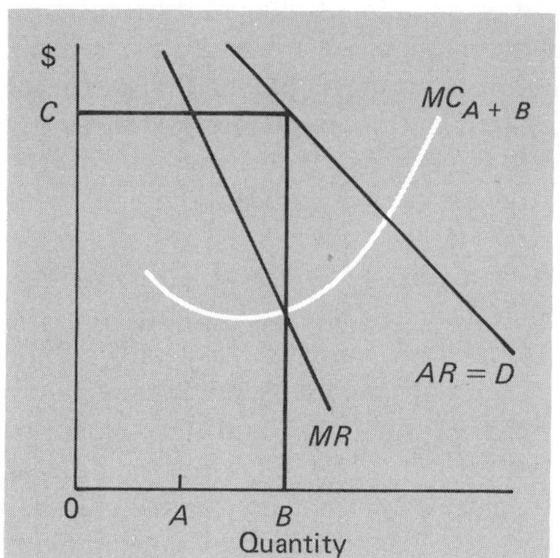

If one firm is a monopoly before the entry of the second firm, adjustments are likely to reach a workable distribution of the market. The late-entering duopolist encroaches upon the established firm's market in direct proportion to its output leverage. The greater the production capability of the entering firm, the more influence it exerts on the market price and, therefore, the behavior of its rival. Since successful encroachment by the late-entering duopolist is more effective if its output capacity is large, initially the duopolist industry may be considerably larger than a pure monopoly. The duopolists together will be able to produce more than would be sold by a monopoly. As a result, unless each firm shows extraordinary prescience in adjusting its market share to anticipate its rival's behavior, price will fall below the monopoly level. (The alternative, of course, is for the firms simply to collude and go directly to the monopoly output that maximizes return, distributing the rewards by prearrangement.) As the market shares of the duopolists are worked out over time, the excess productive capacity that is a consequence of the encroachment period is not replaced and, eventually, the duopolists settle at monopoly capacity and monopoly price.

But if one firm can encroach upon a monopolist, other firms can do the same, and the lucrative market may attract other entrants.

Oligopoly—first a few, then many

Once market encroachment starts, there may be no stopping it, and the duopoly that behaves as a monopoly may be short-lived, as mutuality of interest becomes diluted and unworkable. While two or three firms, or even four or five, may recognize the wisdom of refraining from price-cutting because of the prospect of retaliation, as the number of firms sharing the market increases, the temptation for any one firm to break away from the established price becomes stronger. By shading price only slightly below that established through mutuality of interest, the errant oligopolist can greatly expand sales at the expense of rivals who hold to the original price. Figure 9.7 shows the opportunity open to the chiseling oligopolist.

If all oligopolists adhere to the mutuality-of-interest price OE, established in Figure 9.7 by the aggregate output OP, they all can share the market equally, with sales of OT, TS, SR, and RP respectively. The oligopoly price is set by output OP and determined by the intersection of Curves MC_{TO} (marginal cost for the typical oligopolist) and MR_{AO} (marginal revenue for all oligopolists). The demand curve D_{AO} (demand for all oligopolists) shows what prices are paid for different amounts of oligopoly output. For the wayward oligopolist, the gain obtained by cutting below the mutuality-of-interest price OE is indicated by Line CL, the horizontal extension of the demand curve, D_{AO}. By cutting price slightly below OE to NC (which is equal to OK), the price-chiseler can capture sales of NM from rival oligopolists, approximately one-half of the aggregate oligopoly mar-

Figure 9.7. The Oligopolist as Price Chiseler

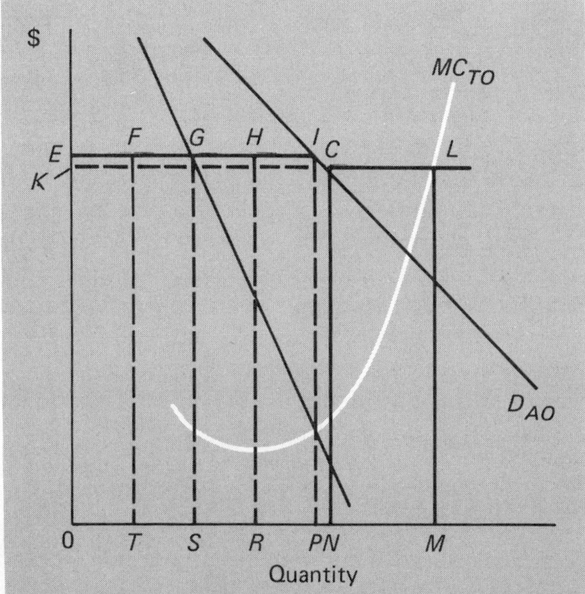

ket. The chiseling oligopolist determines output by expanding to the point where his marginal cost, MC_{TO} (which is identical for all oligopolists) intersects with the price-chiseling line, CL. Since the price does not change as a single oligopolist takes sales away from the established market, Line CL represents the chiseler's marginal revenue curve.

The chiseling oligopolist is, of course, living in a dream world. The gain obtained by cutting prices is short-lived because it is not possible to conceal from his rival oligopolists that the cause of their reduced sales is his price cutting—an avenue equally open to them. Indeed, when the number of firms is small, as in the case of the four firms illustrated in Figure 9.7, price cutting is hardly tenable behavior, since it leads to the immediate disorganization of the market and to the subversion of optimum profitability for all. The transient gain of the price-cutter is quickly replaced by lower returns for all as the other oligopolists retaliate. Only when the number of oligopolists is large enough so that the behavior of any one firm goes undetected for a significant time will the gain from price-cutting compensate for later losses.

Rigid prices

Oligopoly prices are not only likely to be uniform throughout the market, but they frequently appear to be rigid as well. For example, the published price of sulfur in the United States remained unchanged at $18 a ton from 1926 to 1938, and the price of steel rails was quoted without modification for an even longer period prior to the Great Depression. This apparent stability may be illusory, however; it may conceal price-bargaining. Oligopolists may meet price cuts by rival firms but refuse to raise prices when another does, thus preventing the price-cutter from gaining sales. Since firms know the consequence of price-cutting in advance, its appeal to the restive firm quickly disappears.

Actually there may be less to price rigidity than meets the eye. What appears to be a rigid price may simply be a starting point for bargaining. Published prices are likely to be better known than modifications made through private bargaining. In fact, rigid prices may in the main reflect the oligopolistic industry's willingness to accept suboptimum price-output adjustments in place of disruptive price change. Of all the areas in which to compete—prices, service, product quality, advertising, innovation—price competition is the approach least favored when the number of firms is small and the impact of price competition plays back upon the price-cutter. A more benign way to attract customers is generally preferred, such as emphasizing product differences and other nonprice kinds of persuasion.

Product differentiation: the foundation of monopolistic competition

What cigarette appeals to you most—one that conjures the image of a rugged western male, the Marlboro Man; one that supports the women's movement, at least indirectly, by offering equal prize money to women in tennis tournaments, such as Virginia Slims; or a cigarette that competes for customers by emphasizing taste; or another that points to its low tar content? This is but the smallest sample of the varied offerings of the advertising industry, an industry that works with great persistence and some ingenuity to endow products that are actually much alike with an apparent uniqueness. To the extent that brand distinctions, advertising, packaging, and other means of differentiation succeed in setting one product apart from another in the market, the producer is able to build a clientele that identifies with a particular brand and may even be willing to pay a little more for it than for another.

Because consumers react to differentiated products by expressing a preference to some, all cigarette brands, or autos, or beers, cannot be lumped together in a single demand curve for a particular industry. Whether the brands are in fact really different is not the point. As long as the consumer acts as if they are, and develops product loyalty for no obvious reason, the product is economically different. As such, it occupies territory of its own that combines elements of both monopoly and competition, which is the basis for the term *monopolistic competition*.

The monopolistic competition hybrid is a dilute mixture of the two elements, less monopolistic than monopoly and less competitive than competition, but nonetheless a flourishing market type. Table 9.3 lists its major characteristics and locates it within the spectrum of types of market control.

Monopolistic competition, a subcategory of oligopoly, is a much more diverse market type than either pure competition or pure monopoly. Table 9.3 includes the three main variables that are the cause of this diversity: (1) the number of firms; (2) the degree of product differentiation; and (3) the efficacy of advertising and various promotional activities. If the number of firms is large for an oligopoly, advertising is ineffectual, and product differentiation undistinguished, the industry will be more competitive than monopolistic. But if the opposite is the case, the result will more closely approach monopoly.

Whatever the mixture of competition and monopoly, the price and output decisions of firms in a monopolistic competitive industry can be explained in terms of the market characteristics described in Table 9.3. Thus the monopolistic competitive firm faces a downslanting demand curve because the brand it sells is in some degree different and therefore

Table 9.3: A comparison of pure competition, monopolistic competition, and monopoly

	Pure Competition	Monopolistic Competition	Monopoly
Number of firms	Many	Few to more than a few but less than many	One
Nature of Product	Identical	Differentiated	One with limited substitutes
Mobility and freedom of entry	High mobility of resources and complete freedom of entry	Freedom of entry, but produces similar, not identical products	Closed entry
Knowledge of product and market	Complete knowledge of producers and consumers	Incomplete knowledge, especially by consumers: advertising	Complete knowledge by producer and consumers

not perfectly commensurable with other producer's brands. Fords are in some ways different from Plymouths and Chevrolets, even though they serve the same basic purpose and share the same market. This difference affects demand in two ways: (1) The demand curve is downslanting because the firm has a direct and inescapable impact on the market supply of its differentiated product, such as Fords; and (2) separate curves must be constructed for each brand, since differentiated products cannot be lumped together on the same curve.

The demand for most monopolistic competitive products, such as Utica Club or Phoenix beer, Wilson or Bancroft tennis balls, or Arrow or Manhattan shirts, is much more elastic than the demand for a monopoly product. The reason for this is that the products of a monopolistically competitive industry are substitutable, even when differentiation is highly developed. When differentiation is weak, however, it is easier to substitute one brand for another, and the firm demand curve is more elastic.

Retail gasoline sales: monopolistic competition in action

Weak product differentiation, as in the case of gasoline brands, contributes to price wars. Gasoline brand differentiation is based on marginal considerations such as additives that allegedly protect the automobile motor or improve its operation. But since differences in performance are not readily apparent to most motorists, claims of product superiority are largely unconvincing. In such cases, the consumer is likely to base purchase decisions mainly on price differences, which may be as little as a penny or two per gallon, or—given identical prices—to patronize the station that is most conveniently located, provides superior service, or affords side benefits such as crockery or contest offers.

Retail gasoline distribution fits the pattern of monopolistic competition well. There is product differentiation among brands, a high degree of resource mobility and freedom of entry among filling stations, extensive advertising, and sufficient retail outlets to saturate some market areas. A hypothetical but realistic chronology of how retail stations adjust to changes in demand can be reconstructed in three stages, as follows.

Phase 1: The gains of the early entrant

The population is spreading to the suburbs, accompanied by a variety of retailers. Since gasoline is an essential of the suburban commuter's way of life, the filling station that gets to the suburbs first or obtains a preferred location gains an advantage over late-arriving competitors. Figure 9.8 shows a situation in which a retail gasoline dealer enters a new suburban market before competitors and, as a result, makes a profit that initially resembles that of a pure monopolist.

Figure 9.8 Phase I: The Single Monopolistic Competitive Firm in a Lucrative Market MC = MR; AR > AC

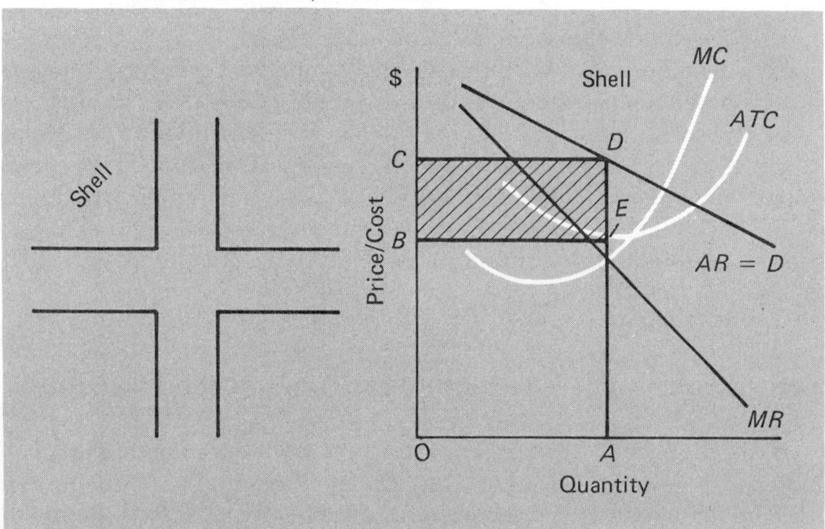

The schema to the left of the familiar cost/demand diagram in Figure 9.8 shows the early entrant, Shell Oil, as the only seller in the new suburban market. The cost/demand diagram describes Shell's adjustment to this favorable demand situation: Output is carried to the point at which marginal cost equals marginal revenue OA, resulting in a price of OC and a profit of BCDE. This monopoly profit, albeit temporary, is possible because Shell is the only source of gasoline in this market area. Shell cannot set its prices as if it were the only filling station in the New World, however. The station has a locational advantage, but one that is vulnerable because of the mobility of the automobile. The suburban Shell price will not greatly exceed that charged at more competitive service centers, but the absence of nearby competitors permits some price spread.

Phase II: Overreaction of competitors

With freedom of entry, mobility of resources, and vacant sites across the street, Shell's hold on the market is tenuous. Marketing scouts of Exxon, Mobil, Gulf, or White Rose are sure to spot this better-than-average opportunity for expansion. Indeed, Phase II may be marked by an overreaction to the gains of the early entrant. Suppose that two other stations, Exxon and Mobil, obtain sites adjacent to Shell to encroach upon the latter's market. This situation is shown in Figure 9.9. What originally was a good thing for one firm is now a losing proposition for three, and the invasion of Exxon and Mobil into Shell's territory results in below-cost

Figure 9.9 Phase II: Below-Cost Market Sharing by Three Monopolistic Competitive Firms MC = MR; AC > AR

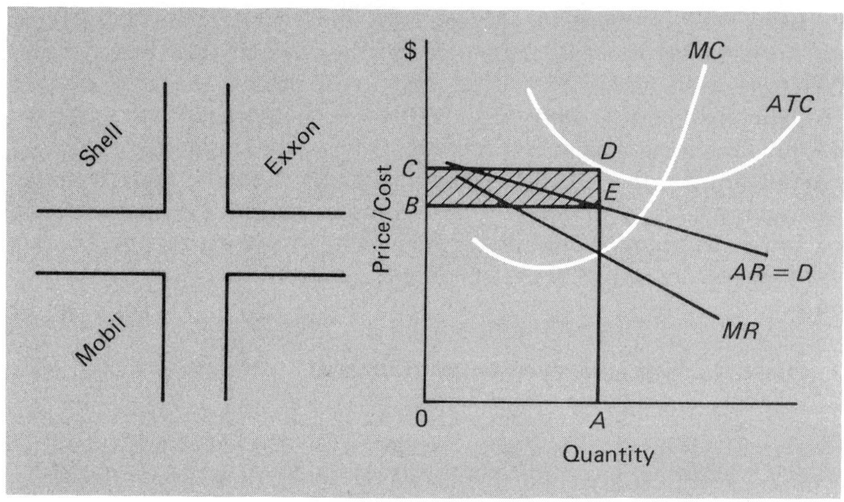

operations for all three. This is shown by Shell's adjustment to the changed market situation.

The Shell station now sells less, OA, at a price of OB, which is below average total cost. Although the firm's marginal cost is still equal to marginal revenue, profit has turned to a loss of BCDE because Exxon and Mobil have cut into Shell's sales. The result is that Shell's demand curve AR, is pushed to the left. In Phase II the market is oversupplied by the three entrants and the losses experienced by Shell are more than matched by Mobil and Exxon, since they are less well established. During Phase II all three firms share an inadequate market, and none is able to sell enough to cover all costs. Presuming that price is above average variable cost, however, the firms are in short-run equilibrium, and they will continue to oversupply the suburban market until forced out or attracted to a more lucrative market prospect elsewhere.

The monopolistically competitive demand curve

Shell's Phase I demand curve was drawn slightly steeper than the demand curve for Phase II to indicate the firm's locational advantage. When Exxon and Mobil opened across the street, however, Shell's market was altered. It sold less, pushing the demand curve to the left, and it lost its locational advantage, flattening the demand curve. But even though Exxon and Mobil brought overcapacity to the market, the demand curve did not flatten to the horizontal curve typical of pure competition, since station sales are not unlimited at the established market price.

Product differentiation is a central feature of monopolistic competition, encouraging consumers to express brand perferences and making it impossible to aggregate the demand for different brands. As a result, industry changes must be shown indirectly through their effect upon a given firm. Industry changes affect Shell in the present case in such a way that the demand curve shifts to the left as competitors enter the industry, and shifts to the right as firms drop out. This course is followed in Phase II: Demand shifts to the left as Exxon and Mobil enter the market. When all three firms share the market in Phase II, however, price drops below cost and causes economic discontent. This in turn leads to further change, which eventually brings about stability in Phase III.

Phase III: Firm and industry equilibrium

The adjustment made in Phase III is a consequence of all firms producing at a price below average total cost in Phase II. Losses during Phase II encourage withdrawal of one of the stations so that those remaining have a

Figure 9.10 Phase III: Long-run Equilibrium in Monopolistic Competition MC = MR; AC = AR

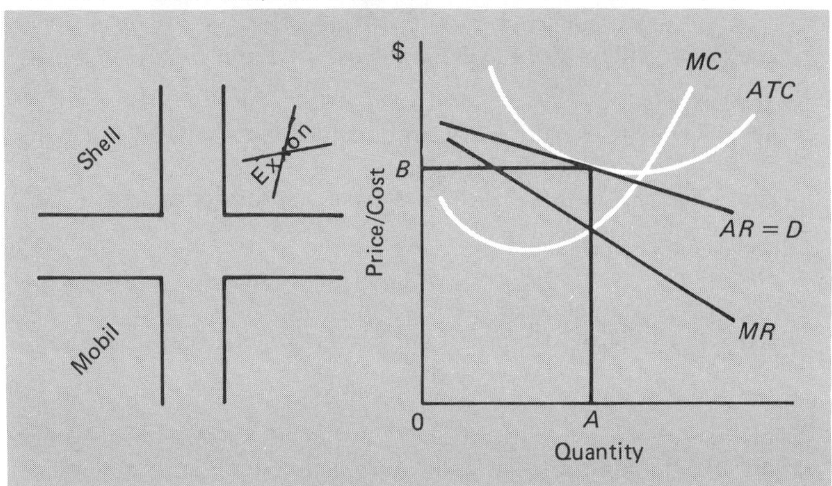

larger market share. This adjustment is illustrated in Figure 9.10 by moving the Shell demand curve to the right, but not so far to the right as in Phase I when Shell was the only station at this location.

In Phase III, the capacity adjustment is most likely to take place by one of the stations closing and relocating elsewhere. This is shown in Figure 9.10, in which Exxon withdraws, leaving a larger market share for Shell and Mobil. These two remaining firms adjust output as usual by equating marginal cost with marginal revenue, but in the long-run adjustment of Phase III, average cost also equals average revenue at this output point. This is long-run equilibrium.

Neither Shell nor Mobil makes a profit or loss, but each covers cost fully, and generates a sufficient return to keep the fixed factor (capital) employed in this station location. For long-run equilibrium to prevail, all firms in the industry have to produce when average cost coincides with average revenue (demand) at the output where marginal cost equals marginal revenue. Both stations operate at a no-profit/no-loss output, thus bringing long-run balance to the industry.

The principles of price and output determination

A summary of the principles of price and output determination under various market conditions reveals major areas of overlap.

Pure Competition
Short-Run: MC = Price (MR); price can be anywhere above average variable cost.
Long-Run: MC = Price (MR) at lowest total unit cost. (AC = AR)

Pure Monopoly
Short-Run: MC = MR; price can be anywhere above average variable cost.
Long-Run: MC = MR; price above average total cost. (AR > AC)

Monopolistic Competition
Short-Run: MC = MR; price can be anywhere above average variable cost.
Long-Run: MC = MR; price equals average total cost to the left of LTUC. (AC = AR)

In all market situations, the MC = MR principle is supreme in both the short run and the long run. Firms in pure competition and monopolistic competition are forced by the entry of firms and the substitutability of competitive products to a long-run price that is neither above nor below the full costs of production. (It should be remembered that *full cost* as used here includes what is sometimes considered *profit* by the recipient.)

The long-run adjustment of firms in monopolistic competition and pure competition differs somewhat during the long run, even though neither makes a profit during this period. The purely competitive firm produces at LTUC, whereas the monopolistically competitive firm produces slightly to the left of LTUC. As a result, a monopolistically competitive firm in long-run equilibrium produces at a higher cost than its pure competitive counterpart, if their cost structures are equivalent. As the number of firms in monopolistic competition approaches that of pure competition and the differentiation of products becomes less effective, however, there is little to choose between the long-run adjustments of purely competitive firms and monopolistically competitive firms.

Pure monopoly stands apart from both pure competition and monopolistic competition in its insulation from rival producers and, consequently, its higher-than-competitive return from sales.

Summary

The range of market control by the producer extends from pure monopoly, in which one firm is the only supplier of a good or service, to pure competition, in which there are many firms supplying identical products. Before World War II, the Aluminum Company of America had no effective competition in aluminum production in the United States, and the International Nickel Company of Canada dominated both the Canadian and the American markets. (Public utilities—railroads, airlines, electric companies, telephone companies, and the like—are also monopolies, but they are special cases since public regulation is designed to prevent them from behaving as monopolies.) Some areas of retail sales and certain aspects of agricultural production represent reasonable approximations to pure competition. As a result, in some of the agricultural industries market control is achieved by the formation of cooperatives or through political pressure upon legislatures for government intervention in the market system, rather than through individual producer action.

Pure monopoly is distinguished from pure competition by its downslanting demand curve, whereas pure competition has a horizontal demand curve. The downslanting demand curve has a further important consequence: marginal revenue, which is derived from the demand curve, falls more rapidly than the downslanting demand curve. By contrast, for the purely competitive firm, marginal revenue and the demand curve coincide. Since price doesn't change when the competitive firm sells more or less output, total revenue changes by the same amount for each unit sold. In monopoly, however, additional output can be sold only by reducing price, which causes marginal revenue to fall more rapidly than price.

Since marginal revenue traces the revenue obtained from successive product sales, the firm adjusts marginal revenue and marginal cost to determine the optimum point of output. (Optimum output for both the competitive firm and the monopoly firm involves equating marginal revenue and marginal cost, since price and marginal revenue are identical in pure competition.)

The concept of marginal revenue serves the further purpose of identifying the elastic and inelastic portions of the demand curve. When marginal revenue is positive, for example, the segment of the demand curve lying above it is elastic; when marginal revenue is negative, the segment above is inelastic. The firm facing a downslanting demand curve produces in the area of elastic demand because for output to take place in the inelastic portion of the demand curve, marginal cost and marginal revenue would have to be negative. When demand is elastic, total revenue is inversely related to price and when inelastic, directly related to price.

Between the extremes of pure competition and pure monopoly, there is a large area of oligopoly in most market economies. Strictly speaking, the term *oligopoly* means a small number of firms, but the term has been extended beyond this limitation. The number of firms in imperfect or monopolistic competition, for example, may vary substantially in different markets with the result that these concepts are sometimes described as applying in cases of few firms and sometimes with many.

In addition to the number of firms, other characteristics of monopolistic competition are product differentiation, freedom of entry by other firms to the industry, and the emphasis upon advertising and promotion in selling the firm's product. In the short run, the monopolistic competitive firm produces where marginal cost is equal to marginal revenue, but average cost may be above or below average revenue so long as price exceeds average variable cost. In long-run equilibrium, the firm produces where average cost is equal to average revenue as well as where marginal cost is equal to marginal revenue. This constitutes a no-profit output for the firm.

Key terms and concepts

Marginal revenue the incremental change in total revenue as sales increase or decrease.

Average revenue (demand) total revenue divided by output.

Duopoly a special type of oligopoly involving two sellers.

Rigid prices prices that remain unchanged for an extended period of time.

Product differentiation distinguishing characteristics of products that are otherwise similar.

Discussion and review questions

1. In the American economy, pure monopoly is even more rare than pure competition. The Sherman Antitrust Act aside, what has prevented monopoly from developing and becoming entrenched in the United States?

2. Marginal revenue is most meaningful when conceived as a flow of revenue increments resulting from changes in price. Why? What does marginal revenue show that the demand curve or average revenue doesn't show?

3. Why is the demand curve also called the average revenue curve? Why does the demand curve slope downward in the case of the noncompetitive firm?

4. If the monopolist faces a perfectly inelastic demand curve, what prevents the monopolist from raising prices as high as the market will bear? Does this happen in some cases?

5. Marginal revenue is an indicator of price elasticity. How does it show whether a given portion of the demand curve is elastic or inelastic?

6. In establishing service charges for a public utility, such as an electric company or the telephone company, the regulatory commission may impose a price that does not equate marginal cost and marginal revenue. What are some of the consequences of this and why would the commission impose such a price?

7. Why is firm profit greatest or loss least where marginal cost equals marginal revenue?

8. Is duopoly a form of market control encountered very often in the modern economy? What about market control at the local level? If a duopoly does exist, what price-output practices are likely to take place in the absence of government regulation?

9. Oligopoly covers a wide range of market behavior. Some oligopolists ignore their rivals, some recognize a mutuality of interest. What are the causes for the different practices? What implications do they have for public policy?

10. What causes a price war? What stops it?

11. What encourages chiseling by an oligopolist, and what discourages such behavior? Is chiseling by an oligopolist in the public interest?

12. Are rigid prices necessarily as inflexible as they sometimes appear to be?

10 Growth in the firm and industry: cost in the long run

Japanese and British shipbuilders have been busy for some time with the designs and dockyard preparations for what must surely be the penultimate in vessels, a million tonner, although some shipping men already have started talking about a 1,250,000 tonner, and, God knows, the way things have been going, there is bound to be somebody already thinking beyond that!*

A tanker is a production unit, quite as much as is a factory or a railroad or a retail store. And although it takes little acquaintance with the ways of ocean transport to know that tankers have increased enormously in tonnage in the past ten years, it may be less than obvious what this has to do with long-run cost. The answer is that the pressures to build the megaton tanker and its only slightly less impressive predecessors are almost entirely economic. The lower costs of construction and operation of these monstrous ships illustrate an important area of long-run cost mentioned earlier, economies of scale.

The construction of large tankers was greatly accelerated by the closing of the Suez Canal in 1967, which had held tonnage below 100,000 for ships using this waterway. With the canal closed, shippers were required to make a longer haul around the Cape of Good Hope, and the ocean shipping industry has steadily increased the size of tankers it has put in service. These huge ships bring more than lower shipping costs to the sea lanes, however; they greatly increase navigational risks and raise the likelihood of massive ocean pollution. But the operating economies of the larger ships are irresistible.

In the last year of the Suez Canal's operation, an 80,000-ton oil tanker made the round trip from Kuwait to Rotterdam at a cost of $3.29 per ton of crude oil. In the early 1970s, a 200,000-ton tanker made the same round

* Noël Mostert, *Supership* (New York: Alfred A. Knopf, Inc., 1974), p. 23.

trip, but taking the longer route around the Cape, for less than $2.50 per ton of oil. Ocean shipping, and especially tanker transport, aptly illustrates decreasing cost based on economies of scale. Scale economies are found in numerous undertakings, although recent developments in ocean transportation show them most dramatically. Before saying more about economies of scale, however, we need to distinguish between the short-run cost function, which has received most of our attention up to now, and the long-run cost function.

The nature of long-run cost

In describing short-run cost in Chapter 6, we emphasized the limiting effect of the fixed factor on output. In the long run, the production organization is freed from this constraint, and change in firm size, modification in technology, and adjustments to market conditions can be carried out without hitch or mishap—*and without encountering diminishing returns.* The long-run curve may initially dip down, to rise later as the industry grows, but this is not because of diminishing returns. Only in the short run is there a fixed factor. Although costs may rise in the long run, this is not because of successively less productive input combinations: Technology can be modified and input combinations arranged in the optimal relationship in the long run. In the short run, the cost pattern is always the same—first down, then up as output increases. In the long run, costs may rise, fall, or remain unchanged. As an industry increases in size, it may experience increasing cost, decreasing cost, or constant cost, and as it passes through different development phases it may encounter different cost functions, such as decreasing cost during infancy and increasing cost during maturity.

Why should costs differ?

If there is enough time in the long run to choose the best technology and the optimal factor relationship, why do some industries experience lower costs as they grow, while others experience higher costs? Basically, the reason is that the technological opportunities and the availability of factors in different industries are not the same. Some industries can use lower-cost methods of production as firms build larger plants, while in other industries higher prices for raw materials from expansion affect all firms. Table 10.1 summarizes the main factors that are responsible for increasing and decreasing cost. (Constant cost is not included in the table because this cost function is largely unaffected by changes in the size of the firm or industry.)

Table 10.1 does not cover all of the causes of decreasing and increasing costs. Its purpose is to establish categories in which the causes of increasing and decreasing costs can be fitted and explained. These categories are reasonably self-explanatory, but we should note that the term *internal* economies or diseconomies refer to the firm, indicating, for example, better or poorer management of the United States Steel Corporation as it grows larger. The term *external* applies to cost changes that are not directly related to expansion in the size of the firm, such as lower transportation costs or higher raw materials prices, which result from an increase in the overall size or output of the industry.

How an industry grows

Whether an industry belongs in the decreasing or increasing cost category depends upon what happens to per-unit cost of production as the capacity of the industry grows. An industry's capacity can be enlarged by the addition of more firms of the same size, through an increase in the size

Table 10.1: Typical causes of long-run decreases and increases in cost

Decreasing cost

Internal Economies (Economies of Scale)—Large firms may have lower per-unit costs as a result of their ability to use mass production techniques, purchase in large quantity, and undertake more effective research programs than smaller firms. The long-run causes of increasing and decreasing cost can be identified as *technical* or *pecuniary,* the former illustrated by mass production techniques and the latter by quantity discount in purchasing.

External Economies—Lower costs for all firms in an industry may result from developments in the industry's infrastructure, such as an improved labor market or more efficient transportation system, or from lower prices for materials and resources purchased from industries that have encountered long-run decreasing cost.

Increasing cost

Internal Diseconomies—After they reach a certain size, large firms may exhaust economies of scale and encounter rising per-unit costs because of the fragmentation of the decision-making process and the increasing complexity of administration and control.

External Diseconomies—As an industry increases in size and the demand for some inputs rises, for example, the demand for iron ore in a growing steel industry, lower-cost sources of supply may be used up, thus raising input costs.

of existing firms, or by a combination of the two. If an industry's capacity is increased because of the enlargement of existing firms, long-run cost changes may be the result of internal factors (within the firms) or external factors (changes in costs of ancillary firms). But if industrial expansion is brought about by the entrance of more firms of the same size, cost modifications are confined to external factors (changes in costs of ancillary firms). These relationships, which are unduly abstract as they are stated above, can be clarified by returning to the example of the supership.

Internal economies

At the beginning of this chapter we pointed out that a ship is a production unit with cost and output characteristics that are similar to other economic undertakings. The ship is equivalent to the production unit or plant. In most industries there are a variety of firm-plant combinations such as those illustrated below.

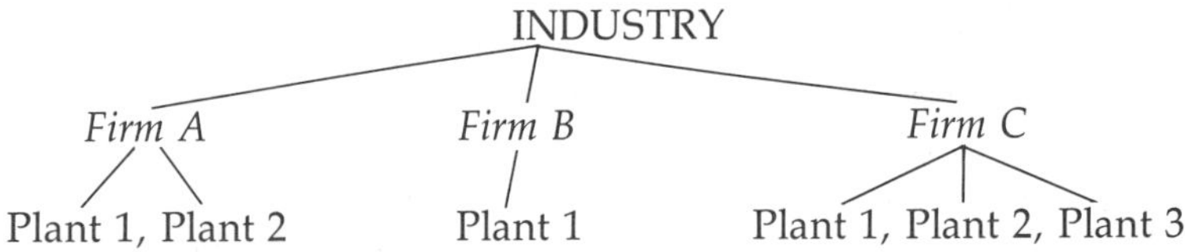

An *industry* is made up of firms that produce similar or identical products. The *plant* is the place where production takes place, and administration and policy are the responsibility of the *firm*.

Tankers as plants

Large tankers cost less to construct in terms of tonnage than smaller vessels because relatively less material is required. A 25 percent increase in a ship's dimensions, for example, brings almost a fourfold increase in capacity as well as less draft relative to tonnage. This means not only that the larger ship requires less construction time and materials in relation to capacity than a smaller ship, but also that the water resistance of the larger vessel is less per ton carried. The second factor reduces energy costs. Finally, the personnel required for the operation of a larger vessel does not increase in proportion to capacity. Fewer crew members are required to work one ship that has twice the capacity of two smaller vessels, while administration expenses, pilot fees, and port charges are less in terms of tonnage for the larger ship.

The lower cost of operating a larger ship comes about in part because the volume of a vessel increases more rapidly than its surface area. This phenomenon is not limited to ships; smelters, storage tanks, blast furnaces, pipelines, pumps, and similar structures require proportionately less material as capacity increases, and personnel maintenance and operation requirements of larger installations generally do not rise in proportion to capacity. Again, this means a cost advantage for the larger operation.

Ships, pipes, and tanks come in all sizes, large and small, and even though larger units may be cheaper to operate, smaller sizes are nonetheless available. This is not the case with some kinds of production processes and some kinds of machinery and equipment, however. When a machine or production process cannot be adapted to a wide range of output but can be used economically only when operations reach a certain scale, it is said to be *indivisible.*

Indivisibilities and internal economies

Indivisibilities are a common feature of the operation of the plant and firm; the special talents of a metallurgist employed in a steel mill represent an indivisibility, as does the use of capital equipment, for example, the presses that stamp out parts of automobile bodies or the machines that bore and tap engine blocks. The assembly-line process, which maximizes specialization of the labor force, is also an example of an indivisiblity. In each of these cases, a certain level of output—scale of plant operation—must be attained before the specialized talent, the large-capacity equipment, or the ideal division of labor can be employed by the firm or plant. Automobile factories are not designed to produce five hundred cars a year, largely because the most efficient machinery and assembly techniques cannot be economically employed at such low output levels. Indivisibility establishes a lower limit to the size of production facilities in the automobile industry, which in turn influences the size of the plant and firm.

Indivisibilities do not bring larger and larger machines, however, or increasingly extended assembly lines, or continually expanding plants. Eventually a point is reached where a further division of assembly-line tasks is either useless or counterproductive. In cases where the task is performed on a machine designed to be operated by one person—typewriters, drill presses, or delivery trucks, for example—output is increased by employing more machines, rather than by designing larger, multioperated machines. Similarly, a plant cannot be expanded indefinitely as the firm grows.

Branch plants are established not only to be near material and labor supplies and sales territory, but because decentralization of production may increase the flexibility of the firm's operations, while at the same time avoiding the problems of control that might arise within a single massive production unit. Indeed, if internal economies continued indefinitely as plant size grew, one huge installation could conceivably supply all of an industry's output. But even where economies of scale are extensive, as in the case of electric power production, the larger utilities, such as Consolidated Edison of New York, employ a number of generating plants. Similarly, American Telephone and Telegraph (AT&T) operates nationwide, but not on a single-plant basis.

As a firm expands, it may outgrow the ideal single plant size. In this case, just as the optimum-size machine can be added to the plant, so the ideal-size plant can be reproduced to expand the firm's capacity.

The indivisible administrator

In distinguishing between the plant and the firm, the separation has been overdrawn. The firm overlays the plant(s), exercising administrative control and determining policy while the plant is the production unit. But

---

Think little . . . and divisible

Bigness—some would say wasteful, unnecessary bigness—is one of the legacies left to the present managers of Pan Am [Pan American Airways] by its founder, Juan Trippe, a visionary who pioneered low-cost foreign travel. Never a man to cut his cloth to suit a purse that was sometimes badly depleted, Trippe indulged from time to time in gambles of imperial proportions. In 1966 he set off a global capital-investment binge by placing an order for twenty-five Boeing 747's at a cost of $600 million. Every other big airline followed suit, though a lot of executives were cursing on the way to the loan window at the bank. As it turned out, a new generation of big, expensive aircraft was the last thing the industry needed when they finally went into service in 1970. Fully loaded with paying passengers all the year round, a 747 is the nearest thing to a money machine imaginable. Half empty, as most of them are these days, the enormous aircraft eat up money.[1]

---

[1] Thomas O'Hanlon, "The Mess That Made Beggars of Pan Am and T.W.A.," *Fortune*, October 1974, p. 125.

the two functions tend to merge rather than to be sharply separated, and indivisibilities show up in both administration and production.

The specialized administrative talents of market analysts, personnel directors, tax accountants, economic forecasters, and others are as indivisible as those of metallurgists and time-and-motion engineers—and even less likely to be fully utilized by the small firm. But if such white-collar specialists increase the efficiency of the firm, they too constitute an internal economy, a cost advantage to the larger firm.

Beyond indivisibilities, the larger firm is likely to have an advantage over the smaller firm because of its purchasing power and its ability to support larger absolute outlays. Large purchasers sometimes bring disproportionate bargaining influences over price, while a small percentage outlay of a large firm's income makes possible the support of research and development beyond the reach of a smaller firm. Product promotion and advertising campaigns may also require large absolute expenditures before they attract consumer attention, another advantage of the large firm, and the costs of underwriting stocks and bonds are likely to be a smaller proportion of large issues.

Firm costs are also affected by the price of the resources it uses, which change because of industry expansion whether the firm grows or not. When such cost changes are favorable, they are called *external economies.*

External economies

External economies occur in Industry A, say the iron and steel industry, when growth and development generates internal economies in Industries B and C—for example, iron ore mining and shipping—that lower the costs of Industry A. Over the years this has happened to an extraordinary degree in the development of the Lake Superior iron ore industry. Striking economies of scale—*internal* to the shipping industry, but *external* to the iron and steel industry—have taken place in the transportation of iron ore on the Great Lakes. Iron ore brought from Lake Superior mines to Eastern blast furnaces has to be carried down the Great Lakes and around the rapids at Sault Ste. Marie, Michigan.

Until the opening of the Soo Canal in 1855, the shipment of Lake Superior ore to Eastern furnaces was not economically feasible.[2] But in the

[2] The construction and later enlargement of the Soo Canal at Sault Ste. Marie, Michigan is an obvious example of an external economy brought about by the increased traffic on the Great Lakes. Such cost-reducing developments are sometimes referred to as social overhead capital because they are beneficial to society as a whole and involve a large-scale capital investment.

late summer of 1855, the shipment of 132 tons of iron ore as deck cargo on the *Columbia,* a 91-foot brigantine, marked the beginning of ore shipments that later brought about unparalleled specialization in Great Lakes ore handling and transport. In moving from sailing ships to the huge ore carriers of the present day, the evolution has been accompanied by a succession of economies of scale. Vinton Coney has described the first carry of ore down the Lakes and through the Soo locks, contrasting it with current practices.

> *The* Columbia *had one advantage over the . . . ships that sailed on Lake Superior: her decks were low enough so that wheelbarrows could be used to transfer the iron ore from the dock to the deck. Even so, it took the better part of two days to bring the ore aboard and trim the load.*
>
> *With no specialized machinery available for taking the ore ashore [at Cleveland], it is probable that this first load was handled by men with wheelbarrows walking across a gangplank. However, when the steamers began to carry ore in their holds a crude form of automation was developed. The red cargo was pitched by shovel gangs to deck level. There it was loaded into buckets which were lifted to the dock by pulleys literally operated by horsepower. When the contents had been dumped, the horses were backed up to let the buckets down again. Unloading was thus improved to the rate of 300 tons per week.*
>
> *The iron industry of the United States of the period was made up of relatively small units. Many furnaces were dependent upon neighboring ore deposits, some of which were becoming depleted. The industry was ready for a major new source. . . .*
>
> *In comparison with the crude conditions of 1855, [today] vessels are loaded in Lake Superior at the rate of more than 18,000 gross tons per hour. They travel from the western end of Lake Superior through the Soo Canal to Cleveland in 2-1/2 days. They can be unloaded by a single Hulett machine in the rate of 20 tons a minute; usually several such machines work simultaneously.*[3]

The cost-reducing innovations in ore handling that marked the early growth of the US iron and steel industry are typical of internal economies encountered in the development in manufacturing and heavy industry throughout the world. As the scale of the industry undertaking increased, opportunities for specialization, mass production, and the use of larger equipment were exploited and the per-unit cost of production fell. Eventually, however, both plants and firms exhausted the opportunities for technical scale economies, although pecuniary scale economies for the firm have been more persistent.

[3] Vinton Coney, "White Sails/Red Ore," *Steelways*, March/April, 1968, p. 24.

That plants and firms may both outrun internal economies does not mean that there will be an abrupt halt in expansion either of the firm or the industry. Whether costs fall or rise in the long run, an industry continues to expand as long as the product price fully covers the costs of production. But long-run costs are only one of the pressures on the firm.

The narrow compass of long-run cost

Because an industry outruns internal and external economies does not mean that a firm's unit costs will forever rise thereafter. Costs rise and fall because of factors other than the size and output of an industry; for example, bumper crops or crop failures, inflation or deflation, variations in taxes, and developments in technology and new materials that are unrelated to firm or industry size can all affect cost. The cost-reducing influence of a widely available innovation, however, is a basic feature of a dynamic economy. There are numerous examples of such developments: the computer, which has established itself in such diverse areas as monitoring steel mill rolling operations, calculating bank balances, and addressing junk mail; plastics, which are used in car bumpers, canoes, IUDs, and building materials; and synthetic fibers, which are spun into clothes, made into tire fabric, and molded into machinery parts.

Innovations as widely used as computers and synthetics are responsible for lowering cost in numerous industries, some otherwise characterized by constant and increasing cost. These do not represent long-run cost economies, however, unless they are induced by industrial expansion.

It is obvious that costs—and prices—have not generally followed a downward trend over the years. From time to time, cost reductions have occurred, and in some cases upward pressure has been held in check by scale economies and innovations, but historically the trend has been inexorably upward. An important factor in this general price rise has been inflation. Inflation, of course, does not set aside the benefits of long-run decreasing cost, but as an economy continues to grow, another long-run influence may emerge in the form of internal and external *diseconomies*.

Internal diseconomies

Some forms of organization appear to be better able than others to check the dilution of decision making and the frustration of central control that often plagues the very large firm. Decentralization of operations and subsidiary competition, as practiced in the General Motors Corporation, or

Scientific management at Bethlehem Steel—specialized economies in shovels

Frederick W. Taylor [father of scientific management, 1856-1915] recounted his experience at the Bethlehem Steel plant. On his arrival there he had found that each laborer brought his own shovel to the yard and used the same shovel to move all sorts of material. "We would see a first-class shoveler go from shoveling rice coal with a load of 3½ pounds to the shovel to handling ore from the Mesabi Range, with 38 pounds to the shovel. Now, is 3½ pounds the proper shovel load or is 38 pounds the proper shovel load? They cannot both be right. Under scientific management the answer to this question is not a matter of anyone's opinion; it is a question for accurate, careful scientific investigation."

After gathering data on the tonnage of each kind of material handled at Bethlehem by each man each day, Taylor had designed his own shovels and supplied them to the men. He then noted the result as he changed the length of the handle. He found, for example, that by cutting off the handle so that the shoveler picked up 35 (instead of 38) pounds in each shovel-load of ore, he could increase the shoveler's daily handling from a total of 25 to 35 tons. Taylor continued to cut off the shovel handle until he found that at 21½ pounds per load, the men were doing their largest day's work. By pursuing this kind of study, he found that the best results in the plant as a whole were obtained when there were fifteen different kinds of shovels, each for moving a different kind of material—ranging from small flat shovels for handling ore up to immense scoops for handling rice coal, and forks for handling coke.[4]

a dominant personality, such as Andrew Carnegie, may stay the enervating influence of bureaucratic growth upon managerial efficiency. Sooner or later as the firm continues to grow, however, increasing administrative complexity is likely to raise costs. Professor George Stigler of the University of Chicago finds in this complexity a source of administrative diseconomy.

As the firm becomes large, . . . [the] center of decision loses all contact with the details of operation. The entrepreneur deals only with large issues (which, however, are composed of and entail numerous minor issues) and the decisions must rest more and more upon brief memoranda and estimates of subordinates' capacities.

[4] Daniel J. Boorstin, *The Americans—The Democratic Experience* (New York: Random House, Inc. 1973), p. 366.

> *If the individual has enormous energy, a fly-paper memory, and the knack of finding able subordinates, the limitations of size appear only slowly and weakly. Industry geniuses . . . can build and manage gigantic firms. Executives are usually men of more ordinary clay, however, and under them the rigidities and stupidities increase rapidly with size.*[5]

Why do firms expand if costs rise?

If the large firm encounters rising costs from the diffusion and disruption in managerial control, why do firms continue to grow—especially conglomerates, which bring under one corporate roof undertakings of massive proportions and highly diverse operations? The answer is that the overall benefits of large size frequently outweigh the costs. The diseconomy of a large corporate bureaucracy may be a small price to pay for the market control and political influence that comes with increasing firm size. Indeed, conglomerates may achieve the power without the penalty; the product diversity of the conglomerate affiliates may ensure that the central decisions are limited primarily to financial and ownership matters in a kind of multifirm federation.

Whatever the diseconomy of the large firm, it will occur at the plant or factory level only through mishap. Machinery is not designed that is too large, nor assembly lines too long, nor factories too high. Instead, if demand increases beyond the capacity of the most efficient plant size, the optimum in machinery, assembly line, and plant capacity are duplicated at another location. Although scale overdesign is an infrequent occurrence in most advanced industrial economies, "giantism" did plague early Soviet economic development. The Russian enthusiasm for bigness undoubtedly stemmed in part from the pressure to catch up technologically with Western economies, but large-scale operations also facilitated central control, as in the case of the huge state farms that have brought hundreds of agricultural workers together under a single Soviet management. Although elements of giantism linger in the Soviet system, it has been guarded against in recent plans—although not with complete success, however, as the account of the Kama truck works shows.[6]

Whether the factory or plant is in a socialist or capitalist economy, production costs may rise due to forces that are beyond the control of the

[5] George J. Stigler, *The Theory of Price* (New York: The Macmillan Company, 1952), pp. 139–40.

[6] The tendency to overdesign projects, especially capital-intensive undertakings such as hydroelectric installations, was initially abeted in the Soviet Union by the reluctance of the planning authorities to use the interest rate as an indicator of the cost of capital. Interest was considered by the Marxists to be a form of capitalist exploitation. The role of interest in production will be examined in Chapter 12.

Would you believe—a plant as big as the Bronx?

The U.S.S.R. has always favored big projects, for its leaders equate size with efficiency whatever the economic circumstances. Yet even by Soviet standards, Kama [truck complex] is a monster: when the $5-billion facility goes into production in a couple of years the plant alone will cover forty square miles of land, an area almost exactly the size of the Bronx. The equipment will include about a half billion dollars' worth of U.S. machinery and technology.

Kama is being designed to produce 150,000 three-axle, heavy-duty trucks and 250,000 diesel engines a year to help modernize the Soviet Union's backward, inefficient transportation system . . . .

The plant itself will consist of six huge installations—foundry; forge; pressing and stamping; tooling and repair; engines, gears, and transmissions; and assembly. In addition, the project will include factories to produce the building materials for the plant as well as those needed to construct the entire city for 95,000 workers and their families.[7]

private firm or the managers of the socialist enterprise. When the pressures that increase a firm's cost come from outside, they are called *external diseconomies.*

External diseconomies

In an expanding industry, firms may find that their costs rise because collectively their demand for raw materials depletes higher-grade supplies, or because growing industrial wastes overburden the environment and raise disposal costs, or because labor becomes less tractable and its supply less elastic as demand increases. Under these and other circumstances, a firm's costs rise because of external diseconomies, whether or not it expands its capacity.

External diseconomies are more likely to develop when an industry is mature than during its infancy. As an industry attains large-scale operation, internal and external economies reduce certain costs, as illustrated

[7] H. E. Mayer "A Plant That Could Change the Shape of Soviet Industry," *Fortune*, November 1974, pp. 150–52.

above in the case of the US iron and steel industry. But the steel industry has come full circle; internal and external economies have been fully exploited and continued expansion of the industry has turned costs upward.

Where there is a heavy concentration of industrial capacity, for example, the location of steel production in Pittsburgh, Gary, and Youngstown regions, the impact of industry growth upon the physical environment and the market for resource inputs may raise firm costs. To locate large industrial capacity in one area accentuates air and water pollution, and increased steel output means more demand for iron ore, coking coal, limestone, and other special ingredients such as nickel and chromium. The result is higher costs for *all* the firms in the industry—large or small—whether they have been responsible for increasing the capacity of the industry or not.

If wages in the steel industry rise, the producers in a given labor market are affected more or less equally. If stricter regulations against air and water pollution are imposed in Pittsburgh, Gary, or Youngstown, plants in these locations are faced with higher costs. And if high-grade Great Lakes iron ore deposits deteriorate—as they are—the need to import ore from more distant sources such as Quebec-Labrador or Venezuela raises the materials cost of iron and steel. Industry-wide bargaining may be encouraged in a large industry, promoting substantial uniformity in wage payments and working conditions. Industry-wide bargaining may thus increase labor costs not only for those firms that expand production, but also for those that do not alter their capacity.

Internalizing costs of waste disposal

The environmental awakening in the early 1970s has raised costs for many industries in the United States. The disposal of industrial wastes, which previously went largely unremarked and uncharged, has become a matter of public concern and private cost. Industrial plants can no longer treat the earth, from the land below to the atmosphere above, as a free dump. Pretreatment or pollution abatement of waste water discharges may be obligatory; industries in large cities are almost universally restricted to using fossil fuels with a low-sulfur content; and precipitators and stack modifications may be required to reduce discharges of particulate matter and sulfur dioxide. In short, where environmental deterioration results from large-scale industrial growth, redressing the grievances costs the polluting firms money. Where the responsibility for preventing the deterioration of the environment is placed on the firm, pollution costs previously borne by the public are said to be *internalized*—made an internal cost of the firm.

Whether internalized disposal costs should be classed as external diseconomies is a fine point, which depends on how environmental deterioration occurs. If damages to the environment, say, oil spills, are the result of the increased output of a particular industry, the industry as a whole may be subject to stiffer controls and a uniform clean-up assessment. This represents an *external* diseconomy. If the pollution is caused by a single large firm, for example, by the Reserve Mining Company's disposal of mining wastes in Lake Superior, compliance with abatement orders constitutes an *internal* diseconomy. But environmental deterioration frequently is caused by a melange of industrial wastes, by-products of many firms in different industries. Regulations to protect the environment, such as those calling for the pretreatment of waste water or prohibiting the burning of high-sulfur fuel, are likely to apply to all firms in an area, whether large or small, and whether members of the same industry or not. The link between an industry's growth and its contribution to environmental deterioration is at times tenuous and difficult to establish.. Moreover, establishing such a relationship may be beside the point. A moderately polluting industry may be subject to abatement controls quite as stringent as those imposed upon heavily polluting industries that are primarily responsible for the decrease in environmental quality. The external diseconomies of some industries thus raise costs for all.

Whatever their long-run cost function, all firms and industries have some impact upon the environment, but the least economic pressure is exerted by firms in constant-cost industries.

Constant cost

None of the glamour of the industrial giant is associated with the constant-cost firm; its factories are not mammoth and it is not involved in struggles over a depleting resource supply. Constant cost is the mom-and-pop grocery store, the family farm, the roadside frozen custard stand, the small contractor, and some larger enterprises, all of which are mostly immune to cost changes from modifications in the size of their operations. Usually, textbooks dismiss constant cost with an illustration or two of small-scale operations—the retail clothing store or the bobby-pin manufacturer—which do not encounter economies of scale, administration complexities, or rising raw material prices, even if they double or triple their size. This does not mean that such undertakings are of little consequence to the economy. Individual proprietors and small partnerships and corporations contribute importantly to economic output. These include carpenters turned building contractors, appliance sales and service shops, a large part of agriculture, much of retailing, and many firms in manufacturing and transportation. These firms are too small to achieve scale advantages, and their collective impact does not carry enough weight to bring either external economies or diseconomies in the supply industries.

Constant-cost industries—ripples, not economic waves

Take a closer look at the bobby-pin industry and at construction by the carpenter-contractor. The bobby-pin industry attracts little attention when it enters the market to cover its raw materials needs. The steel industry, its major material supplier, is indifferent to its growth or decline, and unless a bobby-pin manufacturing firm is the only source of employment in a small town, a labor market of any size is unruffled by the industry's expansion or contraction. Bobby-pin production is not likely to promote scale economies or affect resource input prices.

The small-scale builder is in much the same position as the small manufacturer. Having little leverage in the purchase of materials, the builder cannot borrow at the prime lending rate and is unlikely either to introduce or adopt innovations in building practices. Building a house or two at a time, techniques such as precutting and prefabricating are of little purpose and a limited work force permits only the most basic specialization in building techniques.

Housing construction is not a fertile field for production innovations, but scale economies do occur as building operations are enlarged. The builders of Levitt Town in New York, "Flat Top" Smith's developments in Los Angeles, and the prefabricated National Home line all employed factory-like production methods that were beyond the reach of the small contractor. In an intermediate stage, the moderately large contractor with a work load of twenty-five or more houses at a time is able to purchase in quantity, employ a highly specialized labor force, and fully utilize heavy construction equipment. Thus construction of housing in the United States takes place under different cost conditions: Standardized units are erected by large-scale developers, and custom units are built by moderately large and large contracting firms as well as by small-scale building contractors. Constant cost is typical of small-scale construction; moderate economies of scale occur in the larger undertakings.

At any one time costs of production reflect a multitude of pressures—temporary materials shortages or surpluses, innovations available to more than one industry, diligence or laxness of the work force, general shrinkage in the resource base or development of new materials—and more. In singling out the long-run factors for examination, we necessarily neglect other forces of equal or greater importance. But in spite of this, the special attention given to long-run cost is justified. Dynamic cost influences bring variations around the long-run equilibrium, but the basic structure of the firm and industry is shaped largely by long-run cost.

The graphics of long-run cost

The first stage of development in heavy industry, manufacturing, and transportation is usually characterized by decreasing cost. Per-unit cost falls as labor and equipment specialization takes place and plant and firm size increases. Eventually, however, scale economies and technological innovations fall behind the rate of growth or cease completely. Intermittent cost reductions may still be stimulated by expansion, but decreasing cost is no longer the dominant force in the industry. An upturn in costs occurs and firms may enlarge beyond the optimum size, only to find that their outlays for administration and control have begun to increase more rapidly than output. This evolution of firm cost is shown in Figure 10.1.

The cost curves in Figure 10.1 cut across two time periods of analysis. The SAC curves represent the familiar firm cost curve resulting from the interplay of fixed and variable factors of production. Curve LAC traces modifications in costs as the industry expands without the constraint of a fixed factor. The movement of Curves SAC_1 through SAC_5 records firm per-unit cost as capacity is increased. The long-run average cost curve in Figure 10.1 carries firm expansion through decreasing to increasing cost. For some industries only a portion of the LAC curve may be applicable,

Figure 10.1 Long-run Average Cost

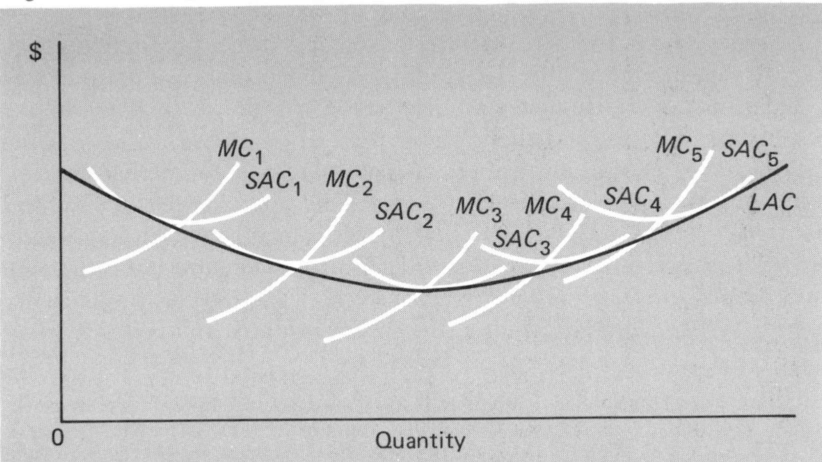

Figure 10.2 Long-run/Short-run Competitive Equilibrium

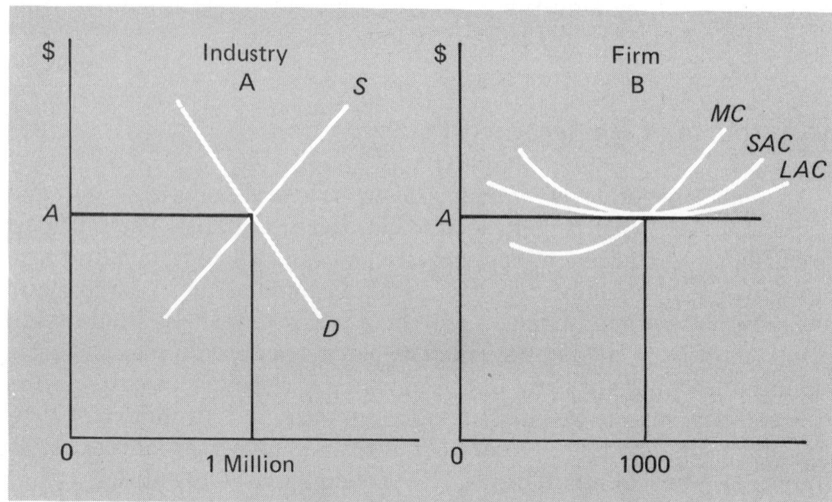

such as SAC_1 through SAC_3, and expansion beyond SAC_3 may take place under constant cost rather than increasing cost.

If the forces of competition bring about the ultimate short-run and long-run adjustments, a twofold equilibrium is reached: (1) In the short run, the industry equates supply and demand and the firm produces where marginal costs equals price. (2) In the long run, the firm produces where MC equals price at LTUC with an optimum firm size. The optimum firm size rests at the point at which the short-run average total cost curve coincides with the lowest point of the long-run average cost curve.[8] This dual equilibrium is shown in Figure 10.2

External cost factors, which raise or lower a firm's production costs, are illustrated in Figure 10.3. To simplify the illustration, we assume that the expansion of the industry's output results from an increase in the *number* of firms in the industry, rather than from adding to the existing firms' capacity. In this illustration of increasing cost, all firms are confronted with higher costs as factor prices are bid up, whether they expand capacity or not. The sequence of adjustments is as follows: An increase in industry demand moves D_1 to D_2 and has the long-run effect of increasing supply from S_1 to S_2, thus raising price from OA to OB. As the industry responds to the increased demand, the cost of resource inputs is driven up

[8] Combining the two time periods of analysis on the same diagram risks confusion, especially when the long-run and short-run cost curves are roughly the same shape, as they are in Figure 10.2. At the risk of emphasizing the obvious, the U-shape of the SAC curves results from the constraint of the fixed factor, while the more gradual but similar shape of Curve LAC in Figure 10.2 is caused by the modification in plant/firm capacity.

for all firms in the industry—even those whose capacity remains unchanged, such as the firm illustrated in Figure 10.3B. For this firm costs rise from ATC_1 to ATC_2. The higher input price also shows up in the cost structure of the new firms attracted by the shift in demand from D_1 to D_2, as well as in outlays of the established firms. For the industry as a whole, output expands along the long-run supply curve LRS in Figure 10.3, which follows an upward course as costs increase.

If costs decrease in the long run, LRS falls, and if costs are constant, LRS is horizontal. The expansion of a constant cost industry through enlarging established firms is shown in Figure 10.4, which illustrates a case in which a typical firm expands firm size from SAC_1 to SAC_2, increasing firm output from Oc to Od and industry output from OC to OD.

With long-run constant cost, both the industry and firm can expand without affecting per-unit cost. Neither economies nor diseconomies occur as firms increase in size or the industry expands. This does not mean that firms in constant cost industries are somehow immune to the inefficiencies and complexities of administrative growth, but rather that they do not generally attain the size at which such problems arise. For this reason, enlarging the size of a typical firm in a constant cost industry (say, from SAC_1 to SAC_2 in Figure 10.4), does not change the level of LTUC. Larger firms have the same minimum average total cost as smaller firms. By connecting the LTUC points for all firms we can trace Line LRS, the industry's long-run supply curve.

The foregoing discussion has been cast against a background of competition. But what happens if there is monopoly?

Figure 10.3 Long-run Increasing Cost

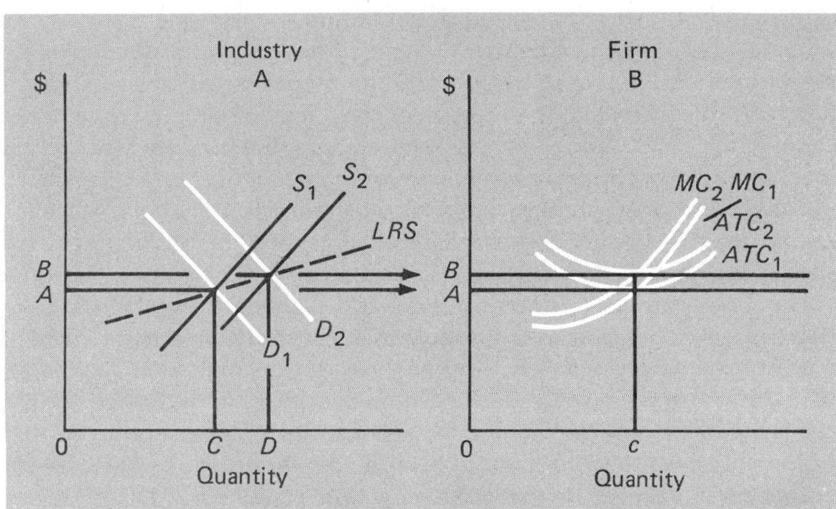

Figure 10.4 Long-run Constant Cost

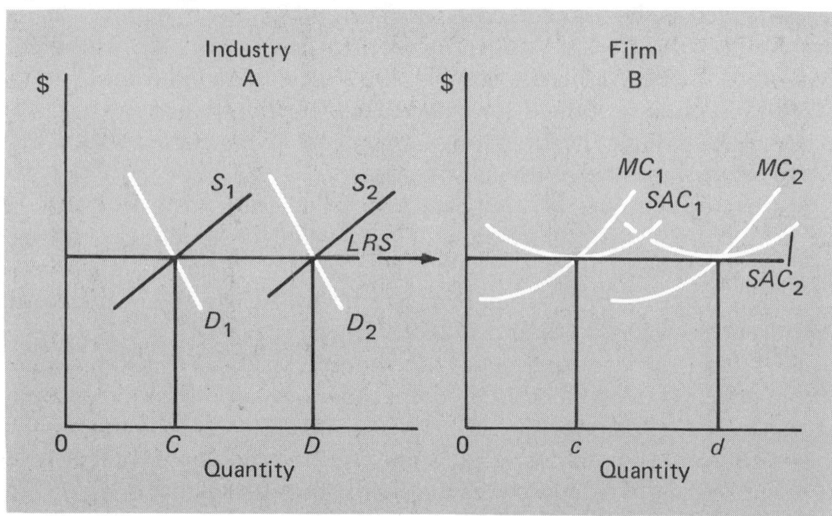

Long-run cost in the absence of competition

Monopoly and oligopoly restrict output in order to raise price above the competitive level, but because the noncompetitive firm exercises control in the product market doesn't mean that it can escape the constraint of cost. There are applications of long-run cost principles to the noncompetitive case that deserve attention. If a single firm controls output, production is lower than if the industry is competitive, but since only one firm supplies total demand, its size may exceed the optimum.

In the absence of competitive market pressures that induce firms to conform to optimum size in the long run, monopolies and oligopolies can expand into the increasing cost region of the long-run supply curve in the pursuit of sales. Expanding beyond optimum size, the noncompetitive firm adjusts to the long-run forces as shown in Figure 10.5.

But there is an optimum, long-run position for monopoly, which—save for the profit incurred—is similar to that of the competitive firm. This is shown in Figure 10.6.

The monopoly is in short-run/long-run equilibrium in Figure 10.6, with a price OA and output OB. Output OB constitutes the most efficient use of firm resources at LTUC on the short-run average total cost curve SAC, which also represents the optimum-size firm, as indicated by the coincidence of the low points of SAC and LAC. This does not mean that the ultimate monopoly short-run/long-run equilibrium is the same as for pure competition. Even if the monopoly firm produces at LTUC at op-

Figure 10.5 Noncompetitive Firm Beyond Optimum Size

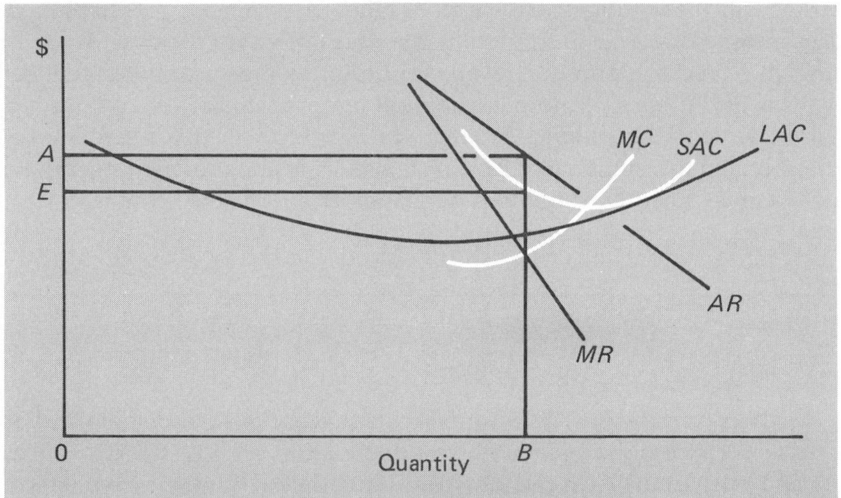

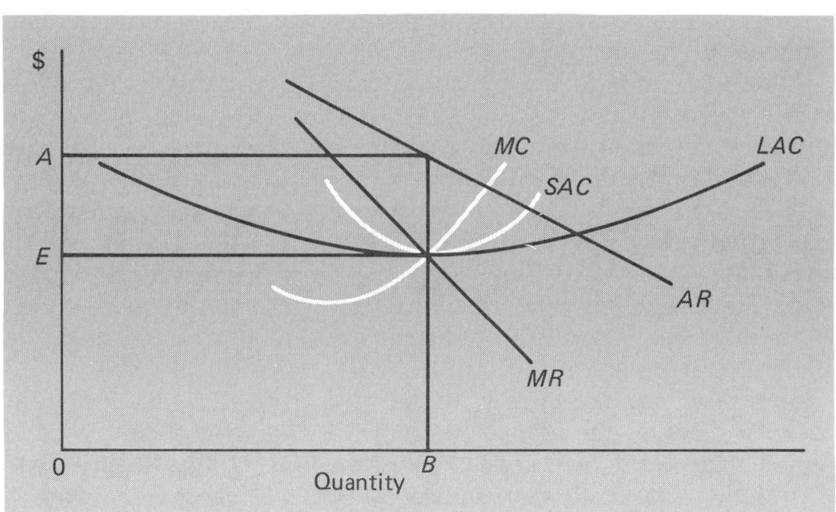

timum firm capacity, its higher price leads to less output than would be the case with a competitive firm.

The perfect adjustment shown in Figure 10.6, while not a complete will-o'-the-wisp, represents but one of a medley of forces that confronts the monopolist. Long-term growth in demand can encourage capacity expansion beyond the optimum size, as shown in Figure 10.5, and at times the monopolist may hold back from extracting the ultimate tribute that the market will yield from fear of encouraging government prosecution. In other instances, perfect output adjustment is not worth the cost. To determine the precise optimum level of output requires sophisticated cost analysis, and it may be more economical to approximate the optimum by trial-and-error adjustments. Finally, the long run is not a fixed point, inflexibly tied to a stationary LTUC; it is a shifting and moving target that is pushed and pulled by the forces of change in a dynamic economy.

Summary

In the short run, the firm faces some costs that are fixed and some that are variable because not all factors of production are equally sensitive to the pull and push of price. In the long run, however, all but the unusual factor of production responds to price. As a result, the conditions responsible for the U-shaped cost curve in the short run are not present in the long run. In the long run, costs may decrease or increase, but the causes are different from those of the short run.

Long-run cost is of three types: decreasing cost, constant cost, and increasing cost. For long-run cost, the distinction between the firm and the industry is important since cost changes may take place because of an increase in the size of either the firm or the industry. Decreasing cost, for example, may occur as a firm grows larger and experiences economies of scale. Economies of scale result from such factors as the superior bargaining position of the larger firm, the opportunity for discounts—such as shipping in carload lots—the use of mass production techniques—such as the assembly-line method of production—and other practices associated with large-scale production.

Firm costs may also increase or decrease, not because the firm grows larger, but because the industry to which it belongs expands, bringing about increased or decreased costs for *all* the firms in the industry. In the case of firms using costly raw materials supplied by another industry, for example, lower costs (economies) in the raw material supplying industry may pass on lower costs to the firms that buy the raw materials. Costs do not always go down in the supplying industries, however. Pressures upon the raw material supply from expansion of the manufacturing industry may raise costs for the firms in the latter industry.

Firm costs may rise as it grows larger, but not because plants increase in size. In some cases, large firms may exhaust the cost-reducing opportunities of large-scale production techniques and encounter problems in the administration and control of firm affairs. In short, higher costs associated with bureaucratic inefficiency may arise as the firm grows, just as similar developments are encountered in governmental and other administrative organizations. Conceivably, a larger, higher cost of production plant might be built instead of a smaller, lower-cost plant, but the obvious remedy for this planning mistake is to duplicate the smaller plant to increase output.

If long-run decreasing cost results from firm economies of scale, as is the case in some public utilities, competition is likely to be a transition step to monopoly. Since the larger firm has lower per-unit costs with scale economies, the large firm can drive the smaller firm from the market by cutting price below the latter's cost. To prevent such destructive competition and to forestall monopoly by the large firm, government permits the more efficient, larger firm to operate in a specified area. The telephone and power industries illustrate this arrangement. Although granted the sole right to a given market, the rates and service of the utility are controlled by the government so that the economies of large-scale production are passed on to the consumer rather than resulting in monopoly profits for the public utility.

Key terms and concepts

Long-run cost the cost of expanding industrial output either by enlarging existing firms or by adding firms, or through a combination of the two. In the long-run period, all factors of production can be varied and the technique of production modified.

Decreasing cost

Internal economies (Economics of Scale) large firms may experience lower costs than smaller firms because they are able to make use of large-scale buying, mass production, extensive research and the like.

External economies lower costs for all firms in an industry may result from favorable developments in the industry infrastructure, such as an improved labor market or a more efficient transportation system, or from lower input prices brought about by economies in related industries.

Increasing cost

Internal diseconomies after they reach a certain size, large firms exhaust economies of scale and encounter rising per-unit costs because of the increasing difficulty of administration and control.

External diseconomies as an industry increases in size and the demand for some inputs rises, lower-cost sources may be used up, thus raising input prices.

Constant cost

In constant-cost industries neither the size of the firms nor the aggregate output of the industry is large enough to bring about internal or external economies or diseconomies.

Indivisible input a factor or production, either capital or labor, that is available in units that cannot be subdivided; for example, a high-speed rotograveur printing press or a certified public accountant.

Internalizing costs shifting costs of production that were previously imposed upon third parties back upon the producer or consumer. An industry is forced to internalize costs when it is required to eliminate airborne waste discharges.

Discussion and review questions

1. Large tankers lower costs of transport; they also raise serious problems of pollution of the sea and the coastlands. Why does the disadvantage not check the development of larger ships?

2. Why doesn't diminishing returns occur in the long run? What does this mean for the output of the world?

3. How can short-run costs for firms follow approximately the same pattern whether the firms experience decreasing or increasing long-run cost? What is the distinction between the short run and the long run?

4. Why is an industry more likely to encounter decreasing cost during its early development than after it reaches maturity? Do the experiences of industrial nations illustrate this tendency? What exceptions to this generalization are there?

5. What are the different costs incurred at the plant level as opposed to the firm level and how do they affect long-run cost? Why is the distinction between the plant and firm particularly relevant for long-run cost? What happens to the variable cost and fixed cost distinction in the long run?

6. Do indivisibilities become larger and larger as industry develops and the size of the plant and firm increases? Is there any relationship between firm size and indivisibilities?

7. Is management a major bottleneck in firm size? Has the computer eased this problem? How do other developments, such as rapid transportation and communication, affect managerial capacity? Does the development of the conglomerate or multinational corporation indicate that management is no longer a bottleneck?

8. Is scientific management mainly just a systematic application of the idea that what is worth doing is not necessarily worth doing well?

9. Why do firms expand if their costs rise with expansion? Will larger plants be built if this causes a higher per-unit cost of production?

10. Is the bureaucracy of the large firm the main cause for long-run increasing cost? Is a smaller administrative unit the answer? Is a large bureaucracy an end in itself in some cases?

11. Increased concern about the environment has confronted industry with a new range of external costs. What industries are most likely to be affected by this development and what will be the impact on long-run cost?

12. How does constant cost differ from increasing and decreasing cost? Why is it treated so briefly in Chapter 10? Are you more or less familiar with industries based on constant cost than with those that operate under increasing and decreasing cost?

IV Factor returns and income distribution

11 Division of the spoils I: wages

When the most celebrated bidding war in American sports history ended last week, the New York Yankees had one of baseball's best pitchers and Jim (Catfish) Hunter had a five-year contract valued at $3.75 million, a record for baseball. [In 1974 he received $100,000 from the Oakland Athletics.]*

While $100,000 for a season of baseball pitching is not likely to impress most people as a case of worker exploitation, this is exactly what most baseball players and some economists have contended because of the hiring procedures in major-league baseball. Catfish Hunter's 1975 contract brought this issue to the courts and appears to have changed the character of the employment relationship. Major league baseball is big business, but by comparison with other businesses it has operated in a privileged status. It is exempt from federal antitrust regulation and before the case of Catfish Hunter, after signing an initial team contract, players were not permitted to negotiate with any other baseball team so long as the team with which they originally contracted wished to retain their services. This was more restrictive than it appears.

The exclusive option to renew was granted the employer by the so-called reserve clause, which tied the player to the team of his original contract, unless this agreement is breached or the player released. In Catfish Hunter's case, the court held that the Oakland Athletics had been guilty of a breach of contract, thus voiding the reserve clause and making Hunter a free agent. Since the Hunter case, other ball players have challenged the reserve clause. When the reserve clause is in effect, however, the player's bargaining power with the employer is severely limited; if the team wishes to retain his services he cannot negotiate with any other. He must either play ball for that team or seek employment outside baseball.

The jump in salary which Catfish Hunter received by moving from the Oakland Athletics to the New York Yankees indicates the improved bargaining position brought about by his availability to all major league teams. But it undoubtedly overstates the effect that eliminating the reserve clause

* *The New York Times*, January 5, 1975, Sec. 4, p. 18. © 1975 by The New York Times Company. Reprinted with permission.

would have for all players. Catfish's spectacular boost in pay was largely the result of the fact that one established player became eligible for hire by any major league team. If all major league players had been equally available for hire—that is, not subject to the reserve-clause restraint—the greater supply choice afforded employing teams would hold down the demand for any one player. If Catfish had been one of many job seekers, his reward would have been considerably less impressive, although undoubtedly better than if he had been negotiating with a single employer under the reserve clause. So it would appear that there has been exploitation of the baseball superstars—a clear case of the rich robbing the rich.

When is a worker exploited?

In the economic sense, a worker is exploited if he or she receives less than he or she contributes to production, whether that contribution takes the form of hitting home runs, assembling an automobile, cooking hot dogs, mining coal, or cutting hair. This generalization raises the question: How can we separate the contribution of a worker from the contribution of the rest of the factors of production employed in the productive process? In some cases, such as that of a hair cutter, the contributing factors can be ignored without seriously distorting the case, but what about the case of a Yankee pitcher or a McDonald's chef? Although a pitcher and a chef are key employees, both are but a part of a larger labor force, to say nothing of the other inputs required to win ball games and produce hamburgers.

In a firm's hiring and investment decisions, the question takes a slightly different form: Is the worker added to the labor force or the equipment installed in the factory worth what it costs? The answer is found by focusing attention on changes in output that accompany the firm's hiring or its acquisition of capital equipment.

Here comes marginalism again

Under competitive conditions in hiring, a firm continues to add workers as long as the market value of the output for which they are responsible is equal to or greater than their wage cost. This adjustment involves marginal analysis. John Bates Clark, a professor at Columbia University at the turn of the twentieth century, is credited with one of the earliest applications of the marginal principle to the determination of wages. Clark explained its application as follows:

The actual and practical test of the productive power of one unit of labor is made, if one unit only is taken out of a complete force and if the ensuing reduction of the product is noted. . . . The effective value of any unit of labor is always what the whole society with all its capital produces, minus what it would produce if that unit were to be taken away.[1]

Clark went on to say that the measurement of the marginal output of a worker by withholding the worker's contribution from the market can be extended to explain the worth of other workers with equivalent ability. In such cases, the loss of the output of the worker first employed is in no way different from the loss which occurs when a worker hired later is released. With an unchanging fixed factor, however, it does make a difference how many workers are employed. Diminishing returns is still a dominant consideration of the firm in the short run.

In order to measure the contribution of a labor input by the changes in firm output that occur when the work force is increased or decreased, the amount and quality of other inputs must remain unchanged. More capital equipment cannot be employed, the technique of production cannot be improved, and the quality of raw materials must not be raised. If such modifications take place in the nonlabor factors, the change in firm output cannot be attributed solely to labor. This is familiar territory: To measure the marginal contribution of labor, we have posited the conditions under which diminishing returns takes place. In fact, the short-run demand for labor is really an application of the principle of diminishing returns and we can use the stages-of-returns diagram as the starting point for our explanation of wage determination.

The return of diminishing returns

When we left the concept of diminishing returns in Chapter 6 it had provided the basic explanation for the shapes of the marginal cost and average variable cost curves. We can build upon this information in explaining wage determination.

We know from our previous encounter with the returns diagram that the firm produces beyond the point of diminishing average returns (Stage II in Figure 11.1) and that the marginal returns curve declines continuously within this output range. This relationship is shown in Figure 11.1 for the input range of five to ten units of labor, which confines the production between the points of diminishing average returns and absolute diminishing returns. Absolute diminishing returns, where ten workers are employed, is the point beyond which the producer will not add variable inputs no matter what they cost, since to do so causes *total* output to fall. Actually, well before output approaches the range of negative marginal

[1] J.B. Clark, *The Distribution of Wealth* (New York: The Macmillan Company, 1914), p. 173.

Figure 11.1 The Stages of Returns

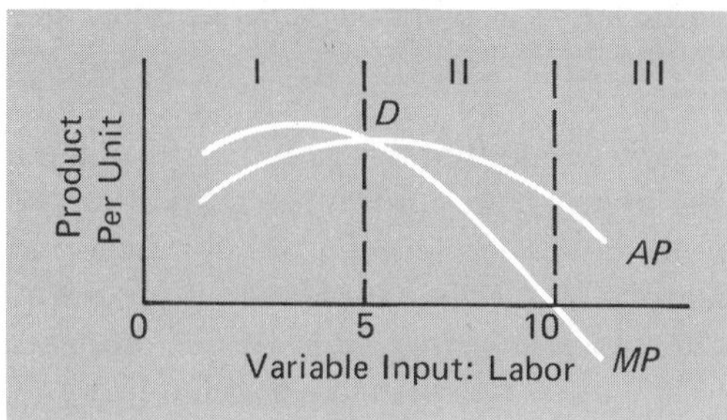

contribution by the variable factor, the employer will find that hiring additional workers costs more than the workers are worth.

Output into revenue

For the producer, physical output is a means of attaining revenue. We know, however, that as successive units of labor are employed by the firm, the marginal output of labor declines throughout Stage II. The marginal product curve, MP in Figure 11.1, is expressed in physical units, but these can be converted to a *value* measure by multiplying output times the price of the firm's product. When marginal output is expressed in value terms, it is called *marginal revenue product* (MRP). What happens to MRP largely determines the firm's hiring decisions. If the marginal revenue product is greater than the wage, the firm adds workers; if MRP is less than the wage, it fires workers. Before discussing wage determination further, however, we need to note the embarrassing richness of the economist's terminology.

In explaining payments to factors of production, economists have been anything but inhibited in their use of terms. *Returns, output,* and *product* are frequently employed interchangeably to mean goods or services produced for sale in the market. When the terms *revenue* and *product* are combined, however, as in *marginal revenue product,* the measure is converted to a dollar value. In Figure 11.2, the basic marginal product curve is lifted from Figure 11.1 and expressed in dollar terms by multiplying physical product times product price. Curve MRP now shows how much workers added to the firm's labor force are worth in terms of revenue from the sale of additional output. Since the firm hires labor to obtain revenue, the MRP curve traces the firm's demand for labor. The curve indicates that the firm pays higher wages when labor's productivity is high and lower wages when the productivity of labor falls off.[2]

[2] The above explanation for input or factor payments is usually called the *marginal productivity theory of distribution*. In this case, the word *productivity* means the value contribution of an input and is synonymous with the term *revenue product*.

Figure 11.2 The Demand for Labor

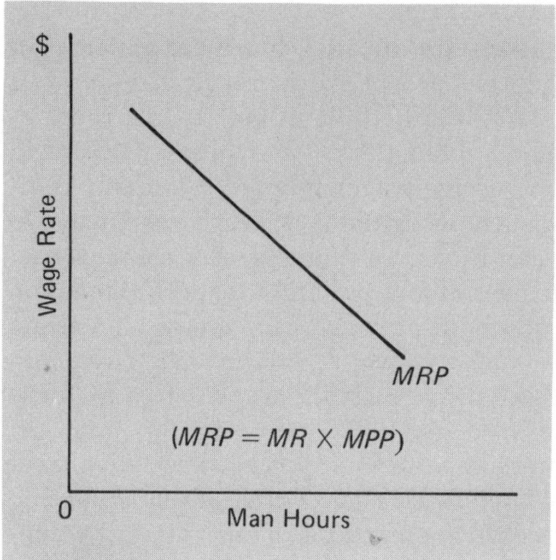

The demand for labor: derived demand

It is sometimes said that the demand for labor, or for any other productive input, is a derived demand. This statement means that an input has value only because it contributes to the production of a commodity or service. Its value is derived from that of the product or service that sells in the market.

The demand for labor is determined by two forces—the physical output produced by labor and the price that output sells for in the market. As labor's physical output or the market price of that output rises, the demand curve for labor shifts to the right, indicating an increase in the value of labor.

Wage determination in a competitive labor market

As we noted earlier, an economy is made up of many markets. One of the most important is the labor market, although it does not usually operate in such public view as the New York Stock Exchange or the Chicago Board of Trade. At times, however, wage bargaining does receive extended public exposure, generally when it is unsuccessful. When wage determination does not take place more or less automatically, but involves a struggle between employer and workers, this is presumptive evidence that the process is not highly competitive. As in the case of product markets, a labor market is competitive if neither the employer nor the workers can influence price—in this case wages— by control of supply or demand.[3]

Highly competitive labor markets are unusual, but there are areas in which both employers and employees accept the market's decision as a factor beyond their influence by submitting to the wage rate that is established. Unskilled workers, waiters, retail clerks, and office workers in many metropolitan labor markets receive wages that are essentially competitive. The supply of labor for such occupations is clearly responsive to price; more workers apply for waiter's jobs, for example, as wage rates rise, and fewer apply as wages fall. In like fashion, undergraduate enrollment in pre-law, pre-engineering, and pre-medical programs increase as starting salaries in these professions rise and decrease as salaries fall. Thus both occupations and professions respond to much the same forces as those which generally determine price.

The supply and demand forces at work in a typical competitive labor market, such as the market for waiters in a large city, are illustrated in Figure 11.3. The supply curve records the reactions of entrants and potential entrants into the labor market as the wage rate varies; more seek employment as waiters at higher wages than at lower rates. The demand curve is based on marginal revenue product and, as in all competitive markets, the interaction of demand and supply brings about a wage rate of $3.50 per hour for 4,000 waiters.

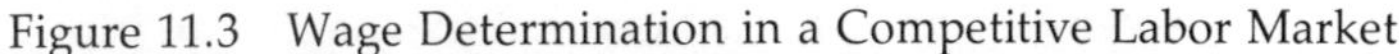
Figure 11.3 Wage Determination in a Competitive Labor Market

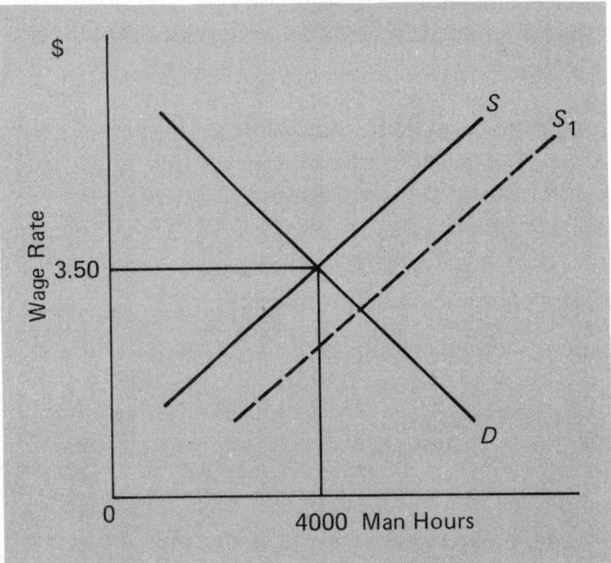

3 As we shall note later, control of supply can sometimes be achieved indirectly by enforcing a wage rate that effects a change in the supply of labor.

The supply of labor

The amount of labor offered for sale—that is, how many individuals seek employment—depends on more than whether wages go up or down. Sometimes when wages fall more people enter the labor market than when wages are high. During a severe recession, for example, unemployment and falling wages go together and the loss of a job by the major income earner of a family may cause others in the family to seek employment even though wages have dropped. Under such conditions, there are increasing numbers of individuals looking for work as wages fall; but of course it is the unemployment rather than the low wage that causes the increase in the supply of labor. The labor supply curve is designed to show the reactions of workers and potential workers to different wage rates. When conditions change, as during a recession, a different supply curve is called for, one such as Curve S_1 in Figure 11.3

Although the upward-sloping labor supply curve shows the conventional reaction to wage rates, some individuals work less when wage rates are high. Fewer workers are available for employment when wage rates are high in such instances than when they are low. This is illustrated by a backward-bending portion of the labor supply curve S_1 in Figure 11.4. The quantity axis in Figure 11.4 records "man hours," which facilitates expressing diagrammatically the reduction in work hours as wages rise.

Not too much should be made of the notion of the backward-bending labor supply curve, however, since it is anything but commonplace in most developed economies with a trained and specialized labor force. In the

Figure 11.4 The Backward-bending Supply Curve of Labor

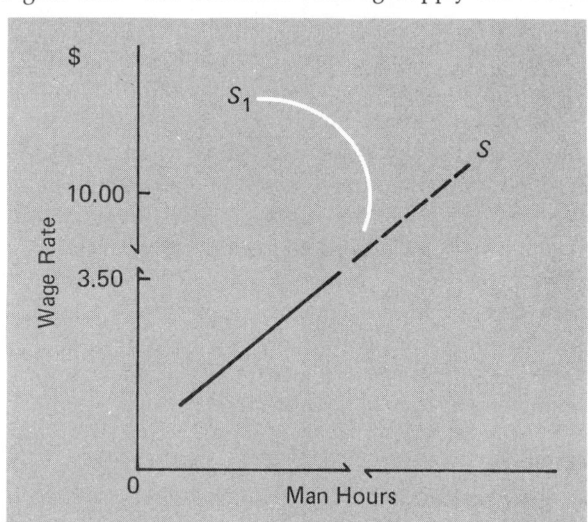

highly acquisitive societies of the Western world, trading income for leisure is an infrequent event, save in the refuges of the counterculture where meditation and idleness are increasingly valued as wages rise. Since the Industrial Revolution there has been an intermittent decrease in work hours in industrial society. At the same time, wages have generally increased. This is clear evidence of the long-run choice of leisure over further wage increases, but it does not necessaily mean that the leisure option is equally available in the short run, contributing to the backward slope of the labor supply curve. Most workers are locked into a pattern of employment and a way of life that require more than the short-run span of time to change.

Whether backward- or forward-sloping, the short-run labor supply curve relates the offer of work to a single variable—change in wage rates. Over time, factors other than wage rates affect the supply of labor, such as the decision of a wife to enter the labor market because of a drop in the husband's earnings, or the abandonment of employment by a newly married wife (or, in these days of egalitarian liberation, by a newly married husband), or graduation from high school or college, retirement, winning the Irish Sweepstakes, or being wiped out in Vegas. Such events shape the individual's reaction to the offer of employment, in some cases encouraging and in others dissuading entry into the labor market, quite as much as the prevailing wage structure. These factors are largely beyond the control

---

Oh, to be with the Tlingits now that April's there . . . or the backward-bending supply curve for labor

[I] n 1965 a man representing a pulp mill in southeastern Alaska spoke to the Juneau Chamber of Commerce to tell . . . what was wrong with the Indians. His company had chosen the area, he explained, not only for the lush forest but because it had a lot of unemployed Tlingits. It looked like a good labor market and had worked out well in the beginning. All the Indians signed on and proved to be excellent workers.

"But in two or three months, when those Tlingits had a little more money than they needed, they quit. Went off to hunt and fish," he reported, still struck with the incredibility of it all. "And then, three or four months later, when they were broke, they came back and wanted to go to work for us again."

"Now, what we've got to teach these people is that they have to work an eight-hour day, a five-day week and a fifty-week year."[4]

---

[4] Lael Morgan, *And the Land Provides: Alaskan Natives in a Year of Transition* (Garden City, N.Y.: Doubleday & Co., 1974), p. v.

of the employer recruiting a labor force, and the one safe generalization is that the employer can hire more if he pays more. Sometimes, however, an employer can hire all the labor necessary with no change at all in the wage offered.

The firm in the competitive labor market

A single firm that is one of many employing the same kind of labor, such as a restaurant employing cooks and waiters, does not have enough of an impact on the supply of labor to affect wage rates, particularly in its marginal hiring or firing. The labor supply curve for such a firm is unaffected by whether one or ten or twenty workers are hired or fired; the wage rate remains unchanged. This supply of labor to the firm is represented by the horizontal line in Figure 11.5B.

In the short run, the firm adjusts the size of its labor force so that the marginal revenue product of the last unit of labor employed is equal to the wage rate. For a wage rate of $3.15 per hour, as shown in Figure 11.5, fifteen workers are employed to bring MRP into agreement with the wage rate. If either the wage rate or the marginal revenue product changes, the firm's employment practices are modified, unless other changes take place. If there is a shift in labor demand from D to D_1 in the industry, for example, the wage rate moves from $3.15 to $4.00. This confronts the employing firm with a higher input price and brings about a reduction in its employment from fifteen to thirteen workers. The adjustment is not necessarily

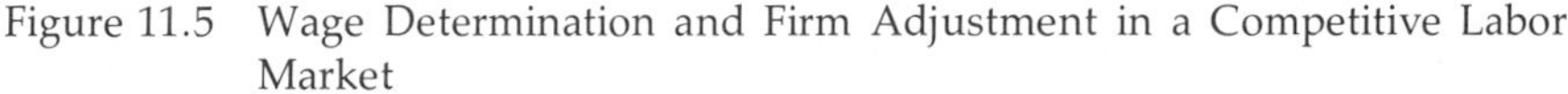
Figure 11.5 Wage Determination and Firm Adjustment in a Competitive Labor Market

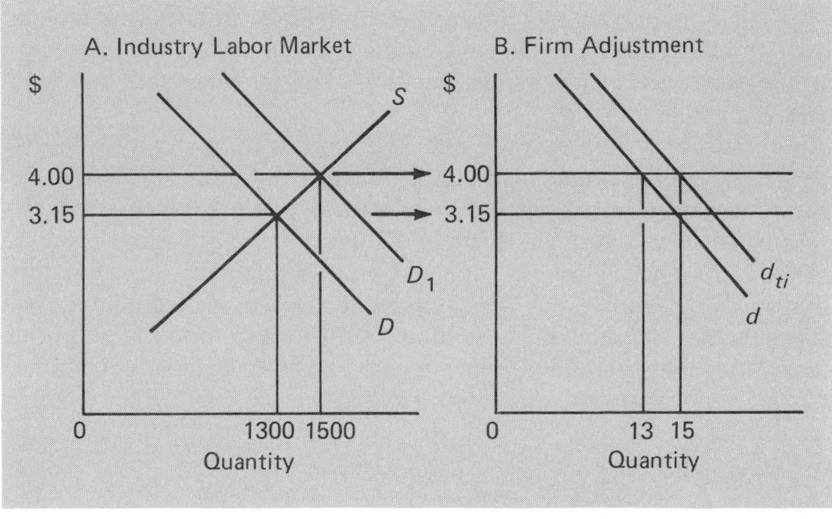

instantaneous, however, and if the wage rise results temporarily in paying workers somewhat more than their MRP, the difference must be made up from somewhere in the firm, either by reducing the return to another factor, eliminating some expenditures, increasing debt, or decreasing surplus. But eventually either employment must be cut back to thirteen workers or the MRP of the work force must increase. If an increase in MRP shifts firm labor demand to Curve d_{ti} in Figure 11.5, no layoff of workers is necessary. But why should firm demand increase? In general, for the same reasons that the industry demand increases.

The demand for labor may increase because the product or service which labor helps produce rises in value, or because labor's physical productivity increases. Labor's output is affected by many things other than the worker's talent—the available capital, the technique of production, the quality of materials, and morale, to name the most obvious factors. The shift from d to d_{ti} in Figure 11.5 may result from a technological improvement in production that raises the physical product of the firm's labor force as well as output throughout the industry, thus justifying employment at a higher wage rate. Which comes first, higher wage rates or increased physical productivity?

Do higher wages bring unemployment or innovation?

A firm's capacity to adjust to an increase in cost—absorbing it or passing it on to the consumer—depends in part on how much time it has to respond to the cost increase. In general, the less time available for adjustment, the greater the likelihood that the firm will bear the increase because of its inability to reorganize its production arrangements. If there is time to cut back on high-priced variable inputs, the firm has the option of adjusting employment, as is shown in Figure 11.5 when the wage rate increases from $3.15 to $4.00.

Over time, the higher wage rate may both induce innovation and reduce employment. Some firms such as coal mines, which face wage pressure from the United Mine Workers, may adapt by increasing the output of a smaller labor force through the use of more advanced production techniques and improved capital equipment. Higher wages in this case are an inducement to the development of labor-saving techniques and more productive equipment. These innovations in turn raise the output of the work force that is retained. In achieving higher wages for coal miners, the United Mine Workers Union has increased the wage return for those in the unionized segment of the industry by raising output per miner and decreasing employment.

Minimum wage standards

In the above discussion of wage determination, all factors affecting wages have been expressed in terms of marginal revenue product. This tends to conceal individual influences upon wages and to focus attention on the process of the determination of the wage rate. One of the important influences upon wages are national or state minimum wage standards.

In the United States a minimum wage must be paid by employers engaged in activities that are related to interstate commerce. The federal minimum-wage rate has been raised by Congress from time to time, as have state standards, and the question of the effect of the rate increase on employment is an important consideration. If we follow the mechanistic approach of the supply-and-demand diagram, the answer is straightforward. An increase in the wage rate decreases employment. This is illustrated in Figure 11.6.

An increase in the minimum wage from $2.25 to $2.50 causes a cutback in employment from 85 to 84 million, assuming a US labor force of around 90 million workers. Only a fraction of the labor force is affected by an increase in the national minimum-wage rate; some workers are exempt, such as farm workers, and most others are employed at jobs that pay more than $2.50 an hour. The impact of an increased national minimum wage shows up mainly in marginal employments—in undertakings that require

Figure 11.6 A Possible Effect of an Increase in the National Minimum Wage Upon Employment

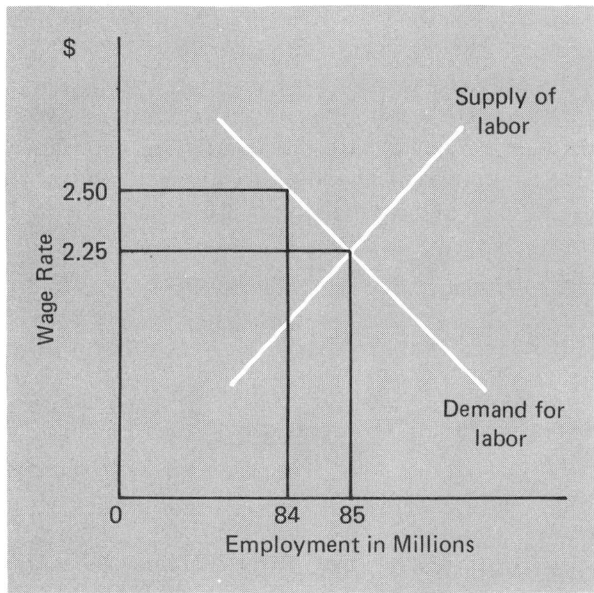

little skill, such as those supported by the most meager productivity-enhancing equipment, and in areas in which labor is overabundant relative to opportunities for employment, such as some parts of the Deep South, Appalachia, and New England. Because these employments are marginal does not mean they are unimportant. The reduction in job opportunities that results from higher minimum wages cuts most heavily into the employment of low-productivity minority workers and teenagers, those at the bottom of the income scale.

The producer and marginal revenue product

In adding or cutting back on the use of inputs, the firm is best off when the cost of the marginal factor is just covered by the revenue from the sale of the output that the factor produces. This is not a new principle. It is a refinement of the general rule that the firm produces to the point where marginal cost is equal to marginal revenue. Generally the firm is faced with the decision of using different amounts of various resources.

In employing different factors, the firm works toward an arrangement in which each factor makes an equivalent contribution to production in relation to what it costs. This relationship can be expressed as follows:

$$\frac{MPP_A}{P_A} = \frac{MPP_B}{P_B} = \ldots = \frac{MPP_N}{P_N} \tag{1}$$

In the above equation (1), MPP_A designates the marginal physical product of Input A and P_A designates the input price; MPP_B is the marginal physical product of Input B and P_B is its price, and so on for all the factors employed by the firm. If the MPP/price ratios for the different factors are unequal, the firm has not achieved the optimum input relationship. In a canoe factory, for example, if employing an additional worker at \$40.00 per day increases output by one canoe, whereas adding two power sanders at \$40.00 per day increases output by two canoes, the factor equation would be

$$\frac{\text{MPP Labor 1 canoe}}{\$40.00} < \frac{\text{MPP Sander 2 canoes}}{\$40.00}$$

Additional sanders would have to be employed to balance factor returns in relation to price such that

$$\frac{\text{MPP Labor 1 canoe}}{\$40.00} = \frac{\text{MPP Sander 1 canoe}}{\$40.00}$$

If the wage-rate rises or the cost of sanders falls, while other factor prices remain unchanged, a rearrangement of factors will take place in which less labor is employed and more machinery is used.

In equation (1) the price of canoes is conspicuously absent. We can ignore product price when the issue is the relationship of different factors to the total of the firm's productive resources, but when we wish to know *how much* of the factors-in-balance should be employed—that is, what is the optimum firm output—we must consider product prices. The following equation (2) takes price into consideration.

$$(2) \qquad MPP_A \cdot px = PA,\ MPP_B \cdot px = PB,\ \ldots,\ MPP_N \cdot px = PN$$

In the above equation (2), MPP represents the marginal physical product of the factors employed by the firm, px is the price of the firm's product, PA is the price of Input A, PB the price of Input B, and so on. This equation shows the market value of the marginal output of the different factors to be equal to the price (cost) of these factors. In terms of hiring inputs in a competitive factor market and selling output in a competitive product market, the firm has carried production to the most efficient point.

To recapitulate, equation (1) shows that the firm's internal distribution of productive resources is in balance. Adding more of one kind of input than another will not result in a more productive resource combination, factor costs considered. Equation (2) shows that the firm has attained optimum output: If fewer factors were employed, revenue would be reduced more than cost, and if more factors were employed, cost would rise more than revenue. Finally, both equations (1) and (2) assume competition in the factor market and in the product market. There is more to factor pricing than the competitive case, however, as the discussion below indicates.

Factor pricing: a closer look at demand

Factor pricing is simplest when competition prevails in both the factor market and the product market. There may be competition in the sale of the product, however, and monopsony in the purchase of a factor. This occurs, for example, in the case of a coal mining company that offers the sole source of employment in a region while it sells coal in a competitive market. By contrast, during the years when Alcoa was the only producer of aluminum in the United States, it sold its product monopolistically but hired labor in competition with other employers in the Pittsburgh area, bargaining with a union that exercised some control over the sale of labor.

The possible combinations of competitive and noncompetitive product and factor markets are extensive. They can be best illustrated using supply

Wage determination in colonial Virginia—spiritual division

Almost from the beginning the compensation of clergymen [in colonial Virginia] had been defined and paid in tobacco. After 1695, the annual salary of a clergyman was fixed by law at 16,000 pounds of tobacco. Since the tobacco in which a minister was paid was that of his particular parish, the money value of his wage depended very much on the quality of that crop. "Some Parishes," the Rev. Hugh Jones lamented, "are long vacant upon account of the badness of the tobacco." The minister who found himself in a parish which raised the cruder "Oranako" type considered himself unfortunate compared with his colleague who preached to parishioners who grew the milder, broader-leaved (and higher-priced) tobacco called "Sweet Scented." When Commissary Blair wrote back to the Bishop of London in 1724 requesting more clergymen for Virginia, he compared the vacancies in "five sweet scented Parishes" with "about double that number of Oranaco ones vacant." . . . [I]n colonial Virginia . . . the so-called "Parson's Cause" (1763) . . . was simply whether, in a period of high tobacco prices, vestries should be permitted to pay their clergymen in money-values of an earlier age of cheap two-penny tobacco.[5]

and demand curves. Figure 11.7 shows the demand for labor when there is competition in both the factor and product markets. (This same demand function was illustrated in Figure 11.2, accompanied by an explanation of its derivation.)

The diagrams in Figure 11.7 show the relationship between the marginal physical product curve and the marginal revenue curve when there is product competition. As was indicated earlier, the marginal revenue product curve is obtained by multiplying the increment of physical product (MPP) times the marginal revenue (MR) to obtain marginal revenue product (MRP). Marginal revenue product is thus a blend of two forces, marginal physical product and marginal revenue. When the product market is competitive, increasing or decreasing output does not change the product price, thus the MPP component becomes the dominant factor that determines the slope of the MRP curve, since MPP is multiplied by a constant MR. When the firm sells its product in a noncompetitive market, however, MR is no longer horizontal but downslanting, and both MPP and MR contribute to the downward slope of the MRP curve. Figure 11.8 shows factor demand by a noncompetitive firm.

[5] D. J. Boorstin, *The Americans—The Colonial Experience* (New York: Random House, Inc., 1958), pp. 128-29.

Figure 11.7 Factor Demand By a Competitive Firm

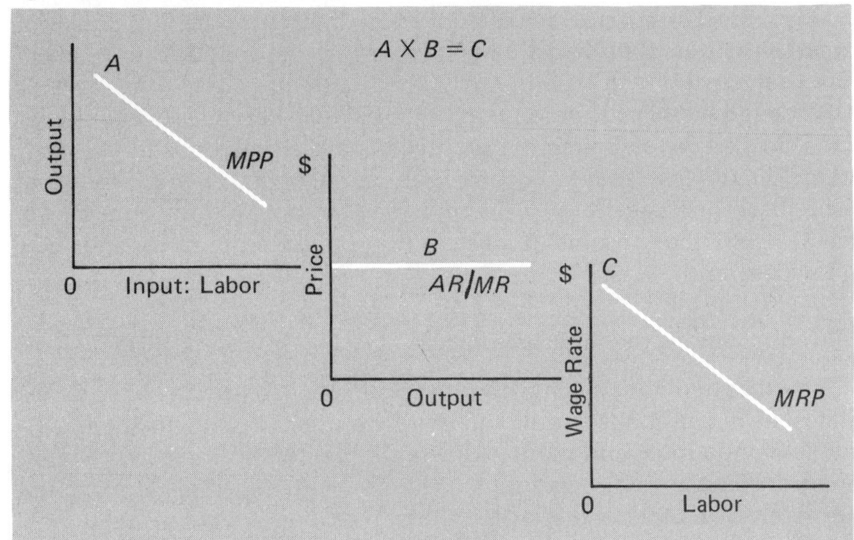

Factor pricing: a closer look at labor supply

The price of a factor reflects a number of different influences. Generally, the more extended the time, the more elastic the supply of a factor. Employers may sometimes be pawns of the labor market and sometimes

Figure 11.8 Factor Demand by a Noncompetitive Firm

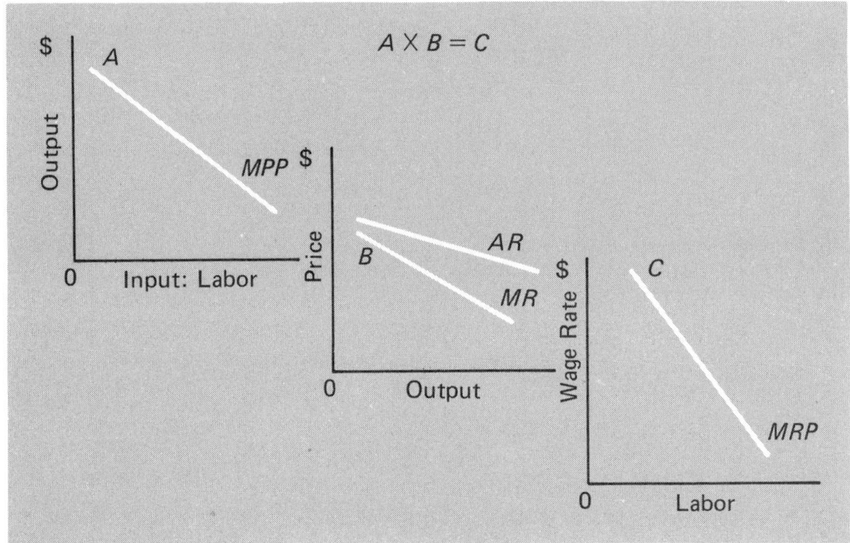

not. Clearly such employers as General Motors in Pontiac, Michigan, or Bethlehem Steel in Sparrows Point, Baltimore, Maryland, are not pawns of the market, nor are their bargaining adversaries, the United Auto Workers or the United Steel Workers unions.

Although neither the union nor the employer is the sole seller or buyer of labor in Pontiac or Baltimore, each exerts a real influence in the labor market. The union exercises a degree of monopoly power if it serves as the primary bargaining agent for the work force of a firm, and the employer is something of a monopsonist if a single firm provides the major source of employment in the area.

Monopsony in the labor market

Pure monopoly (in selling labor) or pure monopsony (in hiring labor) is almost as rare as a Ross's gull, but there are situations in which approximations of monopoly and monopsony occur together in the labor market. Monopsonistic control of hiring by the employer—especially if exercised repressively—at times generates counter measures, such as aggressive union bargaining. The classic case of labor monopsony is that of a mining town dominated by a single company: for example, the Anaconda Copper Company in Butte, Montana, or the Peabody Coal Company in Black Mesa, Arizona. In Butte and Black Mesa, the main source of employment stems from a single firm, and other employment opportunities have only limited impact on the company town's wage structure. This leads to the demand and supply forces illustrated in Figure 11.9.

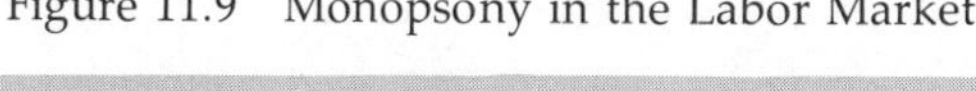
Figure 11.9 Monopsony in the Labor Market

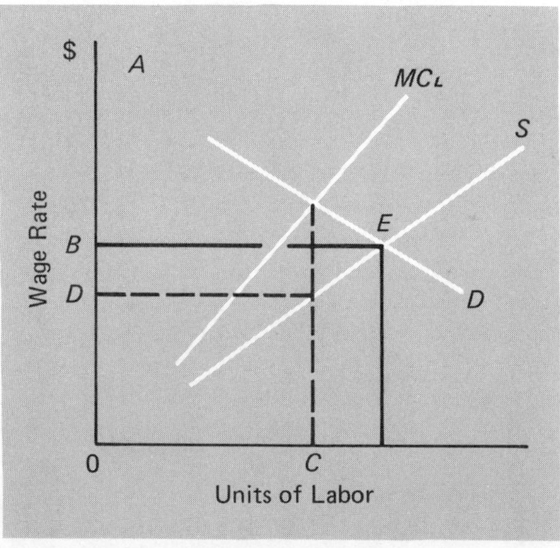

Every hiring action of the monopsonist is reflected in the supply price of labor. When the monopsonist hires more workers, the wage rate goes up; when the monopsonist hires fewer workers, the wage rate falls. But there is more to it than this: The monopsonist's domination of the labor market shows up in a marginal cost for hiring labor as well as in an upward-sloping labor supply curve. In Figure 11.9, the marginal cost of hiring labor intersects with the firm's demand for labor, thus setting a wage rate of OD when OC workers are employed. In the situation illustrated, the employer dominates the labor market but sells in a competitive product market. The monopsonist's marginal cost of labor rises not only to attract labor from other areas, but because the wage for all employees goes up when new employees are paid more. Or, conversely, the wage goes down for all when workers are laid off.

Under monopsony, fewer workers are employed at a lower wage rate than is the case in a competitive labor market. If the labor market were

---

Which sex is best? . . . or why can't a woman be more like a man? —to employers, that is

Employers are always finding reasons for not employing women. Some are justified and some are not, according to a study published by the Department of Employment.[a] Men are stronger than women (by about 80 percent), but more vulnerable to disease (twice as many boy babies die in their first three weeks of life as girls). Men are twice as likely to have an accident as women, three times as likely to commit suicide, see better but hear worse, are more practical but have less vocabulary, are worse at arithmetic but better at mathematical problems, are worse at clerical work, are more emotionally stable, mature, realistic, thick-skinned, liberal, analytical, suspicious, self-opinionated, hard-to-fool, aggressive, stubborn and probably slightly more intelligent. Women are more warm-hearted, sensitive, easy-going, conventional, calculating, penetrating, tense, frustrated, and troubled.

A separate survey[b] shows that more and more women go out to work nevertheless. Some 42 percent of wives now work [in England], compared with 22 percent in 1951. Women's pay has begun to catch up with men's in the last few years, after two decades in which they stayed the same distance behind them.[6]

[a] *Women at Work: Sex Differences and Society* (London: Her Majesty's Stationery Office, 1975.)

[b] *Women at Work: A Statistical Survey* (London: Her Majesty's Stationery Office, 1975.)

---

[6] From *The* [London] *Economist*, November 9, 1974, p. 96.

competitive, OB would be the wage rate and OA workers would be employed, rather than OD wage and OC employment.

Neutralizing monopsony

If the exercise of monopsony power encourages the formation of a strong union, the employer's dominance in the labor market may be largely offset by the monopoly power of the union. If the union is able to establish a wage rate of OB for example, the labor supply curve in Figure 11.9 is reshaped to BES. BES is also the monopsonist's marginal cost curve for hiring labor.

If the union is able to gain control of the labor supply and raise the wage to OB for all labor hired up to OA, the employer carries employment to E, at which point marginal cost equals demand. At this wage rate the union and employer neutralize each other, producing the same employment and wage rate that would occur in a competitive labor market. Can unions really exert such authority in the labor market?

Do unions raise wages?

According to some economists, the answer to the above question comes very close to being, "They don't."

Attempts to measure the effects that unions have on wages have not been very successful. At best, careful statistical studies have been able to demonstrate only slight impact on the part of the union. (You should keep in mind, however, that only about 25 percent of the labor force is unionized in the United States and 30 percent in Canada.) But common observation provides evidence of another sort; we can see the unions' impact in employment-maximizing work rules by the Railroad Brotherhoods (more bluntly called "featherbedding"), the negotiation of cost-of-living escalator arrangements, supplementary unemployment compensation payments, early retirement by the Auto Workers union, and the ability of the United Mine Workers to push the union wage scale significantly higher than that paid in nonunion mining operations. It is not possible to consider all of the practices that are attributed to unions, but we can examine briefly the nature of union power.

The power offset

The character of a union is largely determined by the industrial environment in which it develops. The bargaining climate—labor-market dominance by a few strong firms, a struggle for union recognition, or negotiations with many weak employers—largely determines the goals and tactics of a union. But whatever the bargaining climate, if the union is to offset the employer's power, it must exercise some form of control over the labor supply. Direct control occurs if the union holds down the labor supply by limiting entry to a trade, thus raising wage rates. Indirect control is the result of bargaining for a higher wage and thereby forcing the employer to restrict employment.

Restricting the labor supply

The power to restrict supply is the power to raise price—whether land or capital, physicians or plumbers. A union has very little bargaining influence in the absence of direct or indirect control of the labor supply. Some unions are stronger than other unions and there are different ways of restricting the labor supply. Just as a business firm has greater control over the product market if it is able to block access to the market by other firms, so the union that is able to limit the supply of labor is in a stronger bargaining position with the employer. Some occupations naturally attract fewer entrants than others, and some are blocked to many who would otherwise enter. The supply of physicians, for example, is held down by the long and costly training process and the considerable intellectual qualifications, as well as the limited facilities for training physicians. In addition, the American Medical Association, although not a trade union in the sense of serving as a bargaining agent for physicians, diligently promotes the economic interests of physicians by supporting restrictive licensing practices, opposing what it considers to be "socialized" medicine, and the like.

The supply of plumbers is also held below what might be expected in some areas. High union initiation fees and extended apprenticeship training periods at lower wages discourage many from becoming plumbers, thus raising the ultimate rewards of those who do undergo initiation and apprenticeship. High-steel construction, an occupation in which one might expect the labor supply automatically to be limited, is held below full employment needs in some areas by union restrictions. Work permits are issued to nonunion workers when job opportunities in high-steel construction exceed the available union members. In this manner, the union meets the employers' needs for a flexible supply of labor at the same time that it insulates union members against job loss during recession. The success of this approach depends on the employers' acceptance of preferential hiring of union members, which is a form of union control of the labor supply. Assertion of a wage rate by the union is another form of labor supply control.

Sometimes a union is strong enough to assert a wage rate and enforce it through bargaining, shifting to the employer the responsibility to limit hiring to the labor force that establishes the desired rate. The effect of this tactic does not differ basically from the more direct approaches, but takes advantage of the employer's obligation under federal labor relations regulations to bargain in good faith with worker representatives.

Figure 11.10 shows similarities in the effects of these two approaches to wage determination.

Through restriction of the labor supply, the supply curve shifts from S to S_1 in Figure 11.10A, raising the wage rate from \$3.50 to \$4.50. By asserting the higher wage rate of \$4.50, the union reduces the demand for labor to 700 workers, in effect shifting the supply to S_1 in Figure 11.10B. Raising wages by assertion is not a feasible approach for the union unless it can prevent more than 700 workers from being accepted for hire at the new wage rate of \$4.50. Instead, rather than imposing the higher wage rate on the employer, it will attract up to 900 job seekers and lower the wage rate below \$4.50.

The demand for labor is affected primarily by two forces: (1) changes in the price of the product or service produced by labor, and (2) changes in the output of labor. Only part of the changes in labor's output are due solely to labor. Other factors include improved techniques of production, better management, superior materials, and more efficient capital equipment. Most of these raise labor's contribution to firm output and shift the demand for labor to the right, from D to D_1 in Figure 11.11. With the increase in demand, the wage rate rises to \$4.50 when the amount of labor is fixed, or to \$4.00 in the absence of restriction.

Figure 11.10 Control of the Labor Supply and Wage Determination

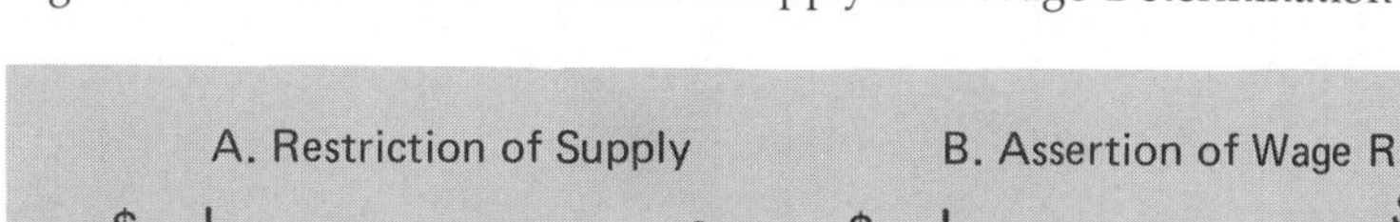

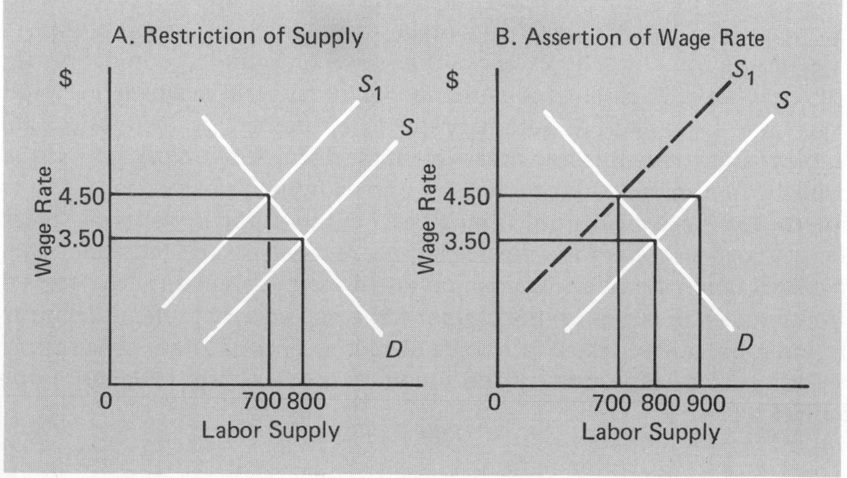

Figure 11.11 An Upward Shift in the Demand for Labor

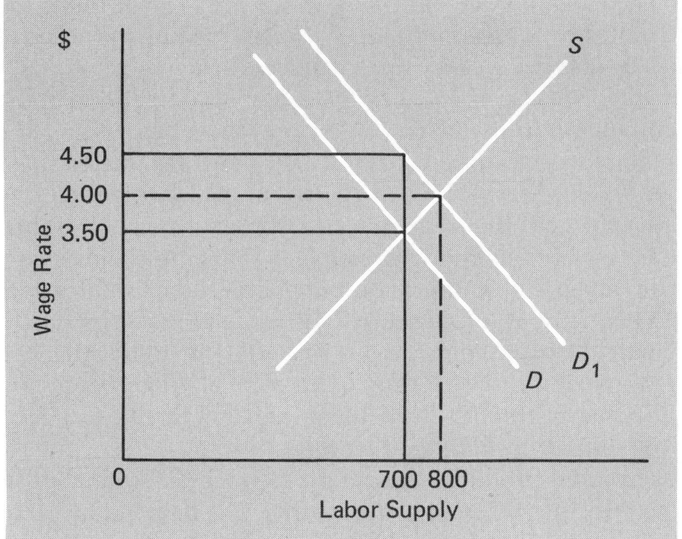

Can a union encourage a shift in demand to the right or must it operate solely upon the supply curve?

Most reports of union control of output involve efforts at limitation—assembly-line slow-downs, restricting the size of paint brushes, holding down output goals for a "fair day's work." But at times unions have encouraged, even coerced, the employer to adopt more productive methods and equipment, thus raising worker output and providing the basis for higher wages. At the turn of the century, the International Ladies Garment Workers' Union provided small employers with loans to increase their capital equipment, thereby increasing labor's output and wages. At the same time, the union attempted to strengthen the market for union-made clothing by advertising the improved working conditions that had been achieved through unionization. Both of these approaches, to the extent that they are successful, shift the demand for labor upward.

Summary

Economists generally explain returns to factors of production by reference to marginal revenue product (MRP). In the case of wage determination, marginal revenue product is the value of the worker's contribution to the output of the firm. MRP can be measured for the labor input by holding the other factors constant and varying the amount of labor employed. If labor inputs are homogeneous and interchangeable in the firm's labor force, the wage rate will be uniform for those employed, determined by the value of output that would be lost if a worker were dismissed.

Wage determination is also affected by the extent of competition in the labor market. Competition in the labor market prevails when neither the employer nor the employees can exert control over the wage rate through the supply of labor or job offers. With competition in the labor market, the employer will hire labor until the wage rate and the labor force's marginal revenue product are equal. This hiring principle is similar to the marginal cost equals marginal revenue rule of firm output policy. If the firm does not add workers up to the point at which the MRP is equal to the wage rate, it forgoes return it would obtain from output that sells for more than the labor input adds to cost; if it carries hiring to the point at which wages are higher than MRP, however, it adds more to its wage bill than it gets back from the sale of the output of the added workers.

The marginal revenue product explanation of wage determination is an extension of the principle of diminishing returns. The demand for labor by the firm, for example, can be derived from the marginal physical product curve of the diminishing returns diagram. The marginal physical product curve measures the increase in output from adding variable inputs, labor in combination with land and capital for example. By multiplying the marginal physical product curve by the price of the firm's product, it is converted to a curve of marginal revenue product. The marginal revenue product curve traces the revenue changes attributable to labor when it is the only input that is varied. Under these circumstances, the MRP curve is the firm's demand curve for labor.

For the economy as a whole, wage rates are dependent upon labor's contribution to the economy's output. This contribution depends not only upon labor's innate skills and abilities, but upon a multitude of other factors: training, experience, techniques of production, quality of resources, and the extent of capital equipment. The return to the labor factor increases as capital becomes more abundant, raising labor's output. Although marginal revenue product determines the return to labor for the economy as a whole, the firm in a competitive labor market adjusts its labor force to the point at which MRP equals the wage rate, rather than establishing its own rate. If the wage rate in a competitive labor market falls, the firm will add labor until MRP and the wage rate are equal; if the wage rate rises, the firm will lay off workers, thus raising the MRP of the reduced work force.

Labor market conditions are not always competitive, however. Employers and workers may at times exert control over the hiring process and supply of labor that either modifies the marginal revenue product of labor or, in some cases, results in wages temporarily above or below MRP. The government may also intervene in the labor market to establish conditions of hiring and set minimum wage standards. All of these influences upon wage determination make the marginal revenue product a point of departure in understanding what happens in the labor market rather than a precise model of what takes place.

Key terms and concepts

Returns, output, product physical units of goods or services produced for sale in the market.

Marginal revenue product (MRP) the value of the marginal physical output. This figure is obtained by multiplying marginal physical product (MPP) times marginal revenue (MR).

Competitive labor market wage determination in the absence of control by either the employer or workers.

Derived demand the demand for a factor, such as labor, which is dependent on the demand for the product or service that labor produces.

Monopsony a single buyer, for example, the sole employer of labor in a company mining town.

Discussion and review questions

1. What is the reason for the bargaining restrictions on baseball players? Do these restrictions really represent exploitation of baseball players? How do you define exploitation?

2. How does marginalism enter into an explanation of wage determination? What was J. B. Clark's contribution to the theory of wage determination and how did he measure the marginal productivity of labor?

3. How is the principle of diminishing returns related to marginal revenue product?

4. What do we mean by derived demand? How is it possible to trace the effect of the demand for a product or service back through the production process to the demand for one of many factors such as labor?

5. What makes a labor market competitive? What factors prevent the market for physicians, lawyers, plumbers, and school teachers from being competitive? Would society be better off if these labor markets were competitive?

6. The national Wages and Hours Act prescribes a minimum wage for workers employed in firms that sell their products in interstate commerce. What are the economic and social effects of the minimum wage? Do you consider it a desirable or undesirable intervention in the market system?

7. In what industries do you expect to find the backward-bending supply curve for labor? Does the historical decline in hours of work in most industrial nations represent a case of the backward-bending labor-supply curve?

8. How are marginal returns equalized when different input combinations are employed? What happens if the factor balance is modified by a technological innovation that raises the output?

9. What effect does monopoly in the sale of the firm's product have on its demand for labor? How does this show up in marginal revenue product?

10. How may wage determination in a company town differ from that in a less isolated labor market?

11. How effective are labor unions in raising wages and improving working conditions? What is the labor union's ultimate source of power?

12. How does assertion of a wage rate work? Does it differ fundamentally from controlling the entry to a trade?

12 Division of the spoils II: interest, rent, and profits

We built the 2,300,000 kilowatt Lenin Volga Hydroelectric Station in seven years. . . . But with the same money we could have built in less time several thermal plants with a total of 11,000,000 kilowatts. —*Nikita Khrushchev**

Premier Nikita Khrushchev, who took over control of the Soviet Union from Malenkov two years after Stalin's death, points out a miscarriage of the Russian planning process in the above statement. Khrushchev was aware that thermal power plants require fuel to drive the generating turbines, while no-cost water power fuels hydroelectric plants. But even with the most generous allowance for fuel costs in thermal generation, a hydro capital cost that is more than four times that of the same thermal capacity clearly is a misallocation of resources, particularly when time is critical. How could this happen, especially in a society where the scarcity of capital is such an overriding fact of economic life?

Undoubtedly many factors contributed to the Soviet planning mishap, but two stand out: first, the Russian's prediliction for bigness, and second, their distrust of the interest rate. Russia is a land of massive parades, monstrous tanks and tractors, large-scale factories and huge hydroelectric plants. Given Russia's bias for bigness and the spectacular nature of the Lenin Volga Hydroelectric Station, a project that demonstrates to the world Russia's engineering talent, an economic justification for the project may have assumed secondary importance. But the Soviet planners' reluctance to accept interest as a legitimate cost of capital formation made the Lenin Volga decision much easier.

To the followers of Karl Marx, the nineteenth-century advocate of the overthrow of capitalism, labor is solely responsible for the creation of the world's wealth, and charging either interest or profit in an economic undertaking is a form of worker exploitation. Consequently, in banishing capitalism from the Soviet Union, the planning authorities also excluded

* *Pravda*, August 24, 1958.

the payment of interest. But ignoring interest led to planning errors: Projects with low return were sometimes favored over those with higher return, and undertakings that yielded a remote benefit were not sufficiently distinguished from those that afforded more immediate output. So the interest rate was reintroduced into Soviet planning, though somewhat disguised, through specifying the payoff period for a project. Thus a payoff period of twenty years is in effect an interest rate of 5 percent, a payoff period of ten years equals 10 percent interest, and so on.

What is interest and how does its payment or nonpayment affect the allocation of capital resources?

Capital and capitalism

Capital has different meanings. It is employed to describe both the monetary value of various economic assets, such as a commercial bank deposits, and specific agents of production such as machinery and equipment. Although this dual usage may be confusing at times, it has a logical basis. In a modern economy, such as that of Canada or the United States, the construction of machinery, a thermal power plant, or an automobile factory requires that resources be directed to capital formation. One way to achieve capital formation is for individuals and business firms to consume less than they produce. In a primitive economy the creation of capital, such as tools for canoe-making or knives for carving argillite dishes, is a fairly casual process. The Kwakiutl Indians added to their capital stock of tools, fishing gear, and other equipment by simply taking time off from activities that were more immediately related to consumption, such as brewing beer or catching fish. Whether an economy is advanced or relatively undeveloped, however, the essence of capital formation involves abstaining from present consumption in order to devote resources to production facilities that will yield more consumer goods later.

Capital formation is thus a delayed route to consumer goods production, whether totem poles or television sets. Building machinery prior to producing consumer goods is the first stage in the *roundabout* method of production. The roundabout method ultimately increases output: In agriculture, an iron hoe is an improvement over a sharp stick, and in steel production, a pressurized, oxygen-fed blast furnace increases pig-iron production well above that of its earlier counterpart. Whether the capital involved is sophisticated or simple, however, the roundabout method initially holds the output of consumer goods below what it would be if the resources were devoted directly to the production of consumer goods.

Later, when the capital innovation is brought to bear in the production of consumer goods, the effect of the roundabout method is to raise output.

Although the output advantages of capital creation are obvious and substantial, capital formation is easier in some economies than in others. The less capital a country has, the more difficult it is to hold back consumption in order to devote resources to capital creation. Indeed, in underdeveloped countries the pressure to maintain the current output of life's essentials may be so urgent that there is little opportunity to take advantage of the roundabout method of production—even though the standard of living would ultimately be raised by doing so. The low-output economy is unable to build up a sufficient backlog of consumer goods, particularly food, to allow much of the labor force to be shifted to capital production. By contrast, the wealthier developed economy can divert a substantial part of its manpower and material resources to capital creation because of previous high output. New capital in turn pushes the economy still further ahead of the subsistence economies. As a result, the gap between the rich and most poor nations of the world is increasing, in spite of attempts to raise the output level of the poorer nations by aid programs.

To some degree, however, all economies—rich or poor, market-

Shropshire, England in the early eighteenth century . . . where the roundabout method took a quantum jump

There is a small brick chamber in the depths of rural Shropshire, England, where one of the most momentous revolutions in history was forged. Here, one winter's morning early in 1709, a dour Quaker piled ore and limestone on a bed of incandescent coke, blew air through the mass with waterwheel bellows, and, 16 hours later, tapped off a trickle of pure iron.

With this experiment Abraham Darby proved that it was no longer necessary to decimate hundreds of acres of trees to fuel a single blast furnace. By perfecting the use of "coak'd" coal—a purified, smokeless distillate of England's most abundant natural resource—he at one stroke made the production of iron easy and cheap. That first trickle became a stream, and then a flood that seethed and hissed out of the furnaces of Shropshire for almost two centuries. Thus was born the Industrial Revolution, and the world was irrevocably changed.[1]

---

[1] Edmund Morris, "Ironbridge: Where the World Was Irrevocably Changed," *The New York Times*, April 20, 1975, Sec. 10, p. 1. © 1975 by The New York Times Company. Reprinted by permission.

directed or planned—make use of the roundabout method of production. The fact that the market-directed economy is usually called *capitalistic* and the planned economy *socialistic* is no indication that the former is more committed to capital creation than the latter. How much capital is employed in an economy—how capital intensive the economy is—depends on the stage of its economic development and the priority it assigns to capital creation. The Soviet Union, with only slight deemphasis since the Communist revolution, continues to stress capital creation at the expense of consumption. Through a series of Five-Year Plans, the Soviet Union has sought to catch up with the more technologically advanced Western nations, and in pursuing this objective, expansion of the consumers' sector of the Soviet economy has been held well below what it would be under free-market direction.

The Soviets' anxiety about catching up with the West has led them to emphasize the expansion of heavy industry. Development of hydroelectric power has been given priority over housing; steel mills have been expanded in preference to shoe factories; and the machine tool industry has had easier access to material resources and manpower than has textile production. Control of resource allocation is the main source of capital creation in the Soviet system, although there is some encouragement of private saving through bond sales. When Russians purchase government bonds, they voluntarily relinquish the resource-directing power of their income in much the same way that individuals in a capitalist economy do when they save.

In the market economy, voluntary saving by individuals generally plays a much more important part in capital creation than government command, although both occur. In wartime, for example, the central government of a market economy assumes an important role in encouraging capital expansion of defense industries. It uses various means to do so, including direct allocation of resources, bond sales to individuals, and heavier taxes in support of public expenditures. During more normal times, however, the private sector of the market economy has the greater responsibility for capital creation, and entrepreneurs rely mainly upon the persuasion of price—in this case the interest rate—to obtain capital, since they do not have the coercive authority to raise funds by taxation or to command the use of resources.

The demand for loanable funds

Whether an economy is socialist or capitalist, advanced or underdeveloped, the essence of capital formation is to produce more than is consumed. In the private market, the interest rate is the reward that encourages the abstinence from consumption that is the preliminary to capital creation. And although later we shall qualify the strict cause-and-effect relationship between the rate of interest and capital formation, we turn first to a consideration of the factors responsible for the demand for loanable funds.

Loanable funds are money for hire—and obviously money has many uses. One use is the purchase of resources to build machinery and equipment. Other uses, such as an individual's expenditures for clothing, vacations, and medical services, or a business firm's use of loans to meet payrolls or underwrite advertising campaigns, do not directly increase capital creation.

Personal loans for the purchase of a new car, payment of income taxes, or a trip to Europe almost always cost more than loans in the form of corporation bonds, which are likely to be used for expansion of a firm's production facilities. For business firms with high credit ratings, the cost of borrowing is close to the prime rate—the lowest bank charge for the use of money. A high credit rating implies at least two things: first, and most important, that the risk of lending money is low—that is, that there is a high probability of repayment of the loan, and second, that the loan will be used productively, thus contributing to the borrower's capacity to repay. These two factors, minimum risk and productive use of the borrowed money, occur in different combinations among borrowers. Personal loans are likely to involve greater risk than business loans, a condition that results in higher borrowing charges for the individual and emphasis by the lender on collateral as security against nonpayment.

The demand for capital

Borrowers pay different rates for the use of loanable funds, depending upon such factors as risk and the administrative costs. As mentioned above, the lowest bank price for money is the prime rate, which is available only to the best loan applicants—"best" in terms of lowest risk. Well-established business firms such as American Telephone and Telegraph, General Motors, and Exxon Corporation are examples of low-risk borrowers. The demand for loanable funds for, say, a bond issue by one of these firms is based mainly on the contribution of the loanable funds to the firm's profitability when used to expand or rationalize its productive capacity.

In order to determine the economic worth of capital and to isolate its contribution to the firm's output, the amount and quality of labor and land must remain unchanged. The determination of the rate of interest illustrated in Figure 12.1 is based on the supposition that these other factors can be held constant for analysis.

Figure 12.1 Determination of the Rate of Interest for Production Loans

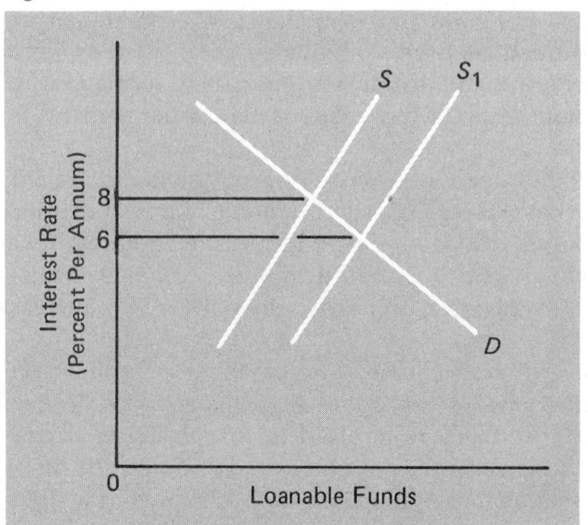

The demand curve for capital slopes downward in the short run because, as increments of capital are added by the firm, additional capital inputs yield successively smaller contributions to firm output. As capital is increased relative to the other factors of production, diminishing returns to capital occur, just as is the case when the labor factor is increased and capital and land are held constant.

When capital is scarce, the return from added inputs of capital is greater than when it is abundant, since it is directed to more productive roundabout uses. As the supply of capital increases relative to other factors, however, investment is carried to less productive undertakings. Since less productive capital employments do not yield so high a return, the price of capital—the interest rate—must be lower if firms are to use capital in such undertakings.

The supply curves S and S_1 in Figure 12.1 represent two different time periods. Curve S_1 represents a later, more affluent period when the economy has more loanable funds and a larger capital stock. With the shift in the supply curve, the interest rate on production loans falls from 8 percent to 6 percent, extending investment to undertakings that otherwise would not be profitable. Although we show no change in the demand curve in Figure 12.1, it will shift over time as a result of modifications in the price of the firm's product and changes in its productivity. These modifications can be traced to the use of capital.

Capital's contribution to output, as that of any factor of production, depends on production techniques and the quality and quantity of other factors. Over time all of these change. Innovation in production techniques is especially likely to shift the demand curve for capital. When innovation increases capital's output, that is, when the roundabout processes become more productive, the demand curve for capital shifts to the right and the rate of interest for production loans rises. Two forces are at work here: (1) technological innovation makes capital more productive, shifting the demand curve upward, and (2) diminishing returns reduce capital's contribution to the firm's output, decreasing the incremental contribution of additional units of capital. Which force has won in the past, diminishing returns or technological innovation?

Actually, innovation appears to have won hands down. Diminishing returns has been consistently set aside or vitiated. As a result, the interest rate for production loans, although the lowest of the loan rates, has held well above zero. In spite of abundant capital stock in mature industrial nations, technological advances have steadily raised industrial output, thus making continued capital investment worthwhile.

Invention and discovery have been a bulwark of the interest rate, a major reason why the rate stays well above zero. But not all innovations increase capital. Some innovations are capital-saving; they decrease investment in certain kinds of production equipment. We have already identified capital-saving innovations such as the coaxial cable and the pressurized blast furnace. These kinds of innovations hold the demand for production loans below what it would be if the innovations were capital-increasing, although any replacement of capital at the time generates a demand for loanable funds.

Giants in collision . . . the New York money market, March 30, 1975

On [March 30, 1975], the General Motors Corporation came to market with a two-part $600-million financing, its first fixed-income issue in nearly 23 years and the largest ever from an industrial corporation. [On the same day, a US Government bond issue of $1.25 billion was put up for auction.]

The head-on competition between the most creditworthy borrowers from the public and private sectors left the bond market in disarray. . . . For GM, it meant offering the new issue at a yield to investors of 8.05 percent for $300-million of 10-year notes and at 8.672 percent for $300-million of 30-year debentures. The yield on the 15-year Treasury issue was an average 8.31 percent.[2]

---

[2] Edwin L. Dale, Jr., "Financier for the U.S. Debt," *The New York Times*, April 20, 1975, Sec. 3, p. 7. © 1975 by The New York Times Company. Reprinted by permission.

We have emphasized production loans in discussing the determination of the interest rate not only because risk and administrative costs are generally lower for these loans, but because the use of loanable funds in production sets a floor on the rate of interest. *Consumption loans* involve more risk and a higher cost of administration per loan dollar and therefore generally command a higher interest rate. Whether used for production or consumption, however, the demand for loanable funds is not the only determinant of the interest rate. The *supply* of loanable funds shares with demand in establishing this price, and there are numerous factors that affect the supply of loanable funds.

The supply of loanable funds

In one way or another, the supply of loanable funds involves abstinence from consumption. Either voluntarily or involuntarily, saving restricts consumption. In the simplest case of voluntary saving, income that might otherwise be spent on food, clothing, recreation, or durable household goods is withheld from consumption and made available for loans.

Personal saving and the rate of interest

Individuals save voluntarily when they buy a government bond, open a savings account, or purchase a corporate security.[3] Corporate securities, as was pointed out in Chapter 3, are classed mainly as stocks or bonds, the former representing ownership in the corporation and the latter constituting a nonequity loan. Both involve a tradeoff between present consumption and later return, although deferring consumption in order to save and invest does not necessarily involve privation, as the phrase "abstinence from consumption" implies. Indeed, in some cases, it may be difficult for those in the upper-income brackets to consume all their income; therefore some must necessarily be saved.

For those in middle- and lower-income brackets, saving—giving up present consumption for future return—can involve an economic sacrifice. Motives for borrowing differ. The expectation of rising income, especially when linked to a preference for present consumption, provides an incentive to borrow in order to raise consumption when preferences are high and pay back later, when income is larger and needs are less pressing. The interest rate rations income between present and future use for much of

[3] Assuming, of course, that these funds come from current income rather than from a transfer of previously saved income.

the economy. From the borrower's standpoint, the interest rate is the cost of transferring income from the future to the present; for the lender, the rate of interest is the payment received for delaying until the future the use of present income.

Individuals and institutions react differently to the rate of interest as a supply price for savings or loanable funds. Some individuals save little even when the rate of interest is very high, and others save about the same amount whether the rate is high or low. Even negative savings are encountered at times among those who default on installment payments and other financial obligations.

At the other extreme, the very wealthy are more or less forced to save and invest a portion of their income—or give it away. The super rich may shift their savings among different investment opportunities, but their saving and investment decisions are not likely to be greatly influenced by changes in the interest rate. Middle-income families are inclined to save for a purpose—for example, a child's college education, the down payment on a house, or a contingency fund against emergencies. Whether the interest rate is high or low, setting aside a portion of income or borrowing for such purposes is justified for those involved.

Beyond these elemental motivations for saving and borrowing, a higher interest rate is likely to encourage more individuals to save than a lower rate, and borrowing is clearly stimulated by a lower rate. Home ownership financing, for example, picks up when the interest rate falls and decreases when it rises. The supply of loanable funds involves more than individual decisions, however. Institutions, such as corporations and governments, save or dissave by taking in more or less than they spend, and banks have the special capacity to expand credit, thereby increasing loanable funds.

Institutions and saving

Corporations save when their revenues exceed their expenditures and they do not distribute these earnings to their stockholders. Certain business firms, such as insurance companies, have earnings available for loan as a matter of course, and they periodically underwrite various developments, such as housing projects, or purchase securities of other corporations. Corporations are an important source of savings in a developed economy. In the United States, for example, corporate saving is somewhat less than personal saving, but it nonetheless contributes substantially to capital formation in the American economy. For the most part, corporate saving goes directly into capital expansion. Internal financing from retained earnings is usually preferred by the business firm over other forms of financing because there is no debt created and no payment of interest or dividends involved. Plowing earnings back into the firm adds to the firm's capital assets and generally raises the market value of its stock. Wealthy investors frequently favor this method of saving over annual dividend payments because of the lower capital-gains tax that applies to increased stock value compared to the personal income tax that must be paid on dividends.[4]

The rate of interest reflects more than the reactions of savers and investors; in a modern economy, the banking system and government exert great, possibly dominant, influence upon the level of this rate.

The banking system—custodian of the interest rate

The banking system channels savings into investment, and the actions of central banks and government debt policies are critical forces in determining the interest rate. Through the expansion or contraction of credit, the banking system can influence the interest rate, and the government can do so through the way it finances its expenditures. Changes in the rate of interest brought about by such actions affect many personal and business decisions. While the supply of loanable funds from personal savings and business earnings may be largely unresponsive to slight movements in the interest rate, a change of a percentage point or two in interest affects many decisions, such as whether to buy a home or replace plant equipment.

The supply of land and rent

Twentieth-century economists usually do not draw the sharp distinction among factors of production that the classical economists did. In the early nineteenth century when economics was emerging as an independent discipline, the different economic characteristics of land, labor, and capital were considered to be highly significant. The supply of capital was generally regarded as elastic, responsive to price change and subject to human control. The supply of land, by contrast, was held by the classical economists to be inelastic, endowed by nature with fertility, and limited in

[4] A capital gain is an increase in the value of property realized by sale. For example, a share of US Steel stock purchased in 1976 for $25.00 and sold in 1977 for $28.00 represents a capital gain of $3.00. If taxed as a capital gain, the rate would probably be 25 percent. If, instead, the stock were held, and it paid a dividend of $3.00, the tax rate would be at the level of the income bracket of the stockholder, which would undoubtedly be higher than 25 percent. This is not to suggest that capital gains may replace dividend payments, although some firms, such as IBM, are noted as "growth" investments that emphasize rising stock prices over dividend payments.

extent by the area of the earth's surface. The classical economists found this inelasticity of the land supply to be a cause for concern. If the supply of land is truly fixed, population growth raises land rent at the same time that diminishing returns brings about a decreasing marginal output in food production. Figure 12.2 shows the effect of a perfectly inelastic land supply on rent when demand increases.

To modern economists the supply of land is much more flexible than it was to the classical economists, especially in the long run. Modern economists point out that modifications in agricultural practices and developments in supporting inputs, such as insecticides, fertilizer, improved seeds, and capital equipment, have raised agricultural output as if the physical supply of land had been increased. Until very recently in the United States, for example, agricultural output increased annually, while less and less land was cultivated. Although this did not decrease the price of land, land values and rent have risen less than they would have in the absence of yield-increasing innovations. If future population growth surpasses the rise in agricultural productivity, however, as seems increasingly likely, land values and rent will accelerate.

For many years, the pressure of population on land has been apparent in many urban areas. New York's Manhattan Island has accommodated a larger and larger population by building skyward, as have Tokyo, Chicago, Montreal, and Hong Kong. Costly building practices are justified by the return from real estate investment in such high-rent areas. Noting the effect of population concentraction on land values in the United States in the late nineteenth century, Henry George advocated a land tax designed

Figure 12.2 Rent with Fixed Supply of Land

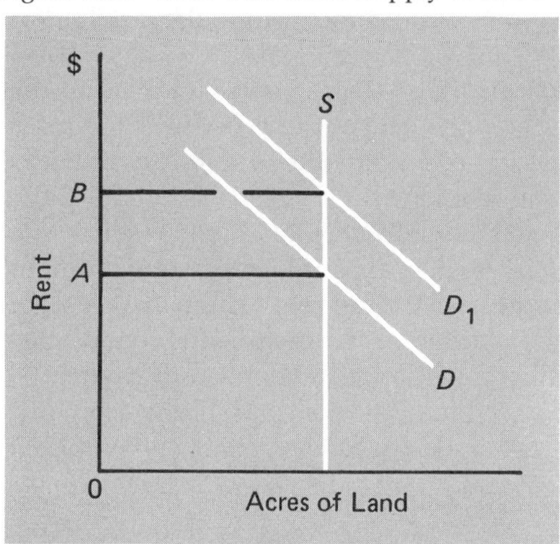

A British farm machine . . . capital-saving, labor-saving, energy-saving

Each spring it takes four operations to convert each ploughed field in Britain into a seedbed: (1) a tractor has to pull a cultivator to break up the clods; (2) another tractor with a flat harrow follows to level the land; (3) the seed, and sometimes the fertilizer with it, is drilled; and, finally, (4) another set of harrows ensures that the seed is covered. If conditions are bad, farmers often have to go through all this twice.

A new invention has now made it possible for a single tractor to perform all these tasks in one operation. Pulling a power-harrow, which breaks the clods and levels at the same time, a tractor can also haul a seed and fertilizer drill and a set of harrows. A "bridge," developed by the National Institute of Agricultural Engineering, enables all these implements to be towed down the field. The obvious saving in manpower, machinery and energy are offset only by a slight loss of speed compared with traditional methods—and hence a smaller area covered per day.[5]

to prevent increasing inequality of income and wealth from land ownership.

Henry George and the single tax

Henry George believed he had found a panacea for a basic cause of mankind's social ills. According to George, poverty was caused primarily by the fact that a rising share of the nation's income went to the landlord as population pressed upon limited land resources. In turn, George held, much of society's crime and social disorganization could be traced to the poverty brought about by the landholder's gain at the expense of the mass of renters. For George, the solution was simple and straightforward: Tax away rent, the cause of poverty and inequality. He called his proposal the *single tax* because at the time it was advanced in his book *Progress and Poverty*, which was published in 1879, the expenditures of government were small enough so that revenue from taxing rent would make other levies unnecessary. Now the story is different. Government expenditures have mounted now to the point that more than the nation's rent payments, implicit and explicit, would be required to cover the costs of government.

But what about the effect of the single tax on the economy? Wouldn't

[5] "Toads, Watch Out," *The* [London] *Economist*, March 1, 1975, p. 81.

such confiscation of a return to a factor of production seriously disrupt the use and allocation of land? Not at all, according to Henry George. Whether rent is paid to a private landlord or taxed away by the government, the land is no less useful. It still is a necessary ingredient in agricultural output or as a site for building. But the single tax would have largely eliminated fortunes based on land ownership, which George considered to be ethically and economically unjustified. He believed rent to be *ethically* unjustified, considering it primarily the result of population growth rather than improvements in productivity by the land owner; he believed rent to be *economically* unjustified, considering that higher rents simply increase the income share of the land owner without increasing the supply of land. He called the land owners' return an "unearned increment."

There are other examples of unearned increments in certain natural endowments; the opera singer's voice or the looks of the movie star are two such unearned increments. To the extent that such commercially valuable attributes are not produced by study and training, the extraordinary high returns these talents sometimes bring represent a fortuitous gain. Such unearned increments turn up throughout the economic system wherever the demand for a good or service outruns the supply. Society has not been unmindful of the inequalities produced by these gains, and inheritance, estate, and income taxation have been designed in part to hold down the inequity they create.

In distinguishing land from other productive factors, early economists were likely to emphasize that land was God-given rather than man-made. During the frontier period in Canada and the United States, land could frequently be acquired by occupancy, but even though there was extensive unused land in the hinterlands, rent was charged for locations in which population concentrated. No longer is there an abundance of land, and rent has risen in accord with its economic value. In allocating land, just as in allocating capital and labor, the optimum economic arrangement is attained by employing the land resource so that its marginal revenue product is greatest. Efficiency in any economic system depends upon its capacity to move and shift resources to those uses which yield the highest return. Rent, the measure of the scarcity of the land factor, guides land away from lower-output uses and into higher-return undertakings. In similar fashion, profits are an indicator of where resources should be employed in a market economy. With mobile resources, profit beckons investment to the area of the economy in which price most exceeds costs and, conversely, brings disinvestment and reduced output in those economic undertakings that do not cover cost. By following these guides to economic efficiency, an economy is bound to develop inequalities in the distribution of income. These inequalities, in turn, are likely to call for remedy through government programs of taxation and expenditure. These issues are discussed in separate chapters. Here we consider only the economic function of profit.

Profit

It will be recalled from Chapter 6 that in the economist's view profit is mainly the result of monopoly restraint or fortuitous market events. It is clear what we mean by monopoly restraint and how it operates, but what constitutes a fortuitous market event is less apparent. A fortuitous market event, sometimes called a *windfall gain*, is one that causes the firm's product price to rise or its cost of production to fall through little responsibility of the firm. If the firm is able to sell its product at a higher price because of improved design, or if the cost of production falls because of better management, this does not lead to profit. If management becomes more efficient and the redesigned product more valuable, the marginal revenue product of the factors responsible rises. But if the firm finds that the demand for its product increases because consumers change their tastes and place the product higher in their scale of preferences, this revenue increase is profit.

Are profits never a reward for an action originating with the firm that improves its financial position—a payment for the daring, cunning, or innovating entrepreneur, for example? On the whole, economists contend that the daring, cunning, or innovative entrepreneur can take these talents with him, and therefore command a price for their use. Some conceptions of profits, however, even those of economists, do not adhere to the foregoing strict construction. As already noted, business people are likely to view profits with a simple directness—profit is what they get to keep.

Profit and risk

A frequent defense of profit is that it is a reward for risk-taking. The less prospect of gain from a business venture, the greater the return must be when it does occur. In a high-risk venture, returns must compensate for the probability of nonreturn. In wildcatting for oil, for example, many dry wells are usually sunk for every producing well, and the return from the producing wells has to be high enough to offset the loss incurred from the dry wells. To economists, the high return from the producing wells is not profit, but compensation in part for the risk of drilling dry wells.

Where risk is great, a higher return is required to induce investment.

But profit lies beyond this. Most economists subscribe to the distinction drawn by Frank Knight between risk and uncertainty. Risk is reserved for predictable events that one can insure against, whereas uncertainty occurs in cases where no actuarial determination of probability is possible. The risk of fire, death, or flood can be predicted on the basis of large numbers—that is, the probability of fire, death, or flood can be assigned a percentage likelihood in certain cases, even though the specific case is unpredictable.

Uncertain events defy actuarial determination. For example, how can one say whether there will be a general depression ten years from now? Will a new product be a best seller? Will war occur in the Middle East? True, predictions can be made about such events, but it is not possible to establish a true probability of occurrence. In general, the more distant the event, the greater the uncertainty. It is more difficult to forecast what will happen in the economy two years hence than two months from now because present economic forces may be completely reversed, heavily reinforced, or variously diluted over time.

Uncertain events do not necessarily turn out to be bad, of course; there may be a boom instead of a depression, or the new product may outsell all its competitors. If market uncertainty is resolved favorably for the firm, profits result; if it is resolved unfavorably, losses occur. In either case, certain signals are raised that provide direction for the flow of resources.

Summary

The basic explanation for the determination of the interest rate and rent is the same as that for wage rates: marginal revenue product. The measurement of the marginal revenue product of different inputs cannot be done simultaneously, however. To measure capital's MRP, the other factors of production employed by the firm have to be held constant while capital is varied; to measure the MRP of land, labor and capital must remain unchanged. If more than one factor changes, it is not possible to isolate the contribution of each factor.

Although the marginal revenue product doctrine is applied in the same way for the determination of interest and rent as for the explanation of wage rates, there are differences in these factors that should be noted. The classical economists, for example, considered the supply of land to be highly inelastic, which caused them to anticipate an increasing income share to land as population increased over the years; the supply of labor and capital, by contrast, was considered to be much more elastic, especially over time.

Improvements in farming practices and the development of agricultural machinery and equipment, commercial fertilizers and other output-increasing developments since the Industrial Revolution have had much the same effect as expanding the area of land available for cultivation, holding down the return to land.

The payment of interest was opposed by the church in the Middle Ages and by Soviet planners following the October Revolution. The church opposed interest as a form of exploitation, which is also the case for the followers of Karl Marx. Interest is a necessary payment for the use of capital in the productive process, however, and it directs capital to the more productive economic activities. If there were no charge for the use of capital—if the interest rate was zero—low-yielding investments would compete for capital on equal terms with high-yielding investment, and returns in the future would be appraised the same as present consumption.

The use of machinery and equipment and other forms of capital in the productive process is the basic cause for a positive rate of interest. What are frequently called interest rates—household finance fees, department store installment charges, and car financing costs, for example—are higher than the MRP interest rate since they include costs for administration and protection of the lender from risk.

Profit—unlike wages, interest, and rent—is not a return to a factor of production, although businessmen at times may view profit as their reward for superior managerial ability. If the return to a firm is higher because of the superior ability of the business manager, in a competitive economy this talent is recognized by a higher salary. Economists consider profits to result mainly from windfall gains over which the firm has no control or monopoly restraint. When competition is vigorous, profit is a purely short-run phenomenon, but it is an enduring feature in both the short run and long run for monopoly.

Key terms and concepts

Capital a term used to describe the money fund invested in factors of production such as machinery and equipment as well as the factors.

Prime rate of interest the cost of borrowing for those with low risk and good credit ratings.

Technological innovation inventions and discoveries that increase the productivity of capital.

Capital gain the increase in the value of property as measured by its price at the time of purchase and its sale price.

Henry George (1839–1897) the American founder of the Single Tax movement and author of *Progress and Poverty* (1879).

Single tax a tax on land proposed by Henry George. The tax was designed to transfer to the government the economic rent of land. George contended that the single tax would make other taxes unnecessary.

Unearned increment the increase in the value of land that is brought about by concentration or growth of population.

Risk the prospect of an undesired event, such as fire, flood, or death, which can be predicted if the number of previously recorded cases is large enough.

Uncertainty an unpredictable event that may be either desirable or undesirable, such as a windfall gain or a decrease in a firm's demand. (Frequently risk and uncertainty are considered to be synonyms, but they are differentiated here in defining profit and loss.)

Profit a return to the business firm that is in excess of its full resource costs of production.

Discussion and review questions

1. How does capital formation take place in a modern economy? What is the difference between capital formation by voluntary saving and capital formation by forced saving?

2. The roundabout method of production is the basic cause of the high productivity of the modern industrial economy. How does the roundabout method increase productivity and what effect does this have on payments to the factors of production?

3. When asked to name the invention that had brought the greatest return through the course of history, a Vermont Yankee suggested that the invention of the rate of interest must lead all others. Do you agree? What function does the rate of interest perform in a market economy? Why did the church try to prevent its use in the Middle Ages?

4. What causes the supply of loanable funds to fluctuate? How are loanable funds related to time preference, to corporate savings, to capital innovation?

5. Is more capital used in the production process in a capitalist economy than in a socialist economy? What are the basic differences between the two forms of economic organization with respect to capital formation, the rate of interest, and payments to factors of production?

6. What is the prime rate of interest? How is it established?

7. What causes the demand curve for capital to slope downward in the short run? Can the demand curve shift to the right? To the left? What causes the demand curve to shift?

8. How responsive are personal savings to changes in the rate of interest? What income groups do most of the saving in a modern economy?

9. How can there be such a thing as negative savings? Who are the negative savers?

10. What is a capital gain? In the personal income tax, why are returns from increased corporate stock value, and not returns from stock dividends, given preferential treatment? Is there an economic or ethical justification for this?

11. Why did the classical economists consider land to be a very inelastic factor of production? What is the view of modern economists? Do the classical and modern views lead to quite different theories of rent?

12. What was Henry George's single-tax proposal? Why did it not receive more support? To what extent is an unearned increment present in returns to factors other than land? What are the implications of the unearned increment for social policy?

13 Economic inequality, poverty, and discrimination

*The US economic system clearly has yielded an extraordinary increase in material well-being since the end of the Great Depression. . . . The average citizen's income has far outdistanced price rises. Median family income before taxes, for example, nearly trebled between 1939 and 1973. While government during those years grabbed more and more of their income, the consumer still came out way ahead. By 1973 the average American's disposable income was 2.4 times as large, in constant dollars, as it had been thirty-four years earlier.**

The Law, in its majestic equality, forbids the rich as well as the poor to sleep under bridges, to beg in the streets, and to steal bread.—Anatole France†

Since the industrial revolution, Western nations have steadily added to their wealth and raised their level of income, but they have not thereby escaped the twin scourges of poverty and inequality. Even in the United States, a nation more dedicated than most to material well being, output that has more than doubled since the Great Depression has not wiped out widespread areas of poverty and inequality—evils made all the worse by the grand affluence that rising income has brought to most of society.

If nearly trebling income in thirty years doesn't erase poverty and inequality, what does it take to do so?

Were the earlier dismal scientists right, from Thomas Malthus, who found poverty unavoidable, to Vilfredo Pareto, who believed mankind to be incapable of significantly altering the existing distribution of the world's output? Pareto believed that "essentially nothing can be done about inequality. The basic forces determining inequality are too strong to be

* Edmund Faltermayer, "Ever Increasing Affluence Is Less of a Sure Thing," *Fortune*, April 1975, p. 92.

† Quoted in John Cournos, *A Modern Plutarch* (London: Thornton Butterworth, Ltd., 1928), p. 35.

affected by state intervention." The persistence of poverty and inequality in the industrial nations of the world, in spite of concerted efforts to bring about change, keeps such gloomy appraisals alive.

What are the costs of eradicating hunger, improving housing, and raising the living standard of the needy? The answer depends on how much housing is improved, the extent to which the standard of living is raised, and what income levels are considered "poor." Beyond direct outlays to assist the poor, there are hidden costs of increasing equality from decreased efficiency of our economic system. And finally, how important is discrimination as a cause of poverty and income inequality, particularly for those minority groups that chronically find themselves at the bottom of the economic heap?

These are hard questions to answer. Moreover, they involve value judgments that at times generate disagreement and high emotion. There is no way to avoid the controversy in discussing inequality and discrimination, but starting with the recent data on income distribution in the United States and how government programs have affected this distribution should be reasonably unprovocative.

The distribution of income in the United States

The US Bureau of the Census has for many years collected data on the distribution of income in the United States. This information has been analyzed in a number of different ways, but one of the most revealing presentations has been to compare the income shares of different segments of the population. By dividing the population into five equal parts *(quintiles)* and comparing income shares, we get a broad view of the pattern of income distribution. Such a statistical breakdown is presented in Table 13.1.

According to Table 13.1, over a period of twenty-five years the percentage distribution of income has remained virtually constant in the United States when measured in terms of quintile income groups. In the face of increasing expenditures for public assistance, the trivial increase of less than one-half of one percent in the lowest income quintile from 1947 to 1973 appears to confirm Pareto's gloomy prediction. Fortunately for the lowest income quintile, however, the statistics shown in Table 13.1 are measures only of "money" income. When data on non money, or "in-kind," income are added for the lowest quintile, the distribution is altered substantially. Before turning to this aspect of the case, however, we need to examine further the nature of the pattern of quintile distribution.

Table 13.1: Percentage income shares for families before direct taxes, selected years, 1947–1973

Income Group	1973	1966	1960	1947
Lowest quintile	5.5	5.6	4.8	5.1
Second quintile	11.9	12.4	12.2	11.8
Third quintile	17.5	17.8	17.8	16.7
Fourth quintile	24.0	23.8	24.0	23.2
Highest quintile	41.1	40.5	41.3	43.3

Source: U.S. Bureau of the Census, "Money Income in 1973 of Families and Persons in the United States," *Current Population Reports,* Series P–60, No. 97 (1975), Table 22.

The pattern of quintile income distribution in the United States

What does it mean that the lowest fifth of the families in the United States in 1973 received 5.5 percent of the money income, while the highest fifth received 41.1 percent? It means that the highest quintile had almost eight times as much money income as the lowest. Perfect income equality would be represented by a 20 percent share for each quintile: 20 percent of the population would receive 20 percent of the income. Note, however, that the money income distribution shown in Table 13.1 represents income before direct taxation, which is to say that the effect of such levies as the personal income tax has not been taken into account. To the extent that taxes are progressive—that is, take a larger percentage of tax from the upper quintiles—the disparity in after-tax income among the quintiles is reduced. The redistributional effect of progressive taxation is of course not confined to the highest and lowest quintiles, but decreases the income inequality after taxes throughout the population.

Comparing *family* incomes instead of *individual* incomes also moderates income inequality. The family is a more appropriate indicator of inequality, however, because its collective resources are usually available to meet household needs, particularly in the case of lower-income families. Although there has been little relative change in money income distribution between 1947 and 1973, there has been a steady rise in the absolute level of real income for almost all income recipients during this period. *Real income*—the goods and services that money income buys—was approximately twice as high for the lowest quintile in 1973 as it was in 1947. Since this was also true for all the other quintiles, however, the lowest quintile's percentage share of the nation's income did not change. The real-income increase does not show up in the statistics in Table 13.1, even though a doubling of real income represents an important economic gain. What is poverty and how much of the population finds itself in this unhappy condition?

Poverty and the level of income

During the Great Depression, Franklin D. Roosevelt in his second inaugural address in 1937 dramatized the plight of the nation by saying, "I see one-third of a nation ill-housed, ill-clad, ill-nourished." Twenty-seven years later, in March 1964, Lyndon Johnson returned to the same theme in a message to Congress, saying "There are millions of Americans—one-fifth of our people—who have not shared in the abundance which has been granted to most of us, and on whom the gates of opportunity have been closed." From Roosevelt to Johnson, from the Great Depression to the Great Society, poverty has remained a perplexing American problem, gradually diminishing, but at the cost of larger and larger public expenditures. When does a family drop below the poverty line and why is it so hard to raise families above this level?

The Philadelphia story—a short walk to the welfare office

[I]n Philadelphia and elsewhere across the U.S. [during the recession of the middle 1970s], many workers who never dreamed they would ever apply for public assistance are making the dreaded trip from the unemployment office to the welfare office.

The trip can be a psychologically devastating last resort that, in the words of one recipient, "destroys any shred of self-respect you had left after being unemployed for over a year." For others, who legally must use up most of their assets before qualifying for welfare payments, the transition destroys dreams as well as self-respect.

Taking the two-block trip from the unemployment office to the Department of Public Assistance office in Philadelphia recently was James Elmore, a 59-year-old former construction worker. . . . If his DPA application is cleared his family will get about $80 a week plus food stamps, against the $95 a week he received as unemployment compensation.

"It's degrading," he says, awaiting his turn at the drab DPA office in Philadelphia. "I just can't understand why they put you through this." . . . He fears the switch to welfare will ensure that he will never work again. "At my age, I can't get a job. Who's going to hire a 59-year-old welfare recipient?"[1]

[1] "As More Unemployed Run Out of Benefits, Many Turn to Welfare," *The Wall Street Journal*, October 27, 1975, pp. 1, 10. Reprinted with permission of *The Wall Street Journal*,

The poverty line is a moving target

What is commonplace to most families now, in Charlemagne's time would have been unparalleled luxury even for the wealthy. What we consider poverty today is influenced by rising standards of consumption—the moving target—as well as the failure of some members of society to fill a productive role in the economy. In the United States an officially defined poverty line, established by the federal Social Security Administration in 1965, is based on the cost of a "minimally adequate diet." Food costs of the minimally adequate diet are tripled on the assumption that food constitutes approximately one-third of total necessary family expenditures. Table 13.2 shows the 1959, 1966, and 1973 poverty lines for families of different size.

Although the official "poverty line" is located with precision at $4,540 for a family of four in 1973, by 1975 it had risen to $5,500. This does not mean that families below this level turn blue from hunger, or that those above prosper in ruddy health. The poverty line is not the point of subsistence; families can survive on less income or experience economic privation with more. But by middle-income standards, the good life is either nonexistent or spread very thin at the poverty line. To the extent that poverty is defined by a fixed real standard—a given amount of food and clothing, for example—the poverty line sinks *relatively* as the nation's per capita output rises. Through 1959, 1966, and 1973, for example, the poverty

Table 13.2: Poverty lines for nonfarm families, by family size, 1973, 1966, and 1959

Family Size	Money Income 1973	1966	1959
1	$2,247	$1,628	$1,467
2	2,895	2,107	1,984
3	3,548	2,588	2,324
4	4,540	3,317	2,973
5	5,358	3,908	3,506
6	6,028	4,388	3,944
7 and over	7,435	5,395	4,849

Source: U.S. Bureau of the Census, *Current Population Reports,* Series P–60, No. 98 (1975), "Characteristics of the Low-Income Population: 1973," Table A–3; 1966: U.S. Bureau of the Census, unpublished data; and 1959: U.S. Bureau of the Census, *Current Population Reports,* Special Studies, Series P–23, No. 28, "Revision in Poverty Statistics, 1959–1968," Table C, from E. K. Browning, *Redistribution and the Welfare System* (Washington, D.C.: American Enterprise Association, 1975), p. 11.

line for a family of four dropped from 55 percent of median family income in 1959, to 45 percent in 1966, to 38 percent in 1973. As family income rose between 1959 and 1972, while the poverty line remained unchanged, the official poor decreased from more than 39 million in 1959 to approximately 23 million in 1973. This big decrease in poor over the fourteen-year period was brought about by holding the standard of poverty fixed during a period of economic growth. Table 13.3 shows the decrease in the number of poor between the years 1959, 1966, and 1973, along with the age and family characteristics of those who remained below the poverty line during this period.

In-kind income transfers: an increasing part of the poor's income

In-kind income transfers are forms of public assistance, such as food stamps, public housing, and medicaid, that provide important additions to the standard of living of the poor. Although in-kind transfers have been expanded greatly in recent years, they do not show up in the statistics of money income, which is the reason for the remarkable stability of the before-taxes quintile income distribution reported in Table 13.1.

An income transfer may be either in cash or in kind. If cash, the transfer is recorded in the statistics of money income distribution. Cash transfers include such payments as welfare checks to supplement in-

Table 13.3: Selected characteristics of persons below the poverty level, 1973, 1966, and 1959

	1973	1966	1959
Number of poor persons	22,973,000	28,510,000	39,490,000
65 years and over	3,354,000	5,111,000	5,679,000
Under 65 years[a]			
Family with female head	9,460,000	7,841,000	8,115,000
Family with male head	10,160,000	15,558,000	25,695,000
Decrease in total number of poor from prior period	5,537,000	10,980,000	—

[a] Includes single person households.

Source: U.S. Bureau of the Census, "Characteristics of the Low-Income Population: 1973," *Current Population Reports,* Series P–60, No. 98 (1975), Table 1.

sufficient or zero earnings. Whether in cash or in kind, however, the transfer shifts income from one segment of society to another. According to the ability-to-pay principle, the income should shift from the upper income groups to the lower income groups. In the United States, the tax structure is moderately progressive overall mainly because of the importance of the federal personal income tax, which is graduated in terms of income—the tax rate increasing as taxable income rises. Equally important for redistribution, tax revenues have increasingly been devoted to cash and in-kind transfers to the poor. Table 13.4 shows this change in federal outlays for the poor over recent years.

The growth of in-kind transfers

In-kind transfer programs have expanded rapidly, as shown in Table 13.4, moving from 19 percent of federal outlays benefiting the poor to 57 percent. In-kind transfers add importantly to the real living standard of the

Table 13.4: Federal outlays benefiting the poor, selected fiscal years, 1964–1975

	1975 (estimate)	1973	1969	1966	1964
Federal outlays ($ billions)					
Cash payments	13.7	11.1	8.2	7.1	6.4
Food and housing transfers	5.4	3.5	0.7	0.3	0.3
Education	2.2	1.9	1.2	0.6	0.1
Health	6.8	5.4	3.5	0.8	0.7
Manpower	2.3	2.5	1.4	0.9	0.2
Other	1.8	1.9	0.9	0.5	0.2
Total	32.2	26.2	15.9	10.3	7.9
Total federal cash transfers ($ billions)	13.7	11.1	8.2	7.1	6.4
Total federal in-kind transfers ($ billions)	18.5	15.1	7.7	3.2	1.5
In-kind as percent of total	57	58	48	31	19
Number of poor persons	NA	23.0	24.1	28.5	36.1
Federal transfer per poor person (dollars)	NA	1,039	660	361	219

(NA = not available)

Source: U.S. Department of Health, Education and Welfare, Office of the Assistant Secretary for Planning and Evaluation, Office of Program Systems, "Federal Outlays Benefiting the Poor—Summary Tables," March 1974, Table 1 for the figures in the first seven rows. Other figures are estimates of E. K. Browning, *op. cit.*, p. 23.

poor, raising it well above the 1973 5.5 percent share of money income for the lowest quintile (see Table 13.1). Correcting the data to account for in-kind transfers raises the lowest quintile's 1973 income share to 8 percent.[2] At 8 percent, the lowest quintile falls well short of 20-percent equality, but it makes substantial progress, rising to 40 percent of the average US family real income in 1973.

A further point needs emphasis. Income redistribution depends both on what the family pays out in taxes and what it gets back in cash and in-kind transfers. When a balance is struck between the tax cost and transfer benefits, in recent years, the burden of taxes on the lowest income quintile is more than neutralized. In 1973, for example, the families in the lowest income quintile paid taxes of $22.5 billion but received transfers of $100.7 billion, giving them a net benefit of $78.2 billion, which amounts to almost half of all such transfers in 1973.

This is not a trivial contribution to income redistribution—yet we have not abolished need. Our programs of public assistance have not penetrated some of the more resistant pockets of economic distress in our society. The strongholds of poverty, from big-city ghettos to Appalachia, have more than their share of the poverty prone types. What are they like?

The lower the income, the higher the price

From coast to coast, mainly in our urban areas, those who can least afford to pay are paying unconscionable prices for junk, pawned off on them through trickery, deceit, and fraud. By signing contracts containing the most inhumane clauses, these poor people legally bind themselves into misery. And when they cannot pay or refuse to pay, they find themselves pushed even further into destitution by a legal system which is incomprehensible to them and which has become perverted from a device for protecting the innocent to a means of abetting the dishonest. Although this is a strong indictment, it is not exaggerated. It is no more than what anyone who has worked in ghettos or studied these problems will confirm.[3]

---

[2] The 8 percent estimate is that published by Professor Edgar K. Browning of the University of Virginia in the study that is cited as a source for Table 13.2. The study has been followed closely in the above material.

[3] From the book, *The Dark Side of the Marketplace* by Senator Warren G. Magnuson and Jean Carper, © 1968 by W. Magnuson and J. Carper. Published by Prentice-Hall, Inc., Englewood Cliffs, New Jersey.

Who are the poor?

The poverty profile

Poverty is predictable. If you are poorly educated, not white, old or quite young, and a farm worker, the chances are high that you are also poor. You don't have to be all these things to be poor, but each helps. Of course you can be poor in a big city as well as in a rural area, but on the average poverty is more prevalent and public assistance is less available in rural regions, particularly in the South. Whether you live in a city or on a farm, however, you are more likely to be poor if, in addition to being a school drop-out and the rest, you are a member of a female-headed family, that is, a family without a live-in father. Since many of the poor possess more than one of these characteristics it is difficult to isolate the effect of any one, but some factors stand out sharply from the rest. Such is the case with educational attainment, whether one is white or nonwhite,[4] as is indicated in Table 13.5.

Table 13.5: Average weekly earnings of males 35–41 for the year 1973[a]

Educational Attainment	White	Nonwhite
0–4	$150	$ 96
5–7	173	149
8	202	165
9–11	211	165
12	231	178
13–15	265	209
16	321	241
Over 16	333	284

[a] Data are from a survey made in May 1973. A full-time worker is defined as one who usually works 35 hours or more per week.
Source: Bureau of Labor Statistics, U.S. Department of Labor, reproduced from *Annual Report of the Council of Economic Advisers* (Washington, D.C.: Government Printing Office, 1974), p. 146.

[4] The classification *nonwhite* is not a coy avoidance of *black*. In his autobiography, Arthur Ashe, the superb tennis player, suggests that the term *nonblack* be used for whites instead of *nonwhite* for blacks. In census data, nonwhite covers more than blacks, including Mexican Americans, Puerto Ricans, and Native Americans (Indians), although blacks make up about 90 percent of the nonwhite category in the United States.

Education and earnings

The positive relationship between education and earnings for both whites and nonwhites is demonstrated convincingly by the data in Table 13.5, as is the familiar contention that minority workers are paid less. It is generally assumed—especially by educators—that education increases productivity, but there are those who believe that higher educational attainment mainly reflects abilities that were present all along. According to the latter view, the education system serves primarily as a screening device to sort and drop out students at attainment levels equal to their abilities. Attempts to validate the sorting hypothesis have not been successful, but there is evidence that the educational system performs both training and sorting functions.

Discrimination and employment

Hiring and promotion decisions are seldom based entirely on productivity. J. Edgar Hoover, the long-time director of the Federal Bureau of Investigation, had an active dislike for men with small heads. (Hoover had one of the largest heads of any public official in Washington.) When he encountered a job applicant with a less-than-average-size head, he was alleged to instruct his subordinates to "Get rid of the pin head." This was certainly discrimination in hiring—a senseless prejudice against applicants with less than 7¼ hat size—but it was hardly a matter of national concern. Not so when discrimination extends to a large segment of the labor market, such as blacks and women, and is practiced by more than the occasional employer.

Equal opportunities in employment and job advancement have frequently been denied because of age, sex, race, marital status, religion, and ethnic origin, which do raise issues of national concern. When discrimination in hiring is widespread, it contributes seriously to income inequality and poverty: Output is lost because some members of the labor force are employed below their full productivity capacity, and both the nation and those discriminated against are worse off economically.

Narrowing income differentials

A glance at Table 13.5 is enough to indicate that equal educational attainment does not overcome racial discrimination insofar as wages are concerned. It is possible—even likely—that the attainment of the eighth grade by a black is not the same as a similar attainment by a white, given the black's grass-roots inequality in educational facilities and dissimilar cultural motivations. But even so, the spread in wages for the same educational level is impressive. Is it being reduced? The answer is: "Yes, gradually over the long run."

Minorities fare best during prosperity when labor is scarce. During such times, the barriers of discrimination are relaxed and minorities find it easier to get jobs. Unfortunately, this breakthrough in the job market may be short-lived if there is an economic downswing, since those hired last are generally fired first. As a result, minority groups are likely to be whiplashed in the labor market—hired during prosperity, bringing them important economic gains, and let go during recession, separating them once again from the mainstream of the working force. But over the longer view, when a trend is struck between the troughs and peaks of the business cycle, a narrowing in the wage differentials for minority groups is clearly evident.

According to the 1974 *Annual Report of the Council of Economic Advisers,* the median wage for black males in the United States increased at an annual rate of 3.2 percent between 1947 and 1971, compared with an increase for white males during the same period of 2.6 percent. For black females the increase was 4.9 percent and for white females it was 1.7 percent during this period. The nature of the changes in wage differentials requires further examination.

The gains of black women in the labor market

The employment gains of blacks are the result of more than a conversion of employers to equal-opportunity hiring. They reflect improved schooling for blacks, brought about by more nearly equal educational expenditures for the black and white races, and by the migration of blacks from the South, where wages are lower, to other parts of the country where they are higher. Over a thirty-year period, the black population of the South dropped from 77 percent in 1940 to 53 percent in 1970. During this same period, changing attitudes and the stimulus of the 1964 Civil Rights Act helped blacks break out of the "back of the bus" in the labor market.

Domestic employment of female blacks, long their major job opportunity, for example, declined markedly in the 1940–1970 period—indicating their acceptance in other occupations—and on a national basis the wage differential between black and white females was virtually eliminated. Indeed, in areas outside the South, black females earn more than white females with equivalent educational attainment. But the closing of the wage gap between black and white female workers overstates the breakthrough of the blacks. Simple wage comparisons ignore the different work histories of the two groups. Black women as a group have more work experience than whites and, therefore, have acquired more on-the-job training. Female white workers are not only less experienced generally, but their employment record is more intermittent. Under these circumstances, equal pay is not equal treatment.

The uneven gains of black males in the labor market

The narrowing of wage differentials that has been so pronounced in the case of black and white females has not occurred with males. According to 1970 census data on occupational earnings, whites as a group were paid 50 percent more than blacks. Slightly more than a third of this difference in white-black earnings appears to be due to occupational differences—blacks were more generally employed at lower-paying occupations than whites—but this may be in part the result of lesser black educational attainment. When black and white male earnings are compared for those with roughly equivalent education, the spread in earnings is greatly decreased—to 8 percent more for whites, for example, among those who have completed twelve to fifteen years of schooling.

When blacks are compared to whites who have equal educational attainments, the wage differential between the two groups is narrowed, but when young, educated black families are compared with less-educated young black families, the wage differential here has been greatly increased: Rich blacks are getting richer, while many blacks have not been able to get the education that would raise their earnings. This has increased income inequality sharply among blacks.

Sex discrimination in employment

Sex discrimination, which is usually directed against women, takes the form of (1) lower earnings in a given occupation than those paid to the opposite sex, and (2) barriers that confine employment to lower-paying occupations. Table 13.6 shows the combined impact of these factors as well as other less apparent influences on male and female earnings. According to the findings of the Council of Economic Advisers, over a span of twenty years from 1949 to 1969, the position of women appears to have deteriorated in the labor market. This is certainly a most paradoxical development just at the onset of the women's movement. Can we explain it?

Women's earnings are lower than men's for many reasons: education, ability, experience, length of employment, and discrimination. Some men's earnings are lower than women's for these same reasons. In the past, these "reasons" have been more applicable to the status of women in

Table 13.6: Female earnings as a percentage of men's

Type of earnings	Earnings of women as percent of earnings of men		
	1949	1959	1969
Mean wage and salary earnings:[a]			
Annual	56	50	47
Hourly	67	66	63
Hourly adjusted for education[b]	63	65	63
Mean total money earnings:[a]			
Annual	([c])	48	46
Hourly	([c])	65	62
Hourly adjusted for education[b]	([c])	64	62

[a] Earnings for any year are for those in the experienced labor force the following year.
[b] Approximate adjustment based on differences in the educational distributions of men and women in the labor force in 1950, 1960, and 1970.
[c] Not available.
Source: *Annual Report of the Council of Economic Advisers* (Washington, D.C.: Government Printing Office, 1974), p. 158.

the labor market than men, mainly because, for the majority of women, employment outside the home was not a permanent arrangement. But the changing structure of society and the women's movement have increased the numbers and the permanence of women in the labor force. Recent female entrants into the labor market have significantly affected the earnings relationship reported in Table 13.6. It is difficult to appraise the factors responsible for the differences between the earnings of men and women. Discrimination is certainly a factor, but there are others. Even when adjustments for educational differences are taken into account, however, the spread between male and female earnings is not reduced significantly. Why? Mainly because *more* women are seeking employment than ever before.

This may seem strange. When women are overcoming occupational and professional barriers more rapidly than ever before, how can they have lower earnings? Remember that the percentages in Table 13.6 represent mean earnings, not totals. The change in the mean earnings of women, compared to those of men, reflect two forces working in opposite directions: (1) the increase in the number of inexperienced females in the labor market, which exerts downward pressure on the mean earnings, and (2) the success of barrier-breaking entrants, which exerts upward pressure on the mean earnings.

There she sits like a queen in her cowhide seat on the lookout for the smokies

Somewhere on Interstate 495, Md.—Judy Kuncher, a small platinum-blond woman of 27 years and 124 pounds, eased her 15-ton tractor-trailer onto the interstate the other morning. Threading deftly through the heavy rush-hour traffic, she headed toward Damascus, Md., to deliver a load of aluminum doors and replacement windows.

The huge GMC Astro 95 tractor chugged, puffed and snorted as Mrs. Kuncher shifted among its 10 different speeds. On the dashboard a Citizens Band radio crackled with reports from other "gearjammers" (truckers) about the whereabouts of the "smokies" (state police).

Another day in Judy Kuncher's two-year career as a truck driver had begun.

"It's the freedom; that's what I like," she said, sitting like a queen in her high cowhide driver's seat. . . .

Why the increase in women truckers? "I think it's because of women's lib. . . . Most of us got hired at a time when everybody got to thinking they had to hire women. . . . I really didn't care about it. But the more I watched it on the news and stuff, I realized it's because of women's lib that I got my job."[5]

For the years assessed in the Council of Economic Advisers' study, the mean-lowering effect of new, inexperienced female entrants into the labor market has overcome the mean-raising impact of women moving up the occupational ladder. Put another way, the spread in the experience differential between employed men and employed women increased during the twenty-year period. New female entrants to the labor market reduced the experience level of employed females at the same time that the labor supply curve for women shifted to the right. Moreover, even for the highly educated, the drop-out rate from employment for white females is very high, leading to lower earnings because of lesser experience than men of equal education. These factors produce a statistical distortion that overstates the actual discrimination against women in terms of earnings.

In spite of the breakthrough to higher-paying occupations that some women have made during this period, the demand curve for female labor did not shift to the right as much as the supply curve. This led to lower mean earnings for women. Figure 13.1 illustrates this situation.

[5] Judy Klemesrud, "New Breed of Woman Driver—Chugging Along in An Astro 95," *The New York Times*, November 10, 1975, p. 38.

Figure 13.1 The Demand and Supply for Female Labor During a Time of Change

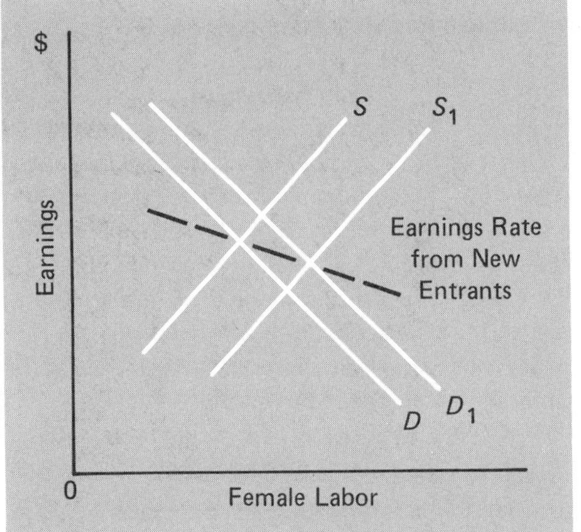

Occupational segregation

To the extent that the lag in mean earnings of women has been brought about by their accelerated entry into the labor market, the earnings gap will be closed over time as new entrants gain job experience. If the initial acceptance of women in higher-paying occupations promotes further breakaway from lower-paying jobs, such as waitresses, nurses, and laundry workers, an additional upward pressure will be exerted upon female earnings.

Occupational segregation, long a cause of lower female earnings, depresses the wages of blacks, Chicanos, and Native Americans even more. Much occupational segregation is the result of discrimination cumulated at the point of hiring, but actually brought about by a complex of prior events: less education, early entry into the labor market, unequal regional job opportunities, and indifferent job motivation. As a result, breaking down occupational segregation involves more than changing the attitudes of employers; it requires greater equality in education and training, improved mobility among poorer workers, and in some cases a generous transfusion of the work ethic. These are major undertakings.

Raising the productivity of minority groups to increase their share of the national income is not only difficult, it is tortuously slow and uneven in effect. For these reasons, it cannot replace the present approaches to poverty and income redistribution except as a long-term goal. Public assistance programs are not likely to wither away even with increased emphasis on equal treatment for minorities, and welfare reform will continue to attract attention and generate controversy.

Welfare—pleasing all of the people none of the time

Welfare has been indicted for encouraging family dissolution, promoting illegitimacy, degrading and alienating recipients, papering over the sins of a society that generates poverty, shielding the dissolute and lazy from their just deserts, failing to support life by providing too little assistance, and fostering sloth by providing too much. Conservatives, liberals, and radicals unite in attacking the welfare system but are divided over its specific faults.

Much of the controversy about welfare systems and welfare recipients rests on resolvable ethical and philosophical differences, and some of it on persistent, if unconscious, racial and ethnic prejudice. Welfare recipients are disproportionately black, Chicano, and Puerto Rican. Adult recipients are largely deserted mothers and mothers of illegitimate children—and illegitimate children and their mothers continue to provoke antipathy.[6]

Welfare in the United States: genesis and growth

The list of federal, state, and local programs to assist the needy is very long and complex.

Before the Great Depression of the 1930s, the needy poor who could not turn to friends or relatives for help had to rely upon the charity of churches or limited local public assistance. The American Way was self-reliance and employment for those willing to work. The Great Depression brought traumatic disenchantment to many—job opportunities were few and self-reliance was no answer to hunger. The assistance offered by church groups and local governments quickly ran out and states provided little additional help. Only the federal government had command of the financial resources necessary to cope with the massive unemployment of 25 percent of the labor force. But the federal government was a sleeping giant; it took time for it to be roused to the task of providing programs of temporary relief and longer-run protection against insecurity.

Since the passage of the federal Social Security Act in 1935, additional income supplements and antipoverty programs have been added at all levels of government, but the 1935 act is still the foundation of our system of social security. Best known for its provisions for old-age retirement and unemployment compensation, the Social Security Act also involved the federal government in public welfare through the program, Aid to Families

[6] Henry J. Aaron, *Why is Welfare So Hard to Reform?* (Washington, D.C.: The Brookings Institution, 1973,) p. 1. © 1973 by the Brookings Institution.

with Dependent Children (AFDC). Old-age pensions and unemployment compensation benefits are based on prior contributions by the recipient, supplemented recently from general revenues, whereas AFDC payments are purely income transfers.[7]

Aid to Families with Dependent Children

When a family is described as being "on welfare," the chances are that it is receiving AFDC payments. AFDC is a mutual undertaking of federal, state, and local governments, and eligibility and other program features vary from state to state. In New York and New Jersey, for example, welfare benefits are over six times as high as those of the lowest-paying state. Eligibility standards also differ as to how "property-poor" a family must be to qualify for welfare. In 1976, for example, California permitted a welfare recipient to retain $600 cash and to own a home valued as high as $5,000, while Illinois limited the welfare client's total assets of cash and property to one month's living expenses.

AFDC benefits are not available to all poor, but are limited mainly to families headed by a single female parent, that is, families with underage children who have no live-in male parent. (An exception is the AFDC supplementary program for families with an unemployed male parent, but this recent change is a minor part of the overall program.) By limiting welfare to female-headed families, the program ignores an important segment of the poor, those families with both parents and those with a single male parent. Moreover, it is sometimes suggested that limiting welfare eligibility to female-headed families leads to family disorganization by encouraging the male parent to separate in order to qualify the family for AFDC benefits. Originally, the idea of limiting welfare to female-headed families was based on the presumption of greater need in families with no employable male and the fear of encouraging idleness if welfare benefits were extended to families with an able-bodied male parent.

Welfare and the work disincentive

Because initially it was assumed that the welfare mother would remain at home, caring for her children rather than working, the employment disincentive effect of deducting employment earnings from benefits was not a matter of concern. Later, however, as attitudes changed and as

[7] In addition to the contributory old-age pension program, the Old Age and Survivors Insurance (OASI), which pays benefits during retirement that are determined in large part by the wage received before retirement—the higher the wage, the higher the pension—the Social Security Act also established Old Age Assistance, a program for those whose preretirement income is insufficient to provide adequate retirement benefits under OASI. The OASI program is not solely contributory, however, since inflation has prompted Congress to adjust OASI payments for cost-of-living changes from general revenues.

coverage of the AFDC program increased, as shown in Table 13.7, a frequent criticism of the welfare program has been that it discourages those receiving welfare from seeking employment. When welfare benefits are reduced dollar for dollar by earnings, there is little economic motivation to get off welfare until earnings rise well above AFDC benefits.

Later the employment disincentive effect was modified by an amendment to the Social Security Act in 1967, which cut back welfare benefits on a fractional basis, rather than dollar for dollar. Welfare recipients were encouraged to seek employment through provisions for work training and child care.

The administration of the AFDC program is primarily the responsibility of state and local governments, and the prevailing practice is to require a means test for welfare eligibility—proof that the family is in need—plus considerable supervision of welfare-family affairs by a social or welfare worker. The supervision is sometimes resented by the welfare recipient, many of whom consider it demeaning, and criticized by others who believe that welfare families can learn to manage their affairs best by making their

Table 13.7: AFDC benefits and families, 1950–75

		AFDC families[a]		AFDC cash payments		
					Monthly average per recipient[b]	
Year	AFDC recipients (thousands)	Number (thousands)	Percent of all female-headed families with children	Annual total (millions of current dollars)	Current dollars	December 1974 dollars[c]
1950	2,233	651	51.3	547	21	44
1955	2,192	602	32.2	612	24	46
1960	3,073	803	38.3	994	28	49
1965	4,396	996	40.2	1,644	33	54
1970	9,659	2,394	81.8	4,857	50	65
1971	10,653	2,783	82.7	6,230	52	66
1972	11,065	3,005	83.5	7,020	54	66
1973	10,815	3,068	80.8	7,292	57	64
1974	11,006	3,219	78.9	7,991	66	66
1975	11,300	3,395	77.1	—	71	68

[a] Excludes families with unemployed fathers. The number of AFDC families is for December of each year except 1975 which is for September. The percents are based on the number of female-headed families in March of each year except for 1955, which refers to April.

[b] Data are for December of each year except 1975 which are for September.

[c] Deflated by the consumer price index.

Sources: Department of Health, Education, and Welfare and Department of Commerce (Bureau of the Census). Reproduced from *Annual Report of the Council of Economic Advisers* (Washington, D.C.: Government Printing Office, 1976), p. 97.

own decisions. Finally, supervision requires supervisors—social workers—and adds to the cost of the program.

All of the foregoing factors indicate that almost everyone finds something undesirable about the present system of welfare, although not necessarily the same thing. There have been frequent suggestions for revisions of the system. Since its inception, the AFDC has been slightly modified and greatly expanded. More important, other programs have been added, as Table 13.8 shows, particularly in-kind transfers. The enlargement of the

Table 13.8: Federal welfare transfers, 1973

Program	Total expenditure (millions of dollars	Number of recipients (thousands)	Monthly benefits per recipient[a]	Percent of recipients in poverty[b]
Social Security:				
Old age and survivors insurance	42,170	25,205	$139	16
Disability insurance	5,162	3,162	132	24
Public assistance:				
Aid to families with dependent children	3,617	10,980	([c])	76
Blind	56	78	([c])	62
Disabled	766	1,164	([c])	73
Aged	1,051	1,917	([c])	60
Other cash programs:				
Veterans' compensation and benefits	1,401	7,203	74	([d])
Unemployment insurance benefits	4,404	5,409	68	([d])
In kind:				
Medicare	9,039	10,600	71	17
Medicaid	4,402	23,537	([c])	70
Food stamps	2,136	12,639	14	92
Public housing	1,408	3,319	([c])	([d])
Rent supplements	106	373	24	([d])
Homeownership assistance (section 235)	282	1,647	14	([d])
Rental housing assis; tance (section 236)	170	513	28	([d])

[a] The numbers represent individual recipients, not families.
[b] Poverty is defined relative to the money income and size of the recipient's family. Money income includes money transfer payments, but excludes income received in kind. All percentages are estimated.
[c] Programs with federal-state sharing of expenses.
[d] Not available.
Source: Office of Management and the Budget, quoted in *Annual Report of the Council of Economic Advisers* (Washington, D.C.: Government Printing Office, 1974), p. 168.

Food Stamp program is the most important recent addition to the welfare programs.

Food stamps: aid for the low-income food budget

The federal government's Food Stamp program has been around for a long time. It originated in 1964 primarily to provide a market for farm commodities that were in oversupply. The program started on a small scale to help hold farm prices up, but it has been converted to an antipoverty program of massive proportions, providing aid for almost 20 million Americans. At least 20 million more are eligible for Food Stamps who have not applied, and already there are more nonwelfare stamp users than welfare clients. In areas of low income, Food Stamp eligibility is very high; in Puerto Rico, for example, over half of the population is covered. Overall the program is second only to AFDC in federal income maintenance expenditures.

The calculation of food stamp benefits

The Food Stamp program is a restricted form of guaranteed income. Benefits are based on income, but payments are made in stamps that can be used only for food purchases. This frees income for other purchases, but at the same time obligates the stamp recipient to make larger food purchases than would be likely if the assistance were in the form of cash.

The program works as follows. In 1976, a family of four with an income of $6,480 was eligible for $24 a month in food-stamp assistance, obtained by paying $138 per month for $162 in stamps, while a family of four with no income received $162.00 per month in stamps free. By basing eligibility solely upon income, the Food Stamp program introduced a major change in public assistance in the United States, extending coverage to recipients ineligible by other standards, including students, above-poverty-level families, striking workers, and those disinclined to work.

Although families with assets of more than $1,500 are not eligible for food stamps ($3,000 if the family includes a 65-year-old member), assets *exclude* house and lot, personal belongings, household furnishings, and a car if it is used for work. Moreover, the upper limit of eligibility in 1976—$6,480 for a family of four—is raised substantially by liberal deductions for a host of expenditures such as medical fees, taxes, alimony, union dues, and tuition.

Food stamps—humanitarian innovation or rip-off?

The growth of the Food-Stamp program has brought the criticism that an expanding Food-Stamp clientele may generate pressure for ever-increasing benefits. Secretary of the Treasury William Simon labeled the program a "rip-off" of the American public, for example. To others, however, the program is a bold and desirable step in the drive to eliminate hunger in America, in spite of some questionable coverage. How the various income brackets have shared in the distribution of Food Stamps in recent years is shown in Table 13.9.

Whether the program represents a humanitarian innovation or a crass rip-off, however, it is well-established as a federal income transfer. It is not likely to be eliminated, but it will be modified. In turn, it has altered the government's approach to poverty in the United States, extending coverage of federal benefits well beyond the AFDC program. In doing so, Food

Table 13.9: Distribution of food stamps, 1974–75

Income class	Percent of total food stamp households		
	July 1974	March 1975	July 1975
Annual income[a]:			
Total food stamp households[c]	100.0	100.0	100.0
Less than $6,000	88.4	78.1	82.8
$6,000–$7,499	5.2	7.3	6.8
$7,500–$9,999	3.2	6.9	5.0
$10,000–$11,999	1.2	3.2	2.5
$12,000 and over	2.0	4.6	2.9
Monthly income:[b]			
Total food stamp households[c]	100.0	—	100.0
Less than $500	90.2	—	87.7
$500–$599	4.7	—	6.1
$600–$749	2.9	—	3.2
$750–$999	1.2	—	1.9
$1,000 and over	1.1	—	1.1

[a] Annual income is for 12 months ending in July 1974, March 1975, and July 1975. Households include single-person households. Annual income shown here may be understated compared to data derived from more detailed surveys of income.
[b] Monthly income data were not collected for March 1975.
[c] Detail may not add to totals because of rounding.
Sources: Department of Commerce (Bureau of the Census) and Department of Health, Education, and Welfare.
Reproduced from *Annual Report of the Council of Economic Advisers* (Washington, D.C.: Government Printing Office, 1976), p. 103.

Stamps have reduced pressures for welfare reform, but those who favor unrestricted cash grants for income maintenance still find the negative income tax preferable to the existing system.

The negative income tax

Negative income taxes reverse the usual direction of money collections by the government. Subsidies are paid to individuals on the basis of their income rather than taxes being collected from them. As generally conceived, the negative income tax has certain features in common with the food-stamp plan: It is based on income and does not employ a means test to determine eligibility; cash benefits are standardized throughout the country, rather than varying by state and locality as in the case of AFDC payments; and the recipient's expenditures are not supervised.

Over the years unsupervised cash welfare payments have gained advocates, but the alleged work disincentive of this approach still concerns many. Economists are fond of stating this issue as a tradeoff between income equality and economic efficiency.

Equality versus efficiency

As we mentioned earlier in this chapter, until recently AFDC payments were reduced dollar for dollar if the welfare recipient's earnings

---

Equality and efficiency—can we have both? Okun says "no"

[W]hile the provision of equal political and civil rights often imposes costs on society . . ., the attempt to enforce equality of income would entail a much larger sacrifice. In pursuing such a goal, society would forgo any opportunity to use material rewards as incentives to production. And that would lead to inefficiencies that would be harmful to the welfare of the majority. Any insistence on carving the pie into equal slices would shrink the size of the pie. That fact poses the tradeoff between economic equality and economic efficiency.[8]

---

[8] Arthur M. Okun, *Equality and Efficiency: The Big Tradeoff* (Washington, D.C.: The Brookings Institution, 1975), p. 48. © 1975 by the Brookings Institution.

increased. This is equivalent to a 100 percent tax on marginal earnings and, understandably, is not likely to encourage an additional work effort. The negative income tax, which drops the requirement of the single female-headed family as the basis for welfare eligibility, substitutes income as a test of eligibility, making the effect of benefits on work incentives a matter of greater concern. Most negative income tax proposals permit the welfare client to keep a large part of additional earnings—50 percent is the usual suggestion—in order to counteract the disincentive work effect.

Can work incentives be designed into a negative income tax plan? No conclusive answer can be given, but the New Jersey-Pennsylvania Graduated Work Incentive Experiment was a long and costly attempt to answer this question.

The New Jersey-Pennsylvania experiment

In 1967, the federal Office of Economic Opportunity undertook an experiment to determine the effect on work incentives of different levels of cash benefits and various discounts of earnings. Over 1,350 low-income families in New Jersey and Pennsylvania were monitored closely for a period of three years by intensive interviews every three months. The major findings of the experiment are published in the *Final Report of the Graduated Incentive Experiment in New Jersey and Pennsylvania.*[9]

Eight experimental groups of differing ethnic and racial composition were provided with unsupervised cash benefits over the three-year period. Varying discounts were applied to additional earnings. Two groups received a cash-benefit base of 50 percent of the poverty line[10] with a discount or "tax" for extra earnings of either 50 percent or 30 percent; three groups received 75 percent of the poverty line and discounts of 70, 50, or 30 percent; two groups received 100 percent of the poverty line and discounts of 70 or 50 percent; and one group received 125 percent of the poverty line and a 50 percent discount.

What did three years of data collecting and many more years of analysis show? The study showed primarily that there was very little disincentive effect from the negative income tax in *any* of the experimental groups. The most notable findings were the work reductions by white wives, which were attributed to the benefit payments, and the absence of any significant withdrawal from the labor force by blacks in the experiment. There were also small reductions in hours of work by white males

[9] Published by the Institute for Research on Poverty, University of Wisconsin, Madison, Wisconsin, 1973.

[10] It will be recalled from earlier discussion in this chapter that the *poverty line* is the official annual federal estimate of poverty.

and increased unemployment by Spanish-speaking males. Finally, there is tentative evidence that a discount of more than 50 percent on additional earnings had a disincentive effect on work. Overall, however, the most significant conclusion is that the different versions of the negative income tax employed in the experiment did not produce important disincentive effects.

How meaningful are these findings? This question will be argued for years, with many contending that the design of the experiment was faulty and others that the very nature of the intensive data-collecting interviews by researchers influenced the welfare families' behavior. Both criticisms are probably true, but the experiment nonetheless provides some support for the negative income tax proposal.

Summary

Economic inequality—the unequal distribution of income and wealth—has not been eliminated among either individuals or nations by the dramatic increase in output that has occurred over the past century in the industrial nations. Indeed, the disparity in income between nations has widened. The developed countries have added greatly to their stock of wealth and level of income, while the undeveloped and developing nations have made little progress, widening the gap between the haves and the have-nots. And within the industrial nations, underprivileged segments of the population have lived a squalid life apart from the rest of affluent society.

In the United States, the serious national concern over inequality first occurred during the Great Depression of the 1930s. Income inequality, which is built into the market economy, was cruelly exacerbated by the mass unemployment of the Great Depression. Insecurity extended beyond the poor and dispossessed and threatened the way of life of the vast middle class. Out of the suffering and distress of the 1930s came national legislation designed to protect against insecurity and to decrease inequality.

The social security legislation passed during the administration of Franklin D. Roosevelt involved the federal government for the first time in a systematic program of welfare, Aid to Families with Dependent Children. This program, later supplemented by many cash and in-kind forms of public assistance, has remained the foundation program of federal assistance to the needy. In addition to the AFDC, the 1936 social security legislation included unemployment compensation, old age pensions, and old age assistance.

A notable recent addition to federal assistance programs is the Food Stamp Plan, an antipoverty cash assistance program of broad coverage. Eligibility for food stamps is based on income, with larger stamp grants for those with lower income. There is no supervision of the expenditure of food stamps as in the case of AFDC payments, although the food stamps can be used only for grocery store purchases.

Most of the poor in the United States are found among the following: old or quite young, farm workers, poorly educated, and members of a minority group, such as blacks or Native Americans. The absence of a male parent in the family is also typical of families on public welfare, partly because of welfare eligibility requirements. Discrimination is an important contributing factor in poverty and income inequality, especially in its impact upon education and training, nutritional adequacy, and the work ethic.

Critics of the present welfare approach in the United States sometimes advocate replacement of the AFDC program with a negative income tax. The NIT would provide an unsupervised cash income supplement on the basis of need. The role of the welfare worker would be eliminated or drastically reduced under NIT and the special place of children, other than as a member of the family unit, would be deemphasized. The New Jersey-Pennsylvania experiment of the federal Office of Economic Opportunity was undertaken to determine the reaction of welfare recipients to unsupervised cash income supplements such as would occur with a NIT plan, but the conclusions of the study are ambiguous.

Key terms and concepts

Poverty line an officially designated level of income which is determined by multiplying the cost of an adequate diet by three on the presumption that food expenditures constitute one-third of all necessary expenditures.

In-kind transfers noncash public assistance, such as public housing, food stamps, and medicaid.

Occupational segregation the limitation of employment opportunities for minorities to lower-paying occupations.

Old Age and Survivors Insurance (OASI) the contributory retirement plan instituted by the federal Social Security Act of 1935.

Aid to Families with Dependent Children (AFDC) the basic welfare program in the United States, instituted by the federal Social Security Act of 1935. The program involves the participation of federal, state, and local governments.

Food Stamp program an income supplement in the form of food stamps for those in lower-income brackets. The food stamps are purchased at a discount that varies inversely with the recipient's income and may be redeemed at face value by the purchase of food.

Negative income tax the payment of unsupervised cash benefits by the government to lower-income individuals.

Discussion and review questions

1. If the output of the American economy has more than doubled since the 1930s, why is there any need for government welfare programs?

2. What was Vilfredo Pareto's contention concerning government intervention to prevent poverty? Do you think Pareto was right?

3. Why is poverty so hard to eliminate? Is it society's responsibility to decrease inequality of income and wealth? Are there costs—other than the obvious money outlays—in doing so?

4. By quintiles, the percentage income distribution before taxes over the last twenty-five years in the United States has been remarkably steady. Why? Does this mean that the standard of living has not changed for the lowest quintile during this period?

5. What is poverty? Why is it said to be a "moving target?" What is the *poverty line* and how is it defined?

6. The basic federal involvement in welfare assistance is the Aid to Families with Dependent Children. When did AFDC originate and why did it take the form that it did? What criticisms are made of the present AFDC approach?

7. What is the difference between in-kind public assistance and money transfers? Why do some favor one kind and some the other?

8. What effects do in-kind transfers have on the income of the lowest quintiles in the United States? Have in-kind transfers increased or decreased in recent years?

9. What effects do taxes have on income distribution?

10. Who are the poor? How can their living standard be improved?

11. There is a high correlation between educational achievement and earnings. Does this mean that education is the cause of higher earnings?

12. The Food Stamp Program is an important recent modification of public assistance in the United States. How does it differ from past programs and what are its implications for the future?

13. It is sometimes said that poverty programs pose a tradeoff between equity and efficiency. Do you think this is true? If so, how important do you think this tradeoff is for society?

14. The negative income tax represents a radically different approach to poverty from that of programs such as AFDC. What is the main difference? Do you consider the negative income tax superior or inferior to the present approaches? Why?

V The public sector and externalities

14 Government: its micro impact

*It is not till it is discovered that high individual incomes will not purchase the mass of mankind immunity from cholera, typhus, and ignorance, still less secure them the positive advantages of educational opportunity and economic security, that slowly and reluctantly, amid prophesies of moral degeneration and economic disaster, society begins to make collective provision for needs which no ordinary individual, even if he works overtime all his life, can provide himself.**

The growth of government in the United States has accelerated dramatically over the past half century. The same trend can be seen in other developed nations where more government takes the form of greater provision for public services and larger output of public goods. This is a natural course of development. As a nation moves from a predominantly agricultural economy to industrialization, changes in the structure of society stimulate an expansion of government. At times, the rate of expansion of government functions may slow, but few expect a reversal of the trend.

The expanding role of government

If we look far enough back in history, government as we know it was virtually nonexistent. The Colonial farmer and merchant turned to government for few needs and complained loudly over the taxes that supported the crucial public functions: a system of justice and limited provisions for law enforcement, a rudimentary network of roads and mail delivery for communication, and—later—arrangements for defense against foreign aggression. These are familiar functions that are still basic to organized society, but present-day expenditures in all of these areas have taken a quantum jump, and new government undertakings have been added. Government expansion has brought growth in the public sector—

* R. H. Tawney, *Equality* (London: Allen & Unwin, Ltd. 1964, 4th ed.), p. 126.

the segment of the economy created largely by decisions of legislative bodies and government agencies rather than through the direction of consumers and producers in the market place.

The public sector

One of the minor deceptions of economists is the overly sharp distinction they draw between economic activity in the public and private sectors of the economy. Actually, private and public economic activity do not occupy separate compartments, but are intermingled. The preoccupation with the nature of the public sector in the early part of this chapter should not be interpreted to mean that business and government decisions are totally unrelated. We shall illustrate some of the interactions between government and business later in the chapter.

The public sector in the United States cuts a broad swath: it ranges from international foreign aid to local school lunches; it includes the bizarre, the indispensable, and the mundane—the federal government's Council of Tea Tasters, the establishment of a standard monetary unit, and the regulation of auto parking. Some functions, such as the defense of the nation, have the broadest possible application, while others, such as flood control and reclamation projects, are primarily of regional or local impact. Growing population and its increasing concentration in metropolitan areas have greatly stimulated such familiar local functions as police and fire protection, while new undertakings have been required of federal and state governments because of economic change. For example, the rise of the industrial system brought the need to check monopoly, provide a system of compensation for injured factory workers, control public utility rates and services, and, later, to devise programs to decrease economic insecurity and income inequality.

Crisis and government expansion

A war or major depression enhances the role of government, greatly expanding some functions and cutting back on a few at the same time that it changes the federal-state-local relationship. During national emergencies the federal government expands and adds new functions. After crises pass, a decline in government activity usually takes place, but seldom does government shrink to the pre-crisis level. Most crises bring about changes that perpetuate the need for continued government functions. Examples are the continued involvement by the United States in foreign affairs after World War II and the expansion of the social security system instituted during the Great Depression.

Inherent forces for expansion

The crisis growth of government creates a bureaucracy to administer the new functions and a clientele that benefits from them. Bureaucracy and clientele work for the continuation of the new functions after the emergency is over. The federal farm programs that were initiated during the 1930s, for example, were retained well beyond the crisis partly because the US Department of Agriculture operated with entrepreneurial skill in gaining Congressional support for the rentention of these programs. At the same time, politically influential farm groups kept steady pressure on Congress to perpetuate and enlarge such functions.

During a crisis, the public's exposure to government regulation creates a climate of acceptance. Government spending expanded to over 56 percent of the national income in 1944 because of World War II—well over twice the prewar level. As a result the postwar 30-percent range of government expenditures seemed less objectionable than it otherwise would have. Table 14.1 shows government expenditures as a percentage of national income and traces the growth of the public sector over two periods of crisis, the depression of the 1930s and World War II.

As income rises, government expands

Up to a certain level of income, the pressure to meet the basic necessities of life—food, shelter, and clothing—does not leave much surplus for amenities. This is true for both the nation and the family. As output and income increase, however, resources can be spared for less essential uses. For the family, affluence permits increased investment in *human capital,*[1] vacations and leisure pursuits, and the indulgence in decorative outlays for high-fashion clothing and cosmetic surgery, for example. For nations, income increases promote investment in *social overhead capital,*[2] the expansion of recreational facilities, such as national parks and public playgrounds, and the staging of world expositions and international games.

A developing nation must devote a larger share of its income to the necessities of life than a high-growth industrial nation, leaving less for expansion of the roundabout method of production. As a nation's output increases, however, gradually a larger amount and eventually a larger share of income becomes available for use by the public sector. In the

[1] *Human capital* consists of productivity-enhancing assets such as skills acquired through education and training and physical well-being maintained by medical care and adequate diet.

[2] *Social overhead capital* consists of such facilities as public roads and water systems that are generally available to all and are prerequisites for further economic development.

United States during the early 1970s, for example, economic growth increased federal tax revenues by as much as $15 billion annually in some years without any change in the structure of tax rates. This automatic increase in revenue is called the *fiscal dividend*. If a tax rate is proportional, an increase in income from economic growth raises the fiscal dividend by a roughly equal percentage; but if the tax structure is progressive, an increase in income from growth diverts a larger share of income to the public sector. To keep the public sector from growing more rapidly than the private sector, periodic downward adjustment in progressive taxes or reduced taxpayer coverage must occur. According to Table 14.1, the public

Table 14.1: Government spending as percentage of national income

	Total Spending[a]	Defense Spending[b]	Domestic Spending[c]
1929	11.9	0.8	11.1
1933	26.6	1.5	25.1
1939	24.2	1.6	22.6
1944	56.4	47.9	8.5
1949	27.2	6.1	21.1
1953	33.2	16.0	17.2
1959	32.8	11.5	21.2
1960	32.8	10.8	22.0
1961	34.9	11.2	23.7
1962	34.9	11.3	23.7
1963	34.6	10.5	24.1
1964	33.9	9.7	24.2
1965	33.1	8.9	24.2
1966	34.2	9.8	24.4
1967	37.2	11.1	26.1
1968	38.0	11.0	27.0
1969	37.6	10.2	27.3
1970	37.8	9.3	28.5
1971	37.5	8.3	29.1
1972	39.1	7.9	31.2
1973	38.0	6.9	31.1
1974	40.1	6.8	33.3
1975	43.4	6.9	36.5

[a] Expenditures of federal, state, and local government, as defined in national income accounts.
[b] Purchases of goods and services for national defense, as defined in national income accounts.
[c] Total spending minus defense spending.
Source: *Annual Report of the Council of Economic Advisers* (Washingon, D.C.: Government Printing Office, 1976), pp. 171, 183, 249.

sector, as measured by all government spending, has increased significantly over the past half century, although it has remained essentially stable for the last decade.

A *progressive* tax rate as applied to income takes a higher percentage in tax as income rises, for example, 10 percent from an income of $10,000, 12 percent from an income of $15,000, and 15 percent from an income of $20,000. If a tax system is progressive overall, a rise in per capita income will thus increase the percentage of national income going to the public sector. A tax system that is *proportional* to income, for instance, a 10 percent tax rate on earnings of $10,000, $15,000, and so on, will increase revenue and the size of the public sector, but at the same growth rate as that of the private sector. With progressive taxation, the public sector grows faster than the private sector. This is not the only financial basis for expansion of the public sector. More frequently than not taxes do not cover all government expenditures. Deficit financing—the sale of government bonds—is relied on to fund government operations, at times raising government spending well above tax revenues.

Government expenditures: exhaustive or transfers?

Earlier we identified government transfer programs in discussing income inequality and discrimination. Various welfare programs were

Expand the public sector? Milton Friedman says, "No!"

The battle over a ceiling on federal spending has spotlighted the major economic problem facing this country in the coming decade: can we halt the growth of Leviathan—to use Hobbes's expressive term of government? Or will Leviathan crush us? . . .

Until 1930, citizens of the U.S. viewed the federal government primarily as a keeper of the peace and an umpire. Today, we view it as responsible for treating every social and personal ill, as the source from which all blessings flow. . . .

There is hardly one among us who believes that he is getting his money's worth for the nearly half of his income that government—federal, state, and local—spends for him. Yet so long as we simply blame waste and bureaucracy, but continue to believe in the omnipotence and beneficience of government, the trend toward ever bigger government will continue.[3]

[3] Milton Friedman, "Can We Halt Leviathan?", *There's No Such Thing As A Free Lunch* (LaSalle, Ill.: Open Court Publishing Co., 1975), pp. 99–101.

classified as cash transfers or transfers in kind. The in-kind transfer provides goods or services to the poor in the form of housing, medical treatment, and job training. In-kind transfers use resources, preventing them from being employed elsewhere in the economy, and this is the reason they are designated *exhaustive* expenditures. Cash transfers do not earmark resources for specific uses, but shift purchasing power from some members of society to others. Cash transfers cover a wide and important area of government expenditures: welfare payments, interest on the public debt, veteran's benefits, old-age assistance, and many direct subsidies such as federal grants to feeder airlines and to Amtrak, and the low-interest student loan program. Exhaustive expenditures cover an equally wide range, including money spent for legal personnel to prosecute monopolies, military systems to defend the nation, highways to improve transportation, waste treatment plants to protect the nation's streams, and fish hatcheries to enhance the angler's prospects in those streams. Both lists could be expanded manyfold.

It is somewhat arbitrary to describe the government's use of resources as exhaustive. Whether income transfers are in cash or kind, resources are used. When a welfare client spends a welfare check on food, clothing, and other goods and services, these items represent resources that have been used up in production in the same way that resources are used up when the government makes an in-kind transfer in the form of a public housing development. The difference is that when the government uses resources, rather than individuals, decisions are political, involving Congress and the Administration, rather than individuals in the marketplace.

The magnitude of government resource use

In the United States, the US Department of Commerce collects statistics on public and private expenditures in computing gross national product and other measures of economic activity. In Table 14.2, government expenditures are classified as either purchases of goods and services or transfers, conforming to the exhaustive versus cash transfer classification defined above. Figure 14.1 presents similar information in the form of a chart.

Exhaustive and transfer expenditures by the federal government have been remarkably evenly divided in the past, but recently transfers have outdistanced exhaustive expenditures, as shown in Table 14.2. This is largely the result of the decrease in defense expenditures, the major federal exhaustive outlay, and the increase in welfare payments, the largest transfer.

The economic impact on the private economy of growth in the public

Table 14.2: Exhaustive and transfer expenditures of governments in 1974

	Federal	State and Local	Total
Expenditures	300.1	201.3	457.5
Exhaustive (purchases of goods and services)	111.7	189.4	301.1
Government employees	54.7	106.4	161.1
Purchases from business	57.0	83.0	140.0
Transfer payments	158.4	20.1	—
To person	114.5	20.1	134.6
To state and local governments	43.9	—	—
Other (interest on debt; subsidies; current surplus of government enterprises [–]; etc.)	30.0	−8.2	21.8
Receipts	288.4	209.4	—
Taxes and other own sources	288.4	165.5	453.9
Transfers from federal government	—	43.9	—
Surplus (+) or deficit (–)	−11.7	8.1	−3.6

Source: Department of Commerce, *Survey of Current Business*, January 1976, (Vol. 56, No. 1), Tables 3.2, and 3.4, pp. 52–57, 58–63.

Figure 14.1 Growth in the Public Sector as Measured by Government Expenditures

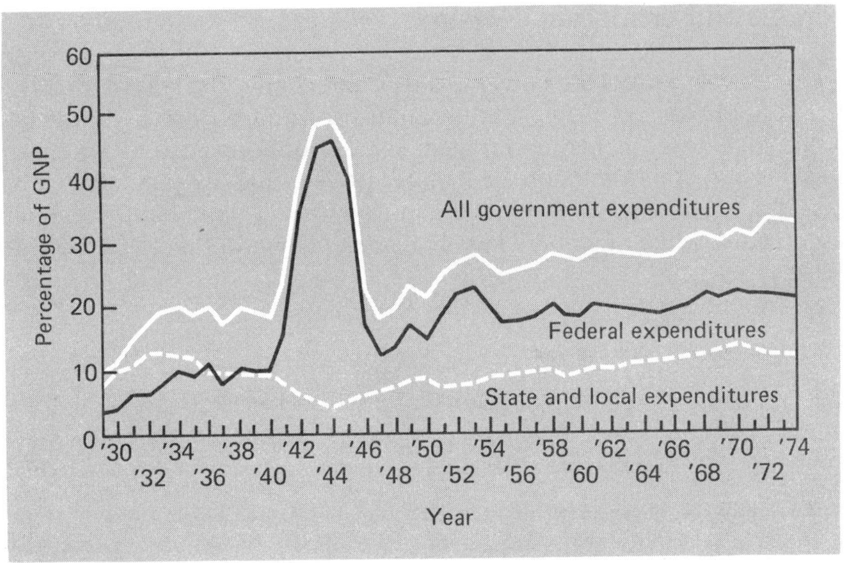

Expand the public sector? Galbraith says, "Yes!"

The family which takes its mauve and cerise, air-conditioned, power-steered, and power-braked automobile out for a tour passes through cities that are badly paved, made hideous by litter, blighted buildings, billboards, and posts for wires that should long since have been put underground. They pass on into a countryside that has been rendered largely invisible by commercial art. . . . They picnic on exquisitely packaged food from a portable icebox by a polluted stream and go on to spend the night at a park which is a menace to public health and morals. Just before dozing off on an air mattress, beneath a nylon tent, amid the stench of decaying refuse, they may reflect vaguely on the curious unevenness of their blessings.[4]

sector shows up mainly in the effects of government taxation and spending on resource allocation and income distribution. In Chapter 13, a case study of government's largest transfer program, we concentrated mainly on the program of inequality and did not look to the source of the transfers to see how different kinds of taxes might affect the operation of the market economy. In this chapter we examine the micro impact of taxes upon the operation of the firm.

Taxation and economic decisions

The power to tax is the power to shape and control the behavior of the taxed individuals and firms. Within limits, consumer purchases can be directed to untaxed items or curtailed; some producers may be shorn of markets while others may prosper under preferential tax treatment. Tax effects differ. Some taxes have a reorganizing impact upon both individuals and firms, while others are largely neutral. How do these effects take place?

The personal income tax

The most important single source of tax revenue for the federal government is the personal income tax, which is also called the individual income tax. Personal income taxes are also levied by many states and some

[4] J. K. Galbraith, *The Affluent Society* (Boston: Houghton Mifflin Co., 1958), p. 253.

localities, but the federal tax is progressive, while most state and local taxes are proportional. The personal income tax should not be confused with the corporation income tax, which is another source of revenue employed by the federal government and numerous states.

The federal personal income-tax rate is levied upon the individual's total annual income—wages, interest, rent, royalties, and the like—for the calendar year after deductions are made for costs of earning income, contributions to nonprofit organizations, certain other taxes and interest payments, hardship medical expenses, and an exemption from taxation of $850 (in 1977) for each taxpayer and dependent. For most taxpayers who use the short form, the computation of the tax liability is less complicated than the above account suggests.

It is sometimes said that a taxpayer can avoid the income tax to some extent by earning less, thereby paying a lower tax rate.[5] Actually, this option is available in only a limited degree to most employed persons. Persons who are self-employed, such as doctors and lawyers, may be able to vary their annual earnings in response to changes in their marginal tax rate. Workers whose services are in heavy demand, or those with the opportunity for overtime work also may do so, but the majority of employed persons are locked into the traditional annual work period.

For almost all taxpayers, the personal income tax is virtually impossible to avoid. Middle- and upper-income taxpayers can invest so they are eligible for a lower capital gains tax in place of the income tax, and of course taxes may be evaded illegally, but there is very little opportunity to avoid the income tax or pass it on to someone else to pay. In technical terms, the *incidence* of the tax remains upon the individual taxed; it is not shifted elsewhere in the economic system.

Tax shifting and incidence

Arturo Toscanini, the famous conductor who was persuaded to leave the La Scala Opera orchestra in Italy to head the NBC Symphony in the United States, is alleged to have insisted on a contract with the National Broadcasting Company that guaranteed a specific after-tax income. Was

[5] Some contend that a taxpayer can be worse off under the federal income tax if his or her earnings increase and are taxed on the basis of a higher income bracket. This is incorrect. In moving to a higher income tax bracket, the rate of the higher bracket applies only to the income in that bracket, *not* to all the taxpayer's income. For example, if a taxpayer's income increases from $20,000 to $21,000, he or she pays a tax of $5,230 on the $20,000, plus 38 percent on the $1,000 increment. Although the marginal rate is 38 percent on the $1,000 increment, the average rate for the total tax is much lower, approximately 26 percent on the first $20,000.

this unique contract an exception to the generalization that the personal income tax cannot be shifted? At first glance the answer appears to be "yes," since NBC had to absorb any tax increase to keep Toscanini's salary unchanged. But in fact the willingness of NBC to accept the risk of paying a higher salary may simply indicate that Toscanini did not bargain to his full potential.

Unlike Toscanini, most of us cannot use salary bargaining in an attempt to shift income taxes—quite aside from whether it actually can be done. Income tax liability is figured on annual earnings and levied *after* the completion of the taxable year. Even if the taxpayer is able to decrease tax liability by reducing earnings, it does not follow that the tax has been shifted to someone else. The excise tax, by contrast, is likely to show up in the price the consumer pays, when levied upon the producer.

The shifting of the excise tax

An excise tax is a levy imposed on the value or volume of a good or service, such as a tax of four cents per gallon of gasoline at the filling station, a levy of 10 percent on the wholesale cost of photographic equipment, or eight cents per package of twenty cigarettes imposed on the manufacturer.

A per-unit excise varies with output and is added to the variable cost of the firm: As output is increased, the firm pays more taxes; as output is decreased, it pays less. Since marginal cost is derived from average variable cost, the per-unit excise tax raises marginal cost, shifting it upward. The excise tax also raises average total cost, as shown in Figure 14.2, because average variable cost is an ingredient of ATC (ATC = AVC + AFC).

If a per-unit excise is levied uniformly upon the producers in a competitive industry, the ultimate effect is to reduce supply and raise price. Before the supply curve is shifted, which raises price from OA to OB in Figure 14.3, a reduction in the output of the industry must take place, shown as a decrease from 50,000 units of output before the tax to 40,000 units after the tax. This long-run change follows the industry's adjustment to the increased costs from the excise tax, bringing about a smaller number of firms in the industry or a reduction in the capacity of the firms that remain, or both.

Unlike the per-unit excise, some kinds of taxes raise the firm's average fixed cost rather than its variable and marginal costs. Taxes that are fixed costs for the firm are unrelated to output. These include the general property tax, which is based on a property valuation that may remain unchanged for a number of years, and various license fees and enfranchise

Figure 14.2 Per-Unit Excise Levied on the Firm

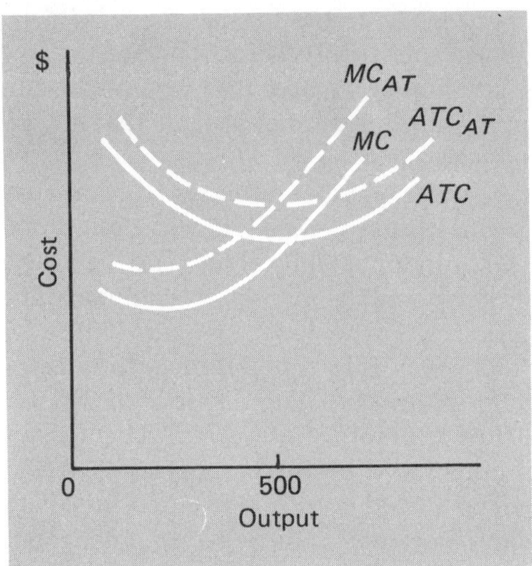

charges. These taxes are sometimes called *flat taxes* or *lump-sum taxes*, and their effect is different from taxes that vary with output.

The flat tax on monopoly

For the firm, taxes are costs. Whether they are paid by the firm or shifted elsewhere depends on the way in which they are levied and the nature of the tax. Excise taxes invite shifting because they are added to the firm's marginal cost. A flat tax on monopoly resists shifting because the tax

Figure 14.3 Effect of a Per-Unit Excise Tax on Competitive Industry

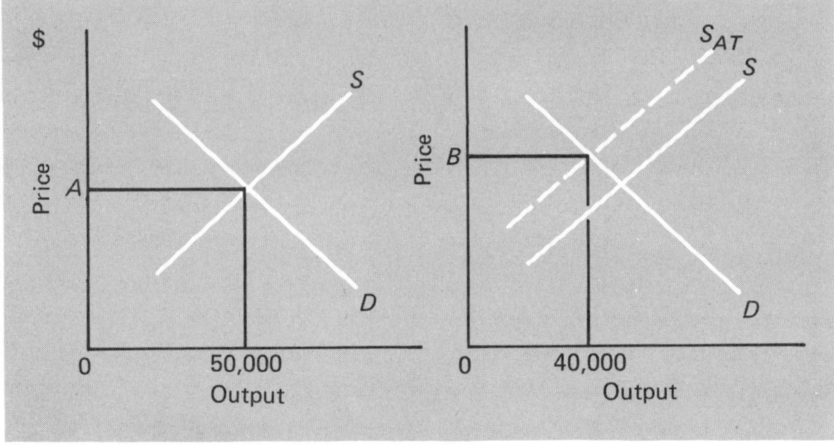

does not change output and the firm's profit provides a resting place for the tax. A flat tax upon a monopoly is illustrated by the case in which a municipality charges a bus company a franchise tax to operate the only transportation system within the city limits. Assume that the franchise tax is $10,000, large enough to encourage shifting but not so large that it wipes out the bus company's monopoly gain.

Unlike an excise, a flat tax is the same whether output is large or small. The tax is a fixed cost to the firm and raises average total cost, but it does not affect marginal cost. Curve ATC_{at} in Figure 14.4 shows the increase in average total cost from the franchise tax and the monopoly's adjustment to the tax.

In the absence of a tax, the monopoly is in equilibrium with marginal cost equal to marginal revenue at an output of OE and a price of OB. This price-output relationship yields the maximum profit of ABCD consistent with the demand and cost conditions faced by the monopoly. When the franchise tax is levied on the firm as a fixed sum, represented by AFGD, average total cost is raised but marginal cost remains unchanged. Maximum profit is still obtained at the point at which price is OB and output is OE after the tax is imposed. Any other price-output combination would reduce monopoly profit without decreasing the firm's tax obligation. Since the monopoly cannot shift the tax by decreasing output and raising price, it absorbs the tax and maintains the established optimum price-output combination.

What conclusion can we draw from these brief examples? Mainly that tax effects differ; indeed, beyond the simple cases considered here there

Figure 14.4 Flat Tax on Monopoly

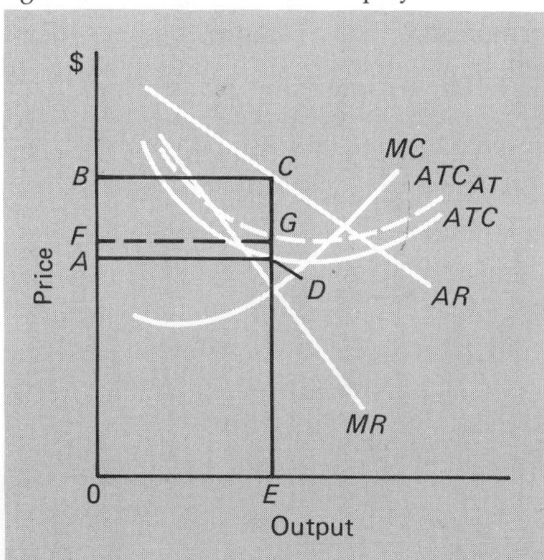

are many different levies, including taxes whose effects are very difficult to analyze. Taxes do more than raise revenue. The way in which they are computed and assessed may attract or repel some firms and discriminate against or favor some industries. Accelerated depreciation and the percentage depletion allowance, which grant preferential tax treatment, have recently received increasing attention because of the energy crisis and concern over the environment.

Accelerated depreciation

In financing capital investments, the business firm relates the payment period to the expected life of the asset. Machinery, buildings, and equipment are capital investments that are used for years, but each year's use generally decreases their remaining economic life. The firm normally pays for its capital by the time it wears out and has to be replaced, although practices vary. The annual depreciation charge may be determined in a number of different ways, the simplest being the straight-line method, in which capital that has a life expectancy of 20 years is charged off at a rate of one-twentieth each year. Two other depreciation practices are sometimes employed: the declining-balance method and the sum-of-the-year's-digits method, which both involve computational mysteries reserved mainly for accountants and their apprentices. Both methods are ways of accelerating depreciation. This acceleration is represented graphically by repayment pattern A in Figure 14.5 in contrast with the straight-line approach of pattern S.

Figure 14.5 Accelerated and Straight-line Depreciation

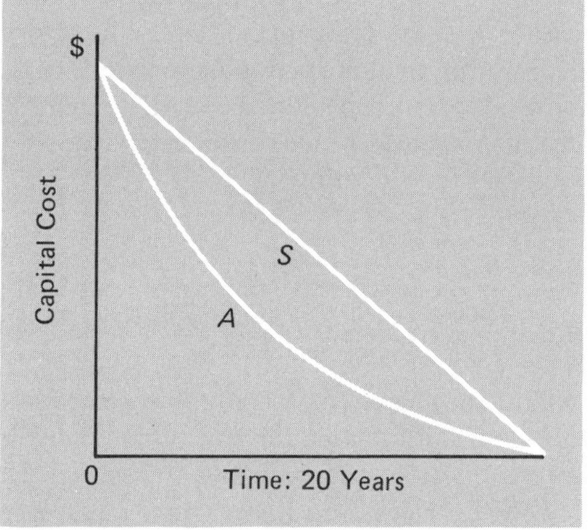

Accelerated depreciation is permitted by tax adminstrations only in special cases when Congress or state legislatures wish to stimulate a depressed segment of the economy, or encourage firms to make socially desirable investments, for pollution abatement equipment to protect the environment, for example. For its own accounting, the firm can employ any depreciation approach it wishes, but in computing the federal corporate income tax and some state taxes, prescribed depreciation practices must be followed. Sometimes the firm keeps two sets of books: one for the stockholders showing lower capital cost and higher earnings, possibly based on straight-line depreciation, and one for the government showing higher capital costs and lower earnings—and therefore lower taxes—based on accelerated depreciation. There is nothing questionable in this accounting duality; it is widely used and accepted.

Accelerated depreciation permits the firm to write off a significantly larger portion of its capital cost in the early years of an asset's life. This is depicted in Figure 14.5 by Curve A, although actual repayment patterns differ from the symmetry of the illustration. By concentrating the write-off of the equipment in the early years, the firm decreases its tax liability during this period: Capital repayment costs are high, earnings are therefore less and taxes lower than otherwise would be the case. In later years, as the end of the asset's life draw near, repayment costs go down and earnings go up, leading to higher taxes. The firm doesn't gain much in the way of tax relief from accelerated depreciation, although the expanding firm may find it advantageous to postpone tax payments until later when it is larger. But accelerated depreciation does more than let the firm postpone taxes.

The firm gains a reduced interest charge because its capital investment is paid off in a shorter time. The longer bonds are outstanding or borrowed money is unpaid, the greater the amount of interest charged. By permitting the firm to pay off creditors earlier and the tax collector later, the cost of capital is reduced. Accelerated depreciation alone is not likely to induce the firm to undertake a capital investment, but it provides encouragement by decreasing capital cost. The *depletion allowance,* by contrast, is a positive encouragement to the firm to expand its operations.

The depletion allowance

The percentage depletion allowance also works through the corporate income tax. Congress, in what some call its wisdom and others consider folly, has given preferential tax treatment to the extractive industries. The most noteworthy case is that of the petroleum industry, now fallen from grace and shorn of its high allowance, but the special treatment remains for firms mining asbestos, coal, lignite, peat, scoria, shale, oyster shells, and other extractive materials. The depletion allowance permits these firms to discount their gross income by a prescribed percentage, which was at one time as high as 27.5 percent for petroleum to a low of 5 percent for oyster shells, gravel, and brick clay. In computing the corporate income tax, the extractive firm is permitted to deduct its depletion allowance from its gross income up to 50 percent of its annual taxable income. (*Gross income* equals product price times quantity sold; *taxable income* is gross income minus costs of production.)

The depletion allowancé is justified by its advocates on the ground that the capital asset of the extractive industries, the deposits of oil, shale, oyster shells, and the rest, are used up in the normal course of operations. Most critics point out, however, that economically there is little difference between wearing out equipment, as General Motors does, and pumping an oil well dry, as Exxon does. Both the equipment and the oil deposit represent an income-producing investment, but Exxon in effect is permitted two depreciation deductions while General Motors is allowed one.

The effect of the depletion allowance, aside from the question of justice in the application of the corporate income tax, is to reduce the costs for the eligible firms, thus extending production beyond what would take place without the allowance. Oyster shell deposits that would be submarginal in the absence of the depletion allowance can be exploited, and wildcatting for oil is carried further than would otherwise be economical. In the extractive industries, the extension of exploration to otherwise submarginal investments is borne by the public and other industries through higher taxes. This is a matter of public policy that we shall not consider here; the purpose of this brief review is to call attention to the micro impact of government on the firm.

The micro impact of government on the private sector is not limited to taxing and spending. In addition to competing with the private sector for resources and altering the distribution of income through fiscal measures, government has the responsibility for the legal framework and economic climate in which the market system operates. This leads to a wide variety of government interventions with the market system.

The varieties of government intervention and control

Government appears in many roles in the private sector: as policeman, as price-fixer, as referee, and as benefactor. We have already noted the efforts of the federal government to preserve competition through the prosecution of monopoly and the prevention of practices that are considered destructive of competition. Using its most extreme federal antitrust weapon, the government can dismember a monopoly firm, which of course has a direct effect on the firm's costs and market power.

When the economies of large-scale production are so pronounced that larger firms are able to cut price below smaller firms' costs, competition cannot be relied upon either to prevent monopoly or to protect the consumer. In this case the government trades its role of antitrust policeman for that of price fixer. It regulates the industry as a public utility. In determining price and output, the decisions of a public utility regulatory commission largely replace those of the private market. While ownership and management remain in private hands, the firm's basic economic decisions are at least monitored and at times determined by the regulatory agency. How well government achieves its purpose in regulating the utility, whether in fact it vigorously defends the public interest or merely pays it lip-service, varies with time and case. Some regulatory agencies are essentially captives of the industries they are supposed to control, whereas others are able to maintain a more aggressive stand in the consumer's interest.

Behavior modification of the firm

The federal government's first all-out commitment to regulation of the firm came almost one hundred years ago with the passage of the Interstate Commerce Commission Act in 1887. This agency, established largely in response to the demands of outraged farmers and small businesspeople who felt they were being gouged by the railroads, is based squarely upon the interstate commerce clause of the United States Constitution, which reserves control of interstate and foreign commerce to the federal government. The commerce clause has continued to provide the main justification for the federal government to intervene in firm decision making.

Two federal regulatory bodies, the Securities and Exchange Commission, which was created in the aftermath of the 1929 stock-market crash, and the National Labor Relations Board, which was designed to prevent the kind of labor-management violence that occurred during the Great Depression, extended government control beyond price and output decisions of the firm. Government undertook behavior modification of the firm, establishing guidelines for employer-employee relations and specifying the requisites for public issuance and trading of securities. These control functions involved the regulatory agencies in more subtle and complex issues than rate regulation, and sometimes influenced the firm's cost structure and market position more than earlier forms of regulation.

What's the latest freight rate on yak fat?

In March, 1965, Tom Hilt, of Hilt Truck Line, Inc., of Omaha, got fed up with the knee-jerk reaction of the railroads in automatically protesting every tariff he filed with the Interstate Commerce Commission. With tongue in cheek, Hilt filed a rate for the transport of yak fat between Omaha and Chicago. Sure enough, the Western Truck Line Committee [a railroad committee] protested on the grounds that the cost of trucking yak fat far exceeded the proposed rate and was therefore illegal. And, sure enough, the ICC suspended the rate. After 30 days, the commission found that Hilt had failed to prove the rate legal, and it was disallowed.

Critics argue that the nitpicking scale of regulation creates a volume of detail work so great that it virtually guarantees inefficiency. In 1973, the ICC handled 373,215 tariffs requiring agency review, received an average of 3,850 pages of tariff material each working day, and heard 8,831 formal cases. The commission, critics say, is trying to make thousands of operating decisions that should be left to management and the market.

More fundamentally, economists argue that regulation feeds inflation, not only where it shuts off competition between truck and rail but also where it prevents true competition between truckers.

The target of the economists is a federal regulatory system that restricts entry into the trucking business, limits what may be carried, delineates routes, and takes a hostile attitude toward rate cuts by railroads to meet truck competition. The result, the analysts say, is that the American public is overcharged on its freight bill.[6]

The establishment of the Environmental Protection Agency consolidated and added to the regulatory functions of the federal government. The EPA increased federal control over water and air pollution, which led to greater restrictions in the disposal of industrial wastes and increased costs for industry. In general, protection of the environment has imposed costs upon the firm to abate water pollution, smog, aesthetic blight, and the like that previously were borne by the public. But government is not all restriction and control. Sometimes it protects firms from competition and helps them keep prices high. The *tariff* performs these functions.

The tariff is a tax imposed on foreign imports, preventing their entry into the United States or raising their price in the American market. Either way, the tariff protects the domestic producer and sacrifices the con-

[6] "Critics Say ICC Policies Inhibit Competition," *Business Week,* November 2, 1974, p. 86.

sumer's interests in the process, keeping product prices higher than they would be with unrestricted foreign competition. Tariffs are not so important as they once were, but they still benefit certain industries.

Farm price supports, like the tariff, have also been employed to shield the farmer from the harshness of the free market. The acreage cultivated has been limited through government intervention to decrease the supply of various farm commodities, and loans have been made available to permit the farmer to withold a crop from the market when prices are low. These interventions in the market process, although generally justified on the ground that farming is an uncertain, low-income occupation, have mainly benefited the high-income farmers and large corporate farms.

In the following chapter we shall examine benefit-cost analysis, a technique that is sometimes used to decide whether the government is economically justified in using resources for such public investments as hydroelectric installations, flood-control projects, and reclamation developments. Benefit-cost analysis is a form of micro analysis that is applied to government economic decision making.

Summary

The growth of government and its role in the economy have accelerated greatly with the rise of the industrial system. As the economic self-sufficiency of early American agriculture gave way to the increasingly interdependent manufacturing economy and its specialized labor force, economic dislocation left the worker without work and income.

The inability of unemployed workers to provide for themselves during the mass unemployment of the 1930s led to the assumption by the federal government of a host of new functions to meet this problem. Other crises, such as war and lesser forms of international discord, added further to the responsibilities and expenditures of the federal government. Growth in the private sector has also increased the size of the public sector. As a nation raises its output and adds to its income, public sector expenditures also increase. Schools, highways, parks, and public amenity services become easier to pay for as society's income increases and relatively more important as private wants are better satisfied.

A progressive tax structure—one that takes a larger proportion in taxes as income rises—automatically gives government a larger share of economic growth for the public sector. This revenue bonus from growth is called the "fiscal dividend" and occurs without any change in tax rates.

Government expenditures and the size of the public sector are not dependent solely upon taxation. Government expansion can occur by borrowing. How the government raises the money that it spends—what kinds of taxes it employs and from whom and how it borrows—have important micro and macro impacts upon the economy. The kinds of taxes levied, for example, largely determine who bears the cost of government and what parts of the economy are affected. Some taxes are shifted from the point at which they are imposed by the government, as in the case of the federal manufacture's excise tax on cigarettes, which is paid by the consumer. Other taxes, such as the personal income tax, are difficult or impossible to shift and the incidence of the tax—its point of payment—remains where it is imposed.

Taxes on the business firm can be either absorbed or passed on to consumers or suppliers depending upon the nature of the tax, the elasticity of demand, the elasticity of material supply, and other factors. Even when a tax is shifted by the firm however, it is likely to affect the firm's sales if not its costs. In some cases, of course, it will affect both.

Government does more than collect taxes and provide public services. It controls and regulates, subsidizes and supports. How well these functions are performed and whether in the public interest or for private gain depend on the activity and agency involved. The percentage depletion allowance and certain tariff provisions, for example, appear designed mainly to protect producers' interests rather than those of the consumers.

Key terms and concepts

The public sector most developed economies are a mixture of public and private economic activity, with resources allocated in the public sector on the basis of political decisions, while private-sector allocation is based primarily upon private decisions.

Human capital such productivity-enhancing assets as skills acquired through education and training and physical well-being protected by medical care and adequate diet.

Social overhead capital public roads, water systems, and similar facilities that are generally available to all and are prerequisites for further economic development.

Deficit financing government expenditures that exceed tax revenue and require the creation of debt, such as the sale of government bonds.

Progressive tax a levy in which the rate increases as the base increases; for example, a 10 percent rate on a $10,000 income and a 12 percent rate on a $15,000 income.

Proportional tax one in which the rate remains the same as the base changes; for example, a 10 percent rate on both a $10,000 income and a $15,000 income.

Transfer expenditures government outlays that redistribute income from one group in society to another, such as taxing upper-income individuals to support welfare programs for lower-income individuals.

Exhaustive expenditures government outlays for programs that use resources in their fulfillment, such as a housing project or a flood-control dam.

Personal income tax sometimes called the individual income tax, this levy is used by the federal government, many states, and a few localities. The personal income tax is the most important source of revenue for the federal government and its rate structure is moderately progressive, whereas state and local levies are generally proportional.

Tax incidence the point at which the tax is ultimately paid, which may not be where the tax is imposed.

Tax shifting movement of a tax from the point where it is levied to where it is paid, as an excise tax levied on the manufacturer but included in the price of the item produced, thus paid by the consumer.

Excise tax a tax levied on a commodity, based on volume or value, as 8¢ on a pack of twenty cigarettes.

Flat tax a fixed-sum or lump-sum levy that does not change with the output of the firm.

Franchise tax generally a flat tax charged for the privilege of doing business within a governmental jurisdiction.

Depreciation the apportionment of the cost of a capital asset such as machinery and equipment, over the expected life of the capital.

Accelerated depreciation a repayment schedule for a capital investment that concentrates repayment in the earlier years of the life of the investment. Sometimes called *rapid amortization*.

Depletion allowance a tax privilege available to extractive industries which allows a special percentage deduction in addition to normal depreciation in computing tax liability.

Discussion and review questions

1. What is the public economic sector and why has it grown so rapidly since colonial times? Why do people generally deplore its growth? Do you think R. H. Tawney, the author of *Equality*, would be more or less critical than most of this growth?

2. How have crises contributed to growth of the public sector? To what extent does contraction in the public sector take place after the crisis is over?

3. When is the fiscal dividend largest? How does the fiscal dividend affect growth in the public sector?

4. What is the difference between an exhaustive and a transfer government expenditure? Is one kind of expenditure preferable to the other?

5. The personal income tax is a progressive tax. How does a progressive tax differ from other kinds of taxes? Is a progressive tax necessarily more productive, that is, does it raise more revenue? Is it fairer?

6. Why should anyone but an economist be concerned about the incidence of taxes? What are some of the things that must be considered in determining whether a tax is likely to be shifted? What kinds of taxes are most likely to be shifted?

7. How does where the tax falls in the cost structure of the firm—whether on fixed or variable cost, for example—affect shifting?

8. What is accelerated depreciation? Why does its use stimulate some industries and some kinds of investment?

9. What is the purpose of the percentage depletion allowance? Does it encourage or discourage conservation of the resources eligible for the allowances? Is the allowance justified economically and ethically?

10. In what areas does the government act as a price-fixer? Why does it assume this role?

11. Why do some say that certain regulatory agencies are captives of the industries they are charged with regulating? How does this come about and what are its consequences?

12. The main purpose of the Sherman Antitrust Act is to prevent restraint of trade and monopoly, but some kinds of government intervention decrease competition. What are these interventions and why did they develop?

15 Benefit-cost analysis: resource allocation in the public sector*

Stuart, Fla.—When the U.S. Army Corps of Engineers began work on a flood control project some 20 years ago, alarmed townspeople tried to halt it. They feared ruination of their picturesque river, the St. Lucie. But the Corps assured residents its project would enhance boating, swimming, and fishing, and the project went ahead.

The people were right and the Corps was wrong.†

The duties of the Civil Works Directorate of the US Army Corps of Engineers are nonmilitary. Examples of its activities are the St. Lucie flood-control project, the dredging of rivers and harbors, and recently, its assignment to revive the 1899 Refuse Act as a means of protecting rivers and lakes from pollution. The top administrative and policy positions in the Civil Works Directorate of the Army Corps are staffed by Army officers, but the majority of its personnel consists of Civil Service government employees and its projects are carried out by private contractors. Most Army Corps projects relate to water resources, such as dams to protect against floods, channel dredging to improve navigation, and hydroelectric installations to generate electricity.

Members of Congress are usually eager to have the Army Corps undertake projects in their districts because the federal expenditures they bring are generally considered evidence of the representative's ability to get things done for constituents. As a result, the Water Resources Development Act, known as the Rivers and Harbors Act previous to 1974, is a well established congressional "pork barrel" appropriation. Most representatives uncritically accept each other's projects in order to ensure acceptance of their own. Although largely the agent of Congress, the Army

* This chapter is a revision of Chapter 6 of *Environmental Issues* (New York: W. W. Norton & Co., Inc., 1973).

† Tom Herman, "Embattled Corps—Army Engineers Draw Increasing Critical Fire for Disturbing Nature," *The Wall Street Journal*, January 6, 1970, p. 1. Reprinted with permission of *The Wall Street Journal*,

Corps is also responsive to Presidents who have favored its activities. President Kennedy turned to the Army Corps in the aftermath of the 1960 election to pay off an election promise.

The case of the Cross-Florida Barge Canal

In what was a futile attempt to induce Florida to support him in the 1960 presidential election, John F. Kennedy promised to undertake the Cross-Florida Barge Canal project, an Army Corps proposal of extended history and uncertain validity. The state of Florida went Republican in 1960, but Kennedy nonetheless made good his pledge and ordered a benefit-cost feasibility study of the project in 1961. This was by no means the first federal involvement with a canal across Florida.

During James Monroe's administration in 1824 such a canal was proposed to improve mail service between New Orleans and the East Coast and to protect shipping from West Indies pirates. Later, in 1850, the War Department authorized a survey for a possible canal route, but the undertaking was interrupted by the Civil War. Finally, a survey was made between 1909 and 1911, and a report issued in 1913 found the projected $15,538,055 investment in the canal entirely unjustified on military or commercial grounds.

During World War II, when the Atlantic submarine menace was at its peak, a cross-Florida canal was urged as a means of protecting shipping from the Gulf to the East Coast. This led to Congressional authorization of the canal in 1942—by a vote margin of one—and the Army Corps estimated the benefit-cost ratio for the project at 0.18 to 1, a payback of eighteen cents for every dollar invested, certainly one of the lowest benefit-cost ratios in recent times. (This is *not* an 18 percent return on investment, but a *loss* of 82 cents for every dollar invested.) The Cross-Florida Barge Canal had no economic justification on the basis of the Army Corps' feasibility study. The canal was not built during the war; instead, an oil pipeline across Florida was constructed in less time and at less cost, but the World War II Congressional authorization for the canal was not rescinded, and it became the basis for President Kennedy's revival of the project. The earlier benefit-cost ratio of 0.18 to 1 in no way justified appropriating federal funds for the project, however. According to traditional standards, benefits should at least equal costs, which is to say a ratio of 1 to 1 or above.

Fortunately for the Kennedy Administration, the project had been refigured in 1958, and the addition of such benefits as "transportation savings," "recreational boating," and "commercial fishing boat passages" raised the benefit-cost ratio to 1.05 to 1—hardly impressive, but at least not ludicrous. Still, the economic feasibility of the project was marginal at best and not likely to withstand competition for appropriations with other projects. Moreover, the ratio went from bad to worse when it was brought up to date in 1962 using a 2⅝ percent interest rate, which was then employed in federal benefit-cost analysis, instead of the earlier 2.5 percent, and when higher construction costs were acknowledged. Nevertheless, the project was presented to Congress in the fiscal 1962 budget. The ratio was still too low, so a restudy was ordered.

The restudy added two new categories of benefits, flood control and waterfront-land enhancement, and the benefit-cost ratio was refigured for a hundred-year project life as well as the earlier fifty-year period. The result was predictable. The benefit-cost ratio moved upward—to 1.2 to 1 for the fifty-year life and to 1.6 to 1 for the hundred-year life. Dredging started March 1, 1964, and slightly less than eight years and 70 million dollars later, President Nixon brought the project to a halt in 1971, when it was one-third completed. He acted in response to the mounting concern for the environment and the appalling ecological havoc wrought by canal construction in an area of unusual natural beauty and abundant wildlife. The courts have since held that the President does not have the legal authority to terminate an undertaking authorized by Congress, and the Army Corps can be expected to press for a revival of construction of the canal.

The origin and milieu of benefit-cost analysis

What is benefit-cost analysis—a charade, as it appears to be in the foregoing case, or rigorous economic analysis?

In most cases, it is neither. A product of the American political process, benefit-cost analysis responds to the pressures of the political system—pressures from Congress, the Administration, the bureaucracy, and the public and its pressure groups. Benefit-cost analysis came into being with the Flood Control Act of 1936, which established the federal policy that the "Government should improve or participate in the improvement of navigable waters or their tributaries, including watersheds thereof, for flood-control purposes if the benefits to whomsoever they may accrue" exceed the costs of the project. This congressional directive was the basis for the development of benefit-cost analysis by the Army Corps of Engineers and was later extended to other federal agencies.

In its early applications benefit-cost analysis emphasized the dollar value of project benefits and costs in the form of a benefit-cost ratio. Ignoring nonmarket factors that cannot be expressed in dollar terms, the project with the highest b/c ratio was considered to represent the most efficient use of resources. For example, if Projects A, B, and C have b/c ratios of 1.7/1, 1.4/1, and 2.7/1, respectively, the most efficient use of resources would take place in developing first Project C, then Project A, and finally Project B. Since each of the above projects has a b/c ratio that is greater than unity (1.0/1.0), the benefits of each project exceed costs and the ratio justifies the undertaking of the project. For a project to be justified economically, its b/c ratio generally must be above *unity,* although favorable considerations that cannot be quantified—so-called *intangible benefits* that are not included in the ratio—may lead those responsible to approve a below-unity project. *Intangible costs* can also lead to rejection of an above-unity project.

Recently the b/c ratio has been deemphasized by the federal government in favor of the *system-of-accounts* approach, which details factors that cannot be measured in dollars. We shall discuss the system-of-accounts approach later. It does not change the basic character of benefit-cost analysis but decreases the reliance on criteria of the private market in federal investment decisions and quantified benefits and costs.

Originally employed by the Army Corps to determine the economic justification of public investment in flood control projects, the use of benefit-cost analysis has spread to other federal agencies, such as the Bureau of Reclamation and the Federal Power Commission.[1] It is also used for more general nonfederal applications in analyses of programs of preventive medicine, highway construction, and investment in education.

Those responsible for the early application and development of benefit-cost analysis were mostly federal engineers and administrators. When the academic economists discovered benefit-cost analysis in the late 1950s, it was a period of full employment. As a result, they viewed the technique primarily as a means of answering the question of whether resources should be shifted from the private to the public sector of the economy. With the strong commitment to the goal of economic growth following World War II, the issue of whether resources produced more in the public sector or the private sector was one of major concern.

Those examining the federal use of benefit-cost analysis in the late 1950s and early 1960s emphasized that with full employment in the economy the opportunity cost of a federal project was the loss of private-

[1] The Bureau of Reclamation, originally responsible for irrigation projects in the West, has become one of the largest developers of hydroelectric power in that part of the country. The Federal Power Commission, among its other responsibilities, undertakes hearings and investigations to determine the desirability of hydroelectric power projects. Both of these federal agencies make use of benefit-cost analysis in the course of their duties.

Pareto optimum is the goal of benefit-cost analysis

A Pareto improvement is defined as a change in economic organization that makes everyone better off—or, more precisely, that makes one or more members of society better off without making anyone worse off. A *potential* Pareto improvement is, then, defined as a change which—if costless transfers of goods and/or money among members of society are assumed—*can* make everyone better off. It is, in other words, a change which produces gains that exceed in value the accompanying losses; a change, therefore, such that gainers *can* (through costless transfers) fully compensate all the losers and remain themselves better off than before.

It is now asserted that the rationale of existing cost-benefit criteria is ultimately that of a potential Pareto improvement. . . . A person who agrees to apply the principles of allocative efficiency needs no new assumption to extend his agreement to the application of existing cost-benefit analysis. In sum both the principles of economic efficiency and those of cost-benefit analysis derive their inspiration from the potential Pareto criterion, and a person cannot with consistency accept the one and deny the other.[2]

sector output. The guns-or-butter tradeoff of the war years was replaced by the issue of private-versus-public-sector output in the postwar period. A tightening of analytical standards by the government was called for by those economists who felt there was overexpansion taking place in the public sector.

The rationale behind benefit-cost analysis is that government projects are economically justified if the market value of their benefits exceeds their costs. But this is not all there is to the matter, by any means. Two areas must be examined further: (1) What do benefits and costs cover and what do they leave out? (2) Is the market standard an appropriate criterion for public investment decisions?

Opportunity cost and public expenditures

Everyone but economists thinks of cost as the amount of money given up to obtain commodities, resources, rights, or services. Economists, although at times chided for their preoccupation with money matters, insist

[2] E. J. Mishan, *Economics for Social Decisions* (New York: Praeger Publishers, 1973), pp. 14, 17. © 1973 by Praeger Publishers.

on looking behind the dollar sign to the "real costs" of economic production. *Real costs* are the resources used in production—land, labor, capital. Sometimes the impact of government projects on the private sector is represented as if all firms—GM, Exxon, and IBM included—were in danger of losing resources to the pull of the public sector. But such firms have too strong a hold on resources because of their high return on investment to be directly affected by the public sector's resource use. Actually, only marginal firms with a low return on investment find that expansion of the public sector curtails their activities.

The foregoing assumes full employment. If there is extensive and well-distributed unemployment in the economy, an increase in resource use by the government need not decrease private output. Sometimes this proposition is stated in another way: The use of resources in the public sector during mass unemployment involves zero opportunity cost. If private output is not curtailed, government resource use during a depression has a money cost but not an opportunity cost. Zero opportunity cost for government projects does not mean, however, that it makes no difference what public projects are undertaken.

A higher benefit-cost ratio represents a more efficient use of resources than a lower ratio, zero opportunity cost or not, and a carefully drawn benefit-cost study can help decision makers to choose which projects to undertake, during depression or full employment. But it makes a great difference how benefits and costs are measured. If the private sector is the model for efficient resource use, market prices and costs are the basic data of analysis. Sometimes, however, problems arise in choosing which prices and costs to use. The rate of interest poses such a problem.

The interest rate for project analysis

The benefit-cost analysis of federal agencies mainly involves water resource projects, which almost invariably are large-scale capital structures such as dams that last for a long time. This makes interest one of the key factors in project cost. For large-scale capital projects, success is a low interest rate. A low interest rate holds down the cost of capital. At the same time, the future benefit stream of the project is discounted less when the rate is low, thus leading to a higher benefit than when the interest rate is high.

Discounting

Most societies—which is to say, most individuals—prefer present satisfactions to future satisfactions. If confronted with the choice between having $1,000 as a lump sum *now* or $1,000 as a stream of $100-per-annum payments over the next ten years, the lump sum is the choice of all but the eccentric. Future satisfactions are worth less to most individuals and they instinctively discount them—that is, value them less than present satisfactions. The economy's appraisal of future satisfactions is expressed by the interest rate, which can be used to discount future payments—or benefits or costs—to convert them to present value.[3] Two factors determine the extent of the discount of a future event: how distant the event is from the present and the rate of discount. Both of these factors are illustrated in Table 15.1, in which discount rates of 5 and 10 percent are employed to convert to present value a ten-year stream of $100 payments.

At a 5 percent discount rate, the 10-year payment stream has a present value of $772.17, while the 10 percent discount rate brings the present value of the $1,000 stream to $614.46. This shows the effect of different discount rates. The yearly increment column in Table 15.1 indicates the influence of time on present value. At a discount of 5 percent, for example, one dollar five years from now has a present value of 78 cents; ten years

Table 15.1: 10-Year $100-per-annum payments discounted to present value at 5% and 10%

	5 Percent discount			10 Percent discount	
Year[a]	Cumulative	Yearly Increment	Year[a]	Cumulative	Yearly Increment
1	95.24	95.24	1	90.91	90.01
2	185.94	90.70	2	173.55	82.64
3	272.32	86.38	3	248.68	75.13
4	354.59	82.27	4	316.99	68.31
5	432.95	78.36	5	379.08	62.09
6	507.57	74.62	6	435.53	56.45
7	578.63	71.06	7	486.84	51.31
8	646.32	67.69	8	533.49	46.65
9	710.78	64.46	9	575.90	42.41
10	$772.17	61.39	10	$614.46	38.56

[a] 1st annual payment deferred one year from present.

[3] For those who are mathematically inclined and who are indifferent to tedious computations, the discounted present value of a series of future payments can be derived through the use of the following formula:

$$P_0 + \frac{P_1}{(1+r)} + \frac{P_2}{(1+r)^2} + \frac{P_3}{(1+r)^3} + \cdots \frac{P_N}{(1+r)^N}$$

where P is the payment for subsequent years and r is the rate of discount. Those with higher opportunity costs will consult a discounted present-value table which supplies such information readymade.

from now it has a present value of 61 cents. At 10 percent discount, one dollar five years from now has a present worth of 62 cents, and ten years from now 39 cents.

To summarize, the lower the interest rate used for discounting in project analysis, the higher the benefit component in the numerator of the b/c ratio and the lower the cost component in the denominator for those costs that are spread over the expected life of the project. Interest enters at another important point in the analysis, however—as a measure of capital costs which add more to project costs when interest is high than when low. As a result, the lower the interest rate, the higher the benefit-cost ratio; the higher the interest rate, the lower the benefit-cost ratio. For this reason, the choice of the interest rate that is used in project analysis has a great effect upon whether projects pass the b/c test or not.

If the government's use of resources is to conform to private market standards, the prime rate of interest is a logical candidate for benefit-cost analysis. The rate chosen should measure the opportunity cost of capital in the private sector, but no single rate reflects this at all times. The capital market is imperfect, and the prime rate as well as other rates is influenced by government attempts to control income and employment in the economy. In recent years, for example, the prime rate has varied from 5½ percent to 12 percent, largely as a result of actions of the Federal Reserve Banking System.

The history of project interest rates

From 1946 to 1962, federal water resource projects generally employed an interest rate based on the average long-term federal bond rate. During this period, the rate was consistently below 3 percent, ranging from 2⅝ percent in 1962 to 3¼ percent in 1969. At this point the rate was recalculated and raised to 4⅝ percent, rising annually until it reached 6⅞ percent in 1974. In 1976, it was reduced to 6⅛ percent.

The argument for using the average long-term federal bond rate for project analysis is that it represents the cost of borrowing for the government. Economists have generally been critical of the use of the bond-rate, considering it to be an inappropriate measure of project opportunity costs. The federal government is able to borrow in the money market at a low rate because its securities represent the least risk of any widely issued credit instrument, not because water-resource projects are unusually secure investments. Moreover, the bond rate used is an average of outstanding government issues rather than new borrowing. Finally, unlike other borrowers, the US Treasury Department is at times able to prevail upon the Federal Reserve System to provide a market for its securities at a low rate, further depressing the bond rate.

In private investment, the charge for loanable funds reflects the risk of the business venture. Wildcatting for oil, publishing a new magazine, or building a power generating plant have failure probabilities that are weighed against the chances of success by those advancing funds, whether staid bankers or plunging speculators, and the interest rate is higher for the riskier undertaking. The government is different from the private borrower. Its ability to repay borrowed money—bonds, Treasury bills or other debt forms—is unrelated to the success or failure of projects that may be financed by these borrowings. In general, the government doesn't borrow to finance a particular project. The low interest rate on federal bonds does not mean that projects are risk-free, but that the government possesses unique borrowing and taxing power. While the federal government is justified in taking advantage of its lower borrowing rate, it does not follow that this rate is an appropriate measure of the opportunity cost of project capital.

How important is the interest rate as a project cost? This depends on the project. If the project is a large-scale, long-lived capital investment, such as a hydroelectric power project, the interest rate is of critical concern in determining whether the project is economically feasible. If the project is a job-training program in which the major outlay is for teaching personnel and the benefits of the program accrue annually, a high or low interest rate has little influence on the economic feasibility of the project.

The period of analysis

The Soviet planners raise or lower the cost of capital by shortening or lengthening the payoff period—the time designated for the recovery of the project's investment costs. A longer payoff period is equivalent to a lower interest rate in the Soviet system.

A somewhat analogous situation occurs in federal water-resource planning in the choice of the period of analysis. The period of analysis is the length of time, say, fifty or one hundred years, over which it is assumed the project will remain economically viable, yielding benefits and bearing costs. A longer period of analysis means a more favorable benefit-cost ratio. The longer time extends the benefit stream, but the benefit-raising effect of extending the period of analysis is most pronounced when the interest rate is low.

The California Central Valley Water Project is a mammoth hydroelectric, municipal water supply, and irrigation development undertaken by the Bureau of Reclamation. The project brings water from the Cascade Mountains of Northern California to as far south as Bakersfield, California.

In 1962, the Bureau of Reclamation and other federal agencies responsible for water-resource development adopted a 100-year period of analysis, making it somewhat easier for a project to attain an acceptable benefit-cost ratio. The different benefit-cost ratios reported in Table 15.2 for components of the California Central Valley Water Project show this effect.

Table 15.2: Benefit-cost ratios for the California Central Valley Project and separable features

Projects	Time Period	Interest rate 3%	4%	5%	6%
1. "Basic" CVP features; without adjustment for surplus crops	50 years	1.21	1.03	0.89	0.77
	100 years	1.45	1.16	0.96	0.81
2. "Basic" CVP features; using adjusted world prices for price-supported crops	50 years	0.72	0.61	0.53	0.47
	100 years	0.85	0.69	0.57	0.49
3. Shasta Dam; including maximum net benefits attainable along Sacramento channel, but excluding all works south of the Delta	50 years	1.16	1.00	0.86	0.76
	100 years	1.38	1.11	0.93	0.80
4. Delta-Mendota and Contra Costa canals and Friant Division; without Shasta but including allowance for opportunity cost of water use foregone in the Delta	50 years	1.22	1.05	0.91	0.79
	100 years	1.47	1.18	0.99	0.84

Source: Joe S. Bain et al., *Northern California's Water Industry* (Baltimore: Johns Hopkins Press, 1966), p. 558. Published for Resources for the Future, Inc. by The Johns Hopkins Press.

Taxes and federal projects

For the business firm in the private sector, taxes are a cost that must be included in the price of the product and passed on to the consumer, usually reducing the sales of the industry and in some cases the size of the firm; or they are absorbed by the firm through a reduction in resource return or profit. The impact of taxes upon the firm varies greatly depending on the kind of tax and the circumstances under which it is levied, as we demonstrated in Chapter 14. Rarely are taxes without impact on the firm's behavior; frequently they cause the firm to modify its output and price policy.

Federal projects do not pay taxes, although at times federal installations make grants or assist in the collection of state and local levies. There are good reasons why one unit of government doesn't tax another. But if taxes are not included as costs in the analysis of a public project when such outlays are a part of the cost structure of private firms that produce similar output, such as electric power, the benefit-cost analysis does not hold the public project to the same standards as faced by the private firm.

If economy of scale is pronounced, as in the generation of electricity, the size of the installation is critical: The larger the generating plant, the lower the cost per kilowatt. Ignoring taxes may not only keep public project costs below that of the private producer, but it may lead to larger project scale than if taxes were considered, compounding the original difference brought about by ignoring taxes in the analysis of costs.

Externalities and project analysis

Even when the benefit-cost analysis carefully mirrors the private market, it may at times misdirect public investment because some side effects of private production are not recorded in market transactions. A flood control or reclamation dam replaces the natural flow of a river with a fluctuating lake of impounded water. If the flat-water reservoir created by the dam destroys a river that was prized for its scenic beauty, its white-water challenge, and its shore habitat for waterfowl, this loss is not recorded by the market or quantified in the b/c ratio. But if water skiing, pan fishing, and other kinds of flat-water recreation take place on project reservoirs, they are quantified and included as "recreation-day" benefits.[4]

The market gives little help to the analyst trying to decide what benefits and cost to place on a noncommercial use of resources. Undeveloped natural areas are worth something to a highly industrialized nation with increasing population, but the market does not record their value as it does kilowatts. Such intangible factors are ignored in the benefit-cost ratio but acknowledged in the system-of-accounts approach.

Benefits: what not to include

The benefit of a project is the money value of its economic output. Sometimes, however, agency analysts get carried away in their search for project benefits and include things that can be attributed to the project, but

[4] A recreation-day in 1976 might add as little as 75 cents or as much as $9 per project visit to the benefit side of the b/c ratio, depending on the nature of the recreational activity.

Biggest dam plan in the world shelved, Alaska Rampart project put on hold

The proposed Rampart Dam in Alaska would dam the Yukon River and flood an area of the Yukon Flats larger than New Jersey behind a concrete structure bigger and more costly than the Aswan High Dam in Egypt. The reservoir would take ten years to fill and would destroy an extraordinarily productive wildlife habitat in order to produce hydroelectric power. What follows is the statement of the Army Corps of Engineers, the federal agency responsible for the project.

Pursuant to Congressional direction, the District Engineer has investigated the feasibility and desirability of hydroelectric power development on the Yukon River, Alaska, at the Rampart Canyon site. Numerous plans of development were analysed based upon different conditions of streamflow, full pool elevation, and timing with respect to power production. Full consideration also has been given to the matter of fish and wildlife losses and displacements, as well as other effects upon the natural environment that would result from a project. Purely from the standpoint of economic efficiency, the most feasible plan has a benefit-to-cost ratio of near unity, 0.96 to 1. However, current and rising rates of interest on Federal investments and rising construction costs would further reduce that ratio.

. . . Although none of the plans studied for this report is economcally feasible at this time, changes in the load growth or cost of alternative sources of power may warrant reconsideration of the hydroelectric potential of the Rampart site at some time in the future.

Based on the foregoing and other factors set forth in this report, the District Engineer recommends that a project for hydroelectric power generation at the Rampart Canyon site, Yukon River, Alaska, not be undertaken at this time.[5]

that are not net additions to the nation's output. In the case of an irrigation project, for example, the *primary project benefit* is the market value of its agricultural produce—grapefruit, avocados, lettuce, or whatever. This is output that would not have been produced in the absence of the project. *Secondary project benefits* were at one time also included in the benefit-cost ratio for some projects by the Bureau of Reclamation. A secondary benefit is the net increase in the dollar value of economic activities which *stems from* the project's primary product. If the project's primary product is

[5] *A Report on the Rampart Canyon Project* (Alaska District: Department of the Army Corps of Engineers, May 20, 1971), p. 1.

grapefruit, then secondary benefits include the proceeds of canning, transportation, and the like. Secondary benefits have not played an important role in benefit-cost analysis in the past and cannot presently be used to raise the b/c ratio. Including "regional development" as a part of the system-of-accounts approach, however, may represent an acceptance of the substance of what were previously termed secondary benefits.

The system-of-accounts approach to project analysis

In August 1973, President Richard Nixon approved the system-of-accounts analysis approach for federal agencies. This approach was adopted following a task-force report and public hearings that examined the problems experienced in the use of benefit-cost analysis by the federal agencies. Basically, the system of accounts shifts the focus from the benefit-cost ratio, which covers only items that can be measured in dollars, to areas of broader project impact. These areas of impact are: national economic development, environmental quality, social well-being, and regional development. The benefit-cost ratio is based solely upon national economic development, in part because the other accounts deal mainly with factors that are not measurable in the market. (The project impact of regional development may be expressed in dollar terms, but regional benefits and costs are not included in the benefit-cost ratio.) For the areas other than national economic development, the system of accounts requires a systematic description and appraisal rather than identification and measurement. The way information is arrayed in the system of accounts is shown in Table 15.3. This summary covers most of the national economic development benefits for a typical federal project, but only a fraction of the effects—benefits and costs—that may arise in the other accounts.

The role of the agency in the benefit-cost analysis

The benefit-cost studies that support requests to Congress for project appropriations are made by the federal agencies that undertake the projects. Sometimes agencies other than the one primarily responsible for the project contribute to the benefit-cost study. The Federal Power Commission, for example, is responsible for evaluation of the benefits and costs of hydroelectric investment, and the Fish and Wildlife Service appraises the project's impact on aquatic species and wildlife. These outside agencies

Table 15.3: System of accounts and plan effects

Account	Plan effects: Beneficial effects	Adverse effects	Net effects
National Economic Development	Flood control		$1,000,000
	Power production		1,000,000
	Water supply		1,000,000
	Irrigation		1,000,000
	Value of output from external economics in processing		1,000,000
		Project construction costs	−3,000,000
		Power pumping costs	−1,000,000
			+$1,000,000
Environmental Quality	Project creates a lake with high quality of water and excellent access.	Project inundates open and green space along stream near city and destroys wildlife habitat.	No dollar measure
Regional Development	Increases job opportunities in the region.	Irrigation run-off increases salinity of streams in the region.	No dollar measure
Social Well-Being	Flood projection for 100 years	Influx of workers strains educational and other community facilities.	No dollar measure

Source: Adapted from "Water Resources Council: Establishment of Principles and Standards for Planning," *Federal Register*, Vol. 38, No. 174, (September 10, 1973), Part III, pp. 111–113, 123–25.

may be less favorably inclined toward the project than the sponsoring agency. The Fish and Wildlife Service and the Bureau of Outdoor Recreation, for example, sometimes play the "spoiler's" role in a project that has an adverse effect upon recreational activities, particularly in areas of environmental concern. But other forces are sometimes more powerful. Since the energy crisis, for example, it takes a very serious impairment of the environment to forestall the building of a hydroelectric power project. Finally, those responsible for the project and analyses are not disinterested parties. They are agency employees, fully aware that the agency's welfare depends on a steady flow of projects with favorable benefit-cost reports.

Changes in benefit-cost analysis have been pressed upon the federal agencies by critics within and without the government. Bureau of the

Budget directives, reports of panels of experts, Congressional hearings, and extended examination in academic studies have all criticized various agency practices. Moreover, in 1972–1973, the Water Resources Council, the guiding authority for federal benefit-cost practices, undertook a comprehensive reexamination of such issues as the discount rate, the legitimacy of secondary benefits, and environmental impacts.The outcome of this reexamination was the recommendation of the system-of-accounts approach.

Since the Water Resources Council consists of the Secretaries of the Army, Agriculture, Interior, and Commerce, the chairman of the Federal Power Commission, and the administrator of the Environmental Protection Agency, the Council—with the exception of the Environmental Protection Agency—has a considerable self-interest in perpetuating analytical practices that encourage project approval.

Benefit-cost analysis: use with care

In deciding on public resource use, there are two areas in which benefit-cost analysis may be of uncertain worth or counterproductive: (1) Projects that have important intangible benefits or costs that cannot be quantified in the benefit-cost ratio; (2) Projects designed primarily to increase the economic welfare of certain groups.

The first case, that of projects with intangible benefits or costs, may also involve externalities that are not accounted for in the analysis, such as the cost of increased water salinity downstream from an irrigation project or the benefit of improved water supply downstream from a pollution abatement project.

The second case, that of projects designed to improve economic welfare, poses a conflict between the goals of equity and economic efficiency. A project that raises incomes in a ghetto or Indian reservation may be socially justified even though its benefit-cost ratio is lower than one in the Imperial Valley that increases farm income. If the dominant goal of a project is income redistribution, there is still a role for economic analysis, however. Given the priority of the equity goal, projects should be chosen on the basis of the most economically efficient way of attaining this objective. The deemphasis of the benefit-cost ratio and increased reliance upon the system-of-accounts approach in project evaluation affords greater recognition for intangible, nonmarket aspects of project benefits and costs.

It is not possible to compute a dollar benefit payoff for many government functions as it is for an irrigation or flood-control project. In the case of defense, the overall goal is usually accepted—although the question of how much should be spent arises frequently. The main consideration is how to defend the nation in the least costly way. In choosing among weapons systems, the Defense Department sometimes employs *cost-effectiveness* analysis, which is a kind of half-way benefit-cost approach. In deciding how to protect the Atlantic Seaboard from attack, for example, cost-effective analysis compares various methods of defense—airplanes, rockets, submarines, surface craft, or combinations of these—to determine which involves the least resource cost.

Benefit-cost analysis serves decision making best when the proposed public project duplicates or is similar to an economic activity undertaken in the private sector and when market prices and costs adequately reflect the project's economic impact. When these conditions are met, the comparison of project benefits and costs provides a valid measure of the project's worth to the economy. Overall, the major contribution of benefit-cost analysis is its systematic organization of comparative information on project proposals; its greatest weakness is in its application to projects for which it cannot adequately measure the benefits and costs of the undertaking.

Summary

Benefit-cost analysis is a form of economic appraisal that is used to determine the feasibility of certain kinds of public investment projects. Originating with the 1936 Flood Control Act administered by the US Army Corps of Engineers, benefit-cost analysis purports to answer the question of whether during full employment resources should be shifted from the private sector of the economy to the public sector. The issue is whether the resources are economically more productive when employed in the private or public sector of the economy. The opportunity cost of public economic output is considered to be the private output forgone when resources from the private sector are diverted to the public sector.

In its early application to federal water resource programs, benefit-cost analysis emphasized the project features that could be quantified in monetary terms and expressed in the benefit-cost ratio. For a project to be economically feasible, the b/c ratio must be greater than unity, otherwise resources presumably produce more in the private sector than in the public sector. The higher benefits are to costs—a ratio of 2.4/1 as compared with 1.7/1, for example—the greater the justification for undertaking the public project and the higher priority the project merits in the schedule of project development.

Benefit-cost analysis relies on the private market standard in determining whether public projects should be undertaken. Some question the appropriateness of this criterion, but if it is to be applied rigorously, public projects should satisfy the same standards as private undertakings. This means that the same rate of interest should be used in computing the cost of capital for the public investment as prevails in the private market, that the amortization period of the project investment should be a realistic estimate of the project's life expectancy, and that all costs, such as taxes paid by similar private developments, should be included on the cost side of the project b/c ratio. Benefit-cost analysis, relying as it does on the private market standard, is a better criterion for some kinds of public undertakings than for others. In evaluating the desirability of a public investment for the development of hydroelectric power, for example, the private market standard is more appropriate than it would be for public-sector activities that have no private market counterpart, such as welfare programs. The benefit-cost standard is also inappropriate when it is not possible to appraise satisfactorily certain intangible benefits or costs, such as aesthetic and environmental deterioration caused by the project, and when the market does not provide satisfactory guidelines for social goals.

In an attempt to measure intangible factors more adequately than can usually be quantified, the federal government now requires an environmental impact study of proposed projects and employs the system-of-accounts approach to benefit-cost analysis. The final responsibility for an environment impact study lies with the federal Environmental Protection Agency, although it is usually not made by that agency. The system-of-accounts approach to benefit-cost analysis is the responsibility of the federal agency undertaking the project and involves the systematic collection and evaluation of information in four main categories: (1) national economic development, (2) environmental quality, (3) regional development, and (4) social well being. In this approach, the benefit-cost ratio is very greatly deemphasized since only the national economic development account is quantified.

Key terms and concepts

Real cost land, labor, and capital factors used to produce goods or services.

Prime rate of interest the commercial bank loan rate for low-risk borrowers.

Discount rate the percentage decrease of future benefits or costs required to adjust them to present worth.

Period of analysis the assumed economic life expectancy of a project.

Primary project benefits the economic value of the direct output of a project; for example, the price of a kilowatt of electricity.

Secondary project benefits the indirect economic contribution of activity that is generated by the project, such as employment in a plant that processes the agricultural output of an irrigation project.

Cost effectiveness a method of analysis used by the Department of Defense to determine the lowest cost among a number of alternatives of achieving an objective.

System of accounts the analysis of government projects in terms of four areas of impact: national development, regional development, environmental quality, and social well-being.

Discussion and review questions

1. How did benefit-cost analysis arise and what purpose does it serve? Why has it been most extensively applied in the analysis of water-resource projects? Why is it not used to determine the feasibility of welfare programs or farm programs?

2. What is included in computing benefits for a flood-control project and a reclamation project? What are the costs?

3. What difference does it make whether benefits are tangible or intangible? Are there also intangible costs?

4. E. J. Mishan says that the objective of benefit-cost analysis is a Pareto optimum. Do you think this is what the analyst at, say, the Army Corps of Engineers has in mind when preparing a benefit-cost study?

5. Why is a shift of resources from the private to the public sector considered justified if the b/c ratio is greater than unity, but otherwise not? Is there a concealed value judgment in this criterion?

6. If there is mass unemployment, does a greater-than-unity benefit-cost ratio still have the same significance for public project decisions?

7. Why is the interest rate such an important factor in benefit-cost analysis? In what ways does it enter into the analysis, and who decides what rate to use?

8. Why are future benefits and costs discounted in computing the b/c ratio?

9. What effect does the period of analysis (project life) have upon the benefit-cost ratio?

10. Since government projects generally do not pay taxes, why should taxes be included as costs in computing the b/c ratio? Are they included by the federal agencies in their analysis?

11. What is the system-of-accounts approach to benefit-cost analysis and how does it differ from earlier project analysis? Is it an improvement?

12. Is the average government bond rate a socially and economically appropriate measure of the cost of capital for public projects?

Appendix: the Middle Snake hydroelectric development—the role of benefit-cost analysis in a complex public investment decision

By the middle of the twentieth century, the Columbia River system in the Pacific Northwest was laced with hydroelectric dams, and a conflict arose over the use of the remaining free-flowing portion of the Snake River between those who wanted wilderness and those who wanted more power production. The Pacific Northwest's increasing demand for power encouraged a number of plans to harness the Middle Snake, which is an undeveloped reach of the Snake River of approximately 150 miles, from Hells Canyon Dam to Lewiston, Idaho.

The development proposals were impressive: dams for power and dams to check the turbulence of the peak-power water release, mechanical aerating equipment embedded in the river to restore the oxygen lost when the water is impounded behind power dams, devices to trap and transport migrating fish around the man-made obstructions in the river, and hatcheries to substitute for the lost spawning areas of the inundated river. In 1975, an Act of Congress declared most of the Middle Snake off-limits to further power installations, overruling the recommendation of the Federal Power Commission examiner to authorize development, but the case illustrates well the problems that arise in applying benefit-cost analysis.

By market standards, hydroelectric generation is the cheapest and cleanest type of power production. The primary capital cost for the dams and turbines is the main expenditure; little outlay is required for operations and maintenance, and none for fuel. At the same time, no unwanted by-product, such as heat discharge or air pollution, accompanies the generation of hydroelectricity. Hydroelectric generation would be the ideal solution to the country's increased power needs in those areas where suitable sites are available if it were not for one thing—the damming of free-flowing rivers to produce electricity grossly degrades the character of the rivers. It accumulates behind the power dam a large area of slack water that is lowered and raised in response to the needs for power, in the process exposing an unseemly shore area. It may substitute flat-water use—boating, panfishing, water-skiing—for fast-water use—white-water canoeing, game fishing, wilderness travel. The opportunity cost of flat-water use is thus fast-water use. How much we need of one is related to how much we have of the other. As a nation we are just becoming aware of this choice.

Hydroelectric power and the Pacific Northwest

Unlike the rest of the country, where most power installations are thermal plants, the Pacific Northwest has been heavily dependent upon hydroelectric power. Until recently, the Columbia River and its tributaries have provided ample sites for power dams. Figure 15.1 shows the extent to which the Columbia River system has become saturated with power installations. By comparison with other regions, the Pacific Northwest is deficient in fossil fuels, although abundant coal and oil shales are close by in the Rocky Mountain region. Sites for hydroelectric developments are now very scarce in the Columbia River system and plans for future power involve major dependence on nuclear-thermal generation.

Delays in bringing nuclear power plants into production have caused a shift to coal-fired thermal plants, however, and the vast gas and petroleum resources that will be available to the Pacific Northwest in 1978 when the Alaskan North Slope oil fields come into production may change the competitive position of these fuels. The planned Canadian Mackenzie River gas pipeline eventually may also offer a partial solution to the region's need for additional power. The questions are: At what future date will the natural-gas pipeline through Canada be completed? Will Canada find it in her national interest to sell fuel to the United States? In the early 1970s, the Pacific Northwest's power plans for the future were committed to nuclear development at the rate of roughly one plant per year, relegating existing hydro installations to peaking output, but the one-a-year objective has not been achieved. The lag in nuclear plant construction has increased the pressure for development of the remaining hydro sites.

The Middle Snake River as a power plant

The Middle Snake runs free of hydro dams, but it has long been coveted as a site for hydroelectric development. The Snake River has its inception at the foot of the Teton Range in Wyoming and works its way through Idaho and Washington, where it finally joins the Columbia on the way to the sea. For a part of its course, from the Boise River to Lewiston, Idaho, the Snake serves as the boundary that separates Idaho from Oregon and Washington in the region of the Payette and Nez Perce national forests—largely undeveloped and mostly wilderness areas.

This section of the river—the Middle Snake—is the last remant of the wild river that Lewis and Clark traveled in the final days of their westward journey. The Upper Snake, in contrast, is smothered with hydro dams, fifteen are in operation or under construction from the shadows of the Tetons to the Hells Canyon dam. Below the Hells Canyon dam the Snake runs free of man-made obstructions, and the steelhead trout and the Chinook and sockeye salmon that surmount the many dams in the Lower Snake and the Columbia can spawn in their birthplace—the Middle Snake and its tributaries: the Grande Ronde, the Salmon, and the Imnaha.

But the Middle Snake is more than a breeding area for fish. Along with the Salmon river and limited portions of other tributaries, the Middle Snake is one of the last of its kind—a 150-mile reach of a wild, white-water river flowing through the deepest gorge in the country, a sharp contrast to the slack backwaters behind the many power dams on the rest of the Snake and Columbia. Although the Middle Snake flows through a gorge that is spectacularly steep in places, there are points of access to the canyon floor. Wildlife in moderate abundance, including cougar, elk, deer, and a variety of bird life, inhabit the canyon. A power dam in the Middle Snake would not only turn a river into a pond and endanger or eliminate the migratory and resident game fish in the Snake; it would destroy a wilderness and its wildlife.

The Federal Power Commission and the Middle Snake

The Federal Power Commission understands its primary function to be that of "assuring an abundant supply of electric energy throughout the United States with the greatest possible economy and with regard to the proper utilization and conservation of natural resources."[6] The FPC has interpreted this responsibility to mean the promotion of hydroelectric power wherever possible. With an unyielding singleness of purpose, the Commission has promoted the development of hydroelectric power in the United States until there are few economically feasible sites left.

[6] Section 202(a), Federal Power Act (16 U.S.C. 791–825).

Figure 15.1 Hydroelectric Projects of the Columbia River Basin

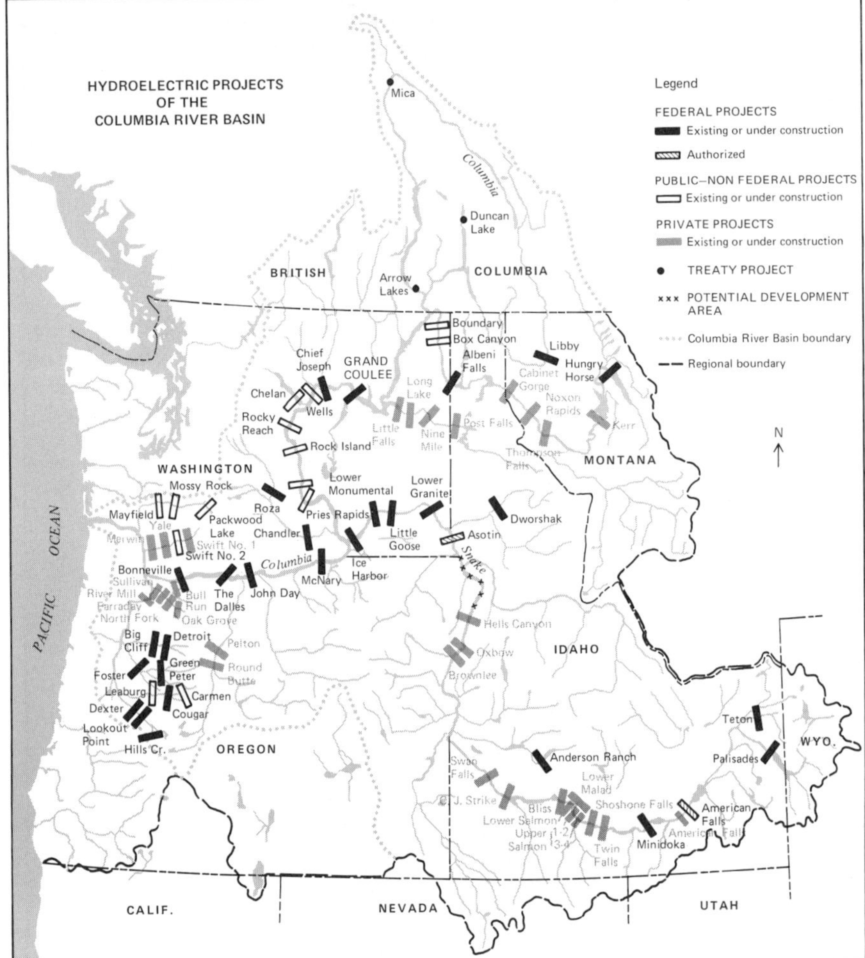

Source: *Resource Study of the Middle Snake* (Washington, D.C.: Department of the Interior, 1968), frontispiece.

Middle Snake power sites

Figure 15.1 shows the extensive network of hydroelectric power plants in the Pacific Northwest.

Part of the river, which is enlarged in Figure 15.2, affords the physical opportunity for four possible hydroelectric dams or combinations of dams: Appaloosa dam and Low Mountain Sheep reregulating dam; High

Figure 15.2 Estimated Distribution of Salmon and Steelhead Trout in the Middle Snake River System

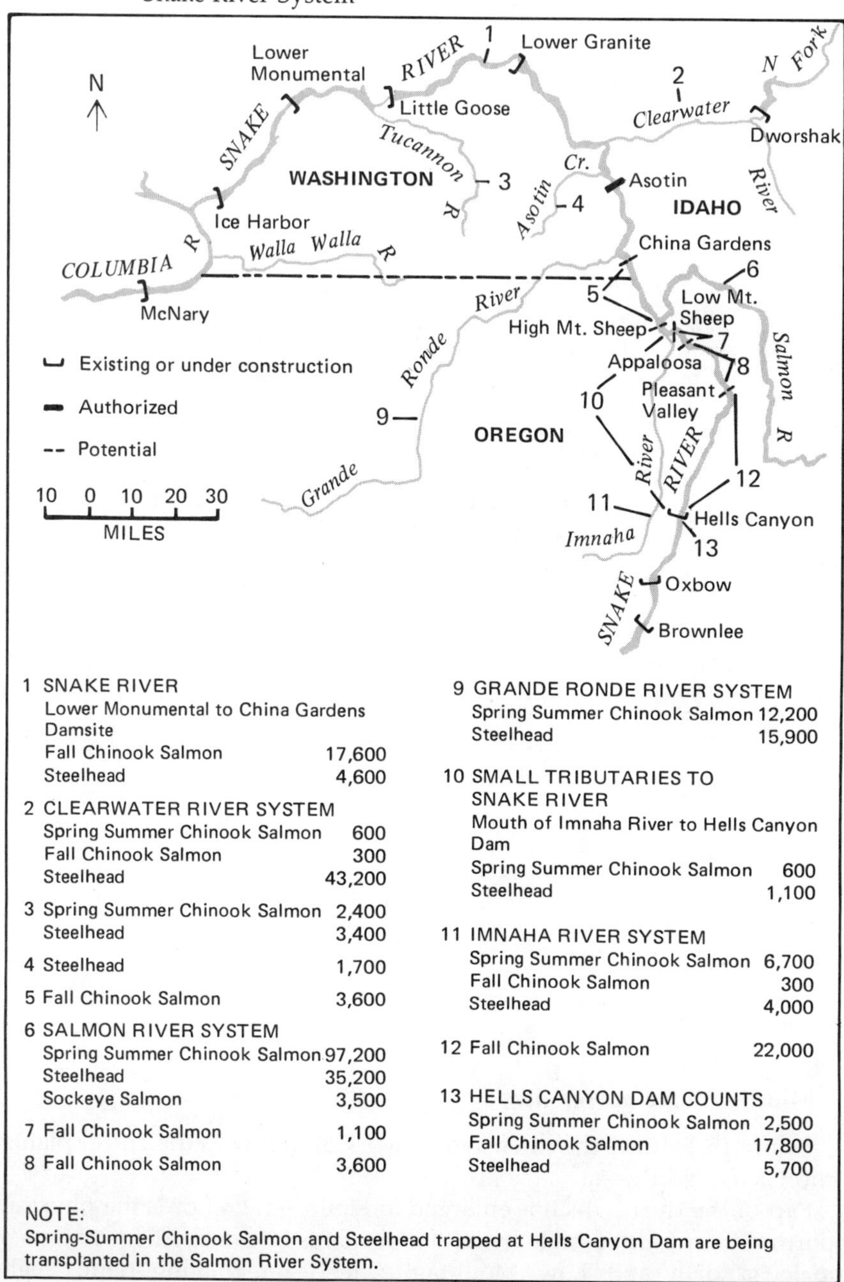

Source: *Resource Study of the Middle Snake* (Washington, D.C.: Department of the Interior, 1968), map insert unpaged.

Mountain Sheep dam and China Gardens reregulating dam; High Mountain Sheep dam without a reregulating installation; and Pleasant Valley dam and Low Mountain Sheep reregulating dam. The main dam, for example, High Mountain Sheep dam, is solely designed for power productions, whereas the lower site, the reregulating China Gardens dam for instance, is a secondary source of power generation, but its main purpose is to check the flow of water downstream, decreasing the surges of the river that result from peaking power releases at the main dam.

The Federal Power Commission's involvement with the Middle Snake has been long and controversial. The dispute started quietly in the fall of 1954 when the Pacific Northwest Power Company, a private electric utility, filed with the FPC for a permit to construct a hydroelectric power project in the Middle Snake. Years later, on February 23, 1971, the FPC examiner recommended that a license be granted to build a hydroelectric dam in the Middle Snake. The license was issued to a consortium of public and private utilities, of which the Pacific Northwest Power Company was a leading applicant. Between the time of the original application and the 1971 decision, however, over 28,461 pages of transcript and 1,436 exhibits had been reviewed and two court actions—one involving the United States Supreme Court—and numerous hearings had occurred. Finally, on December 31, 1975, President Ford signed Public Law 94–199 (94th Congress, S.322), which designated 71 miles of the Middle Snake as wilderness to be protected against development. Before this action, extensive examination and analysis of the proposed power developments were submitted to the Federal Power Commission by the petitioning utilities, government agencies, and the staff of the Federal Power Commission.

The four plans for power

The issue facing the Federal Power Commission examiner was not simply that of dam or no dam in the Middle Snake. If the examiner decided in favor of a hydroelectric development, he was faced with a choice of sites. The Department of the Interior's *Resource Study of the Middle Snake* identified four sites in the Middle Snake, each with a different generating capacity and different envrionmental effects. The installations at the four sites also differ, but we shall consider only the basic plans here.

Plan 1: Appaloosa and Low Mountain Sheep

The Appaloosa project (see Table 15.4) consists of two dams and two power plants. The main power installation located at Appaloosa contains

Table 15.4: Plan 1: Appaloosa and Low Mountain Sheep

Output:	2,500 megawatts		
Benefits:	$56,463,000 annual equivalent		
	Power		$49,267,000
	Fish and wildlife enhancement		6,590,000
	Resident fish	$ 189,000	
	Anadromous fish	$6,401,000	
	Recreation		406,000
	Flood Control		200,000
		Total	$56,463,000
Costs:	$20,770,000 annual equivalent		
	Federal investment		$16,083,000
	Annual operating		4,687,000
		Total	$20,770,000

B/C ratio: 2.72/1
Interest rate: 3¼ percent
Project life: 100 years

Source: *Resource Study of the Middle Snake* (Washington, D.C.: Department of the Interior, 1968), Part VI, pp. 3–6.

six 350-megawatt generating units plus one 400-megawatt unit that is located in the reregulating dam at Low Mountain Sheep. The combined output for the complex is 2,500 megawatts. Compared to other sites, such as those proposed in Plans 2 and 4, the Appaloosa complex preempts a relatively short stretch of the Middle Snake. Because it lies above the Salmon and Imnaha rivers, the project would interfere less with the migration of salmon and trout than would a dam at High Mountain Sheep, which would cause massive destruction of the fish population. The Appaloosa development would impair spawning of anadromous fish[7] in the area of the Snake River below Hells Canyon dam, but this is the last stop of the migrants in any case. Fish that reach this point cannot ascend beyond Hells Canyon dam and those than can be trapped are artificially propagated in hatcheries. Additional fish loss would take place because of the obstruction of the Appaloosa dam, but the *Interior Resource Study* contends that the Appaloosa project would actually increase the fish population of the Middle Snake.

[7] Anadromous fish, such as salmon and steelhead trout, are born in fresh water and migrate to the sea, where they grow to maturity, later returning to the river of their birth to spawn.

A unique feature of the Appaloosa power project is a multilevel intake system to permit water to be withdrawn from five different levels of the reservoir to use in generating power. By selecting water from a lower level, the Middle Snake below the Appaloosa dam could be cooled, thereby improving fish habitat during the summer and fall. Since the oxygen content in water decreases when it is impounded, however, it would be necessary to reintroduce oxygen into the cooler water by aeration. This would be achieved by injecting air into the reregulating area from a network of pipes beneath the surface of the river. The map (Figure 15.2) shows that the Middle Snake inherits moderately low-quality water from the slack-water storage areas of Brownlee, Oxbow, and Hells Canyon dams. The combination of slack water with high phosphorous and nitrogen content has produced floating algal slimes in the storage areas, which further deplete the oxygen supply when the algae die.

Because it would restore the oxygen content and improve the temperature of the water so that it is more hospitable to fish life, the Appaloosa project is assigned an annual benefit of $6,590,000 for fish and wildlife enhancement. But the Appaloosa pool would destroy a spawning area for approximately 44,500 fall Chinook and a lesser number of spring Chinook and Steelhead, requiring the construction of collection and hatchery facilities at the reregulating dam in order to compensate for their loss. The capital cost of these facilities is estimated at $22,600,000 with an annual operating cost of $1,018,000. (These costs are *not* included in Table 15.4.) In addition, the Appaloosa pool would displace and therefore eventually destroy an estimated 960 deer and 1,840 game birds. Other wildlife losses are neither estimated nor evaluated, but they would be of equivalent magnitude.

At an interest rate of 3¼ percent and a project life of one hundred years, the Appaloosa installation has the highest benefit-cost ratio of the four projects—2.72 to 1. The project is also assigned the highest annual equivalent for recreational benefits of any of the plans, although the difference among projects is not great. Flood-control benefits—the value of property that would be saved from destruction by checking high river flow—is the lowest of all the benefits and relatively unimportant. All the projects are much the same in regard to flood-control benefits except Plan 4, the Pleasant Valley project, which is less than half that of the others.

John Krutilla, senior research associate for Resources for the Future and a leading water-resource economist, disagrees with the conclusion of the *Interior Resource Study*. He testified at the FPC hearings that in terms of 1967 prices the Appaloosa project was the least desirable economically. Employing a 9 percent rate of interest, which he considered a more realistic measure of the opportunity cost of capital than the 3¼ rate used in the

Interior Resource Study, Krutilla found only Plan 2, High Mountain Sheep and China Gardens, to be economically feasible—that is, to represent an investment in which the benefits exceed the costs—and this only by totally disregarding environmental destruction.

Plan 2: High Mountain Sheep and China Gardens

Plan 2 would produce the greatest power output of any of the plans, 3,100 megawatts (see Table 15.5), but it would virtually eliminate the large anadromous fish population that spawns in the Salmon and Imnaha rivers, unless a satisfactory fish passage around the dams were devised. The Federal Power Commission had previously concluded that fish passages could be constructed around dams that would permit the Columbia-Snake River fish populations to be maintained without serious depletion. Later, however, fishery authorities determined from experience at Hells Canyon dam and other installations that fish-passage structure are generally unsatisfactory. As a result, attempts to maintain fish passage beyond China Gardens, High Mountain Sheep, and Hells Canyon dam have been abandoned, and it was proposed instead those fish that can be trapped be subjected to artificial hatchery propagation. Such procedures are costly

Table 15.5: Plan 2: High Mountain Sheep and China Gardens

Output:	3,100 megawatts	
Benefits:	$61,329,000 annual equivalent	
	Power	$60,748,000
	Fish and wildlife enhancement	none[a]
	Recreation	336,000
	Flood Control	245,000
	Total	$61,329,000
Costs:	$24,275,000 annual equivalent	
	Federal investment	$18,705,000
	Annual operating	5,570,000
	Total	$24,275,000

B/C ratio: 2.53/1 (acknowledged as misleading)
Interest rate: 3¼ percent
Project life: 100 years

[a] Very large adverse effects on anadromous fish.
Source: *Resource Study of the Middle Snake* (Washington, D.C.: Department of the Interior, 1968), Part VI, pp. 14–15.

and generally result in a decrease in the fish population as compared with natural conditions.

The High Mountain Sheep and China Gardens project provides—as does Plan 1—multilevel intakes to the main dam's generating turbines and mechanical aeration of the downstream discharge, but the extraordinary disorienting effect of blocking off access to the Salmon and Imnaha rivers, quite aside from the questionable efficiency of the trapping devices, is likely to have harmful effects on the fish populations. The benefit-cost ratio of 2.53 to 1, which is based on a 3¼ percent interest rate and a one hundred-year project life, does not reflect the adverse effect on the migratory fish population of this reach of the Snake—one of the most productive aquatic environments along the whole Columbia-Snake system. The harmful effects of the project on the fish population are acknowledged, but not included as a cost in computing the 2.53 to 1 ratio. In 1965, the net value of the Columbia River anadromous fish run was estimated at $13,805,500 with the Snake and Salmon rivers responsible for the largest single runs of spring Chinook and steelhead as well as fall Chinook (see Figure 15.2).

With or without fish passages, eventual total loss of the Salmon river and Imnaha river anadromous fish population will take place. Spawning waters for 48,000 fall Chinook would be eliminated by the reservoir pool, and 1,450 deer and 2,570 upland game birds would be lost through inundation of habitat. The fishery loss is impressive, estimated by the Fish and Wildlife Service at 2,104,000 angler-days and 5,745,300 pounds of commercial fish harvested annually.

Although the destructive impact of the High Mountain Sheep-China Gardens project on the migratory fisheries was not accounted for in the benefit-cost ratio, there is no doubt that the pressure from commercial and sports fishing interests was an important factor in the decision against development of this site in spite of the examiner's conclusion that it provided "greater power benefits than Pleasant Valley or Appaloosa with reregulation at Mountain Sheep."[8]

Plan 3: High Mountain Sheep without China Gardens

The High Mountain Sheep project without the reregulating dam at China Gardens produces less than half the power of Plan 2—1,400 megawatts instead of 3,100 megawatts (see Table 15.6). Based on an interest rate of 3¼ percent and a project life of one hundred years, Plan 3 has a benefit-cost ratio of 2.69 to 1, which is higher than the ratio for Plan 2,

[8] William C. Levy, *Presiding Examiner's Initial Decision on Remand, Projects Nos. 2243 and 2273* (Washington, D. C.: Federal Power Commission, February 23, 1971), p. 12.

Table 15.6: Plan 3: High Mountain Sheep without China Gardens

Output:	1,400 megawatts	
Benefits:	$36,525,000 annual equivalent	
	Power	$35,944,000
	Fish and wildlife enhancement	none[a]
	Recreation	336,000
	Flood control	245,000
	Total	$36,525,000
Costs:	$13,557,000 annual equivalent	
	Federal investment	$10,377,000
	Annual operating	3,180,000
	Total	$13,557,000

B/C ratio: 2.69/1 (acknowledged as misleading)
Interest rate: 3¼ percent
Project life: 100 years

[a] Very large adverse effects on anadromous fish.
Source: *Resource Study of the Middle Snake* (Washington, D.C.: Department of the Interior, 1968), Part VI, pp. 19–24.

including the dam at China Gardens. But as in the former case, this ratio is acknowledged to be deceptively high because it does not account for damage to the migratory fish population. Although a dam at High Mountain Sheep does not seal off the Salmon river tributary from the Snake, the extraordinary water turbulence below the dam would be seriously disruptive of the fish life. In fact, the absence of the China Gardens dam and after-bay makes it more difficult to aerate the water below the High Mountain Sheep dam, even though aerating devices are a part of the equipment of Plan 3. Flow surges of water during the production of power for peak demand could therefore be expected to reduce the oxygen content of the water below the power plant as well as to cause severe temperature variations. As a result, the construction of Plan 3 would eventually be likely to eliminate all anadromous fish upstream from China Gardens. Much the same wildlife habitat loss as in the case of Plan 2 would result from Plan 3.

Plan 4: Pleasant Valley and Low Mountain Sheep

This complex of two dams is one of the smallest of the four plans, measured either in terms of reservoir storage or power production (see

Tables 15.7 and 15.8). The original plant at Pleasant Valley would yield 1,700 megawatts of power and the Low Mountain Sheep reregulating dam would produce 400 megawatts. Ultimately, however, the capacity of Pleasant Valley-Low Mountain Sheep could be raised to 3,200 megawatts through the addition of pumped storage.[9] Since the usable storage behind the Pleasant Valley dam is limited, however, Plan 4 does not incorporate devices for downstream temperature control or oxygen restoration.

The impounded waters of the Pleasant Valley reservoir would suffer oxygen loss at the lower levels, and algal bloom on the surface waters would occur during the summer. The algal bloom would impair the use of the Pleasant Valley reservoir for recreation as well as eliminate much of the resident fish population in this reach of the Snake. The loss of high-quality stream fishing—smallmouth bass, trout, salmon—is estimated at 15,000 angler-days, and could only be compensated for in part by hatchery production of reservoir-tolerant fish, which are generally considered inferior by the dedicated angler.

The Pleasant Valley dam complex would result in the destruction of the spawning grounds for a moderately large number of fish—44,500 fall

Table 15.7: Plan 4: Pleasant Valley

Output:	1,700 megawatts	
Benefits:	$44,544,000 annual equivalent	
	Power	$44,165,000
	Fish and wildlife enhancement	none
	Recreation	305,000
	Flood control	74,000
	Total	$44,544,000
Costs:	$18,987,000 annual equivalent	
	Federal investment	$15,021,000
	Annual operating	3,966,000
	Total	$18,987,000

B/C ratio: 2.35/1
Interest rate: 3¼ percent
Project life: 100 years

Source: *Resource Study of the Middle Snake* (Washington, D.C.: Department of the Interior, 1968), Part VI, pp. 24–29.

[9] Pumped storage involves taking advantage of lower off-peak electric rates to pump water above a generating dam. The water is then drawn down again to generate electricity during high-demand peak periods.

Table 15.8: Plan 4A: Pleasant Valley-Low Mountain Sheep (the pumped-storage addition to Plan 4)

Output:	400 megawatts
Benefits:	$11,504,000 annual equivalent
Costs:	$6,721,000 annual equivalent

B/C ratio: 1.71/1
Interest rate: 3¼ percent
Project life: 85 years

Source: *Resource Study of the Middle Snake* (Washington, D.C.: Department of the Interior, 1968), Part VI, pp. 24–29.

Chinook and smaller numbers of spring Chinook and steelhead trout. In the absence of the Appaloosa dam, the Pleasant Valley dam simply obstructs the same fish that run higher in the Middle Snake. (See Figure 15.2.) But in comparison with Plans 2 and 3, both of which employ dams at High Mountain Sheep, fish destruction would be less with the Pleasant Valley development, and downstream recreational opportunities would be relatively unaffected. The creation of the Pleasant Valley reservoir would inundate wildlife habitat, however, and it is estimated that 500 deer and 960 upland game birds would be lost as a result. Other wildlife losses of equivalent magnitude would occur under this plan.

The spawning loss from the Pleasant Valley reservoir could be mitigated by building collection facilities in the Low Mountain Sheep reregulating dam at a capital cost of $22,600,000 and an operating cost of $1,018,000 annually. A cost for the loss of wildlife habitat can be assessed on the basis of the days of hunting forgone, but since this is but a partial measure of the worth of wildlife in the natural setting of the Middle Snake, such an estimate is an understatement. Neither of these costs is included in Table 15.7.

The Fish and Wildlife Service, which is responsible for the determination of losses that result from the destruction of game species and their habitat, is concerned almost exclusively with opportunities for hunting and sport and commercial fishing. But there is a vast army of outdoor enthusiasts who neither hunt nor fish—hikers, canoeists, rafters, nature photographers, bird watchers, and simply scenery lookers—who value the sight of a bald or golden eagle on the wing quite as much as the hunter prizes a Hungarian partridge in the bag. Such uses are rarely quantified in a benefit-cost ratio.

A conflict of values difficult to compromise is involved between the position of the Federal Power Commission, which is dedicated to the development of hydroelectric power, and those taking a different view of the public interest. Indeed, the hydropower advocates find the suggestion that the last undeveloped reach of the Snake remain free of power plants little less than subversive.[10]

The Bonneville Power Administration, the federal agency with jurisdiction over power produced at the Bonneville Dam and other installations on the Columbia River, understandably views the Snake River mainly in terms of kilowatts. In the Department of the Interior study, the Bonneville Power Administration report says:

The Middle Snake Canyon location is extremely strategic in the Pacific Northwest water and power economy. To weaken this system by depriving it of the major remaining potential storage project of the Middle Snake River subverts and undermines the legislative policies and intent of Congress in its enactment of the Bonneville Power Act.[11]

The Bonneville Power Administration and—to only a degree less—the FPC examiner see the undammed area of the Middle Snake as an incompleted hydroelectric system, unproductive and wasteful; others, such as the economist John Krutilla, see this undeveloped region of the Snake as increasing in value if it retains its unique wilderness character, free of power development. Krutilla's position is that the Middle Snake canyon

. . . may have few, if any, close substitutes. Moreover, if the present environment is adversely altered, its reproduction is not possible. In short, while rare natural phenomena can be reduced in supply, they cannot be expanded by the works of man. They represent irreplaceable assets not subject to reproduction. Now if the supply is thus fixed but the demand for the services of this asset increases, it is an irreplaceable asset with an increasing annual benefit.[12]

[10] A dialogue between Floyd Dominy, one-time commissioner of the Bureau of Reclamation, and David Brower, former executive director of the Sierra Club and later head of the Friends of the Earth, presents the conflict in values of a power/irrigation advocate and a wilderness preservationist. Against the background of a float trip down the Colorado river—which contains a number of Bureau of Reclamation dams and plans for more—Commissioner Dominy finds the river better off as a result of Reclamation's dams, and regards conservationists as little more than obstructionists. He boasts to Brower, "I'm a greater conversationist than you are, by far. I do things. I make things available to man. Unregulated, the Colordao River wouldn't be worth a good God damn to anybody. . . ." John McPhee, *Encounters with the Archdruid* (New York: Farrar, Straus & Giroux, 1971), p. 240.

[11] *Resource Study of the Middle Snake,* p. II–4.

[12] John V. Krutilla, *Testimony Before the Federal Power Commission on the Middle Snake Issue* (Washington, D.C.: mimeographed, 1970), p. 29. See also John V. Krutilla and A. C. Fisher, *The Economics of Natural Environments* (Baltimore, Maryland: The Johns Hopkins University Press, 1975).

At the same time that the pressure to add hydroelectric installations rises with the demand for power in the West, the value of the Middle Snake as a wilderness area also increases. Using a variant of the familiar supply-and-demand illustration, we can illustrate the changing worth of a commercially undeveloped Middle Snake. In the usual supply-demand relationship, supply responds to price with increased offerings as prices rise and reduced offerings as prices fall. Demand conventionally reacts in just the opposite way; a higher price discourages sales, while a lower price increases purchases. In Figure 15.3, however, the diagram shows that the supply of Middle Snake wilderness cannot be increased in response to higher prices or increased demand, as is indicated by the perpendicular supply lines at 1930 and 1977. Destruction of wilderness is not reversible. In 1977 there was approximately 150 miles of remaining wilderness in the Middle Snake.

The demand and supply curves in Figure 15.3 are hypothetical, but they reflect changing attitudes toward wilderness and the impact of hydroelectric development in the Pacific Northwest on its supply. This supply and demand illustration differs from earlier versions, however, since the vertical axis in Figure 15.3 is a scale, which shows only that 6 is higher than 5, 5 higher than 4, and so on, rather than the usual cardinal dollar measure. Another difference is that two time periods, 1930 and 1977, are depicted on the same diagram, which violates the conventional short-run demand and supply arrangement.

What Figure 15.3 shows is that the demand for wilderness in 1977

Figure 15.3 Value of Middle Snake Wilderness Over Time

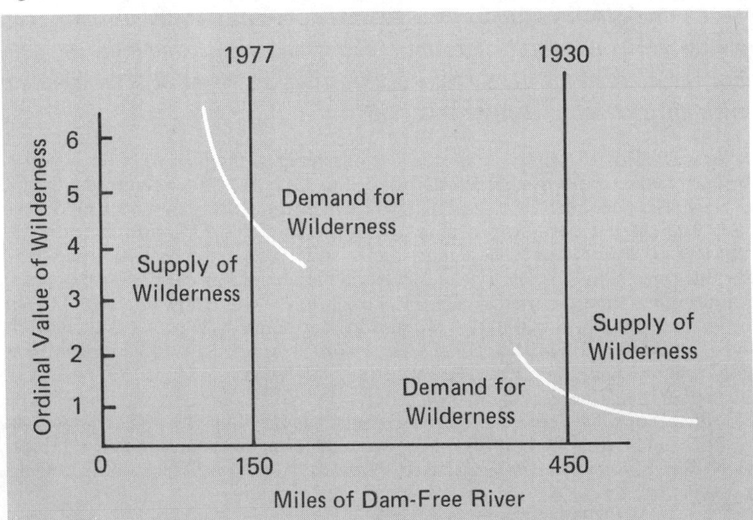

significantly exceeds the demand in 1930. The greater demand, interacting with a reduced supply, results in a higher value being placed on wilderness. The reduced supply of wilderness is self-evident; the increase in demand is the product of a combination of factors including increased population and leisure, higher income, and a basic change in the attitude of many Americans toward the worth of natural areas. In sum, wilderness takes on the character of a scarce and valuable resource in 1977.

How the costs of thermal power become the benefits of hydroelectric power

The "alternate source" approach

In quantifying benefits, some federal agencies employ what they term the *alternate source approach.* Normally, market data are used to compute the benefit side of the b/c ratio, such as the price of the farm commodity raised on an irrigation project or the dollar value of the property protected from water damage by a flood-control project. In some cases, however, instead of computing benefits directly from the price of project output, such as kilowatt rates for a hydroelectric plant or freight rates for a canal development, the measure of benefits is the *cost* of obtaining the output by the most likely alternative source of supply. In the case of power production, for example, the most likely alternative to hydroelectric power is thermal generation.

The reasons for employing the alternate source approach to compute benefits are not completely apparent, and the practice has been criticized on the ground that it inflates the benefit side of the b/c ratio. The Federal Power Commission, which undertakes benefit-cost studies of hydroelectric installations for the other federal agencies, uses the thermal alternative as a measure of the benefits of hydro production, in part because the power rates vary in terms of amount and time of use. Utilities with different customer composition and time distribution of sales experience different revenue returns. Costs presumably do not reflect such variation. But whatever the reason for its use, the alternate source approach provides an extremely favorable frame of reference for the determination of project benefits.

Relying upon the cost of the most likely alternative for the measure of benefits means that there is little danger of understating the project's worth. In the case of hydropower, for example, the thermal alternative is almost always a higher-cost method of producing power. As a result, the alternate source approach yields a higher benefit-cost ratio than if benefits are based on market rates, thereby making it easier for a project to pass the b/c test.

Benefit-cost ratios: no consensus on the Middle Snake

In Plans 1 through 4, the benefit-cost ratios for the Middle Snake hydro projects are sometimes recorded with the stipulation that the ratio is "acknowledged as misleading" because no cost computation is made for extensive fish and wildlife destruction. These ratios were prepared for the Department of the Interior *Resource Study* under the direction of the Bureau of Reclamation, and all plans have benefit-cost ratios above unity, with Plan 1—the Appaloosa project—ranking first.

In benefit-cost analyses prepared by the Federal Power Commission staff for the use of the FPC examiner, however, only Plan 2—High Mountain Sheep with China Gardens—is able to produce power at a lower cost than the most economic thermal alternative. And when the costs of the loss of the free-flowing character of the Middle Snake are assessed against this project, costs computed by John Krutilla to range between $700,000 and $1,100,000 annually, the High Mountain Sheep-China Gardens development also fails to pass the test of economic feasibility.

Considering such environmental factors together with the marginal character of the projects, the FPC staff report to the examiner found *none* of the projects to be economically justified. The examiner did not accept the staff's reasoning, however, contending that "it should be emphasized that feasibility studies, however useful and detailed, remain speculative models of a future that eludes prediction. They are aids, not substitutes for decision making."[13]

The case of the applicants

The consortium of utilities seeking a license to build a power dam on the Middle Snake—the Pacific Northwest Power Company and the Washington Public Power Supply System—also presented benefit-cost analyses to the Federal Power Commission examiner, but they used different considerations from those of the Department of the Interior. The capital investment in the applicants' plans was less, and the benefit-cost ratios were below those of the Interior Department. The applicants' lower benefit-cost ratios, which ranged between 1.426 to 1 and 1.194 to 1, are

[13] William C. Levy, *op. cit.*, p. 28.

primarily the result of using a higher rate of interest to compute costs and discount benefits and a shorter period of analysis. Although the applicants employ a higher rate of interest and a shorter period of analysis, the benefit-cost ratio is kept above unity mainly by employing lower construction-cost estimates and omitting major items of cost, such as those for downstream temperature control, oxygenation, recreation, and taxes.

Relying on minimum design of facilities and low construction-cost estimates may appear to invite later cost difficulty. But unrealistic cost estimates do not carry the same prospect of economic distress for an electric utility that they do for other businesses. Power producers are insulated from some of the harsher forces of the market. They are alloted a market area without competition, and although their rates are regulated, they can be adjusted upward to cover costs. In the strategy of obtaining a hydro license, there is little to lose and much to gain by understating costs, thereby ensuring an attractive benefit-cost ratio. Later, a petition for a rate increase based on full cost will prevent the utility from experiencing financial distress.

What is the economic cost of power development of the Middle Snake?

Perhaps the most ironic aspect of the extended Middle Snake controversy is the failure to identify the economic cost of keeping the Middle Snake as a free-flowing river—especially in view of the Federal Power Commission's use of thermal costs as a measure of Middle Snake hydro benefits.

It is apparent that the opportunity cost of preserving the Middle Snake in its natural state is the market value of the output, such as power production, that would be obtained if the river were commercially developed. This does not mean, however, that the cost of power production is simply the loss of wilderness, or that preservation of the Middle Snake necessarily reduces the supply of power for the Pacific Northwest. There are alternative sources of power—thermal generation using fossil fuels or nuclear energy. These entail higher generating costs but lower transmission costs. The *net* cost of preserving the Middle Snake is thus the increase in the cost of thermal over that of hydro, not the total expenditure. In sum, society can have both wilderness and increased power production if it is willing to pay a somewhat higher kilowatt rate, or it can have increased power production at a lower kilowatt rate and no wilderness. Congress has chosen wilderness preservation and higher-cost power.

Key terms and concepts

Hydroelectric power production the generation of electricity through the use of flowing water to drive turbines.

Thermal power production the generation of electricity through the use of a fuel such as coal or atomic fission to produce steam which drives turbines.

Peaking output power generated during the period of maximum electric use, as from five o'clock to seven o'clock in the evening.

Pumped-storage power production pumping water above a hydro dam in order to draw it down during a peak period.

The alternate source approach a method of establishing the dollar value of project benefits on the basis of the most likely alternative source of supply, for example, the railroad in the case of canal development and thermal power generation in the case of a hydro pwoer project. This should not be confused with the opportunity cost principle.

Discussion and review questions

1. In deciding whether to authorize a hydroelectric project, what factors does the Federal Power Commission consider and how does it go about the authorization?

2. What was the controversy surrounding the authorization of the Middle Snake hydroelectric project?

3. On what grounds may Congress intervene in a decision of the Federal Power Commission?

4. What were the findings of the various benefit-cost studies undertaken on the Middle Snake development? Why are they different?

5. What is the alternate source approach to benefit evaluation and why is it used?

16 Beyond the market: externalities, the environment, and the public interest

*The rise in prices for American Indian art, though it has been good for the collector, has had disastrous consequences for scholarship. One can see the link between the art market and looting by examining the unwanted consequences of a single sale—the auction, in November, 1971, at Parke-Bernet, of the Green Collection of American Indian Art. The sale itself was thoroughly reputable, but as a result of the publicity it gave to record price levels of Indian art, looting, which was already epidemic, intensified with extraordinary rapidity.**

American Indian art objects, particularly artifacts of early South American cultures, have recently become highly prized by wealthy collectors and museums. The result has been predictable—a sharp rise in the price of such collector's items and fierce competition for the limited supply. Since much Indian art is found in archeological sites that are protected by national law, marketing these art objects in another country involves removing them illegally from the site and smuggling them from the country of origin. Little care is exercised in the removal of the artifacts and much site destruction accompanies the thievery. In responding to the high-price bids of collectors and museums, the looters are also wiping out much irreplaceable source material for archeological research. Economists call such side effects of economic activity *externalities*.

Externalities

Not very long ago the subject of externalities was given only the briefest of treatment in economic texts. But the concept of externality,

* Karl E. Meyer, *The Plundered Past* (New York: Atheneum, 1973), p. 8.

although not widely noted until recently, was well established in the economic literature in the writings of the great English neoclassical economists, Alfred Marshall and A. C. Pigou, who taught at Cambridge University at the turn of the twentieth century. This was well before environmental damage from industry was widespread, but not before it was evident that market decisions affected more than those directly involved in the production and consumption of economic goods and services.[1] Indeed, the environmental deterioration that seems so recently to have befallen much of the industrial world has been present for some time in areas where it has been ignored.

Externalities are not all bad, although environmental deterioration in the early 1970s focused attention primarily on the harmful effects. Since beneficial externalities do not raise the same problems of adjustment or compensation, however, they attract less attention; therefore we shall confine our discussion in this chapter largely to external diseconomies. We

"Superstack" internalizes environmental costs by spreading pollution higher and wider over Sudbury, Ontario

"Superstack," the world's tallest chimney, dominates International Nickel's [International Nickel Company of Canada, Ltd.] sprawling 200,000 acre complex at Sudbury, Ontario. Built [in 1971] at a cost of $26 million, the 1,250 foot-stack dispenses gaseous wastes that once spewed from low level stacks and, before that, from ground-level "roasting yards." (These were used in the separation of nickel sulfide ore until 1929, when the smelting process moved indoors.) The sulfur dioxide fumes from the roasting defoliated the countryside, leaving blackened buttes . . . that resemble a lunar landscape.

"Superstack" is only one element in a major environmental effort undertaken by the company since 1969. All together, some $60 million has been spent to meet tougher new government standards. Inco has installed equipment to help purify noxious dust inside its plants; it has also invested in "clarifying systems" to decontaminate water affected by waste fallout from its refineries. In Shebandowan, Ontario, the company put its ore-conveyor belts underground in order to minimize noise on the surface. Shebandowan also features $200,000 worth of landscaping, including some 15,000 freshly planted seedlings.[2]

[1] Externalities are not confined to the market-directed economy. They may also occur in the planned economy, as the pollution of Lake Baikal in the Soviet Union demonstrates.
[2] Lansing Lamong, "Inco: A Giant Learns How to Compete," *Fortune,* January 1975, p. 104.

can distinguish two kinds of externalities, *external economies* and *external diseconomies,* depending on whether the side effects are beneficial or harmful to those beyond the producer-consumer relationship. Broadly defined, an *externality* occurs when an action by A imposes a cost or benefit on B for which no charge or compensation is made through the market.

Externalities and optimum allocation

Only if all benefits and costs are accounted for in the prices of resources and economic output—only, in other words, if there are no externalities—does an otherwise perfectly operating, competitive-market economy achieve the optimum allocation of resources. In considering this issue in his classic study *The Economics of Welfare,* Arthur Cecil Pigou noted that the economy's output was less than optimum when the price system failed to take account of externalities.[3] Pigou distinguished between private and social output and held that society was best off when the two were in balance. With externalities, however, marginal private product and marginal social product are out of balance, private product exceeding social product when there are external diseconomies and the reverse when there are external economies. To correct this imbalance, Pigou advocated intervention in the market to expand those economic activities that generate economies and curtail those producing external diseconomies.[4]

Pigou's plan to improve resource allocation involved taxing economic activity that generated diseconomies and granting a bounty or subsidy to firms encountering external economies. The objective was to equalize marginal social product and marginal private product. Although Pigou examined the externality problem early in the twentieth century, until recently governments generally ignored it. Economists as well showed little interest in the empirical investigation that is the necessary preliminary step to devising a system of taxes and bounties to encourage economies and discourage diseconomies. In the meantime, the critics of the Pigovian approach advocated instead private bargaining between those causing and suffering injury from externalities.

Bargaining as an alternative to taxation of external diseconomies has obvious advantages. Taxes entail costs of collection, and determining the tax rate to be used to curtail the diseconomy is not a simple matter.

[3] *The Economics of Welfare,* first published in 1920 by Macmillan Limited of London, went through four editions with the last appearing in 1932.

[4] Various terms have been used that are essentially synonymous with the term externalities. These include *social cost* and *spill-over cost,* which are equivalent to external diseconomy, and *neighborhood effects* and *side effects,* which are broader concepts that apply to either economies or diseconomies. Pigou's proposition, for example, may be expressed as the relationship between *marginal private cost* and *marginal social cost* rather than product.

Moreover, if there is really the opportunity for a bargain to be made between two parties of essentially equal power, the adjustment of the injury by compensation or internalization may be both more efficient and more flexible than the remedy through government intervention. But in fact private bargaining affords little opportunity of adjusting the more important externalities of an industrial economy.

Internalizing an externality

Internalizing an external diseconomy imposes on the firm costs that previously were shifted to third parties. To internalize pollution costs, a firm that previously discharged untreated wastes into the environment may change the production process, stopping the discharge of wastes, or it may treat the wastes. As the federal Environmental Protection Agency and corresponding state agencies undertake more stringent control of industrial waste-disposal practices, more and more firms are faced with the legal obligation to internalize costs previously shifted to the public. The pulp and paper industry, formerly one of the worst air and water polluters, recently has made substantial progress in internalizing its pollution costs.

The technical modifications undertaken to eliminate paper-making waste discharges raise costs for the producer and prices for the paper consumer, but the higher price more accurately reflects the full cost of paper making. When part of the cost of paper making is shifted to the public in the form of air and water pollution, the lower cost and price stimulate paper output beyond that which occurs when full costs are covered by the firm. With externalities, a misallocation of resources takes place even if the market operates efficiently. The question is: How should firms or government internalize such costs—by taxation, regulation, or bargaining?

Internalizing costs: by bargain or coercion

Sometimes the externality cases discussed by economists—such as the smoke-soiled family wash or an offensive necktie—have been hand-picked candidates for the bargaining approach. So long as the number of injured parties is small, the bargaining approach requires lower administrative cost and less disorganization of production than taxation or regulation of the polluting firm. In most cases, the firm can compensate one or a small number of injured parties at lower costs to all concerned, including society, than if the government becomes involved in regulatory action. As the number of injured parties increases, however, the bargaining procedure becomes more cumbersome and it becomes more difficult to attain a socially optimum solution.

Government regulation is likely to be a more effective way of dealing with externalities that are either widespread or serious, such as some kinds of environmental pollution. Inhalation of asbestos fibers, for example, is a cause of lung cancer, an acknowledged health hazard to those who work or live in the vicinity of certain kinds of construction and building demolition. Not only does such an externality injure the individual, but the latter's disability may impose a burden upon society as well. Therefore the prohibition of practices that lead to airborne asbestos fibers is justified rather than relying upon compensation determined by bargaining.

The bargaining-compensation approach to externalities is totally inappropriate in cases in which the externality irreversibly destroys resources that have value for those *not* represented in the bargaining. Bargaining followed by land purchase or compensation may prevent injury that could

The Reserve Mining Company's externality is Duluth, Minnesota's water supply problem

In 1951, when the Reserve Mining Company constructed its ore-processing plant on the north shore of Lake Superior . . . few people were concerned about the environmental damage to the area; most, instead, looked forward to the stimulating economic effect of the large investment in this somewhat depressed region. The state of Minnesota was anxious to have its declining iron-ore industry shored up by the development of low-grade ore processing, and the federal government had not yet become sensitive to environmental damage. As a result, Lake Superior was selected as a free, bottomless pit in which to dump the plant's powder-fine waste—nearly 25 million tons a year. The rock dust was sluiced into the lake, where it was expected to settle benignly to the bottom.

But the taconite wastes have not stayed in place. They have fanned out from Silver Bay for hundreds of miles and have made parts of this cleanest of the Great Lakes murky with suspended dust. The resulting aesthetic degradation is but one of the unaccounted costs shifted to the public in producing iron ore from taconite. [Another is the contamination of the Duluth, Minnesota water supply with asbestos-like fibers from the taconite wastes.][5]

[5] L. G. Hines, *Environmental Issues* (New York: W. W. Norton & Co., Inc., 1973), pp. 54–5.

result to property owners from damming and flooding a white-water river for hydroelectric power production such as the St. John River in northern Maine, but another group affected by the project—canoeists, fishermen, boaters, and outdoor enthusiasts in general—may be inadequately represented or completely ignored in the bargaining process. Since the change in the character of the river and the surrounding area is permanent, future generations are also affected: Those who would choose white-water instead of flat-water recreation and those who favor thermal instead of hydroelectric power production are disadvantaged.

The bargaining approach to externalities breaks down most seriously in cases where a private transaction ignores the broad public-interest consequences of the bargain, as in the case of contract between a mining company and a land holder. In a mining agreement, neither the land owner nor the mining company may be willing voluntarily to accept a lower return from mining to ensure protection and rehabilitation of the land. The public interest in preventing the mining company from devastating the land needs to be incorporated into the private contract.

Because hydroelectric projects require approval by the Federal Power Commission, there is an opportunity for third parties to express their views in such cases, but about the only role of the third party to coal contracts in Appalachia is that of mourning the demise of the land. The public interest is likely to be underrepresented in the negotiation of such private contracts; moreover the bargaining power of the contractors may be grossly unequal, further weakening the bargaining approach. But even if the hillside Appalachian farmer is the bargaining match for the Peabody Coal Company, the largest coal operation in the world, a private contract is an unlikely vehicle for the expression of the public interest.

Before pesticides and herbicides endangered human and other life forms, when blowouts from off-shore oil drilling were unknown, and when oil transport by tanker and pipeline did not threaten the sea and the tundra, private bargaining may have been an appropriate approach to external diseconomies. But no more. Control of externalities is still unchartered, but proposals to internalize the costs of air and water pollution have recently received attention from legislators and administrators as well as economists. Among the arrangements in operation, the Ruhr system of user charges in the case of water pollution is one of the most noteworthy.

The Ruhr Plan

Although deterioration of the air, water, and land appeared to take place with startling abruptness in the early 1970s, pollution is not a recent development in many highly industrialized areas. There is a threshold effect with air and water pollution. Up to a certain level, the air, the land, lakes and streams can tolerate pollution. A body of water can degrade some kinds of wastes—break them down into their constituent elements—without impairing the normal life processes in a stream or river. If the waste load becomes too great, however, the free oxygen that is needed for the stream's aquatic life is used up in oxidizing the wastes. When this happens, the stream's capacity to support high-oxygen-using organisms, such as game fish, falls off abruptly, producing an observable deterioration in the stream's water quality.

The Ruhr Valley in Germany is one of Europe's more heavily industrialized areas. If the wastes of the industries in the valley were discharged untreated into the Ruhr River, virtually all forms of aquatic life would be destroyed. To prevent this, a system of user charges has been devised by the Ruhr Valley industrial cooperative that is responsible for water management. Over the past fifty years, cooperative associations of the industrial firms in the Ruhr have exercised control over water quality, land drainage, water supply, flood control, and waste disposal. To abate pollution in the Ruhr River, these associations have imposed effluent charges to finance waste-treatment facilities. One basis for the Ruhr effluent charge is BOD, "biochemical oxygen demand," which measures the pollution waste load in terms of the pounds of oxygen required to degrade or neutralize the pollution.[6]

In the few applications of an effluent charge in the United States, such as that initiated by Cincinnati in 1953, the BOD assessment brought about an impressive reduction in waste discharges. After the charge of 1.3 cents per pound of BOD was imposed, industrial waste disposal at the Cincinnati municipal treatment plant fell by more than one-third and continued to decrease annually for the next decade. On any scale, however, the effluent charge is an untried approach to internalizing pollution costs by industry. The United States has relied mainly upon municipal waste-treatment facilities subsidized through a program of federal construction grants.

Air pollution and user charges

Municipal waste-treatment plants cannot be built to abate air pollution, but much the same issue is involved: Should the firms responsible for air pollution be required to modify their operations to decrease environmental damage? Industry is not the only cause of air pollution. The au-

[6] BOD does not take account of many of the more harmful kinds of pollution, such as acids, radioactive materials, viral or bacterial conditions, silts, thermal elevation, heavy metals, poisons, phenols, and substances that affect water palatability. Biochemical oxygen demand is expressed in pounds, making it possible to assess a per-pound effluent charge.

tomobile is a major cause of air-quality deterioration in most metropolitan areas, but industrial wastes—especially particulate matter and sulfur dioxide—are usually more lethal when in high concentration.

The external diseconomies of air pollution range from damage to buildings and vegetation to debilitation and death of humans. Air pollution has contributed to death, as at Donora, Pennsylvania, in October 1948, when twenty deaths occurred during an air inversion.[7] A similar situation in New York City during Thanksgiving Day in 1966 caused two hundred above-normal deaths. Less harmful externalities from air pollution are eye-irritating smog, respiratory and heart disabilities from sulfur dioxide and carbon monoxide inhalation, destruction of plants, shrubs, and trees from ozone and oxide combinations, and accelerated deterioration and soiling of clothes and buildings from soot and oxides.

Although there are still areas of considerable uncertainty about the effects of some kinds of air pollutants, sulfur oxides lead the list of harmful pollutants. Produced mainly through combustion of fossil fuels, sulfur dioxide and sulfur trioxide are prime targets for elimination. Restriction of the use of high-sulfur fuel in generating electric power is presently imposed in most metropolitan areas. A more unusual approach is to internalize the cost of sulfur oxide pollution by imposing a tax on sulfur emissions.

The sulfur tax-rebate proposal

In 1972, the United States Treasury Department and the Environmental Protection Agency endorsed a proposal to tax lead in gasoline and sulfur in fossil fuels. The immediate purpose of the tax on leaded gasoline was to discourage the use of leaded fuel in cars equipped with catalytic emission-control systems. (Lead is destructive of the operation of the catalyst.) A secondary benefit of reducing the use of leaded gasoline is the decrease in lead pollution of the environment. The purpose of the tax on high-sulfur fuels, mainly coal and petroleum, was to reduce sulfur-oxide pollution of the air. The tax was to be levied at the mine or refinery and raised over a period of five years from one cent per pound to ten cents per pound of sulfur. By imposing a cost penalty upon the use of high-sulfur fuel, it was anticipated that the production and use of less-polluting fuels would be encouraged, such as natural gas and low-sulfur coal and fuel oil. The sulfur tax endorsed by the Treasury and the Environmental Protection Agency provided an incentive system of rebates designed to encourage firms to suppress sulfur-oxide emissions. If the sulfur discharged into the

[7] An air inversion, or thermal inversion, produces a cap of cool air that holds down the fumes and particles discharged from combustion which normally rise with the heated air and are dispersed above breathing level.

air is less than originally contained in the fuel, indicating supression of sulfur, the firm is eligible for a tax rebate for decreasing sulfur pollution.

If the sulfur tax is high enough, the tax-rebate system will bring about a change in the technology of fuel use and a reordering of fuel demand favoring low-sulfur or nonsulfur fuels. The short-run effect of the tax-rebate program will be confined largely to raising the price of high-sulfur fuels, thereby improving the relative price position of low-sulfur fuels. Since the short-run supply of low-sulfur fuels is inelastic, the improved price position is not likely to have very much effect upon the supply of low-sulfur fuels. In the long run, however, if the tax rebate system provides sufficient incentive, modifications in the technology of fuel processing and fuel use will take place. Finally, by internalizing these costs, an increase in product prices will occur.

The tax-rebate approach to pollution has the advantage over other

---

Environmental external diseconomies: a regulatory challenge

It is not surprising that a society of increasing population, interdependence, and affluence should discover the need for collective intervention in matters once ignored or left wholly to private decisions. Pollution, congestion, noise, sprawling suburbs, and the decay of central cities are not the dominant problems of a young and sparsely settled nation. And concentration on economic growth was likely to be balanced by considerations of environmental quality, the provision of decent housing for the poor, and other more recent concerns only after the growth itself had generated the resources to address these problems.

While the nation's attention has turned to the need for new types of social policy, we have generally proceeded as if the legislative process and the techniques for governmental action suitable for an earlier set of problems could be carried over without change. But cleaning up the environment, relieving urban congestion, and reforming the health care system are not the same kinds of tasks as building canals and highways and paying out social security benefits. And the legislative genius that finds ways to mold a coalition behind a piece of legislation, though still necessary, is no longer sufficient to devise the instruments of social intervention. . . . Far more than in the past, legislative action must emphasize the creation of new incentives and new institutions that harness the self-interest of individuals and business firms toward socially desirable goals.[8]

---

[8] A. V. Kneese and C. L. Schultze, *Pollution, Prices and Public Policy* (Washington, D.C.: The Brookings Institution, 1975), pp. 119–20.

methods of leaving the choice of how pollution abatement is achieved to the producer, thereby encouraging innovative cost-reducing approaches. In the short run, however, internalizing pollution costs through the tax-rebate approach will be limited mainly to increased marginal cost because of higher fuel prices. This situation is illustrated in Figure 16.1.

Before the air-pollution costs of a product requiring large fuel inputs are internalized, the short-run supply curve for an industry, such as the iron and steel industry, MPC (marginal private cost) in Figure 16.1 lies below the short-run internalized supply curve MSC (marginal social cost). In order to internalize pollution costs, the tax on high-sulfur fuel must make it more costly for the firm to use high-sulfur fuel than to shift to low-sulfur fuels or improve fuel-use techniques. The short-run price increase of high-sulfur fuel from OA to OB decreases purchases from OD to OC, presumably as a result of shifting to low-sulfur fuels, and decreases sulfur pollution.

In the long run, the firm can take advantage of the rebate feature of the tax-rebate plan by installing equipment that reduces the discharge of sulfur into the atmosphere, in effect decreasing the supply price for high-sulfur fuel. For both the short and long run, the reorganization of the industry brought about by the tax-rebate program will move the economy closer to the Pareto optimum. When pollution costs are internalized, product prices more accurately reflect the full costs of using resources and the operation of the private market is made more responsive to the public interest. But there are costs involved in the tax-rebate approach. Monitoring and

Figure 16.1 Tax on Externalities in the Short Run

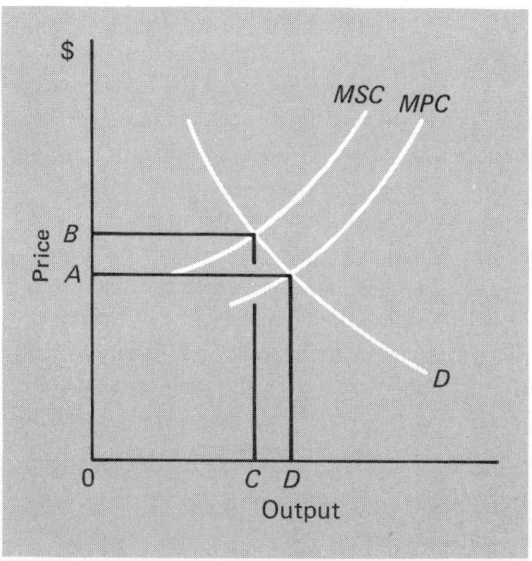

measuring a firm's sulfur discharge is very expensive, and the tax-rebate approach has none of the administrative simplicity of imposing standards of permissible levels of sulfur in fuels, which are more easily measured and enforced. In short, these are costs of reaching a Pareto optimum.

Summary

Externalities occur when an action by an individual or a firm imposes a cost without compensation or confers a benefit without charge on another individual, firm, or a part of the community. A beneficial externality of education, for example, is the increased national output that may result from higher educational attainments of the nation's labor force. The direct benefit is the higher income of the more educated members of the labor force. Undesirable externalities, such as water and air pollution, have received much attention recently. The environmental impact study of the federal Environmental Protection Agency, for example, is designed to identify and appraise externalities that affect the environment.

If externalities are not accounted for in the operation of either a market economy or a planning-board-directed economy, the resource allocation will fall short of the social optimum. This deficiency may be corrected by private bargaining or by government intervention. For the more important externalities, such as toxic industrial by-products, water pollution, and air pollution, government intervention has been increasingly employed. Various approaches to undesirable externalities are available, but economists are likely to favor internalizing these costs. To internalize externalities means to prevent the individual or firm from shifting a cost burden to third parties. Water pollution may be internalized, for example, by imposing an effluent charge upon the polluting firm that encourages a change in waste disposal practices so that third parties are no longer burdened. Requiring automobiles to be equipped with catalytic converters reduces air pollution and imposes the cost on the auto user rather than the breathing public.

Key terms and concepts

Internalizing an externality imposing the cost of an external diseconomy on the party responsible, as by an effluent tax on an industrial firm.

The Ruhr Plan a system of user charges imposed by industrial cooperatives upon its member firms using the Ruhr River for waste disposal.

BOD (biochemical oxygen demand) a measure of the polluting capacity of an organic waste in a stream.

Sulfur tax rebate a proposal to tax fossil fuel on the basis of its sulfur content and to rebate the tax in relation to the fuel user's suppression of sulfur discharged into the atmosphere.

Discussion and review questions

1. What is an externality? Why doesn't the market take account of externalities?

2. What was Pigou's proposal to correct for external diseconomies?

3. What is meant by internalizing an externality? Why do not business firms voluntarily internalize their externalities?

4. What are the advantages and disadvantages of the bargaining approach to externalities? In what areas is this approach likely to work best? In what areas does it work worst?

5. How effective is the bargaining-compensation approach in adjusting the externalities that arise in strip mining?

6. What kind of externalities may arise in the case of hydroelectric developments that are not compensated through normal market transactions? What kind of approach is necessary in adjusting for these? (Hint: This issue arises in the case of intangible benefits in benefit-cost analysis.)

7. Which of the various options to water pollution abatement do you consider preferable? Which represent internalizing the cost of water pollution and which shift the cost to the community?

8. Does air pollution pose a different kind of problem in internalizing costs?

9. In abating air pollution, how would the sulfur tax-rebate proposal work? Compared with other approaches, is this a low-cost or high-cost approach? What are its advantages and disadvantages?

10. In protecting the environment, the optimum economic arrangement is attained when the dollar expenditure on pollution abatement is equal to the dollar benefit from reduced pollution. Why cannot the market be trusted to provide the information and guidelines to achieve this arrangement?

Index

G

H

I

J

K

L

M

T

U

V

W